Conflict Resolution in Early Childhood

Helping Children Understand and Resolve Conflicts

EDYTH J. WHEELER
Towson University

D1280050

PEARSON
Merrill
Prentice Hall

Upper Saddle River, New Jersey
Columbus, Ohio

Library of Congress Cataloging in Publication Data

Wheeler, Edyth J.
    Conflict resolution in early childhood : helping children understand
and resolve conflicts / Edyth J. Wheeler.— 1st ed.
        p. cm.
    Includes bibliographical references.
    ISBN 0-13-087401-9 (pbk. : alk. paper)
    1. Conflict management—Study and teaching (Early childhood)—United
States. 2. Interpersonal conflict in children—United States. I.
Title.
LB3011.5 .W54 2004
372.14—dc22   2003015348

Vice President and Publisher: Jeffery W. Johnston
Publisher: Kevin M. Davis
Editorial Assistant: Autumn Crisp
Production Editor: Sheryl Glicker Langner
Production Coordination: Julie Frigo, D&G Limited, LLC
Design Coordinator: Diane C. Lorenzo
Photo Coordinator: Kathy Kirtland

Cover Designer: Mark Shumaker
Cover photo: Getty One
Production Manager: Laura Messerly
Director of Marketing: Ann Castel Davis
Marketing Manager: Amy June
Marketing Coordinator: Tyra Poole

This book was set in Palatino by D&G Limited, LLC. It was printed and bound by R.R. Donnelley & Sons
Company. The cover was printed by Phoenix Color Corp.

Photo Credits: Anne Vega, pp. 2, 5, 114, 124, 139, 150, 214, 225, 254, 303, 313; Dan Floss/Merrill, pp. 9,
108, 136; Todd Yarrington/Merrill, pp. 13, 106, 236; Teri Leigh Stratford/PH College, pp. 16, 144, 220;
Laima Druskis/PH College, pp. 32, 40, 66, 71, 90, 154; Shirley Zeiberg/PH College, pp. 21, 210; Andy
Brunk/Merrill, p. 45; Pearson Learning, p. 56; Antony Magnacca/Merrill, pp. 84, 163, 263, 276, 290;
KS Studios/Merrill, p. 95; Scott Cunningham/Merrill, pp. 117, 129, 196, 280; John Paul Endress/Silver
Burdett Ginn, p. 174; Marc P. Anderson/PH College, p. 181; Larry Fleming/PH College, p. 185; Barbara
Schwartz/Merrill, p. 300; Frank LaBua/PH College, p. 309.

Pearson Education Ltd.
Pearson Education Singapore Pte. Ltd.
Pearson Education Canada, Ltd.
Pearson Education—Japan

Pearson Education Australia Pty. Limited
Pearson Education North Asia Ltd.
Pearson Educación de Mexico, S.A. de C.V.
Pearson Education Malaysia Pte. Ltd.

10 9 8 7 6 5 4 3 2 1
ISBN: 0-13-087401-9

Preface

As young children face increasing violence in their world, interest in conflict resolution continues to grow in schools and communities across the nation. Conflicts are part of everyday life in our work with young children. Conflict resolution is also part of a larger context of violence prevention, response to national crisis, character or moral education, and peace education.

Conflict Resolution in Early Childhood: Helping Children Understand, Manage, and Resolve Conflicts examines the nature of young children's conflicts, the role of peer conflict in children's development, and ways for practitioners and families to foster children's prosocial interactions and conflict resolution. With its primary focus on children and their conflicts with their peers, this book also explores the idea of adults as positive models for children in conflicts, and it incorporates the roles of family, community, and culture. An additional consideration is the evaluation, selection, adaptation, and development of curriculum program models for conflict resolution.

In order to support children's developing conflict resolution ability, adults need to understand what is happening in children's conflicts. Using real-life examples of children's interactions, this book explains conflicts through several theoretical perspectives and provides a practitioner focus on supporting child-centered resolutions in programs and classrooms for young children from ages two to eight. Constructivist and ecological contexts support an understanding of conflict resolution and peacemaking for all children.

Beginning in the early years, conflict resolution is an area of vital concern worthy of an in-depth study beyond the single chapter or few pages in books of a broader scope. This book presents children's ability to understand and resolve their disputes as a process of learning and development with implications for curriculum, behavior guidance, and child development. The growth of both children and teachers is a focus of this book.

The chapters resonate with the idea of collaboration in support of young children's conflict resolution across a broad spectrum of participants. We will look closely at children themselves, and also at classrooms, schools, families, and communities. Our approach is consistent with recommendations included in a list of

14 proposed solutions for preventing and reducing violence, from a 1994 symposium on violence at Brown University (Lipsett, 1994, p. 91):

- Take a collective moral responsibility for violence and make a long-term, national commitment to its eradication.
- Shift from a reactive to a proactive stance. Focus on tasks such as teaching conflict resolution and guaranteeing day care, instead of installing metal detectors and building bigger prisons.
- Practice prevention. Teach kids as early as possible.
- Teach non-violent conflict resolution to everyone.
- Restrict media violence and promote responsible children's television programming.
- Coordinate communication among kids, parents, schools, police, and communities.

ORGANIZATION

This book is presented in four parts. Part I offers a close look at definitions of children's conflicts, and at the broader context of the violence and peace surrounding children in their world. Part II presents ways to look at and understand children's conflicts and conflict resolution: first with the tools of observing and listening to children, then with characteristics of children's conflicts, and finally with theoretical perspectives to help make sense of what we observe. Part III takes us into the everyday world of classroom decision-making, from creating a caring community to supporting conflict resolution and peacemaking, to curriculum approaches and materials, to guidelines and strategies for intervening in children's conflicts. Part III includes chapters that focus on specific age groups, from young preschoolers to primary grades. Part IV moves the discussion beyond the early childhood setting to working with families and communities, to evaluating and using program models for conflict resolution, and, finally, to taking action and advocating on behalf of children and families in working together toward conflict resolution and peace.

FEATURES OF THIS BOOK

Conflict Resolution in Early Childhood brings together the themes of children's prosocial development, guiding behavior, anti-violence, peacemaking, and caring classrooms. The book encompasses all areas in which an early childhood professional might encounter conflicts: primarily interactions between child peers, but also between siblings and between adults. There is an emphasis on all children, considering diversity of culture, language, and ability. This focus has direct applications to curriculum and professional development. The intent is to further the reader's depth of understanding while providing direct implications for practice.

LEARNING WITH THIS BOOK

This book includes a variety of features for different audiences. Chapters include key points or objectives, practical examples, connections to theory, questions for further discussion, application exercises, "Thinking about All Children" boxes, and chapter summaries. Integrated throughout the book, real-life scenarios provide opportunities for students to analyze conflicts from the viewpoints of both children and adults. The book also discusses implications for classroom decision-making and recommends resources. More advanced students will find useful the sections on theoretical perspectives, research updates, teacher researcher suggestions, and focus on current issues. Those newer to the field will enjoy the application assignments, case studies, classroom strategies, and activities for children. These features will be helpful to instructors as well. Questions for reflection and self-examination are suited to all audiences.

Students, teachers, and others who read this book and then apply what they learn, will

- Have a greater understanding of children's conflicts in the context of their peer, family, and community cultures.
- Develop tools for seeing and understanding children's peer interactions and conflicts by learning *about* children *from* children.
- Think of children's peer conflicts and conflict resolution as complex social, emotional, and cognitive processes, which we can understand using a number of theoretical lenses.
- Recognize elements of children's peer conflicts, issues, strategies, and outcomes.
- Work to create an early childhood setting for peace and conflict resolution, creating a caring community and integrating curriculum activities, materials, routines, and all aspects of the physical and social environment, in a diverse and inclusive setting.
- Use appropriate adult intervention in children's peer conflicts, working toward children's independent and mutually agreeable conflict resolution.
- Develop new ways of working with families and communities to support peaceful, non-violent environments.
- Become familiar with, and be able to evaluate, a variety of models of conflict resolution, violence prevention, and peace education programs.

Acknowledgments

This book is the result of the tremendous help, inspiration, and encouragement that I received from many people. I am deeply grateful to all of them. First of all, I would like to thank the children at the preschools in Northern Virginia where I taught and conducted my research, and who taught me to learn about children from children. I am also deeply indebted to my graduate students at Towson University, whose help has been invaluable in offering suggestions, asking challenging questions, and, especially, bringing their voices to the text.

I owe thanks to my colleagues in the Early Childhood field: Joan Isenberg, who first challenged me to consider children's peer conflicts and then to write this book; Aline Stomfay-Stitz and Blythe Hinitz, who offered great insight on Peace Education; Diane Levin, who shared her passion for peacemaking and confronting violence in children's lives; and Terry R. Berkeley and my colleagues in the Department of Early Childhood Education at Towson University, who have continually supported, encouraged, and occasionally critiqued my writing.

The editorial and production staff at Merrill/Prentice Hall have been wonderful to work with, and I am thankful for their guidance and support throughout the whole process: Ann Davis, who gave me the confidence to begin the project; Christina Tawney, who guided me through writing and revisions; and Kevin Davis and Autumn Crisp. I am extremely grateful to the reviewers of the book for their valuable advice and suggestions: Richard P. Ambrose, Kent State University; Ginny A. Buckner, Montgomery College; Susan Culpepper, Samford University; Richard Elardo, University of Iowa; Pamela Fleege, University of South Florida; Kathy Hamblin, Aims Community College; Eileen Mahoney, Hudson Valley Community College; Karen L. Peterson, Washington State University, Vancouver; Sherriff Richarz, Washington State University; and Deborah S. Zurmehly, Ohio University, Chillicothe.

Finally, I am grateful to my family and friends, who have offered their continuous encouragement, especially my husband, Bill, who, in his role as Encourager-in-Chief, provided technical support as well as patience with my unending time spent at the computer.

Discover the Companion Website Accompanying This Book

THE PRENTICE HALL COMPANION WEBSITE: A VIRTUAL LEARNING ENVIRONMENT

Technology is a constantly growing and changing aspect of our field that is creating a need for content and resources. To address this emerging need, Prentice Hall has developed an online learning environment for students and professors alike—Companion Websites—to support our textbooks.

In creating a Companion Website, our goal is to build on and enhance what the textbook already offers. For this reason, the content for each user-friendly website is organized by topic and provides the professor and student with a variety of meaningful resources. Common features of a Companion Website include:

FOR THE PROFESSOR—

Every Companion Website integrates **Syllabus Manager**™, an online syllabus creation and management utility.

- **Syllabus Manager**™ provides you, the instructor, with an easy, step-by-step process to create and revise syllabi, with direct links into Companion Website and other online content without having to learn HTML.

- Students may logon to your syllabus during any study session. All they need to know is the web address for the Companion Website and the password you've assigned to your syllabus.

- After you have created a syllabus using **Syllabus Manager**™, students may enter the syllabus for their course section from any point in the Companion Website.

- Clicking on a date, the student is shown the list of activities for the assignment. The activities for each assignment are linked directly to actual content, saving time for students.

- Adding assignments consists of clicking on the desired due date, then filling in the details of the assignment—name of the assignment, instructions, and whether or not it is a one-time or repeating assignment.
- In addition, links to other activities can be created easily. If the activity is online, a URL can be entered in the space provided, and it will be linked automatically in the final syllabus.
- Your completed syllabus is hosted on our servers, allowing convenient updates from any computer on the Internet. Changes you make to your syllabus are immediately available to your students at their next logon.

FOR THE STUDENT—

- **Introduction**—General information about the topic and how it will be covered in the website.
- **Web Links**—A variety of websites related to topic areas.
- **Timely Articles**—Links to online articles that enable you to become more aware of important issues in early childhood.
- **Learn by Doing**—Put concepts into action, participate in activities, examine strategies, and more.
- **Visit a School**—Visit a school's website to see concepts, theories, and strategies in action.
- **For Teachers/Practitioners**—Access information you will need to know as an educator, including information on materials, activities, and lessons.
- **Current Policies and Standards**—Find out the latest early childhood policies from the government and various organizations, and view state, federal, and curriculum standards.
- **Resources and Organizations**—Discover tools to help you plan your classroom or center and organizations to provide current information and standards for each topic.
- **Electronic Bluebook**—Paperless method of completing homework or essays assigned by a professor. Finished work can be sent to the professor via email.
- **Message Board**—Virtual bulletin board to post and respond to questions and comments from a national audience.

To take advantage of these and other resources, please visit the *Conflict Resolution in Early Childhood: Helping Children Understand, Manage, and Resolve Conflicts* Companion Website at

www.prenhall.com/wheeler

Educator Learning Center: An Invaluable Online Resource

Merrill Education and the Association for Supervision and Curriculum Development (ASCD) invite you to take advantage of a new online resource, one that provides access to the top research and proven strategies associated with ASCD and Merrill—the Educator Learning Center. At **www.EducatorLearningCenter.com** you will find resources that will enhance your students' understanding of course topics and of current educational issues, in addition to being invaluable for further research.

How the Educator Learning Center will help your students become better teachers
With the combined resources of Merrill Education and ASCD, you and your students will find a wealth of tools and materials to better prepare them for the classroom.

Research
- More than 600 articles from the ASCD journal *Educational Leadership* discuss everyday issues faced by practicing teachers.
- A direct link on the site to Research Navigator™ gives students access to many of the leading education journals, as well as extensive content detailing the research process.
- Excerpts from Merrill Education texts give your students insights on important topics of instructional methods, diverse populations, assessment, classroom management, technology, and refining classroom practice.

Classroom Practice
- Hundreds of lesson plans and teaching strategies are categorized by content area and age range.
- Case studies and classroom video footage provide virtual field experience for student reflection.
- Computer simulations and other electronic tools keep your students abreast of today's classrooms and current technologies.

Look into the value of Educator Learning Center yourself
Preview the value of this educational environment by visiting **www.EducatorLearningCenter.com** and clicking on "Demo." For a free 4-month subscription to the Educator Learning Center in conjunction with this text, simply contact your Merrill/ Prentice Hall sales representative.

Brief Contents

Contents

**PART IV   SUPPORTING CHILDREN'S CONFLICT
RESOLUTION BEYOND THE CLASSROOM:
UNDERSTANDING AND COLLABORATION
IN FAMILY, SCHOOL, AND COMMUNITY   235**

**11   Working with Families and
Communities for Conflict Resolution   236**

Note: Every effort has been made to provide accurate and current Internet information in this book. However, the Internet and information posted on it are constantly changing, so it is inevitable that some of the Internet addresses listed in this textbook will change.

Children's Conflicts with Peers: A First Look

Part 1—Introduction: Chapter 1 introduces the idea of what conflict is and explores the difference between conflict and aggression, and between constructive and destructive conflicts. We will begin to see that children learn through conflicts with peers and will reflect on the experiences and assumptions that we bring to the topic. Chapter 2 addresses broad societal concerns about children's peer conflicts, which may be framed as issues of violence, peace, safety, or character education. These multiple frameworks have an impact on how teachers and families deal with children and their learning about conflicts.

1

An Introduction to Children's Conflicts with Peers

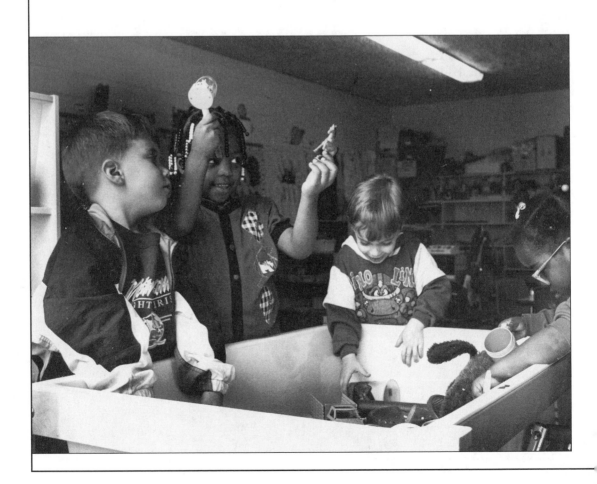

A teacher comments:

"The two year olds are communicating with each other just by virtue of knowing one other. What is amazing is that, when you watch a group of two-year-olds, they are doing what comes naturally and that is the beginning for us in trying to understand them."

Chapter 1 Objectives: Learning about children's peer conflicts, the reader will develop an understanding of what conflict is and what it is not. Also, the reader will examine distinctions between constructive and destructive conflicts, and between conflict and aggression. This chapter introduces readers to the idea that children learn through conflicts with peers.

Chapter Outline:

A FAMILIAR SCENE

Ben, Bruce, and Scott (all age four) are building with small construction toys. Bruce takes a piece from Ben's structure; Ben takes a piece from Bruce's; they roll back and forth, trying to grab the pieces.

Bruce: I need this!

(Both stop rolling and grabbing.)

Ben: You took mine, so I'm taking yours!

Bruce still has the piece he took.

Ben: Well, you can have that part, but not the rest.

They return to building on their own.

FIRST THOUGHTS

Have you heard words like these? If you have, you will recognize the source of the argument (possession of toys), the physical response (grabbing, rolling on the floor), and perhaps the reconciliation. Perhaps you have witnessed such scenes with feelings of exasperation, frustration, wonder, and, finally, relief. What should your response be? What should you do in the face of apparent chaos? How can you help children resolve conflicts peacefully, as Ben and Bruce did?

To answer these questions, we will be taking a journey into understanding children's conflicts by reading this text. We are about to explore a topic that matters a great deal to all of us as teachers, parents, students, and members of our communities and the world. Destructive conflict, violence, hateful prejudice and discrimination, and fear are growing concerns all around us. Potential for conflict confronts us throughout the day.

- In classrooms every day, teachers are concerned about children's arguments and battles over toys, pencils, space, playmates, and rules.
- Families experience sibling rivalry and marital conflict.
- Playgrounds and neighborhoods can be places for play disputes, bullying, hostile competition, and gang rivalry.
- Children witness angry drivers, road rage, and "parking lot rage."
- Daily incidents of criminal issues and violence, such as shootings both random and purposeful, are reported in community newspapers and often cause fear in children's families and teachers.
- Conflict between nations has become very real to children in the United States and across the world as a result of the events of September 11, 2001, and, more recently, the war in Iraq.
- Misunderstandings occur across the boundaries of age, generation, geography, culture, and language.

Conflicts may arise naturally and frequently in an early childhood classroom.

We might wonder, perhaps in despair, how these conflicts are to be resolved. Yet in the face of all this conflict, we are gratified to see children acting with caring, empathy, and understanding. We see children who engage in mediation, conciliation, compromise, and resolution. In the preceding example, Ben and Bruce found a way to resolve their dispute and return to peaceful play. Our task in this book is to explore why and how children are able to do this, and how we can help them.

In the following chapters, we will explore what conflict is, what it is not, how it fits into the context of children's development, where conflicts come from, and how they are resolved. Finally, we will look at the role of an early childhood professional in supporting conflict resolution in the classroom, family, and community. This book asks teachers to ask questions, apply their knowledge and experience, and decide how to bring it all together. Our goal is helping children understand, manage, and resolve their conflicts.

Note: Examples throughout this book will include both male and female children and adults, as well as young children of different ages.

Self-Awareness: Examining Your Understanding and Responses to Conflict

First, let's begin with your understanding of conflict. Think a moment about how you respond to the word "conflict." A useful strategy at this point is to "brainstorm," or make a list of words that you associate with "conflict." Figure 1–1 is an example of a conflict word web.

The thesaurus includes more words for "conflict," such as discord, argument, hostility, strife, friction, antagonism, disharmony, battle, struggle, fight, skirmish, contention, contest, and controversy.

Thinking about the images that come to mind as you consider these words is a good way to gauge your response to the conflicts you experience in everyday life. As you begin to study children's conflicts, it will be important to assess your natural reactions and interpretations of conflicts. Looking at the story of Ben and Bruce, consider your reaction to their conflict. As a teacher, what are your assumptions and expectations for conflict resolution in your classroom?

Adults approach children's conflicts and resolution in different ways, reflecting their individual interactional styles and values. Action-oriented individuals may intervene promptly, while others may first watch and evaluate. Those who value harmony may encourage conciliation. Those who value fairness may feel that it is important to pursue "the principle of the thing." Interpretations of the

Figure 1–1
Conflict word web.

concept of democracy vary from "majority rule" to consensus achieved by all voices participating.

William Kreidler (1984) has described five types of approaches to conflict that teachers may demonstrate:

1. *The no-nonsense approach:* I don't give in. I try to be fair and honest with the kids, but they need firm guidance in learning what's acceptable behavior and what isn't.

2. *The problem-solving approach:* If there's a conflict, there's a problem. Instead of battling kids, I try to set up a situation in which we can all solve the problem together. This produces creative ideas and stronger relationships.

3. *The compromising approach:* I listen to the kids and help them listen to each other. Then I help them give a little. We can't all have everything we want. Half a loaf is better than none.

4. *The smoothing approach:* I like things to stay calm and peaceful whenever possible. Most of the kids' conflicts are relatively unimportant, so I just direct attention to other things.

5. *The ignoring approach:* I point out the limit and let the kids work things out for themselves. It's good for them, and they need to see the consequences of their behavior. There's not a whole lot you can do about conflict situations anyway. (Kreidler, 1984, p. 10–11)

Teachers may see themselves in one of these categories. Typically, however, good teachers will vary their approach depending on the circumstance or the particular needs of children. In Chapter 10, we will explore in depth the different approaches that teachers may use when conflicts occur. At this point, we are using these five types as a starting point to help you figure out your natural and most comfortable approach to conflict.

WHAT WE NEED TO KNOW ABOUT CONFLICTS

Conflicts Will Happen

Conflict is a natural part of the human condition. Achieving harmony and peace is the result of a series of negotiations, either *internal (intrapersonal)* or *external (interpersonal or social)*. Figure 1–2 shows examples of internal and external conflicts. In an *internal* conflict, I might wonder, "Half of our classrooms will move to multiage next year. Should I stay in my first grade or move to a new K-Three?" I hold an internal conversation or dialog with myself as I weigh the options, "listening to both sides" of the issue. My conversation with myself proceeds. "I have read so much about the value of multiage settings for children and their learning, but it will surely mean work and will be a new challenge for me." Eventually I will come up with a compromise or develop a new perspective and in that way will resolve my internal conflict.

An internal conflict or
intrapersonal-one person in conflict

An external or interpersonal
conflict between two people

Figure 1–2
Internal and external conflict

A similar but more complex process occurs in *external (interpersonal or social)* conflicts with others. Conflicts between people, regardless of age, provide us an opportunity to learn about one another and enable us to broaden our individual views to see the world as others see it. "Oh, I didn't think of it that way!" Our goal is to understand the dual nature of conflict. Positive conflict leads to growth and greater understanding. Negative conflict can create a wedge or an obstacle that brings greater misunderstanding, a wall of hurtful words, violence, and pain.

Conflicts, disputes, and arguments occur naturally and frequently between young children as they interact in an early childhood classroom. Traditionally, many adults have viewed conflicts between children as undesirable and have tried to prevent them or intervene promptly when they arise. More recently, there have been greater efforts among early childhood practitioners to help children develop conflict resolution strategies on their own, without adult intervention (Chen & Smith, 2002; Crosser, 1992; Essa, 2003; Evans, 2002; Gartrell, 2002; Kohn, 1991; Ramsey, 1991). Theory and research have long suggested that peer conflict contributes to children's development and represents an important form of social interaction (Arcaro-McPhee et al, 2002; Berkowitz, 1985; Guralnick, 1994; Laursen & Hartup, 1989; Rende & Killen, 1992; Ross & Conant, 1992). We are growing in our understanding of how children learn to manage conflicts with their peers and come to their own peaceful and mutually-satisfying resolutions (Arcaro-McPhee et al, 2002; Wheeler, 1997; see Chapter 4 for more on children's conflict resolution).

In later chapters of this book, we will see conflict in the context of theories of growth and development, and in the context of our early childhood practice, as we facilitate children's harmonious relations with their peers. We will also see children's conflict resolution as one piece of a larger continuum of peace education and anti-violence movements.

Definitions of Conflict

Definitions

According to the *Merriam-Webster Collegiate Dictionary*, conflict is defined not only as a "fight, battle, or war," but also as a "competitive or opposing action of incompatibles: antagonistic state or action (as of divergent ideas, interests, or persons)" or a "mental struggle resulting from incompatible or opposing needs, drives, wishes, or external or internal demands" (Mish et al., 2001, p. 242). Social conflict occurs "when one person does something to which another objects" and is not necessarily intended as harmful (Shantz, 1987, p. 284). Researchers have identified verbal and non-verbal conflicts in terms of mutual opposition: "Child A does or says something that influences child B; child B resists and child A persists" (Shantz, 1987, p. 284). In the preceding example, Ben takes the construction pieces. Bruce objects by taking some of Ben's, Ben persists and Bruce continues, alternately insisting verbally or trying to regain physical possession.

In play, children have opportunities for conflict and peaceful negotiation.

Constructive and Destructive Conflicts

There are two types of conflicts, and it is important to make a distinction between them. *Constructive conflict* involves efforts toward mutual problem solving and continuing social interaction. In our example, Ben offers a rationale for his retaliation and then, perhaps seeing Bruce's need for the pieces in his structure, suggests a limited conciliation. The children return to playing harmoniously.

Destructive conflict, or dysfunctional conflict, is characterized by threats, coercion, and escalation beyond the initial issue (Furman & McQuaid, 1992). Let's suppose that Ben and Bruce continued their scuffle on the floor and began to hurt one another. The issue of block play would be left behind. Perhaps the issue would only end with the more effective fighter taking control. The opportunity for learning reasoning, perspective-taking, and problem solving would be lost. The lesson learned would be that power, violence, and a one-sided solution are the most effective ways to deal with disagreements.

The outcomes of conflict, constructive but most especially destructive, have an impact on both the players in the conflict and the classroom onlookers observing their peers.

Aggression

Contrary to conventional thinking, aggression is only one of several possible strategies children may use in their conflicts. Most conflicts among children do not involve aggression but are a result of social differences as defined above. We will examine the many causes of children's peer conflicts later.

Aggression is defined in the dictionary as a "forceful action or procedure (as an unprovoked attack), especially when intended to dominate or master" and as "hostile, destructive or injurious behavior" or "forceful attacking behavior or outlook" (Mish et al., p. 23). Furthermore, the word "aggressive implies a disposition to dominate often in disregard of others' rights" (Mish et al., p. 23). Aggressive actions are themselves identified as *hostile aggression*, not related to a conflict issue but intended to be harmful, or as *instrumental aggression*, used as a means of achieving the goal of the conflict. If Bruce hit Ben over the head with the blocks in his efforts to keep them, for instance, he would be engaging in instrumental aggression.

This definition notwithstanding, practitioners often associate conflict with aggression and see conflict in a negative light. Thus, the topic of children's conflicts in the classroom has been the subject of books, articles, and workshops dealing with discipline, war play, classroom management, and behavior problems (Carlsson-Paige & Levin, 1992; Crosser, 1992; Essa, 2003; Guralnick, 1994; Katz, 1984; see also NAEYC conference sessions, 1990–2002).

To sum up, we can say what conflict is and what it is not: Conflict is a disagreement between people, and it is an opportunity for children to learn. Conflict is not the same as aggression. Conflict may be constructive or destructive. What children learn from their conflicts may be desirable or undesirable. Conflicts may create harmful aggression or lead to peaceful negotiation. We will explore these aspects of children's conflicts throughout this book.

Conflict and Children's Development

In contrast to this traditional negative view of conflicts, a multi-disciplinary body of literature supports the importance of conflict in human growth and development. Classical theorists Freud and Erikson stressed internal conflict as critical elements in psychological growth (Shantz, 1987; Erikson, 1963). John Dewey included a model for children's conflict resolution as part of his progressive approach to education (1938). More contemporary theory, influenced by the work of Piaget (1962), Vygotsky (1978), and Bronfenbrenner (1979), supports the idea that peer conflict contributes to children's social, cognitive, linguistic, and cultural growth and is interrelated with family and community.

Piaget suggests that, just as children learn through the process of adaptation as they experience internal cognitive conflict, conflicts with peers also provide children with powerful opportunities for cognitive growth. In Vygotsky's theories about internalization, learning from more capable peers, and the relationship between thought and language, children's peer conflict is an important activity that contributes to development. As children argue, they learn to experience and exercise a "rich set of voices" (Goodwin, 1990, p. 239), they hear and interpret what others are saying, and they learn to form responses based on what they are hearing. Peer conflict is also described as a means of social organization in children's peer culture, as well as way to develop social problem-solving skills (Maynard, 1985; Straus, 2002; Vespo et al., 1995).

How do children learn to speak, read, write, and play? The early childhood knowledge base tells us that learning is the result of a combination of developmental sequence, behavioral reinforcement, genetic makeup, and the influence of family, friends, school, culture, and community. Learning to resolve conflicts is not so different, as we shall see. We will examine all of these theoretical perspectives, and others, in greater depth in Part Two of this book.

How Do Conflicts Begin and How Are They Resolved?

If we look closely, we will see that children's conflicts have a pattern or structure. Descriptive studies have investigated children's conflicts and have defined *structural features* as instigating *issues*, oppositional *strategies*, and *outcomes* (Laursen & Hartup, 1989; Shantz & Shantz, 1985; Malloy & McMurray, 1996; Wheeler, 1997; Wilson, 1988). In this type of analysis, the issue between Ben and Bruce is possession of the building pieces. The children use both physical and verbal strategies, and finally, reasoning and negotiation leads to a peaceful and mutually agreeable outcome.

We will look further at this "anatomy of a conflict," and the many variations in children's conflicts, in later chapters. We will also refine our observation and assessment of what is happening when children engage in conflicts. Other important questions are how social or physical surroundings influence the ways in which children begin, conduct, and end their conflicts with their peers. Through observation of children as they interact in natural settings, we can extend our understanding of children's conflicts (Arcaro-McPhee et al, 2002; DeVries & Zan, 1994; Levin, 1994/2003, forthcoming; Ramsey, 1986; Rende & Killen, 1992; Ross & Conant, 1992; Shantz, 1987).

Role of Practitioners

Another focus on children's peer conflicts is an emerging interest in developing conflict resolution skills. Concerned about violence and tension between diverse groups in schools, neighborhoods, and communities across the nation, educators in secondary and upper elementary grades have encouraged conflict resolution through cooperative learning, peer mediation, peace curriculum, and appreciation of diversity (Johnson et al., 1992; McCarthy, 1992; Molnar, 1992). Conflict resolution is gaining greater attention among early childhood professionals (Arcaro-McPhee et al., 2002; Levin, 1994/2003; Wilson, 1988; Ramsey, 1991). A greater understanding of children's social conflicts, including causes, oppositional strategies, and outcomes, supports our goals of providing a peaceful, positive classroom experience.

This book is dedicated to the role of practitioners in children's conflict resolution and peacemaking. In Part 2, we will develop an understanding of children's conflicts as a basis for our practice. In Parts 3 and 4, we will explore in depth our role with children in our classrooms and centers, and with families and communities.

An imperative in our role as early childhood professionals is a commitment to ethical practices. The National Association for the Education of Young Children (NAEYC) Code of Ethical Practice and Statement of Commitment details our responsibility to children, families, colleagues and community, and society (NAEYC, 2001). We will remember these principles throughout our study of children's conflicts.

>>

SUMMARY

Conflicts are a natural part of life, and they present opportunities that are both positive and negative. A contradiction exists between child development theory, which describes children's conflict as a positive contribution to development, and traditional practice, which defines conflict as a negative, undesirable behavior. The bridge across this gap may be an understanding of the processes of children's conflicts that supports development and fosters positive conflict resolutions. An

Constructive conflict contributes to chidren's development.

important question that we will consider: What developmental and environmental factors influence the way children manage their conflicts?

Practitioners have several concerns about classroom conflicts: creating a peaceful classroom environment, managing behavior and maintaining order, and teaching conflict resolution skills. Their questions may include: If conflict is an opportunity for growth and learning, should I allow it to occur? What kinds of conflicts and resolutions can I expect from the children in my classroom, based on my observations of these children? In what ways can I help children find mutually agreeable solutions to their conflicts? Do I support children's conflict resolution in ways that are responsive to differences in culture, language, and ability? Taking the perspective that conflict is a natural phenomenon, and conflict resolution is a developing capability, brings peer conflict into a focus similar to other areas of children's development, such as fine motor ability, language, sense of humor, and sense of self and others. As reflective practitioners, we must ask ourselves about our own understanding of and response to conflict.

The first stop on our journey toward understanding children's conflicts is in the world outside the classroom door. As we welcome children into our classrooms, we recognize that there is a larger context of peace and violence in the world outside. The next chapter will look at the landscape of that world, as we learn to help children resolve their conflicts peacefully.

>>>

SUPPLEMENTARY MATERIALS FOR CHAPTER 1

Research Focus

Review the work of early writers and thinkers in foundations of education, as well as in early childhood education, for themes related to children's conflicts and recommended practices for teachers.

>>>

APPLICATION EXERCISES

1. Using the Kreidler "teacher approach to conflict" categories, think about your own most natural response. Which response most closely matches your own?
2. Speak to other teachers in your setting, or at a school you visit, and ask for their reaction to the Krieder list.

3. Go to the NAEYC Web site (*www.naeyc .org*). In the Position Statement section, locate the Code of Ethical Practice and Statement of Commitment. Print a copy to keep with you in your practice, and share it with others.

>>>

THINKING ABOUT ALL CHILDREN

1. A question for reflection and analysis: Does your approach to conflict change depending on the child's needs? Do you make assumptions about certain children that influence the way you respond to their conflicts?
2. What do we mean by "all children?" NAEYC has defined "*all children*" as "chil-dren with developmental delays or disabilities, children whose families are culturally and linguistically diverse, children who are gifted and talented, children from diverse socioeconomic groups, and other children with diverse learning styles and needs" (NAEYC, 2002).

2 Frameworks for Conflict Resolution: Responding to Issues of Violence, Peace Education, and Safe Environments

>>

"I know what I see every day on my way to school and my children see the same things. My classroom needs to be a place where they will can feel safe." (First grade teacher in an urban school)

>> >

Chapter 2 Objectives: This chapter addresses the broader societal concerns about children's conflicts, which may be framed as issues of violence, peace, safety, or character education. Chapter topics include violence, its causes and effects on children, and responses from a wide range of stakeholders who seek to address violence and provide safe environments for children. This discussion is presented at this stage because readers of this book are well aware of these topics. We will need to consider these issues before we can begin to see peer conflicts through children's eyes and find ways to support children's peaceful resolution of conflict.

Chapter Outline

INTRODUCTION

Our study of children's conflicts includes an awareness of the widespread violence in the world in which young children and their families live. There are reports of shootings in schools and neighborhoods, terrorist threats, child abuse, and domestic violence. Children see violent images on television and video games, and in movies. In response, there has been a greater emphasis on safe schools and a return to teaching about values through character education, peer mediation, and other school programs such as No Put Downs, Second Step, and Character Counts. Community and national efforts such as the Million Mom March in 2000 and Stand for Children, an annual event since 1996, have sought to raise a unified voice against violence in the lives of children and families. In the aftermath of acts of terrorism in the Fall of 2001, adults and children across the United States came together for caring, support for shared grief, and reaching out for cross-cultural understanding. We continually see examples of violence as well as peace, both incidents of tragic violence and examples of committed efforts for peace and children's well-being.

The subject of children's conflicts and conflict resolution is associated with peace education, character education, safe and harmonious schools, and violence prevention. As early childhood professionals hear about these goals and initiatives, it is important for us to sort them all out and think about our reactions to what we are hearing. There are calls for conflict resolution as an antidote to violence in schools and communities. Teachers may wonder what to do when confronted with contradictory messages that tell them to focus on basic academic skills but also to add values programs to an already crowded school day.

Other questions include: Do teachers understand the prescribed conflict resolution/peace education programs that they are asked to use? What do children think of these adult efforts to guide their dealings with their age-mates? Perhaps most importantly, are these mandates based on what we know about children and their learning and development? Are these programs developmentally appropriate and responsive to the diverse needs of all children and families?

Before we answer these questions later in this book, we will look more closely at the violence that can result from destructive conflicts. We will also bear in mind the remarkable resilience of children, families, schools, and communities in the face of pervasive and persistent violence.

VIOLENCE ISSUES

What do violence issues really mean to you in your setting? We know that young children are not living in a vacuum and that classroom conflicts often have roots elsewhere. Teachers need to understand broader issues outside as well as the safe world inside our classrooms. As professionals, we should be prepared to speak with an informed voice in the discussion.

What Causes Violence?

What is violence? "Violence is an aggressive behavior not based on mutual agreement, which inflicts both physical and emotional hurt to the victim; a destructive response, physical, verbal, or emotional; an expression of anger." This "good working definition of violence" was developed in a national symposium on violence (Lipsitt, 1994, p. 99).

There are different forms of violence based on participants, motivation, and strategies.

Interpersonal violence involves behavior that threatens, attempts, or completes intentional affliction of physical or psychological harm by persons against other persons.

Primary violence takes place among persons who are acquainted, and *secondary (instrumental) violence* occurs among those who have no relationship, such as in armed robbery. (Lipsitt, 1994, p. 99. Italics not in original.)

A combination of factors can lead to violence. Lipsitt (1994) cautions that overly simplistic explanations may lead to narrowly focused and overly simplistic solutions. Complex developmental, societal, and cultural influences play a role in the occurrence of violence. In our discussions, it is important to be clear about whether we are discussing violent behaviors of individuals or a general societal tendency to accept and display violent acts. For individuals, both the environment and heredity make a contribution. The following section illustrates the wide range of conditions that may contribute to an individual's violent behaviors. They are *developmental factors*, *family factors*, *school and peer influences*, and *society and culture*.

Developmental Factors

A child's experience with violence as perpetrator, witness, victim, or bystander is a powerful influence on later behaviors. In fact, the American Psychological Association's position is that "the strongest developmental predictor of a child's involvement in violence is a history of previous violence" (Americal Psychological Association, 1993, p. 17). The APA warns that an established level of aggression may be fairly stable and predictable over time. For these reasons, "early intervention for aggressive and violent behavior in childhood is critical, the earlier the better" (p. 17).

Biological factors in development include a possible genetic predisposition to violence, or to characteristics that may lead to violent behaviors. Those with a temperament described as fearless and impulsive may have a predisposition to violence and aggressive behavior (APA, 1993, p. 18). Early indicators may include aggression and violence toward animals, lighting dangerous fires, and other evidence of a lack of inhibition. There has been little research to explore the reasons behind these reported differences (APA, 1993). These findings are to be taken with caution and should not be overgeneralized. More compelling than genetic factors are those related to family, society, and culture.

More violent crimes are reported among males in the Unites States than among females. These differences between males and females may be genetic or due to socialization. William S. Pollack (1998) explains that violence among boys is a result of a "Boy Code": being hurried into adult roles and feeling disconnected from love, care, and support.

Children's emotional and cognitive development also contributes to later violent behavior. Those who have developed little impulse control and have a poor understanding of social cues, and who have a history of violence, may react to situations in violent ways. While it is important to be alert to early signs, it is equally important to avoid falsely labeling individuals as future violent offenders. There is a continuing need for research into why inhibitions break down and violent behaviors follow.

Family Factors

Family factors contribute to the development of violent behavior. These factors include adverse childrearing conditions, ineffective parenting, and child abuse. Poverty, illness, and unemployment may bring about a sense of hopelessness, leading to violent responses. There may be a lack of confidence in the self, the family, or even the community to provide for immediate needs. Awareness of the stresses and risk factors associated with poverty is crucial for those who work with young children and families.

Poverty is widespread and persistent among families with young children. According to data from the U.S. Bureau of the Census, more children than ever, 11.7 million, were living below the poverty line in 2001 ($14,128 a year for a family of three). Of those children, 44 percent lived in families with extreme poverty, living at less than half of the poverty level. Poverty rates are higher for children who are Black (30.2 percent) and Hispanic (28 percent) (Children's Defense Fund, 2002). Even in times of national prosperity, children remain among the poorest citizens in the United States. To follow this trend, we will need to look at current statistics available on the Census Bureau's web site (http://www.census.gov).

Other conditions experienced by contemporary families may provide a context for alienation, disenfranchisement, painful experiences with racism/discrimination, lack of family support structures, or alcohol/substance abuse. These conditions may contribute significantly to violence that children experience at home. These causes are important, but by themselves, they do not bring about violent behaviors (Lipsitt, 1994).

School and Peer Influences

As they grow and learn, children receive powerful messages from their experiences away from home. Peers provide models of behaviors and attitudes. Shared expectations emerge and are understood by children as members of their peer culture. Children may be at risk for learning violence by spending time with others who use aggressive and violent behaviors. Children who have difficulty interacting appropriately with others may band together, perhaps shunned by or avoiding more conforming peers.

School factors may help create a climate for violent responses in children, including overemphasis on academic achievement and authoritarian practices. Consider violence done to children institutionally and violence against children by authority figures. Institutional procedures in schools often show disregard for children's rights. The lack of privacy, strict regimentation, uncompromising timetables, and constant standing in lines are typical school experiences that adults would resent. Fortunately, we are far from the days when children were regularly subjected to the violence of corporal punishment in schools. The violence toward children within today's school institutions is of a different nature and is not always apparent.

Society and Culture

Trends in U.S. society and dominant culture are also contributing factors to violence. Children live in a cultural milieu heavily influenced by media and its representations of both real-life and fictional violence. There is an overall acceptance of violence as part of life. Violence and the use of power are seen as accepted ways of

All three of these children are learning about conflicts from their peers at school.

deciding disputes. Violent words and phrases permeate everyday language, through metaphors based on war and sports. Children hear, and model, adults using violent language, often without thinking and sometimes with frightening irony. A real-life example: "He was so rude, I could have killed him!" Looking around, we notice violent images in the least likely places. One example is the irony of well-meaning slogans for peace-oriented efforts: "War on drugs!" and "Fight crime!"

Accessibility of handguns and the American "love affair with guns" reinforce this idea of acceptance. Handguns make available the means to act on violent tendencies, often with tragic consequences. (Lipsitt in Judy Mann, 2000) Barriers to this breakdown of inhibitions are crumbling. The idea of shooting at classmates and co-workers is no longer unimaginable.

While many educators suggest thorough and wide-ranging approaches, obstacles to effective and comprehensive solutions to this trend toward violence include an attitude that nothing can be done, a helpless shrugging of shoulders. "It's not my problem. It's somebody else's problem." "Nothing will work." "It's a natural part of life." In other cases, overly simplistic solutions may be promoted. In Virginia, state legislators passed a law requiring a moment of silence at the start of the day as a way to help reduce violence in schools.

A Hopeful Note

Throughout this discussion, remember why you are reading this book. It is important to remember that, as teachers and caring adults, we can be agents of change for children and families. A guiding principle is that "if individual violent behavior is caused by learning, then the violent behavior can be unlearned and therefore changed" (APA, 1993, p. xx). The report from the American Psychological Association is one of hope: Violence is learned and can be changed (Slaby et al., 1995). Interventions can counteract these developmental and societal factors that put children at risk for violent behavior. Figure 2–1 shows a continuum of peace and violence that children may see and experience in their daily lives.

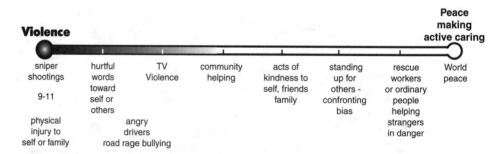

Figure 2–1
What children see and experience: A continuum of peace and violence in their daily lives.

What Do Children See and Experience?

As the first grade teacher quoted at the beginning of this chapter pointed out, children are not living in a vacuum, immune to either the violent or peaceful aspects of their environments. They are aware of, and respond to, what is going on around them. The following stories of two children named Samuel and Peter reveal how violence has shaped their understanding of what will be expected of them as they grow up.

Samuel's Story

A drama enrichment teacher in an urban school uses *role drama*, a technique used to engage children in creative expression. In preparation for the *role drama*, she asks the children to create a character for themselves, someone who is an accomplished explorer or someone who could be a hero. After a group discussion about the characters, the children draw what they think the character would look like.

Samuel is a second-grade student who is labeled a "difficult child" and is often suspended for violent behavior, but he behaves in a very reserved manner during drama time. He is working hard on his picture.

Teacher: I see your character's name is Killer. Can you tell me about him?

Samuel: Everybody thinks he in a gang. It ain't fair.

Teacher: Is he?

Samuel: No, but everybody treats him bad anyhow. He's gonna have to join one if people don't quit.

Teacher: What else? (pause) Is he brave?

Samuel: No, he scared.

Teacher: Is he crying?

Samuel: Yeh.

Teacher: Do you know why he's crying?

Samuel: He don't wanna use his gun. He don't wanna shoot anybody.

Teacher: Will he?

Samuel: He has to. He ain't got a choice.

Teacher: There isn't another way for him?

Samuel: Not for m—uh, him.

Peter's Story

First graders in this east coast suburban school have written about what they will be when they grow up. Peter's illustrated story, transcribed from his invented spelling, reads as follows:

"When I grow up, I want to [be a] trained killer. I have guns. I have to protect my family. I kill bad guys in the snowtime. I kill bad guys in the night. My name would be Strong Man."

The person Peter has drawn is saying, *"I'm gonna get you!!!"*

The teacher later writes to Peter: *I think your writing is great, but please (underlined twice) remember that guns are dangerous! If you want to protect your family, you can be a police officer!*

Both Samuel and Peter express a sense of the inevitability of violence, notably the use of guns, in their lives. Samuel has an expectation that he must become a member of a gang, use a gun, and kill people, although this makes him sad. Peter reflects a message, often seen in television as well as in real life, that it is acceptable for the "good guys" to use violent means to achieve worthwhile ends. As we have seen and will see in later chapters, violence is learned and can be unlearned. There is much that caring adults can do to foster resilience in children and help them overcome the violent messages that they are receiving.

In 1993, a position statement by NAEYC recognized violence in children's daily lives and experiences. Children have direct experiences with violent situations in their families, neighborhoods, and schools. Indirect exposure to violence may come from the daily news, television, video games, certain sports, and the Internet. Children reflect the concerns of adults around them and are aware of violent and frightening events both close to home and far away. In the past few decades, children's own worries about violence have changed from global concerns of nuclear threat in the 1980s, to closer-to-home concerns about street violence and school shootings in the 1990s, to fears about terrorist attacks in 2001 and war in 2003.

An article in the *Washington Post* (Stepp, November 11, 2001) featured the headline "Children's Worries Take New Shape." The article described a study conducted by researchers at the Children's Television Workshop, in which children, ages 6 to 11, drew pictures of their likes, dislikes, hopes, and fears. In May 2001, children's drawings of their fears included snakes, spiders, and monsters. The following fall, the children's pictures showed hijacked airplanes collapsing into buildings, cemeteries, and blackness.

A mother reported in Fall 2002 about her 4½-year-old: "On September 10 of this year my daughter, with no provocation, no reminders, no prompting, drew a picture of the 'burning buildings that the planes crashed into.' I had a wonderful conversation with her about this, and she described the events of a year ago."

Effects of this exposure to television violence include becoming desensitized to violence, copying or reenacting violent actions, and developing a diminished understanding of the reality of violence and its effects. Young children see violence that is unpunished. Acts of violence by television protagonists is portrayed as acceptable and justified (Krcmar, 2001).

To add a positive note, let us remember the ways in which families can not only reduce these negative effects, but also help children develop critical thinking and their own responses to violence. Monitoring children's viewing and discussing what they've seen are key strategies for families (Chang, 2000).

CHILDREN AND TELEVISION

Children's exposure to violence on television is well documented, with statistics showing the number of hours that children watch television and the number of acts of violence they see as they watch:

- Children watch 35 hours a week of television, video games, and videos and, by kindergarten, have watched 4,000 hours.
- Saturday morning cartoons have more than 20 acts of violence per hour, even more than in prime-time programming.
- By the end of elementary school, a child will have seen 8,000 murders and 100,000 other acts of violence. Even the "good guys" use violent methods to save the day (TRUCE, 2002; Levin, 1998; APA, 1993).

Effects of Violence on Children and Families

As we look at the effects of violence on children, areas to consider include physical, social, emotional, and cognitive development; academic progress; and the toll that violence may take on families. According to *Zero to Three* (2000), "infants and toddlers who have been exposed to violence may show the effects of their experience in four key areas: emotional distress; immature and repressive behavior; physical complaints; and loss of skills, especially language" (Groves et al., 2000, pp. 9–10).

The following aspects of children's development are affected by exposure to violence:

- **Trust and safety.** Children see a dangerous world full of enemies in which they will need weapons for safety, rather than a world where, with help and trust, they can overcome their fears.
- **Autonomy and connectedness.** Children see that autonomy comes from weapons and superior force. They associate being connected with others in work and play with weakness and dependence.
- **Empowerment and efficacy.** Physical strength and violence are seen as necessary.
- **Gender identity and diversity.** Stereotyping and exclusion justifies violence and a sense of superiority and entitlement. The "bad guys" deserve to be hurt. Winning is the only acceptable outcome.
- **Play.** Meaningful and creative play gives way to imitative play limited to the scenarios of television scripts (Levin, 1998, p. 28).

According to the NAEYC Position Statement on Violence in the Lives of Children (2001), children have a fundamental need to feel safe. In Maslow's hierarchy of needs, safety is the most basic (Prince & Howard, 2002). From a child's very earliest days, according to Erikson (1963), developing a sense of trust is a critical developmental task. These foundations of development are put at risk by exposure to violence. As a result, children may later have problems in school, and experience difficulties in play and in peer interactions. Children's direct exposure to violence has been described as similar to the *post-traumatic stress disorder* of war veterans (Alat, 2002). It is characterized by inability to concentrate, disturbed sleep, nightmares, images of terror and flashbacks, eating disorders, regressive behaviors, and more (Alat, 2002; Garbarino et al., 1992).

Children who are victims of violence may later become perpetrators of violence. According Jeffrey Pine, Attorney General of Rhode Island, "the journey from the delivery room to the living room can also be a rough one. There is absolutely no question in my mind that there is a direct link between violence in the home and violence later committed by juveniles. And when young people are either victims of domestic violence or are witnesses to acts of domestic violence, they learn that this is a proper response to the problems of the day" (Lipsitt, 1994, p. 11).

Not all children who experience violence suffer these traumatic effects. Similarly, families and communities have "ranges of strength" (Lipsitt, 1994, p. 13). Looking to these protective factors of resilience in children and families will give us direction in confronting violence and supporting children's conflict resolution (Alat, 2002).

Looking at Theory: Ecological Systems

Ecological systems theory has particular relevance in our understanding of how children grow and learn in this context of violence. According to Urie Bronfenbrenner, children's development is influenced by a reciprocal interactive process in the context of five nesting ecological systems (Bronfenbrenner, 1979; Bronfenbrenner & Morris, 1998). See Figure 2–2.

The child's immediate context, or system, is the *microsystem*, which involves direct interaction with family, school, and close neighborhood friends. The *mesosystem* involves the interaction of various settings in the microsystem, such as the relationship between school and home. The elements of the *exosystem* affect the child indirectly: mass media, family workplaces, community, and social services. The *macrosytem* represents the larger context that ultimately affects children's lives: the social, political, and economic environment and the values and ideologies of the culture in which the child and family live. A fifth system, the *chronosystem*, addresses changes in interactions among these systems over time (Berk, 2000; Bronfenbrenner, 1979).

Children learn about violence, and also about caring and peacemaking, in each of these systems. Seeing children's development according to Bronfenbrenner's theory provides insight into the complexity of their sociomoral development. We can see in these systems the potentially harmful influences mentioned in this chapter. We can also see opportunities for collaboration as we support young children in learning peaceful attitudes and developing the ability to resolve conflicts.

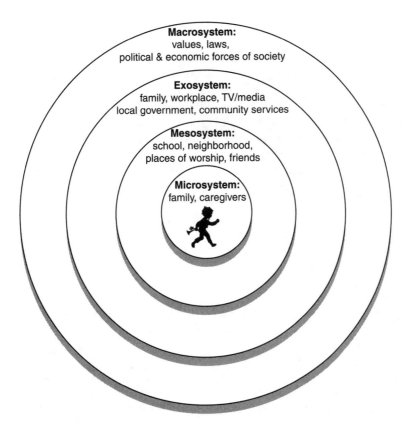

Figure 2–2
Bronfenbrenner's ecological systems: Into which system—or circle—would you find your examples of violence and peacemaking in children's lives?

RESPONDING TO VIOLENCE

Stakeholders in the Issue of Children and Violence

Here are the next questions to ask: "*Who* is involved in these issues of violence prevention, conflict resolution, and peace education? *Why* are they interested? And *how* are they involved?" Stakeholders include families, schools, communities (civic groups, law enforcement, churches), businesses, government officials, and agencies at all levels.

Each group of stakeholders has a different perspective. (This is the "why.") Families care for the safety of their children and have hopes for their future. Schools are concerned about the safety of children and their teachers and seek a peaceful environment for effective teaching and learning. Community groups see violence and safety issues in a number of different ways that include broad concerns for all members of the community and respect for the laws that guide them. Members of the business community are concerned about the safety of workers and customers. Their concerns about children's needs are often related to the idea of children as a future work force. Government officials act in response to their constituencies, based on their own understanding of the issues. The role of early childhood professionals includes protecting children from exposure to violence in the classroom, while helping them make sense of the violence they see and experience elsewhere (Levin, 1998). We will explore what teachers and families can do in Parts 3 and 4.

Collaboration on behalf of violence prevention and conflict resolution may bring these groups together. But how does each group address the problem? Gaining momentum in recent years has been a hardline approach to curbing widespread violence through deterrence: stiffer penalties; strict discipline; and policies such as Zero Tolerance for weapons, drugs, and violent behavior in schools. (Interested readers may want to search the ERIC database at http://www.eric.ed.gov for more on Zero Tolerance, research on its effectiveness, and its implications.) Different approaches that look at some of the deeper causes of violence call for greater support for families and children in terms of quality care and education, anti-poverty efforts, and programs to develop caring communities in schools.

DISCUSSING THE ISSUES

Early childhood professionals should examine these varied efforts in terms of what we know about children and families. Questions to consider: What messages do these approaches send? How do the more punitive approaches see families? Is the message that families have failed in childrearing, or that professionals respect families and consider them to be partners and models?

In examining the range of suggested solutions, we are reminded of the recommendations for preventing and reducing violence listed in the Introduction to this book. (Lipsitt, 1994, p. 91):

A 1994 symposium on violence at Brown University described long-term solutions (Lipsitt, 1994, pp 102 ff):

- Reducing the cultural values and learning experiences that teach that violence is appropriate in some situations
- Real deterrents and "costs for offenders"
- Identification of at-risk children, interventions, and compensatory early education
- Effective dropout prevention and functional skills programs
- Family support and alternative role models for children

The symposium also proposed these short-term solutions:

- Reducing child abuse and domestic violence
- Enforcing gun control

- Reducing everyday occurrences of violence in order to break the intergenerational cycle of violence
- Providing meaningful work in high poverty and unemployment areas
- Eliminating violence in schools by teachers
- Making schools smaller and finding other ways to create peaceful environments
- Collaborating with communities to support recreation, education, secure shelter, medical services, and substance abuse treatment

Obstacles to enacting effective and comprehensive solutions include resistance to involvement of outside agencies; diffusion or duplication of efforts by many groups; limited time, funding, and energy; and lack of persistence and patience in waiting for long-term results.

Collaborating for Safe Environments for Children in School and Community

Many groups are working together in different ways to create safer environments for children. One example is the Adults and Children Together (ACT) Against Violence (see box). There are additional collaborative efforts throughout the United States. A number of character education programs have been developed to help schools reduce violence and encourage conflict resolution. An extensive school-community collaboration is the Resolving Conflict Creatively Program in all of New York City's public schools (Lantieri & Patti, 1996). Efforts have extended beyond schools into communities as well. The city of Gaithersburg, MD, incorporated a program called Character Counts! into its mission statement, beginning with a citywide event in 1996. A quick search of the Internet will provide information about many other collaborations.

ADULTS AND CHILDREN TOGETHER (ACT) AGAINST VIOLENCE

A joint initiative by NAEYC and APA, supported by the Advertising Council, launched a national awareness campaign in 2001. ACT brings together an extensive network of resources from several organizations to help teachers, families, and communities with violence prevention, anger management, and problem-solving. Resources are listed on the web site: www.actagainstviolence.org.

There are four principles in the ACT ad campaign message:

1. Violence is largely learned, often early in life.
2. Violence prevention can be learned, starting early in life.
3. Adults shape learning environments for young children.
4. Adults can learn how to model and teach young children constructive ways to cope with anger, frustration, and conflict.

Community partners have joined to act in response to violence across the United States. In New Orleans, COPS for KIDS is a collaboration of mental health professionals and police officers, with funding support from the business community. Providing healthy activities, developing trusting relationships, and providing needed intervention and outreach services, the program gives "each child a hand up rather than a hand out" (*Zero to Three*, 2000, p. 26). The San Francisco Child Trauma Research Project works to educate community partners about the effects of domestic violence on children. The Child Witness to Violence Program in Boston supports children, families, and caregivers who have been affected by violence. The SAFE HAVENS Training Project in Pittsburgh provides trusting relationships with adults and safe places for children who have witnessed violence.

There are more details about these and other programs in *Protecting Young Children in Violent Environments* (*Zero to Three*, 2000). We will also look closely at family, school, and community collaboration later in this book.

Peace Education

Developed as a response to violence with roots in the international conflict of war, peace education not only advocates *against* violence but also stresses reasons *for* peace. Peace education curricula generally include conflict resolution, cooperation and interdependence, global awareness, and social and ecological responsibility. Additional themes in peace curricula are altruism, empathy, kindness, and caring.

Reflecting the changing times, the focus of peace education has shifted since its inception. Early in the 20th century, in the midst of two World Wars, the peace education movement grew out of a vision for world peace. In the mid-twentieth century, this anti-militaristic thrust gave way to a more positive, society-building approach. The 1980s brought an emphasis on conflict resolution, and finally an integrated view of peace education on multiple levels, from mutual understanding, cross-cultural understanding, and global awareness. As the 21st century begins, peace education advocates span an international network. Crossing the barriers of language, religion, nationality, and customs has increased in importance in the U.S. since 9/11.

Peace education also occurs on a very local level, with peace activities taking place in schools and centers. Peace education writers and researchers are looking at a broad range of issues, including cross-cultural and cross-national understanding, positive relationships among students from warring nations, school violence, equality, the meaning of peace, and ways to develop a culture of peace. Peace education efforts in schools include "peace tables" in classrooms, where children sit together to resolve conflicts, and school-wide peace displays, such as walls of peace murals or decorated "peace poles" that bring a message of peace to the neighborhood. Other examples are Peace Week celebrations, international pen pals, and environmental awareness projects.

Resilience in Children and Families

Children face many situations that pose risks to their healthy growth and social, emotional, and cognitive development. Poverty, uncertain family structures, medical concerns, and other violence-related factors may all be considered risks to children. Some children, in the face of these challenges, are able to "make it." They are effective and well-adjusted, both as children and later as adults. Other children do not fare so well. The difference between those who make it and those who do not has been identified as *resilience*.

A combination of characteristics help children to become resilient. Some characteristics, such as persistence, may be inborn and natural for children. Other traits of resilience can be developed and nurtured by the adults in their world. Early research on the question of resilience was conducted by Emmy Werner in a longitudinal study of children growing up in Hawaii, many of whom experienced one or more risk factors (Werner, 1982, 2001).

Traits of resilient children include the following:

- Gaining people's attention in a positive way
- Planning ahead and solving problems
- Developing a talent or hobby
- Having a sense of autonomy
- Persisting in the face of failure
- Relating to a caring "other person"
- Developing a sense of humor
- Developing a sense of control over one's life
- Judging and acting on right and wrong

We can also look for, and support, resilience in families. Long-term research efforts have helped us understand more about families and family systems (*Zero to Three*, 1994. p. 11).

Five factors help families support and nurture their children in high-risk communities:

- Strong kinship bonds
- Flexibility of family roles
- Strong spiritual/religious orientation
- Strong work orientation
- High achievement orientation

For early childhood professionals, the implication of what we know about children's resilience are clear. First of all, we can become one of those caring "other

Relating to a caring adult supports resilience in children.

persons" in a child's life. We can encourage children to pursue special interests or talents. A classroom arranged around multiple intelligences offers an environment for the expression of diverse abilities and interests. Teachers can provide tools and opportunities to practice planning, problem-solving, positive attention-gaining interactions, and moral reasoning. Over time, we can work to support children in developing a greater sense of autonomy, capability, and hope.

A Resilient Nation and a Resilient World

The sense of confidence and safety from international aggression felt by many in the United States was shaken in the Fall of 2001. Even as the events of September 11 were unfolding, there was an instant and thoughtful response by the early childhood professional community on behalf of children and families. Web sites and publications offered guidance to families and teachers in helping children cope with frightening events and uncertain times. The next phase of the response was an outpouring of acts of caring and sympathy by children, as well as adults, for those directly affected by the attacks.

Responding to Children in Times of Crisis

The first impulse for adults may be to shelter children from what is happening, to assume that children "are too young to know or care." Understanding children, their development, and their particular individual needs is important when helping them in difficult times, as it always is. Jim Greenman (2001) describes how children of different ages may perceive what is happening in times of crisis:

> Children under three years old: "They know something is up."
>
> Preschool children: "They know more than you think, and much of it is incomplete or misconceived."
>
> Elementary school children: "They know much more than you think, and they want to know more."

The following are suggestions from an article in the November 2001 issue of *Young Children* (pp. 6–7):

1. Give reassurance and physical comfort.
2. Provide structure and stability.
3. Let children know that feeling upset is okay, but expect a range of reactions.
4. Help children to talk—if they are ready.
5. Turn off the television.
6. Provide experiences that help children release tension and cope with their feelings.
7. Promote peaceful resolution to conflicts.
8. Respect diversity and oppose bias.
9. Watch for changes in children's behavior.
10. Care for ourselves.

Here is a note that resonates with a message of resilience for young children and families, from *Zero to Three* (2002): "Finding comfort in each other's presence: Our world has changed, but the joys of parenting prevail."

TALKING WITH CHILDREN ABOUT THE TRAGEDY

From the Reggio listserv on September 12, 2001:
  Some general advice from the experts includes:

1. Continuously reassure your children that you will help to keep them safe.
2. Turn off the TV. Overexposure to the media can be traumatizing. If your older children are watching the news, be sure to watch with them.
3. Be aware that your child's age will affect his or her response. Adolescents in particular may be hard hit by these kinds of events. Obtaining counseling for a child or adolescent soon after a disaster may reduce long-term effects.
4. Calmly express your emotions—remember that a composed demeanor will provide a greater sense of security for your child.
5. Give your children extra time and attention, and plan to spend more time with your children in the following months.
6. Let your children ask questions, talk about what happened, and express their feelings.
7. Play with children who can't talk yet to help them work out their fears and respond to the atmosphere around them.
8. Keep regular schedules for activities such as eating, playing, and going to bed to help restore a sense of security and normalcy.
9. Consider how you and your child can help. Children are better able to regain their sense of power and security if they feel they can help in some way.

Resources for Talking with Children About Tragedy

>>

WEB SITES

Professional educational organizations responded immediately to the events of September 11 with resources and links to help children, families, and teachers in difficult times. As always, please note that web site URLs and content may change from time to time.

American Academy of Pediatrics: *www.aap.org/advocacy/releases/ disastercomm.htm*

American Psychological Association: *http://helping.apa.org/therapy/ traumaticstress.html#children*

American Academy of Child and Adolescent Psychiatry: *http:// www.aacap.org/*

Association for Childhood Education International: *www.acei.org*

Children's Defense Fund: *http:// www.childrensdefense.org/*

National Clearinghouse for Bilingual Education: *http://www.ncbe .gwu.edu/library/tolerance.htm* (The site includes a resource called "Promoting Cultural Understanding in the Classroom and Community.")

National Education Association: *http://www.nea.org/*

The Parent Center: *www.parentcenter .com/general/34754.html*

Teaching Tolerance: *www .teachingtolerance.org*

United Nations Refugee Agency: *http://www.usaforunhcr.org* (An international organization, directly assisting Afghan children and their families.)

National Association for the Education of Young Children: *www .naeyc.org*

On line Resources at *www.naeyc.org*

Position Statement on Violence in the Lives of Children Position State-ment on Media Violence in Children's Lives

Early Years Are Learning Years: Safe Schools Can't Save Children

Early Years Are Learning Years: Discussing the News with 3- to 7-year olds

Early Years Are Learning Years: Helping Children Cope with Violence

Additional NAEYC resources:

When Disaster Strikes: Helping Young Children Cope

Early Violence Prevention: Tools for Teachers of Young Children

Remote Control Childhood? Combating the Hazards of Media Culture

Anti-Bias Curriculum: Tools for Empowering Young Children

>>>

PRINT RESOURCES

Greenman, J. (2001). *What happened to the world? Helping children cope in turbulent times.* Bright Horizons Family Solutions.

NAEYC. (2001). Helping young children in frightening times. *Young Children, 56*(6), 6–9

Zero to Three (2002). *Little Listeners in an uncertain world: Coping strategies for you and your child after September 11.* Brochure available at www.zerotothree.org.

>>>

SUMMARY

The idea of resilience may be this chapter's closing message. The tragic reality of violence in the lives of young children may be balanced with their own resilience and with positive steps that adults can take. Several of the traits of resilience may be innate to a child, but many can be facilitated by a caring adult: a parent or family member, a teacher, or another adult in the community. This is the hopeful message for children like Samuel, whose drama teacher may encourage his talent and support him in developing a sense of control, and for Peter, whose understanding teacher may foster these traits. Early childhood professionals should know and understand the issues of violence in children's lives and the appropriate responses to it.

This chapter has addressed the impact of violence on young children. We are reminded of the role of early childhood professionals in understanding the environment that young children live in, supporting their resilience, and collaborating with families and community. As we prepare to move to the next part of this book, we can see how children's conflict resolution fits into this picture.

Speaking of creating an environment of understanding differences and teaching tolerance, Vivian Paley says, "If we can't do it in an early childhood classroom, where in the world can we do it?" (Teaching Tolerance Project, 1997). We can say the same thing about preventing violence through conflict resolution and peace-making with young children.

In our next chapter, we will begin to look more closely at how children understand and experience conflicts with others.

>>>

SUPPLEMENTARY SECTIONS FOR CHAPTER 2

Research Focus

Causes, effects, and responses to violence: Explore recent findings on violence in children's lives and ways that adults are effectively helping children confront violence.

Clarke, S. H., & Campbell, F. A. (1998). Can intervention early prevent crime later? The Abecedarian Project compared with other programs. *Early Childhood Research Quarterly*, 319–343.

Kamps, D. M., Tankersley, M., & Ellis, C. (2000). Social skills intervention for young at-risk students: A 2-year follow-up study. *Behavioral Disorders, 25,* 310–324.

Interventions to support resilience in children: Can you find recent studies to add to our understanding of how early childhood professionals can help children develop resilience?

Lowenthal, Barbara. (1999). Effects of Maltreatment and Ways to Promote Children's Resiliency. *Childhood Education*, 204–209.

Novick, Rebecca. (1998). The Comfort Corner: Fostering Resiliency and Emotional Intelligence. *Childhood Education*, 200–204.

>>>

APPLICATION EXERCISES

1. Examples of violence and peace: The class will share collections of examples.

Using a diagram of Bronfenbrenner's circles (see Figure 2-1), locate your examples within the systems where they may occur (microsystem, mesosystem, exosystem or macrosytem).

2. Continuum of experiences from peace to violence: Think about a child's day. Think about your day. Use the continuum diagram for your children and yourself.

3. Question: Consider a child's perspective in this environment.

4. Fill in an ecological system diagram with specific examples.

5. Look at today's newspaper: Headlines/ articles from a "typical" day in your community, elsewhere. Where do you find news reports of violence? Where do you find positive stories and reports of peaceful acts?

6. Violent phrases in common usage (make a list: consider war and sports analogies used daily.): "He was so rude, I could have killed him" was used by parents (according to preschool teacher).

7. Books for children with prosocial themes and models.

8. Watch TV for a day and evening. Do your own count of violent or peaceful actions.

9. Poll children about what they watch, alone or with adults (wrestling, extreme sports).

>>

THINKING ABOUT ALL CHILDREN

1. Do all children experience and understand violence in the same way?

2. What children may see at home:
   - Violent conflicts within families, battered spouses. Without blaming all families as dysfunctional (a point on which we need to examine our own biases), we must acknowledge this possibility in the lives of some of our children.

   - On the other hand: Adult arguments, fights, and squabbles may be frightening to children and may be seen as more serious that adults intend them to be.

   - Seemingly harmless school practices mentioned in this chapter have embedded violence toward children. Can you think of more?

Peer Conflict and
Children's Development

Part 2—Introduction: In Part 1, we examined children's conflicts in the context of peace and violence in their lives, and we took a first look at their conflicts with peers. In the next part, we will look more closely at how children experience conflicts with each other in early childhood settings. In Chapter 3, we will first explore ways to observe clearly what is happening in children's conflicts. Next, in Chapter 4, we will look at specific characteristics of children's conflicts to further guide our observations. Finally, in Chapters 5 and 6, we will encounter theoretical perspectives on children's conflicts. These theories will provide a framework for understanding what we observe.

3

Observing and Understanding Children's Peer Conflicts

A teacher comments:

"The two-year-olds are communicating with each other just by virtue of know-ing one other. What is amazing is that, when you watch a group of two-year-olds, they are doing what comes naturally, and that is the beginning for us in trying to understand them."

Chapter 3 Objectives: This chapter addresses methods of observing and listening to children in order to understand conflict episodes from children's perspectives. We will examine the shared understanding of language and meanings of conflict in the context of children's peer culture, and we will investigate cultural and individual differences in conflict issues and strategies. Examples and applications will also include conversations with children and with teachers.

Chapter Outline

A TEACHER ENCOUNTERS A CONFLICT

Kendra and Chad are together at the computer, each looking for information for their second grade unit on changes in the earth. There are a number of issues to negotiate: Who controls the mouse, what words to search for, what links to follow, and so forth. There is an ongoing conversation, which varies between loud exclamations, words of insistence and objection, and moments of quiet explanation. The computer has frequently been the center of conflicts this year. The teacher, Mr. Tomasi, busy with other activities in the room, looks over from time to time, wondering if the two children will be able to work peacefully or whether their small conflicts will begin to escalate beyond resolution.

OBSERVING AND LISTENING TO CHILDREN

As the teacher in the preceding scene, what would be your first reaction to this situation? How would you describe what is going on? Do you think that the children would describe the situation in the same way? In your own setting, how often do you see conflicts occur? How often do you notice prosocial and helping behaviors? Do you see acts of aggression, or do you observe acts of mediation or conciliation among children? To answer these questions, we need to observe and listen to children, learning *about* children *from* children.

Early Childhood teachers routinely observe young children to determine their growth and learning in all domains, and to plan environments and experiences for further learning and development. Children's social, emotional, cognitive, language, and physical development all require systematic approaches to observation for effective and appropriate assessment. Observing what children do and say in natural settings provides a context for authentic assessment. Children's conflict resolution is a developing capability that grows along with other areas of development. Conflicts are complex interpersonal interactions that require close, thorough, and objective observation in context. Authentic assessment stresses emerging development (Puckett & Black, 2000) and will guide our understanding of children's conflicts.

The goals for assessment of children's conflicts through observing and listening are to learn ways to help children develop conflict resolution ability, and to determine your role in intervening as conflicts occur. Two different types of situations provide opportunities for observing and assessing conflicts: *spontaneous observation* and *systematic observation*.

Spontaneous observation captures children's conflictual or peaceful interactions as they occur. Mr. Tomasi, the teacher in the preceding example, observes as two children argue over turns at the computer. He watches to see what happens, listens to the negotiations, and observes facial expressions, tones of voice, and gestures. This information will help Mr. Tomasi decide if the children will resolve the dispute agreeably on their own. He may also make notes about the conflict resolution skills that each child has demonstrated and about the computer-sharing system in his classroom for future decision-making.

Systematic observation will provide answers to concerns about children's conflicts and oppositional behaviors. Mr. Tomasi has noticed a number of arguments at the computer center and has decided to make a systematic observation of what is happening there. He wonders if certain children are having difficulty with others in the center, or if there is something in the environment of the center that is contributing to children's conflicts.

> **Important Note:** Throughout this chapter, we will consider ways to understand children's conflicts by taking time to observe what is happening as young children interact in natural settings. We can learn a great deal as we observe without intervening. However, any situation that appears to pose a threat to children's safety calls for immediate adult intervention.

Basic Tools for Observing and Listening

In this section, we will take a brief but not exhaustive look at a number of approaches to learning about children through observing and listening. You will find more details on these methods in most comprehensive texts on child development, observation and assessment, and teacher-as-researcher to apply to your study of children's conflicts.

Observing and listening are our primary ways of finding things out about children. In this chapter, we will focus on ways of finding out information directly from children:

- *Observing children* in natural settings, recording both words and actions in play and work times, structured leaning situations, transitions, and routine times.
- *Interviewing children*, asking them what they think and listening closely to what they say, both in informal and more structured settings.

In addition to these direct (or primary) sources of information about children's conflicts, there are indirect (or secondary) sources. We can learn about children by looking closely at their stories, journals, drawings, dictations, and other artifacts and documents. We can also learn a great deal by talking with families and other professionals. We will consider ways of working with families and others in later chapters of this book.

Observing

When and Where to Observe   Teachers can learn much about children by observing them in many different times and settings:

- The natural context of children's play offers rich opportunities for complex negotiation of rules and roles and interactions in pretend play roles. Routine times during the day are valuable occasions for observation.
- Structured times during the school day, such as story discussions, morning meetings, and group learning, provide opportunities for scaffolding (guiding children's thinking at a higher level), and assessing their potential. Teachers will gain a more complete understanding of children by observing them in different physical and social settings, and even at different times of the day.
- Multiple observations over time offer more complete and valid information than a single observation.

TEACHERS TALK ABOUT CHILDREN:

"There are so many ways that I observe children. Sometimes, I tell the children that I am so interested in their work that I want to watch and write down all that I see. If they are still curious about my reactions, I tell them that I want to remember all of the great things that they do so that I can tell their grownups. At other times, I feel like a spy for the CIA or FBI as I sneak around the room, avoid making eye contact, and quickly write down all that I observe. My goal then is for the children to be unaware of my actions so that I can get an observation that is true, in the sense that the children have not changed their actions due to my presence. A final way that I observe is to take pictures of children's actions and create captions with the children so that we can remember what was occurring."

TEACHERS TALK ABOUT CHILDREN:

"Playing on the floor: I have found as a Kindergarten teacher, spending countless hours on the floor of my classroom, teaching, playing, and communicating, that if I get down on the child's level, literally, I can find out a lot about his/her experiences. When I am standing in front of a child, the distance between his/her head and mine is great. (And I'm not even that tall!) It takes a lot more effort to make his/her voice travel up to mine and be heard ... If I sit on the floor in the middle of a room full of children, they will naturally gravitate toward me, interact with me, and involve me in whatever they are doing. Joining children in play is a great way to get information from them."

Observation Methods   The observation method that teachers use depends on what they want to know about children's conflicts and why they have decided to gather the information. The purposes and goals for observation lead to the choice of the method that will provide the most valuable information. You may choose *categorical (closed-ended)* recording methods or *narrative (open-ended)* methods:

- *Categorical,* or *closed-ended recording:* Specific information about clearly identified behaviors is recorded by means of *frequency counts, checklists, rating scales,* and *rubrics.* Questions for closed-ended recording may include: How many conflicts occur each day? How many conflicts occur in certain areas of your classroom, at certain times of the day, or between certain children? How often are children call-

Observing and carefully recording of children's interactions helps teachers understand their conflicts.

ing names, taking pencils, or pushing others? Which children seem to instigate conflicts? And how often do you observe children using reasoning and negotiation in a conflict?

Mr. Tomasi decides to use a checklist to record children's interactions at the computer. He will learn how often children argue at the computer during work time, how often they come to him to help them resolve the issue, and how often they manage to work things out on their own.

• *Narrative,* or *open-ended recording:* A complete and detailed narrative recording of what is happening may provide a more complete picture of the context of children's interactions. Examples of questions for open-ended recording include: What are children saying to each other, and which words are they using during conflicts? What do children do with their bodies and with objects as they interact? What are these fights about? What else is happening? What happened earlier?

Mr. Tomasi wonders what is happening in the computer center that makes it so peaceful one day and so full of conflict the next. For several days during the class's work time, he takes a few minutes to carefully record everything that he observes as children use the computer together.

The following are different types of observational strategies you may find helpful.

Narrative/Open-Ended Methods

• *Anecdotal Records:* A narrative account written in descriptive paragraphs, usually recorded as soon as possible after the event. The account may be brief but is factual, detailed, and accurate. Teachers may use note cards in a pocket, or a flip chart for notes to expand later.

• *Running Records:* A narrative account that records events as they occur over a continuous period of time. Running records are similar to anecdotal records in factual detail and accuracy, but they are made by an observer who is not part of the action. Note that a specific type of running record is used for reading assessment as children read aloud to an adult, but running records are used for other observations as well.

• *Specimen Records:* A narrative account, similar to the running record, but more detailed. A researcher observing in a classroom may use a specimen. Beatty (1998) suggests that the written record should be complete enough for someone unfamiliar with the setting to be able to visualize or recreate the scene.

Categorical/Closed-Ended Methods

• *Time Sampling:* A method of recording, by means of tallies or check marks, occurrences of specific behaviors that are observed during a predetermined time period. Recording takes place as the behaviors are occurring.

• *Event Sampling:* A method that records predetermined events and includes a brief narrative of conditions preceding and following the specified behavior. As the target behavior occurs, the observer may briefly record the antecedent event, the behavior, and the consequence of the behavior.

• *Checklists:* A method of recording a list of behaviors with check marks, during and after the occurrence of specified behaviors. There is no narrative detail, but information is provided on the presence, absence, or frequency of occurrences.

• *Rating Scales:* A method of recording based on a scale of traits or behaviors. The observation consists of check marks made before, during, and after the specified behavior occurs. Without narrative detail, the observer must decide on the rating at the time of the observation.

• *Rubrics:* A method of recording based on matching what is observed to descriptions of criteria for levels of performance or process. Rubrics are often used by children, as well as by teachers, to evaluate products such as written work.

OBSERVING CHILDREN'S PLAY

Piaget/Parten/Howe Play Scales offer examples of ways to observe children's play, providing information about the social context of children's interactions. As we will see in later chapters, this information is helpful in understanding children's conflicts. The play scales are in the Appendix.

Graphic Documentation and Media Techniques   Additional approaches provide valuable objective information to complement open- and closed-ended written records. These methods include audio and video recording, photographs, drawings or sketches, and classroom maps or diagrams. All graphic documentation needs to be labeled with the date, location, and details of the setting. (Teachers need to be aware of privacy and confidentiality issues, as well as any family concerns about pictures of their children.)

• *Audio and Video Recording:* Full and accurate details of events can be documented by these recordings. As with any observation method, taped information is limited to what is happening in the area where the recording takes place. The major advantage is that the tape can be played and replayed, giving adult observers an opportunity to look at different aspects of children's behaviors and notice details that may have been missed during an one-shot, on-the-spot observation. New technologies, such as digital cameras and small and powerful video cameras and microphones, are adding to our capacity to capture observations for later analysis.

• *Photographs:* Is a picture worth 1,000 words? A still photograph can capture a moment in detail, and frequent photographing may be easier for teachers than video recording. Photographs can also be used as a basis for conversation or interviews with children at a later time.

• *Drawings and Sketches:* Adding drawings to narrative accounts can be especially valuable in capturing the setting and sequence of events. How much clearer and easier it is to make a sketch of children's block construction than to write a lengthy description! A quick drawing of stick figures to show where children are standing allows the observer to focus more fully on the conversation.

• *Child Interaction Maps:* An observational recording strategy uses a diagram of the classroom instead of (or in addition to) a narrative recording in order to document where children interact and play, which children spend time together, and which activities they choose. This idea can be called a *classroom social map, social*

DOCUMENTATION IN REGGIO EMILIA

Drawings and photographs are important components of *documentation* in the municipal schools of Reggio Emilia, Italy, and in Reggio-inspired schools and centers in the U.S. An ongoing process of observation, interpretation, and documentation addresses the challenge of learning "how children know," rather than "what they know." Documentation is "learning made visible" to children, families, administrators, and community in Reggio Emilia (Reggio Children, 2001). For more on the Reggio Emilia documentation process, refer to *The Hundred Languages of Children*, by Edwards, Gandini, and Forman (1998), or visit the traveling display of *The Hundred Languages of Children: Narratives of the Possible.* The exhibit will visit Oberlin College in 2003. For the North American Tour Schedule information, visit http://ericeece.org/reggio/regtour.html.

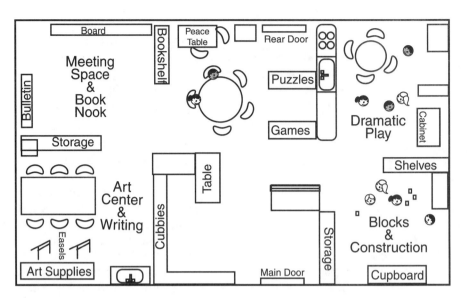

Figure 3–1
Classroom floor plan for social mapping.

Note: Throughout this book, there will be frequent references to Reggio Emilia. The municipal infant/toddler centers preschools in this Italian city have inspired many Early Childhood educators in the United States. The Reggio Emilia approach is not a curriculum or a theory or a set of materials not easily explained. It encompasses a way of thinking, feeling, and acting in settings with young children, which values the environment; collaboration with children, families, and teachers; the competence of children; the humility of adults; and an appreciation of time, space, light, and community. Please read *The Hundred Languages* or *Making Learning Visible: Children as Individual and Group Learners*, by Reggio Children and Project Zero, 2001, to learn more.

activity map, or *classroom interaction map* (see Figure 3–1). Draw a map of your classroom and mark the locations of children's interactions. By taking the time to look closely and by documenting observations on a map, teachers will gain information about the social context of children's interactions. You may be surprised to see where children spend their time and who they spend it with.

Note: A *sociometric analysis* may be displayed with a formal *social map.* In interviews, children are asked to identify best friends, peers they consider friends, or peers they would choose or not choose to play or work with, and a graphic of group preference is created. In our classroom mapping strategy, the graphic is based on observation instead of questioning.

The mapping in the following example helped the teacher understand more about the frequent conflicts between two children in a preschool class of fours and fives.

A Classroom Mapping Example: Phillip was generally considered by adults to be the instigator of the conflicts. The classroom map showed that Phillip, a fairly tall four-year-old, spent most of his time in sociodramatic play with the older children in the dramatic play area. Nick, also four, mostly played in the construction area with the younger children. Looking at the map, the teacher wondered, "Why would Phillip go out of his way, disrupting his own dramatic play with the older children, to begin a conflict with Nick?" Taking this broader view, the teacher began to see what was happening. Nick would come past Phillip's play area and do something that only Phillip would notice, like take a toy or kick the table. Phillip would not react instantly, but later would pass by the other part of the room and knock down Nick's block construction. Phillip's act of retaliation, provoking a loud response from Nick, was always noticed by the teachers, and Phillip was seen as the aggressor.

TEACHERS TALK ABOUT OBSERVING:

"For observing, I mainly use anecdotal records and watch children interact with other children. I have used video cameras to record special events and allow the children to watch themselves during snack time. I use tape recorders to record retelling of stories and pretend phone calls. I don't think I observe differently based on gender. I do use different techniques if the group is small or large. If it is a large group, I don't generally write down the incident as it happens. Usually things happen faster than I am able to write, and I end up missing too much. So I opt for a tape recorder or just watching and then writing down key items after observing."

Interviewing

Reasons for Interviewing Children About Social Understanding The most obvious reason to interview children is that we want to know about them and about what they think. Teachers and researchers often base their knowledge of children on information gathered from other adults, from test scores, and from observations of children's behavior. Teachers who respect children as being capable, self-aware, and reasonably verbal may decide that the most straightforward way to find you what children think is to ask them. More specifically, interviews with children may have two different purposes and outcomes. The role of the adult interviewer varies in these two situations:

1. One purpose is to understand children's perspectives by listening to, and hearing without judgment, their interpretation of the world. In this approach, the adult assumes the role of receptive listener and learner. "Listening is a suspension of certainties" and an opportunity "to open a space for something" (notes from Elena Giacopini in Reggio Emilia, Italy, May 2001).
2. A second purpose is to provide for scaffolding children's learning. The interview becomes a dialog in which children and adults move together to a new place

of understanding. "Listening is at the heart of the teacher's role" (Filippini, in Edwards, 1998, p. 181). In this Vygotskian framework, the image is as follows: "We must be able to catch the ball that the children throw us, and toss it back to them in a way that makes the children want to continue the game with us, developing, perhaps, other games as we go along" (Filippini, in Edwards, 1998, p. 181).

Interviewing Children: What, When, and How to Interview   Interviews with children may be informal and spontaneous, as conversations would be. (Circulating around the room as children are writing and illustrating, the teacher asks Sarah about her story.) Interviews may be planned with a specific focus in mind and at a predetermined time. (Sarah and her teacher meet to discuss her story, and may consider how to edit it or whether to include this one in her portfolio.)

Teachers may take advantage of learning about an occurrence as it happens: "Let's sit down and talk about what is happening with the pencils at your table." Teachers may also ask about feelings, ideas or prior occurrences: "What do you think it means to be fair"? "How do you feel when your friends call you names?" "Let's talk about the field trip we went on last week." Using a process known as *ethnographic interviewing*, teachers can begin to learn about children's ways of seeing the world (Spradley, 1986): "What do you do when you can't agree about the rules of the game at recess?"

Another way to approach an interview with children is through their drawings. For instance, a teacher may listen as a child talks about a picture she is drawing and learn about the child's fears about the dark, or her happiness about visiting her grandmother. In Samuel's story in Chapter 1, a picture led to a conversation about the violence this young boy sees in his future. For his books *The Moral Life of Children* (1986) and *The Spiritual Life of Children* (1990), Robert Coles opened windows into children's ways of knowing, or how they learn and understand the world, as he conducted extensive interviews around children's drawings.

Teachers may interview children in small groups, as well as individually. In a group, teachers may mirror the focus group interview approach. Opening the conversation to all ("What do you think about ...") may provide a safety net for children who are reluctant to speak one-on-one, and can stimulate ideas that might not come out in an individual interview. Morning meetings may be effective opportunities for a brief group interview, if the class is not large.

What do children say when you ask them? There are key points for adults to remember when interviewing children. To learn what children truly think, adults will need to redefine their accustomed roles and status. In the interview, adults will need to establish the child informant as more knowledgeable, with "higher status" in the conversation, and establish the adult as the information-seeker, in a "lower status." Children assume that adults know the answers to questions and may try to offer the "right answer" that an adult is expecting. The adult interviewer must be explicit that they sincerely want to know what children think, will not judge their responses, and do not already know the answers to the questions (Tamivaara, J., & Enright, D. S., 1986).

There is clear evidence that children are aware of their own actions, motivations, and responses to events and are able to recall past experiences.

Example: In an interview about conflicts, Tomas (age five) watched a videotape of play time that occurred two weeks prior and demonstrated his memory of recent events.

A frequent block builder, he watched himself building with blocks and described in detail what he had been making, adding, "I didn't do this today. I did this one other day."

Example: Observed as they sat at a table in the writing center, the following exchange between two children offers evidence of their intentional awareness of their conflicts and the ability to recall and discuss them: Daniel (age five) asked his friend Todd (age four), "Do you remember that fight we had about GI Joes and I wanted all of them?"

WHEN CHILDREN SPEAK: VOICES FROM REGGIO EMILIA

What happens when adults ask children what they think about peace, violence, conflicts, and fighting, and truly listen to what they have to say? In the open and psychologically safe environment of the Diana School, in Reggio Emilia, children share their thoughts on the rights of children:

"Children have the right to have friends, otherwise they do not grow up too well."

"Children have the right to live in peace."

"If a child does not know, she has the right to make mistakes. It works because after she sees the problem and the mistakes she made, then she knows."

"To live in peace means to be well, to live together, to live with things that interest us, to have friends, to think about flying, to dream."

"We've got to have rights, or else we'll be sad."

(Gandini, 1998, p. 161).

Guidelines for Recording Observations and Interviews

- The written record of children's behaviors is objective and describes observed actions, not judgments or interpretation.
- Make a separate place to note interpretations and impressions. These notes can be valuable in your analysis but must be kept separate from your objective observation record.
- The recording is written in sequence, in the order that the events take place.
- The recording is complete and objective, with everything that happens included.
- Words and conversation are recorded verbatim, not paraphrased or summarized.
- Non-verbal actions are described objectively and in detail.
- Observers and interviewers are unobtrusive as they write and/or tape.
- Record the date, location, and time of day.

- Be ready to be surprised and open to the unexpected. This mindset is the basis for objective recording of what you see and hear.
- A final piece of advice: As an observer of children, realize the limitations of what you have observed and recorded. Keep in mind this question: "Do I really know what is happening here?" Words to remind us come from a teacher in Reggio Emilia: "I have captured not what happened here, but what I was able to capture" (Giacopini, Elena, May 2001).

Specifics for Observing Children's Conflicts

The preceding guidelines and suggestions are particularly applicable to the observation of children's conflicts. The following suggestions have special relevance because of the complexity of children's conflicts, the importance of the context of conflicts, and the absolute need for objectivity on the part of the observer:

- **Recording:** Include in the observation record detailed information about the following:
- **The temporal context:** The sequence of events, the duration of the episode, even the time of day or day of the week.
- **The social context:** Children who are engaged in the episode, those who are nearby, adults who are present, and verbal and non-verbal behaviors of all participants.
- **The physical context:** Activities children are engaged in, and the location.
- **The outer boundaries of the episode:** Looking at children's conflicts beyond the immediate action, to the preceding events.

Observational Recording Tools for Conflicts

Checklists, rating scales, and rubrics can be useful in observing children's conflicts. In the next chapter, we will find structural features and characteristics of children's conflicts that can be used for constructing for your own tools, such as checklists and rating scales. Time samples may be used to find out how many conflicts are actually occurring in your setting. Event sampling may clarify the instigating issues and the outcomes or endings of conflicts. A checklist may help to document the types of strategies children use during conflicts. Examples of observation forms and resources for observation tools are included in the Appendix.

Observing the Classroom Environment as a Context for Conflicts

Looking beyond the observation of specific incidents in the classroom, teachers may assess the classroom community as a context for both conflictual and peaceful interactions. (In Chapter 7, we will address ways to create and support creating a caring community, with more on evaluating the physical and social environment.)

Things to look for:

1. Do children listen to each other, and is there evidence of receptive listening?
2. How do children enter a group? Are they welcomed or excluded? Do children know how to join a group and enter the ongoing activity effectively?
3. How many children are in play groups, and what is the group make-up (boys, girls, children of color, or children with varying abilities)?
4. How long is interaction maintained in pairs or groups of children?
5. Is there evidence of shared language about expected behaviors and rules?
6. What general conflict management strategies do you observe? Do children seek adult intervention, tattle, or work on their own to resolve conflicts? Do conflicts seem to escalate or deescalate?
7. Take a step back to notice the sounds of the classroom. Is there a comfortable noise level (busy, but not too loud)? Is there a background of calm voices and laughter? A balanced exchange of voices in conversation? Or are there loud voices, objections, and insistence?

After Observing Children's Conflicts, Then What?

Teachers use information from their observations of children's conflicts to understand and guide children in developing conflict resolution ability. First, they analyze the information from observations, and then they plan for children's further learning and development.

Analyzing

The first step is a descriptive analysis of the observed conflict. Identify issues, strategies, outcomes, and the context of the conflict, such as children's interactions before and after play, the physical setting, the time of day, and so forth. Next, look for any patterns, processes, and relationships that emerge as you look carefully at what is happening. How does your information help answer the questions that prompted your observation? Perhaps what you have noticed raises new questions?

In your role as teacher, you bring your own prior knowledge of the children you are observing. This knowledge, used non-judgmentally, can be valuable in understanding conflicts. What you know about each child's affective and communicative style, daily needs and ongoing concerns, individual differences, and cultural factors can provide a richer context for children's interactions. (Did a new baby just arrive at home? Is the child recovering from an illness?) Knowing children well, however, may lead to preconceived ideas about the role they play in conflicts. Teachers must avoid making assumptions about children. Be especially aware of "typecasting" in the classroom, as in the example of Phillip and Nick.

Planning

Teachers use observational information to plan for individual children, consider changes in the environment, and design and implement group strategies, including curriculum ideas, activities, and materials. For example, teachers may notice that children are unable to find the words they need to work through a conflict. They may provide and model words that the whole class can use to defuse conflicts, and create opportunities for all children to practice using those words. If teachers notice that children are not attempting to hear another's point of view, they may engage children in activities, games, and stories to develop perspective-taking. These everyday classroom strategies will be a major focus of Part 3 of this book.

Red Flags: When What You Are Seeing Is Beyond the Norm

Most of children's conflicts with peers in an early childhood classroom are normal interactions and part of their developing social competence. In some cases, however, what teachers observe may go beyond what is normal. Signs of possible problems, or "red flags," may be frequent, unprovoked aggression; participation in chronic, destructive conflicts; or excessive anger. There are many alternative explanations and possible causes for these behaviors, including physical conditions such as Tourette's and Asperger's Syndromes, ADHD, and others (Kostelnick, et al., 2000; Novick, 1998). Sadly, behaviors that contribute to children's conflicts are among signs for child abuse and neglect (Crosser-Tower, 2002). Children's interactions with peers may be difficult if there are problems with sensory integration (Bakly, 2001). Watch for other signs of sensory integration difficulties, and work with an occupational therapist to understand what you observe.

Other "*persistent* behavioral problems" include actions that hurt one's self or others, keep children from having friends, and cause damage to property. These signs call for close observation, careful and non-judgmental listening, precise documentation, and very likely further team-based assessment and referral (ACT, 2002).

Teachers must not make assumptions or attempt to diagnose or identify causes of behaviors beyond the norm, but should collaborate responsibly with the family to make referrals to other professionals as appropriate. A good source for decision-making in difficult situations is the NAEYC Code of Ethical Conduct for Early Childhood Professionals.

Seeing the Positive

Children's antisocial behaviors are not more natural than their prosocial behaviors, according to Alfie Kohn (1991). Adults are drawn to disruptive behaviors and problems between children. Many instances of children's caring, cooperation, support, empathy, and peer mediation go unnoticed each day. When teachers take time to look for these prosocial occurrences, they are often surprised and gratified. Labeling acts of kindness and making sure that children are aware of the kindnesses around them offer an important balance to the many times that children's attention is drawn to antisocial behaviors and consequences.

TEACHERS TALK:

"While preparing to observe children in conflict and their way of resolving conflicts, I was prepared to witness a plethora of conflicts, and I assumed that there would be an excessive amount of teacher involvement in the resolution to those conflicts. I was extremely surprised by two factors involving conflicts at my center. 1) There were not that many conflicts that occurred during the times that I observed, which are the most hectic times of the day, morning drop-off time and playground time. 2) The conflicts that did occur, children were able to resolve themselves, or one child within the conflict opted not to continue the conflict."

TEACHERS TALK:

"I often hear other children in my third grade class being great mediators. For example, last week I overheard a few students in line discussing another girl who was bothering them in Music. One student, Abby, told Rachel to just ignore the rude things that this girl Caron was saying to her in Music. Abby said, 'Hey, sometimes Caron is mean to me and I just ignore her. I just turn to the person on the other side of me and talk to her.' I watched Rachel's reaction, and she liked what Abby said and thanked her."

Children's Peer Culture: Children's Language and Meanings in Conflicts

Interviewer:	I'd like to know how people solve their problems when they have arguments. What if someone wanted to play and you didn't want to play with them?
April (age four):	I would tell them I wanted to play with Natalie and Mary Peyton and they should change their minds and they probably would.

What Is the Children's Peer Culture?

Culture can be defined as the shared understanding of phenomena, shared experiences, shared language, and meaning among members of a group. Although the term is often used in relation to aspects of ethnicity, color, or national origin, the concept of culture is much broader. Each of us is a member of a number of different cultures that, together, shape our identity and frame our understanding of the world.

When children begin school, they expand from membership in a family culture to a school or center culture. They first learn to "do school" according to the rules, routines, and expectations that are determined, for the most part, by adults. Children's own peer culture exists within and apart from this school culture. As members of their own peer culture, children share commonly understood rules, rituals, humor, expectations, ways of resolving conflicts, and ways to define and demonstrate membership/hierarchy/status in the culture. Using a similar term, Fine (1985) describes an "idioculture" among children that "consists of a system of knowledge, beliefs, behaviors, and customs shared by members of an interacting group," which serves to "regulate group behavior and typically provide for a sense of cohesion" (p. 111).

Within this peer culture, children create meanings that are defined by the culture and, in turn, help to define the culture. "Culture is as much a forum for negotiating and renegotiating meaning and for explicating action as it is a set of rules or specifications for action … It is the forum aspect of culture that gives its participants a role in constantly making and remaking the culture—an *active* role as participants, rather than as performing spectators…. It follows from this view of culture as a forum that induction into the culture through education, if it is to prepare the young for life as lived, should also partake of the spirit of a forum, of negotiation, of the recreating of meaning" (Bruner, 1986, p. 23).

"All children have membership in at least two cultures: one of their own making and the one created by adults" (Tamivaara, J., & Enright, D. S., 1986, p. 233). Linguistic minority children have four cultures or worlds to navigate: The peer and adult cultures of their first language and the peer and adult cultures of their second language.

In their peer culture, children share commonly understood rules.

After becoming aware that there is a peer culture among children, adults may progress through several steps in gaining a greater understanding of children, in spite of their "outsider" status as adults. We move from the assumption that we understand all of children's meanings to realizing that we do not fully understand. And finally, we "crack the code" in order to learn important things about children and gain insight into their world. Adult interpretations of what children say to each other in their everyday peaceful and conflictual interactions are often not what children actually mean.

TEACHERS TALK:

Aware of the shared experience that children bring and build on in their play, a third-grade teacher points out that children have shared experiences based on television programs that they watch: "On occasion, the children will role-play a popular cartoon titled Powerpuff Girls. When they play this game, I usually don't understand what is happening since I am not familiar with the show. I am planning to see an episode to help me understand what they are saying during this role-play activity."

Example   Watching a videotape with children provided an opportunity to listen to children as they explained their conflicts. As she viewed an episode of cooperative pretend play, Meg described their reasoning as three girls decided which color of waffle blocks would be their "beds."

Meg (age five):	There's the red waffle blocks.
Interviewer:	What was your plan when you were doing that?
Meg:	Um. Playing with waffle blocks. (listens and watches, giggles) That was me talking [on the tape].
Interviewer:	So can you tell me what's going on there? I see waffle blocks, and you are dressed up and there are some pillows.
Meg:	I had to clean off the blocks with my dress from people walking on it. (pause) Those were the beds. (pause) Heidi was the guest, so she was in the middle and we figured that Kendra was blue 'cause my favorite color was red'. (narrates action) And then we went to sleep, and then it was time to wake up, and then we went back to sleep.

Observing in the Peer Culture and in Children's Spaces

How can adults observe children within their peer culture and look through that window into the very special world of the child? As adults, we cannot be full members in that peer culture. Graue and Walsh (1998) caution that adults may hope to "enter the world of the child" and study children in the context of the peer culture, but by our very entry, the context is changed. However, we can learn from children as unobtrusive observers or as invited guests.

As unobstrusive observers, adults can be near enough to children to hear and see them, but without making their presence part of the context. Being busy with a routine adult-world task will help teachers blend into the background. In the same way, a tape recorder may be ignored by children. Mrs. H. describes this unobtrusive observation as being "invisible."

TEACHERS TALK ABOUT BEING INVISIBLE:

"This Halloween, I decided I would come to school dressed as the Invisible Teacher. I imagined that when I didn't show up for school on the 31st, I would just smile and tell the administrator, 'Oh, I was there. I was just invisible!' The children would love it. Maybe some day, but not this year. As I put my dreams on hold for yet another year, I have a great thought. I don't need to be invisible, I think. I just need to be five again. I need to get back to reality and see and hear children as they see and hear themselves. This Halloween, Mrs. H. is just another kid in the art class."

As an invited guest, adults may have a closer look at children in their peer culture. Sitting near the children and watching with interest as they play, an adult may be brought into the action as a child spontaneously offers a prop or includes the adult in the "cast." In this way, the adult enters the play on the child's terms, conferring authority, or host status, to the child. This response is described as "reactive entry" into play, responding to children's conversations and invitations to play rather than initiating the interaction (Corsaro, 1985).

Child: "Here's your ticket. The bus is about to leave."

The role of adults within children's peer interactions is critical. If the adult retains an aura of authority, the sense of the children's peer culture gives way to an adult-defined school culture. Minimizing the adult role, stressing the host status of the child, is described by Nancy Mandell (1986) as acting as "least adult." Teachers and researchers sit on the floor with children, follow the children's rules of the game, yield control of the action, and assume a non-directive stance. These approaches also require a conscious effort to refrain from engaging in "teacher talk" with children (using questions and probes to encourage learning) but instead to hold "normal" conversations. In short, adults become followers and not leaders. Trust is another important aspect of this type of interaction.

A researcher recounts evidence of gaining a "least adult" status. On the playground, Latisha (age five) shares a secret. She confides that she is hiding a puppy pull toy that was now a "magic key," something that "the teachers don't know about."

Within an adult-dominated world, children find and create their own "spaces." Knowing where these spaces are offers valuable insight to adults who hope to encounter children's peer culture. In these "backstage" spaces, which are "owned" by children, the peer culture thrives away from the direction and control of adults. With its looser boundaries, the playground is often a space where children can define their world. In transition times during the school day, the rules of the peer culture may supplant those of the adult world. In the following example, children have defined the back seat of the car as their "space."

TEACHERS TALK ABOUT CHILDREN:

"One way that I have been able to listen to and see children is when we ride in the car. When I was a nanny, I learned a lot about how they felt about brothers, sisters, and friends. They were not paying attention to me, so they were talking openly and honestly. I now use this on my own children. I listen to them talk in the car. Most of what I hear from my four-year-old are things that I say to her, like, 'Jordan, don't talk back. That is not nice.' I learn about school and who did what at school."

Children's Language and Meanings

Both children and adults use language to make meaning, and their language is based on their worldviews and experiences. For this reason, adult and child language and meaning are not necessarily the same. A challenge for adults is to translate what they hear from children without imposing an adult-centered interpretation. This is a key point in observations, interviews, and everyday inter-actions with children. Adults need to do three things: abandon our assumptions that we understand, listen fully to what children are saying, and ask them non-judgmentally what they mean. Here are two examples:

A pre-kindergarten teacher listens to Anna and wonders about her meaning, beyond the literal interpretation: "Jaime tells me: 'Anna won't be my friend.' What I think she is really saying is, 'Why can't we play the way I want to play?' and 'Why does Anna leave me alone?'"

Tomas provides his own unanticipated interpretation:

Tomas: He broke something I didn't want him to.

Interviewer: What did you do?

Tomas: I called him corny 'cause it means you're so mean.

A teacher of threes tells us:

Children's language is a complicated thing. Children use language for communicating, self-expression, experimentation, and to gain attention from others. Adults take chil-dren's language too seriously because they believe that language is solely a means of communication and do not value how children express themselves creatively with lan-guage or how they need to experiment with sounds and words as they are mastering their language. An example of this is one that I observe everyday in my classroom. My three-year-old children are hearing many words for the first time, especially words that are taboo and fun for them to say because of the reaction that they cause. Foul language, words such as 'stupid,' and nonsense words are so fun to experiment with when you are three. Maybe they tickle the tongue, maybe it's all about reaction, and maybe it just sounds interesting to their ears. I think it's safe to assume that adults do not know why, and that the reasons switch constantly. Young children need ample space and time in which to experiment and play with language so that they can fully master the language.

Children's Intentions in Conflict

Directly related to the idea of children's language and meaning is the question of children's intentions in conflicts. The purpose of a conflict may be to resolve an issue or settle a dispute. On the other hand, the purpose may be to engage in dispute. In other words, the purpose of an argument may be the process of arguing itself. In an outcome-oriented approach, the purpose of a conflict or argument may be to decide an issue and will have a beginning and definite ending. In a process-oriented approach, the primary object may not be to solve a problem, but to see who is the best arguer (Goodwin, 1990).

As you begin to intervene in a conflict, do you see a bewildered look in children's eyes, as if to say, "What is she talking about? We weren't fighting!" In a common scenario at home, an adult family member hears children's voices and calls to them, "Stop squabbling in there!" The answer floats back, "We're not squabbling! We're playing!" Children engage in verbal rough-and-tumble play, as they do in physical play. We will explore more about this *sociolinguistic* understanding in a later chapter.

Children who are developing conflict resolution ability begin to understand the intentions and reasons for their own actions, and for the actions of others. In the contrasting examples that follow, we see that children develop and demonstrate this understanding at different times.

A pre-kindergarten teacher says:

Sometimes children do something accidentally (a bump or shove in line causes a chain reaction), and children may not be able to distinguish the accidental from the intentional.

A teacher of young threes in a multiage program reports that she asks children:

Did you take that truck because you really wanted to play with it, or did you want to do something mean?

This teacher says that the children know the difference and are willing to tell her their intentions. An important next step in this situation is to consider children's responses to intentional or accidental behaviors. We will address these next steps fully in later chapters.

OPPORTUNITY FOR OBSERVATION AND DISCUSSION:

What are the "rules" in the peer culture of your class? Does it make a difference to children whether an offending action was "on purpose" or "by accident"?

Another aspect of understanding children's intentions is their definition of an acceptable and desirable outcome. Children's resolution of conflict is based on their notion of fairness, equity, or need, and it may not be the same as that of adults. These differences suggest that children's disputes are varied and different from adult expectations. Adults should be aware of *children's intentions* in a conflict situation. Understanding and recognizing children's intentions, and their definitions of acceptable conflict resolution, is an important role for adults.

Cultural and Individual Differences in Children's Conflicts

Early childhood professionals plan teaching and learning in ways that are developmentally, individually, and culturally appropriate in all areas. Understanding and supporting children in their conflict resolution requires the same approach.

Cultural Norms

We have noted that adults and children are members of a number of different cultures. In addition to the peer culture and classroom culture, children are members of a family culture and cultures defined by language, ethnicity, and national origin. Response to conflicts may vary according to the norms of each of these cultures.

Cultural differences may be a cause of conflict as children approach day-to-day situations with different understandings. Conflicts may result from issues regarding cultural interpretations of ownership, space, humor, or turn-taking. For example, individual ownership is an understood value in most Euro-American families, while community property is the norm in other cultures. This difference can lead to cross-cultural conflict over possessions that is quite different from a monocultural conflict. This difference can also be a result of family size and even economic status, which determine whether individual ownership or communal sharing is the norm within the family.

Euro-American dispute: "Give it back. It's mine!" "No, it's mine!"
Cross-cultural dispute: "Give it back. It's mine!" "It doesn't belong to anybody."

Cultural differences are evident in how children manage conflicts, such as in language style, body communication, assertiveness, and degree of persistence. An important question for teachers is, "Are you observing individual cultural diversity in children's conflicts?" As early Childhood professionals, we need to be aware of our own cultural and individual "lenses" and our own approach to conflict management as we observe and interpret what children say and do in their conflicts. For instance, as we guide children in managing their conflict interactions, do we make the assumption that "standing up for yourself" is a universal objective? Deference to others and conciliation may be the preferred value in a child's family culture.

TEACHERS TALK ABOUT CROSS-CULTURAL UNDERSTANDING:

"This year, I have a little boy from Turkey who didn't know any English. We obviously had a language barrier, but we also had some cultural differences we had to figure out together. In his culture, children do not tell an adult 'no.' Since 'yes' and 'no' were two of the first words I thought would be helpful in our survival in the classroom together, I thought I was doing a good thing by teaching them to him. This created a little problem when he went home from school declaring 'No, no, no!' to everything his mother asked of him. He also was taught that to show respect, you don't make eye contact. For me, not making eye contact is a sign of disrespect."

TEACHERS TALK ABOUT FAMILY NORMS:

"Shelby was one of my favorite children in kindergarten that year, but whenever there was a disagreement, I could hear Shelby's loud voice insisting, arguing, explaining to others. As a naturally soft-spoken person myself, I first thought that he must be very angry. I began to notice that he was even loud when there was no argument. I finally asked his mother if perhaps he had a hearing problem. She laughed and said no, that every teacher eventually asked her that, but it was just that, at home, in a very large family, everyone just yelled all the time throughout the house in order to be heard. For Shelby, using a loud voice was a family norm."

In later chapters, we will explore ways to support children's conflict resolution in a caring classroom community that is diverse and inclusive. At this point, it is important to note that as we learn more about culturally defined norms and behaviors, overgeneralization of attributes to an entire group is also inappropriate. There are many valuable resources on cross-cultural understanding that should be part of every early childhood professional's library. You will find some suggestions at the end of the chapter.

Special Needs and Abilities

Conflicts occur in inclusive classrooms, among children of all abilities, with and without special needs. Learning to resolve conflict with others is valuable for all children. Opportunities for learning perspective-taking and empathy are even greater in a diverse and inclusive early childhood setting. Children's natural empathy, caring, and motivation as social beings work to offset difficulties with communication and social competence. Factors that contribute to conflict among young children are lack of effective communication and inappropriate responses to social cues. For teachers, the task is "knowing all children." This means observing what is happening in both peaceful and conflictual interactions and analyzing and planning for teaching and learning. Part of the "knowing" is being aware of the abilities as well as the disabilities of children with a wide variety of special needs. Realizing that each child is unique, a teacher will see that a child with

Down's Syndrome is apt to respond differently and need different social support than, for instance, a child identified with Asperger's.

However, children with special needs, disabilities, and developmental delays need to experience the same play processes as children who are typically developing. Outcomes "associated with social competence apply equally to children with and without special needs" (Guralnick, 1994, p. 45). Assessing social competence is important both for children with already identified needs and for children with needs not yet identified. Social competence issues may be the first signs to teachers that there may be a problem with children's development. Abilities that define peer-related social competence are peer group entry, conflict resolution, and maintaining play (Guralnick, 1994, p. 48).

TEACHERS TALK:

"If a teacher has a child with cerebral palsy in the classroom, and has never dealt with a child with that condition or any other type of special need before, that teacher may be distraught and afraid at the thought of doing something that is not 'right.' By having these feelings, there is a high probability that the child will not be listened to or will not be seen as other children are. Unfortunately, the teacher may shy away from interactions with this child. I think that it is extremely important for us, as teachers, to realize our biases and our misconceptions about special needs, race, religion, nationality, etc. If we can realize these things, we are one step closer to being able to listen and see children for who they are. We will be one step closer to giving every child a fair shake."

>>>

SUMMARY

The primary focus of this chapter is learning about children from children, and respecting them as gatekeepers to their world and their peer culture. Early Childhood professionals have a wide variety of tools and strategies for observing and listening to help understand the social world of children. Truly seeing children and hearing them, however, requires an openness and a feeling of humility. Sergio Spaggiari, Director of the Educational Department in Reggio Emilia, describes "the potential of children and the humility of adults" and quotes Reggio schools founder Loris Malaguzzi: "You have to know that you *don't* know ..." With this awareness, teachers will be ready to learn about children and, for the purposes of this text, about how children manage and resolve their conflicts with their peers in early childhood classrooms.

In this chapter, we have considered ways of observing and listening to children, specifics for observing children's conflicts, children's conflicts in the context of their peer culture, and cultural and individual differences in children's conflicts. In the next chapter, we will explore characteristics of children's conflicts that will give us a specific focus for our observation. We will know what questions to ask as we observe and listen, and we will have a better understanding of what we are seeing and hearing.

>>

SUPPLEMENTARY MATERIALS FOR CHAPTER 3

Research Focus: Teacher as Researcher

Observation is often an important way to collect data for teacher research in your own setting. You may ask a teacher research question about the physical nature of the interaction among children in your group. Using what you know about "aggression versus rough-and-tumble play," you could observe children's play to answer your question.

As mentioned in earlier chapters, aggressive actions are themselves identified as either *hostile*, not related to a conflict issue but intended to be harmful, or *instrumental*, used as a means of achieving the goal of the conflict. The difference between aggression and rough-and-tumble play can be the basis for an assessment tool.

AGGRESSION PLAY VERSUS ROUGH-AND-TUMBLE PLAY

Aggression	Rough-and-tumble
Issue-related, goal-oriented	No issue; process of playing is the focus
Serious affect	Laugh, smile
Usually 2 children	Any number
Children part after	Children remain together
Intent to hurt	Physical mock fighting—no intent to hurt
Taut, stressed bodies	Relaxed bodies
Displeasure	Fun
Non-friend peers	Friends

>>

APPLICATION EXERCISES

1. Are the children really "always fighting?" Explore the validity of your impressions of the children's behaviors. First, define observable evidence of prosocial behaviors and do a time-sample observation. You may also try an anecdotal record, a running record, or a specimen record in order to see what evidence of prosocial behavior may emerge.

2. A Brief Perspective on Seeing Conflicts Through the Eyes of Children: Use these guiding questions to further your under-

standing of children's conflicts *as children se them.*

- How will you plan to observe children in conflict (listening and seeing) in your own classroom?

- Is there a code or key to unlock the language children share in their peer culture?

- What have you learned about the children's conflicts? Their purposes and goals and the intentionality of their strategies?

- What would you say to another teacher or adult who would like to understand the children's conflicts from being with, observing, and hearing children?

- What do you know about friendship, acceptance, and rejection relationships in your class?

- Have you asked children to tell you about their understanding of conflicts when they are not in the middle of one?

- We know that conflicts may happen at any time or in any place. When do they begin? How can you tell?

- Is there something different in the ways you use to observe siblings, boys/girls, or different age groups?

>>>

THINKING ABOUT ALL CHILDREN

Not all evaluation methods are effective with all children. Alternative assessments may be needed for children with developmental delays or disabilities, or even for those whose home language is not the same as the adult evaluator (Losardo & Notari-Syverson, 2001). Remember to use more than one observation method and to look for evidence of bias or stereotypes in any published assessment materials that you use.

Questions for Reflection:

1. Do you consider children's individual differences in culture, language, and ability as you observe and record their conflicts?

2. Do you have any ideas about family, community, culture, and communication styles of the children in your setting?

4

Characteristics of Young Children's Peer Conflicts

"If you don't do what I want, I won't be your friend."
"Because you're friends, you figure it out."

Chapter 4 Objectives: This chapter guides us through the "anatomy of a conflict": the structural characteristics (issues, strategies, and outcomes) of what happens in children's conflicts. Further characteristics of children's conflicts are the physical and social contexts: the who, where, and when. While there is no such thing as "the typical conflict," there are patterns to guide our understanding and support children's positive resolutions in their conflicts. For instance, children playing together before a conflict, and those who use reason and negotiation during the conflict, are more likely to arrive at a positive resolution.

Chapter Outline

A CONFLICT IN DRAMATIC PLAY

In pretend play, a group of children have arranged chairs to make a bus. Rosa (age three-and-a-half) tries to take the chair that Beth (also three-and-a-half) is sitting in.

Rosa: No, this is my chair. I was using it.

Beth: No, it's my turn. You were out of it.

They pull the chair back and forth between them, repeating their words.

Rosa tries to pull Beth's fingers off.

Beth: Stop!

Rosa gets the chair and sits on it.

Beth calls to the teacher.

Teacher: Let's see if there is a chair that is not being used.

April (age four) brings a chair to Beth.

WHAT HAPPENS IN CHILDREN'S CONFLICTS?

Conflict Structure and Context

In this chapter, we will build on the observation and listening tools we discussed in the last chapter to better understand children's conflicts. We will look closely at the structure and context of children's conflicts: what happens in conflicts, when and where conflicts occur, and who is taking part in the conflict. We will begin to see children's conflicts as *structured interactions* with a beginning, middle, and end. In this chapter, we will examine these pieces of the structure.

In addition, it is important to know that conflicts occur in the physical and social context of children's everyday lives.

- The *social context* includes other people in the setting, both children and adults, and the roles, behaviors, and interactions that occur among people in the setting.
- The *physical context* describes the place and objects where interactions take place.

An important implication here is that too often, adults see only part of the picture when they come upon a conflict in progress. To understand conflict, we must see the whole context.

We have defined conflicts in terms of mutual disagreement. Conflicts occur "when child A does something to which child B objects, and child A persists" (Hay, 1984, p. 2). When children are in conflict over an issue that needs a resolution, we see a definite sequence in the structure of conflict: a *beginning*, a *middle*, and an *end* (Arcaro-McPhee et al., 2002; Eisenberg & Garvey, 1981; Hay, 1984; Killen & Turiel, 1991; Malloy & McMurray, 1996; Shantz, 1987). As we shall see, there are other types of arguments, such as verbal rough-and-tumble play, that follow a different pattern because they are not based on an issue to resolve. Here we will focus on conflicts in which children are attempting to resolve an issue.

Fully Developed and Defused Conflicts

Observing children closely, we may see situations that are about to become conflicts but do not (see Figure 4–1). Instead of a fully developed three-turn conflict, a disagreement between children may end after only two turns. These two-turn oppositional interactions have been described as "compliance exchange" or "affiliative interaction," in contrast to conflicts of three or more turns (Gillespie & Chick, 2001; Laursen & Hartup, 1989, p. 291; Wheeler, 1997). These brief oppositional encounters are different from fully developed conflicts. They are less emotionally intense, and children use different strategies to end them. The question is, "What happens to defuse these potential conflicts?" We will think more about this question as we move into Part 3.

A *defused conflict* might look like this: Children begin to argue over a toy. Child A claims "Mine!" Child B claims, "Mine!" No further exchanges occur as Child B decides to play elsewhere.

The same situation might develop into a *full conflict* this way: Children begin to argue over a toy. Child A claims "Mine!" Child B claims, "Mine!" Child A persists.

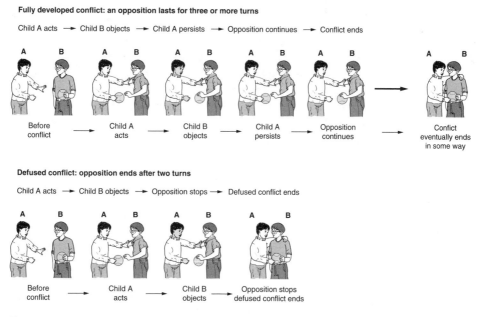

Fully developed conflict: an opposition lasts for three or more turns

Child A acts → Child B objects → Child A persists → Opposition continues → Conflict ends

Before conflict → Child A acts → Child B objects → Child A persists → Opposition continues → Conflict eventually ends in some way

Defused conflict: opposition ends after two turns

Child A acts → Child B objects → Opposition stops → Defused conflict ends

Before conflict → Child A acts → Child B objects → Opposition stops defused conflict ends

Figure 4–1
Fully developed and defused conflicts.

Voices get louder as exchanges continue. The children pull on the toy. Intervention occurs to end the conflict.

Anatomy of a Conflict: Issues, Strategies, and Outcomes

Structural features, the "anatomy" of a conflict, are evident as the conflict develops from its beginning to its resolution. The stages of conflict are as follows:

1. The event that "sets the stage" with a "behavior, request, or statement" by child A

2. The initial opposition, when child B disagrees with or resists the actions of child A

3. Mutual opposition, as child A persists

4. The continuing oppositional strategies, as the children take turns using a variety of tactics in the dispute

5. The ending, when children discontinue their opposition (Shantz, 1987, p. 155)

Conflict features describing these stages can be identified as follows:

- *Issue:* The event that provokes the initial opposition
- *Strategies:* The mutual opposition and subsequent oppositional strategies
- *Outcome:* The ending

Children's conflicts are complex and varied, with a vast array of possible *issues*, a seemingly limitless number of *strategies* (from bargaining and negotiating to hitting and grabbing), and several possible types of *outcomes*. We can also consider the *differences in individual children* and in the *social and physical context* of their interactions. Although there is no single example of a "typical" conflict, we can identify categories of issues, strategies, and outcomes, and begin to understand what is happening in children's conflicts. There are charts of the various types of issues and strategies at the end of this chapter. Observe the children in your setting and see what else you can add to these lists.

TEACHERS TALK:

> "In my kindergarten class children don't fight 'each other.' They fight each other's 'belongings.'"

Issues

Issues in children's peer conflicts have been generally categorized as control of the *physical* environment or control of the *social* environment (Ramsey, 1991; Shantz, 1987; Wheeler, 1997).

The *physical* environment includes objects and space. Conflicts may occur over possession of objects for children's immediate use (like the chair), or over a more permanent claim of ownership ("Hey, that's my pencil!"). Conflicts may also involve possession of physical space or "territory." Possession issues are among the most frequent issues in young children's conflicts. Children may argue about indoor spaces in which to play or build, classroom spaces in which to put a desk or chair, or space on the playground for games or gathering. In the conflict at the beginning of this chapter, Rosa and Beth are engaged in a possession dispute over a chair in their bus play.

In some cases, control over the play environment, rather than a desire for the toy itself, may provide impetus for the dispute. A young child who takes all the toys is often more interested in being "in charge" than in actually wanting to play with everything at once. Issues of possession also involve control over physical space or territory, such as the platform of a playground climber (Shantz, 1987; Wilson, 1988; Singer & Hannikainen, 2002).

Example of an Issue of Control of the Physical Environment: A Conflict at Math Time *In the following episode, the basic issue between Dominic and Donald is possession of a marker.*

Third graders are engaged in a math activity. Dominic takes Donald's marker without asking.

Donald: Dominic, will you please give me the marker back?

Dominic: No! Not till I'm done.

Donald: Dominic, I need my marker, give it to me!

Conflicts often occur over possession of an object such as a riding toy on the playground.

Dominic: No! When I'm finished, I will give it to you.

Donald: You better give me back my marker now!

Dominic: I'm using it.

Donald takes Dominic's paper.

Dominic: Give me back my paper.

Donald: Not until you return my marker!

Dominic: Don't play around, Donald! I want my paper back!

Donald: Well, when you give me my marker, you will get your paper back!

Dominic: Mr. Blake, tell him to give me my paper back!

Donald: Mr. Blake, he took my marker!

Mr. Blake: You guys have to work that out.

Dominic goes to get another marker. He returns Donald's marker. Donald returns the paper.

Control of the *social* environment involves control over the behavior of peers in issues of group entry (inclusion or exclusion from play); social space; decisions within the play activity involving role-play or rules; disagreement over information or facts; superiority of size, age, physical ability, and knowledge; and intentional annoyance or teasing (Arcaro-McPhee et al., 2002; Corsaro, 1985; Guralnick, 1994; Shantz, 1987; Wilson, 1988). Social conflict issues may involve a privilege (such as a preferred place in line), interpretation of rules, and power and authority. Turn-taking disputes are frequently observed issues of control over the social environment. As young children grow older, superiority in ability and physical competence, group affiliation, and status among peers become more frequent sources of conflict or interpersonal friction. Group affiliation may be defined by gender, culture, language, ability, economic status, and even participation in sports teams and clubs.

A serious consideration in the social environment is conflicts that stem from bias, prejudice, and discrimination. Conflicts can be aggravated by differences in language, lack of shared understanding of words and gestures, or different approaches to conflict. Even very young children are aware of hurtful words and racial epithets (Van Ausdale & Feagin, 2001; Katch, 2001). As with adults, sometimes the apparent issue is not the true cause of children's conflict behavior. Underlying the immediate instigation may be a remembered hurt, or a general frame of mind or emotional state, that brings about an oppositional reaction to other children's actions.

Example of an Issue of Control Over the Social Environment: In the Lunchroom
Children are sitting at assigned tables in the lunchroom.

Elizabeth (age six):   Stop looking at me.

Daniel (age seven):   I'm not looking at you.

Elizabeth:	Yes, you are.
Daniel:	No, I'm not.
Elizabeth:	Yes, you are.
(Silence for a few minutes)	
Elizabeth:	DANIEL!!!!
Daniel:	WHAT?!!
Elizabeth:	Stop it!
Daniel:	Stop what?
Elizabeth:	Stop staring.
Daniel:	I'm not looking at you.
Elizabeth:	S-T-O-P!!!!
Daniel:	I can look at you or anything else I want. It's not a crime.
Elizabeth:	I don't care. I don't want you looking at anything by me.
Daniel:	You're such a baby.

The conflict continues until Elizabeth throws her milk carton at Daniel. It misses him and hits the wall behind him. At this point, a teacher intervenes.

Another way to categorize conflict issues is based on children's understanding of the domains of *moral rules* and *social conventions* (Killen & Turiel, 1991). *Moral rules* address physical harm, psychological harm, distribution of toys, and rights. These rules are defined by children's understanding of right and wrong and fairness and justice. ("It's not okay to hurt people.") Issues of *social conventions* involve behaviors governed by social rules or understood ways of acting, such as how children put away their backpacks or how someone is supposed to wear a hat.

Within the domain of social rules and conventions, there is the further distinction between adult/school-determined rules and rules of the peer culture. Let's look at hat wearing. How do you wear a hat? Is there a rule against wearing hats at school? If you are wearing a baseball cap, are you supposed to wear it with the bill in the back?

Strategies

Once a conflict has started, children use a variety of different strategies to manage it. Strategies are either *physical* or *verbal*, and both types may involve either *aggressive* or *non-aggressive* tactics. See Table 4–1.

- *Physical strategies:* The push-pull between Beth and Rosa is focused on the object/chair and is *non-aggressive*. Hitting someone or knocking them down to take possession would be *aggressive*. Non-aggressive physical strategies involve the frequently observed tactic of simply taking a toy or entering a play space.

TABLE 4–1   STRATEGIES IN CHILDREN'S PEER CONFLICTS: TYPES OF STRATEGIES AND EXAMPLES

Verbal Strategies		Physical Strategies	
Non-Aggressive	**Aggressive**	**Non-Aggressive**	**Aggressive**

Insistence
Bargaining
Reasoning/
  negotiation
	Name-calling
	Taunting
	Threats
		Taking disputed
		  object
		Blocking access to
		  an object or space
			Hostile: kicking,
			  hitting, pushing in
			  order to hurt
			Instrumental:
			  pushing a child
			  away from
			  disputed object

Example:
"You're not
  coming to my
  birthday!"
Example:
"You use the chair
  for 3 more
  minutes, and then
  I get to use it for
  3 minutes."
	Example:
	"If you don't do this,
	  I won't be your
	  friend."
		Example:
		Blocking the monkey
		  bars: "This is our
		  space. You can't
		  come up."
			Example:
			"This is my seat!"
			  Child pulls chair
			  out from under
			  another child,
			  who falls hard to
			  the floor.
			Example:
			"I was here first!
			  You're pushing
			  me off!"

- *Verbal strategies:* Verbal strategies exist on a continuum from simple opposition to complex reasoning and negotiation. Verbal strategies can be aggressive if they involve name-calling or threats.

Aggression is the most undesirable and potentially harmful type of conflict strategy, and it is also the most noticeable. However, children use aggression infrequently as a strategy for resolving their conflicts (Arcaro-McPhee et al., 2002; Killen & Turiel, 1991; Malloy & McMurray, 1996; Ross & Conant, 1992; Shantz, 1987). Aggressive actions are themselves identified as *hostile*, not related to a conflict issue but intended to be harmful, or *instrumental*, used as a means of achieving the goal of the conflict.

Affectivity is another dimension within the strategy sequence, seen in the intensity of insistence in oppositional exchanges (Laursen & Hartup, 1989). If children continue to insist without effect, the conflict may escalate to anger and frustration. Losing control or seeing that words are ineffective may lead to physical strategies, hitting, and anger.

An alternative to child-managed strategies that children may use to end a dispute is the strategy of seeking adult intervention. This turn of events alters the conflict episode from peer interaction to an adult-child interaction. Although children are very often capable of resolving conflicts without adult help, when an adult intervenes, the resolution is usually provided by the adult and not generated by the children (Arcaro-McPhee et al., 2002; Killen & Turiel, 1991; Malloy & McMurray, 1996; Singer & Hannikainen, 2002; Vespo et al., 1995; Wheeler, 2000).

We can see what happens as Rosa and Beth argue about the chair. Their strategies are verbal insistence ("No, it's my turn!") and physical strategies (peeling Rosa's hands from the chair). When these strategies do not bring an end to the dispute, Rosa enlists the teacher's help in resolving the issue.

A Negotiated Conflict

First graders are in the Music Room, arranging themselves on the floor.

Jade: No, Willow, I don't want you to sit by me.

Willow: Yeah, Jade. I want to sit next to you.

Jade: I want to be by myself.

Willow: I want to be by you, too.

Jade: Sit on your own cushion.

Willow: I want to sit on your cushion.

Jade: We can still sit next to each other, but I want my own cushion. You can have your own cushion, too.

Willow: My own cushion?

Jade: Yes, see? One for me and one for you.

Ms. H. asks the class if everyone is ready now.

Willow: Yeah, look, Ms. H. We have our own cushions!

Jade (to Ms. H.):   Willow wanted to sit by me.

Outcomes

Children's conflicts have four types of endings or outcomes (see Table 4–2). These outcomes may be controlled by children or by adults. Children acting as peer mediators may contribute to the resolution.

TABLE 4–2   ADULT OUTCOMES VERSUS CHILD OUTCOMES

Adult-Controlled Outcomes	Child-Generated Outcomes		
Direct intervention Scripted peer mediation	Mutually agreeable Spontaneous peer mediation	Compliance/ domination	Unresolved: Issue is dropped without resolution

1. Unresolved: A conflict may remain unresolved as children simply drop the issue or leave the area, moving to different activities and playmates.

2. Compliance/Domination: A dispute may end with one child submitting to the other through conciliation, yielding to dominance, unwilling compromise, or withdrawal.

3. Mutually Agreeable: Children may arrive at a mutually agreeable solution through bargaining, compromise, creating an alternative activity, or turning the conflict into a game. Rende and Killen (1992) describe this type of outcome as "active resolution." Peers may assist as spontaneously mediators in a mutually agreeable child-generated outcome.

4. Adult Intervention: The conflict may be ended by adult intervention, as an adult suggests or imposes a solution. When children act as formal peer mediators following a script and a set procedure, the outcome is similar to an adult-generated outcome.

Each of these outcomes may end the conflict, but only the mutually agreeable solution helps children to develop resolution skills and learn how to resolve conflicts effectively (Arcaro-McPhee et al., 2002; Bakeman & Brownlee, 1982; Chen & Smith, 2002; Dunn & Cutting, 1999; Eisenberg & Garvey, 1981; Genishi & DiPaolo, 1982; Laursen & Hartup, 1989; Malloy & McMurray, 1996; Singer & Hannikainen, 2002; Vespo et al., 1995; Wheeler, 2000; Wilson, 1988).

An Example of Spontaneous Peer Mediation *Julia (age three) and Jonathan (age three) are arguing in the hallway about possession of small plastic bears. Jonathan puts his hands around Julia's throat with an angry look on his face. Billy (age three) rushes into the hall and pushes himself between them.*

Billy to Jonathan: Wait a minute! Wait a minute! Listen to Julia's words! You can't use your bodies!

Jonathan lets go. Julia keeps taking bears. Jonathan turns to Billy with a threatening gesture.

Billy to Jonathan: It's not okay. Use your words.

Jonathan backs away and then suggests a new game. All three play.

WHY NOT "WIN/WIN?"

A word about terminology: In this book, we have been using the term "mutually agreeable solution" instead of "win/win," and "compliance/domination" instead of "win/lose." The phrase "win/win," although it suggests a positive outcome, nevertheless still implies competition. We feel that using the longer term "mutually agreeable" is more consistent with the idea of an active consensus by all children.

WORKING WITH CHILDREN: A PREVIEW

What we know about the issues and strategies children use in their conflicts will guide us in supporting desirable conflict outcomes. Parts Three and Four of this book are devoted to providing applications for teaching and learning. There may be things that you are already doing that are helping, such as these:

Ideas for Understanding Cause-and-Effect, Perspective-Taking, and Generating Alternatives
Books, storytelling, and puppets provide scenarios for discussion. Ask preschool children what else could the characters in the story do, what else could they say, or what would happen if …? These ideas also work naturally with literacy learning at all levels. How about primary writing experiences, as children write a new ending or act out scenes from a story?

WHO'S DOING THE FIGHTING?

All children engage in conflicts, including both girls and boys, and children of all ages who are old enough to engage in interaction with their peers. Do differences among children make a difference in their conflicts?

Gender, Age, and Numbers of Children in Conflicts

Gender

Is there a difference between the conflicts of girls and boys? On the question of gender, studies of children's conflicts have offered contradictory findings. According to some researchers, boys engage in more conflicts than girls and differ in their issues and strategies. Boys are more often involved in issues of object control and use more threats and physical force. Girls are more concerned with issues of social control, such as group entry and role-play decisions, and use more conciliatory strategies (Dunn & Cutting, 1999; Hay, 1984; Miller, Danaher, & Forbes, 1986; Shantz, 1987; Vespo et al., 1995). Other researchers have found no differences between girls and boys in issues, amount of conflict, or use of aggression (Bakeman & Brownlee, 1982; Laursen & Hartup, 1989; Sacken & Thelen, 1984).

A possible reason for the differences may be the type of activity in which conflict occurs. Gender may be a factor in the activities that children choose, rather than their approach to conflict management. Different types of conflict issues will occur between children playing a game with rules and those engaging in rough-and-tumble play on the playground or in sociodramatic play. Conflicts may be more noticeable to adults if children are involved in an activity confined to one area, perhaps arguing about the objects they are using or rules of the game, and less obvious if children walk from place to place carrying on an argument about exclusion from the group, superiority, or other social issues.

In this discussion, we may also consider some gender differences explored by Carol Gilligan (1982, 2001). Women and men in general have different values that are the basis for their moral reasoning and decision-making. Gilligan's findings hold true for girls and boys as well. She found that boys and men make decisions based on justice, fairness, and rules, while girls and women are more likely to decide based on relationships and connections with others and avoiding harm to others. Deborah Tannen (1990) also describes gender-based differences based on conversational styles. Gender issues are complex and changing, as is our understanding of what is happening with girls and boys as they grow (Pipher, 1994; Pollack, 1998). What we know about gender and children's conflicts from research today may be different from what we may see in the future.

Age

Toddlers, preschoolers, and primary age children differ in their conflict issues and strategies. Younger children are more often involved in issues of possession of objects and space. They use more physical strategies, while older children disagree over social issues and use more verbal negotiation and reasoning. Younger children use more conciliatory strategies in non-aggressive conflicts, while older children rely upon insistence (Eisenberg & Garvey, 1981; Ramsey, 1986; Ross & Conant, 1992; Singer & Hannikainen, 2002). Social rules used to decide possession issues among toddlers often involve dominance, while preschoolers may use a rule of prior possession (Bakeman & Brownlee, 1982; Singer & Hannikainen, 2002). As children grow, there are more issues of rule violations, ideas, assertion, and social dominance. Primary age children's conflicts may relate to competition, superiority, or physical and academic accomplishment.

A HUMOROUS LOOK AT TODDLER PROPERTY RULES

1. If I like it, it's mine.
2. If it's in my hands, it's mine.
3. If I can take it from you, it's mine.
4. If I had it a little while ago, it's mine.
5. If it's mine, it must never be yours in any way.
6. If I'm doing or building something, all the pieces are mine.
7. If it looks like mine, it's mine.
8. If I saw it first, it's mine.
9. If you are playing with something and you put it down, it automatically becomes mine.
10. If it's broken, it's yours.

—*Author unknown*

The strategy most often used by toddlers is simply physical force: taking the disputed object away from another child. With increasing verbal ability, children move to insistence and threats, and then expand their repertoire to include calling on adults for help. Older children may use persuasion, tact, citing rules, or pointing out mutual interests in resolving conflicts (Ramsey, 1991). A developmental sequence has been suggested but not established by these observations. Rather than age alone, it may be verbal ability and perspective-taking ability that contribute to children's mutually agreeable outcomes in conflicts. If threes are able to express themselves in words and offer reasons that are understood by their peers, they are as likely to resolve conflicts as five-year-olds (Wheeler, 1997).

TEACHERS TALK:

"In my situation, pre-k, we often interact with the K children. In most situations, the K children win arguments out of intimidation (size). But many times, if a pre-k is being intimidated by a K child, many other children will come to the pre-k's defense, either by telling an adult or by intervening."

Numbers

Conflict episodes may involve pairs of children, or groups of three or more. The sequence of an argument among several children is similar to conflicts among pairs of children, but the alignments among children in defense, alliance, and opposition offer complex variations (Maynard, 1985). Little research has been done, however, on third parties in children's conflicts. The immediate effects of alliances on conflict outcomes have not been evaluated (Ross & Conant, 1992). In his observations, Corsaro (1985) found nine disputes involving group entry issues in which children collaborated in conflict. These limited findings indicated that alliances contributed to the outcome of conflicts. Ross and Conant suggest that the "study of multiparty conflicts is essential for understanding the place of conflict in children's social lives" (p. 179).

TEACHERS TALK ABOUT KNOWING CHILDREN:

Mr. Blake explains more about the math time conflict between Dominic and Donald: "The conflict was resolved and the two students continued to work on their assignments. I chose not to intervene because I expect my students to work out their differences. These two students did not need my intervention. The problem did not escalate, but it might have if these were two different students with different personalities in the same situation. I might have reacted differently also."

Cultural, Ethnic, and Family Identity of Children in Conflicts

In an increasingly diverse world, cultural and ethnic identity is another aspect to explore as we try to understand children's conflicts. There are probably more questions than answers at this time, but it is clear that cultural, ethnic, and linguistic identity play a large role in children's interactions in general, and in their conflicts in particular. It has also been suggested that by looking at children's conflicts, we can also gain a deeper understanding of different cultures (Ramsey, 1987, 1998).

We can ask about cultural influences in children's conflicts in three ways. First, to what extent does conflict occur the same way among young children universally? If friendship is an important factor in conflict resolution, we can expect that, regardless of culture, children will work to resolve conflicts with their friends.

Next, we may look at cultural identity of the peer group as opposed to the family. Is the immediate context of the peer group a greater factor in how children manage their conflicts? Shared understandings and expected behaviors may not be the same at home as at school. In many cases, children will adapt their words and actions to fit the context.

Finally, children, we know, bring their own perspectives and family worldviews to their peer interactions. Differences in language and interactional styles are important factors as well. Awareness of, and respect for, family culture will continue throughout this book. In order to resolve conflicts, children must be able to understand the perspectives of others, and must be able to use verbal strategies of reason and negotiation understood by others. Differences in language and communication styles also include non-verbal communication; body language; and voice volume, pacing, and tone.

Another dimension of family culture relates to ways of responding to and dealing with conflict. In some families, compliance and deference to others are valued and taught. In other families, children learn about assertion, standing up for themselves, and "hitting back." Children from all these types of families bring to school a very different basis for behavior when a conflict arises. In later chapters, we will explore the importance of communication between teacher and family in clearly understanding family and cultural perspectives on conflict.

OBSERVATION AND DISCUSSION

What do adults see? In an urban center, the English-speaking teachers believe that four-year-old Matthew, whose home language is Korean, doesn't speak. In reality, he does speak to other children and effectively negotiates his conflicts. Your reactions?

Children with Special Needs

The skills and abilities needed for successful management of conflicts may be limited in the case of children with special needs. We have noted that some children who are typically developing may exhibit altruism, patience, and caring toward children with atypical development. They may also understand that other children need special consideration as they work and play together. Other peers may not act so favorably toward the lack of verbal and cognitive skills, physical or emotional control, and appropriate social responses on the part of some children with special needs.

Not all children with special needs, disabilities, or developmental delays interact with others in the same way. An important question for a teacher in an inclusive setting to ask is, "What are the behavioral effects of this specific disability on children's social acceptance or rejection?" There are variations among individual children, as well as variables in conditions such as ADHD, autism, and cerebral palsy. Studies have documented caring, consideration, and patience shown toward children with Down Syndrome (Wheeler, 1997). Children have shown helping behaviors toward children with visual impairments, whose conflict issues and strategies were similar to those of sighted peers (Erwin et al., 1999).

Conflict issues among children with special needs may include acquisition of objects, invasion of space, and changes in the course of play, all related to limited social competence, as discussed in Chapter 3. Children with special needs or developmental delays may experience more problems with group entry. Successful group entry depends on learning the rules of the ongoing play and the ability to pick up social cues. Delayed speech among some children results in more physical, non-verbal, though not necessarily aggressive strategies. Inappropriate response to social cues and frustration may bring about strategies that are perceived by others to be aggressive. Teachers can help facilitate decoding on the part of the child with special needs, and can stress the need to clarify the rules on the part of typically developing peers. Like their typically developing peers, children with special needs are often able to resolve conflicts without adult help, but teachers are more likely to intervene in their conflicts.

TEACHERS TALK:

"I have a little boy in my kindergarten class who I will call George. His problem goes beyond conflict, and it breaks my heart. He is a sweet, bright child, but he sticks out like a sore thumb. He is emotionally and socially young, and he just doesn't fit in with the other children. Sometimes with a child like George, the other children kind of take him under their wing and 'mother' him a little, but in this case he is at the center of most conflicts in my class and is often 'left out'. I had been worried about him since school began, but it really hit home when one of my students (a really sweet, nice girl) said, 'Why does George have to be at our table?' She wasn't trying to be mean, she was just frustrated from having to deal with him all the time. We talked about how George would feel if he heard her say that, but she wouldn't let it go and really wanted an explanation of 'Why does he?' I asked her to think of five good things about George, and then told her five good things myself, but she still wasn't satisfied. We have done a unit on 'All about me' and talked about how we are all different, and that is what makes us unique, etc. Any suggestions on how to help that child who just doesn't fit in?"

Friendship and Playing Together: The Social Context of Peer Conflict

The social context of children's conflicts includes their friendship relations and the type of social play in which they are engaged. Children playing together before conflict arises are more likely to resolve their disputes agreeably and continue to play together afterward (Laursen & Hartup, 1989; Rende & Killen, 1992; Sacken & Thelen,

1984; Wheeler, 1997). Using Parten's levels of social play, children engaged in prior associative or cooperative play use less aggression in their conflicts than children in onlooker, solitary, or parallel play. If children are playing apart before conflict, the issue is more likely to involve distribution of toys. Those playing together disagree over "use of space and activity roles" (Rende & Killen, 1992, p. 559).

Conflict issues are related to the type of social and cognitive play. Children engaged in parallel play and functional/constructive/practice play are more likely to be involved in conflicts about possession of objects. Children engaged in associative or cooperative play, dramatic play, sociodramatic play, and games with rules will encounter more conflicts about decisions within play and group entry.

Observing friendship relations among children, researchers have compared interactions among friends, unknown peers in experimental play groups, and non-friend peers in preschool settings. Conflict occurs more often among friends, partly because they spend more time with each other. However, there is less intensity and more conciliation in conflicts, and more socialization afterwards among friends than among non-friends (Hartup, Laursen, Stewart, & Eastenson, 1988). Friends can disagree and argue "safely" and with greater confidence that after conflicts, friends will still be there. (Siblings close in age may experience the same thing, engaging in conflicts and trying out unfamiliar language safely.) Friends give more explanation and criticism and offer more solutions, than non-friends (Dunn & Cutting, 1999; Nelson & Aboud, 1985).

Friendship and effective conflict management may work together. Children who are able to develop friendships may also be better at conflict resolution, and at the same time, being able to resolve conflicts may also help children become better at developing friendships. On the other side of the coin, children who have difficulty with elements of social competence, conflict resolution, group entry, and maintaining play often experience rejection by peers in the classroom. Friendships and the related classroom dynamics of peer acceptance and rejection have clear implications for children's conflict resolution in Early Childhood settings. We will include more about these topics in later chapters.

WHERE DO CONFLICTS TAKE PLACE?

Activities and Locations

Conflicts occur in many different play settings, at school, at home, and in the neighborhood. More studies of peer conflicts have been done in school settings indoors, or in arranged play groups, than in home and neighborhood settings or on playgrounds (Corsaro, 1985). Differences between school and home rules and the supervision of teachers, directly or indirectly, may influence children's conflicts.

Conflicts between children playing in isolated pairs differ from those between two children in a group setting. In a preschool classroom, for instance, children have the option of walking away and finding a new activity, while in pair play, children persist in resolution efforts in order to continue to play (Arcaro-McPhee et al., 2002; Dunn & Cutting, 1999; Genishi & DiPaolo, 1982; Killen & Turiel, 1991). Primary children have fewer unstructured interactions during the day and may find themselves unable to walk away and choose different companions. Toddlers have fewer conflicts when the classroom is arranged for play in groups of two, rather than four, as is typical for preschoolers and primary age children.

Teachers observe conflicts throughout the day in many areas of the classroom and playground. Close observation may suggest that certain areas seem to be the sites of more conflicts due to traffic patterns, space, time, number of children, or materials. Play setting was also a factor in Ramsey's 1986 study of possession disputes. She found that more disputes occurred in closed play areas with a single entrance. The conclusion is that the accessibility of play space, as well as the availability of toys, may contribute to conflicts (Wheeler, 1997). As in the following example, conflicts often occur in transitions as well as in specific activities.

In Line for Lunch

Standing in line for lunch, Connor bumps Brooks in front of him.
  Brooks turns around, yells, "Connor!," and looks toward the teacher.
  Connor pushes again.

Brooks whispers angrily, "Connor! Move! I was here first!"

Connor: "So?!"

Brooks shouts, "Connor! Mrs. Edwards said we can't stand together! I was first, so move!"

Brooks looks around for the teacher, and then repeats, "Connor, move!"

Amy, behind both of them, steps in and says, "Connor, just get behind me!"

Connor: "But I want to stay here!"

Brooks: "You can't! Just move!"

Connor gets behind Amy, huffing and puffing.

The Presence of Adults

As we mentioned in our discussion of children's peer culture in Chapter 3, the presence of an adult alters the context of children's conflicts. Children take responsibility for their interactions and generate their own solutions more often when no adult is present (Laursen & Hartup, 1989). There is more aggression in children's conflicts when an adult is present but not involved in the children's interaction (Killen & Turiel, 1991). Preschool teachers are more likely to be present during long conflicts and to intervene in issues related to moral rules than to the social order (Killen & Turiel, 1991). Attempting to be fair, adults sometimes make mistakes in

Intervening in a conflict, adults may help children come to a mutually agreeable solution that seems fair to both children.

the resolutions they impose. In a study of parents and children, adult interventions also suffered from inconsistency and bias. Endorsing justice and fair play, mothers nevertheless intervened to apply these principles on behalf of other children but not their own (Ross & Conant, 1992).

CHILDREN'S IDEAS OF FAIRNESS

As we consider "mutually agreeable solutions" in children's conflicts, adults in Early Childhood settings need to remember that these sought-after outcomes are what children themselves have determined to be mutually agreeable. Their solutions may not necessarily be the same as what adults would prescribe for them.

An Example of What Is Fair in Preschool *After a simple negotiation, the children at the Play-Doh table have decided that Alonzo needs more Play-Doh than Ethan because he is making a pizza with many toppings. Ethan is only interested in rolling some dough into a snake. An adult passing the table stops, observes the unequal distribution of Play-Doh, and takes some from the pile from in front of Alonzo and places it in front of Ethan. "There," she says, "That's better. Now it's fair."*

In Chapter 3, we introduced the idea of children's intentions in conflicts, and later in Chapter 5, we will look at the development of children's moral reasoning and decision-making. For now, we need to remember that what is important to children at different ages is related to their conflict issues and ways of resolving those conflicts. Very young children can distinguish issues about moral rules, such as hurting others, from issues about social conventions, and can demonstrate decision-making based variously on their definitions of fairness, caring, relationships, responsibility, rights, or needs. Older children are developing an understanding of the effect of conflict outcomes on others.

MUTUALLY AGREEABLE RESOLUTION OF CONFLICT: "MOST LIKELY TO SUCCEED"

What are the characteristics of young children's conflicts that end in mutually agreeable, child-generated resolutions? We can identify some general characteristics or conditions that occur when children are able to resolve their conflicts in a way that satisfies all parties. The two most compelling are as follows:

1. Children playing together before a conflict arises are more likely to resolve the conflict in a mutually agreeable way that allows them to play. Children who are friends and those engaged in cooperative or associative play are more successful in achieving mutually agreeable resolutions.
2. Verbal strategies incorporating reasoning and negotiation are more likely to lead to successful resolution than insistence or non-verbal strategies.

Interviews with children about their perceptions of successful resolutions reflect these same two themes. As they watched videotapes of their own conflicts, these children reported that they resolved their conflicts either because they are friends or because they talked, or "used words."

Interview with Matthew

Interviewer: When you have a problem that causes an argument, what happens?

Matthew (age 5): Because you're friends, you figure it out.

Interview with Tomas

Tomas (age 5) is watching the same taped episode that his friend Matthew watched earlier. His interpretation of the events is the same as Matthew's, but his explanation of how children resolve conflicts is different.

Interviewer: Matthew said people solve their arguments if they're friends. Is that how?

Tomas: No.

Interviewer: How do people solve their arguments?

Tomas: If they talk.

There are other conclusions we can make about children's conflicts:

1. Children's conflicts are complex social interactions. With a wide range of issues and strategies, there is no "typical" conflict. Structural and contextual features of conflicts, such as outcomes, issues, strategies, participant characteristics, and type of social play, are interrelated.

2. There are as many different specific issues that begin conflicts among children as there are among adults. Uncovering these variations through close observation shows the complexity of children's interactions and provides a picture of the rich fabric of their social lives. This detail also helps teachers, as they observe children, to analyze conflicts and decide the most effective ways to help children learn to resolve their disputes.

3. Children are often more likely to resolve conflicts related to issues of control over the social environment than issues of control over the physical environment, possibly because these issues are more often addressed verbally and often occur within ongoing play.

4. Successful conflict resolution is related to children's ability to recognize the perspectives, needs, and rights of other children, as well as the effect on others of their own words and actions.

5. There are two ways that children's oppositional interactions can develop. First of all, we are interested in children's ability to actively resolve the fully developed conflicts of three or more turns that inevitably occur in classrooms. The concern is that children learn to understand another's point of view, generate alternative solutions, and construct mutually agreeable outcomes. We can also learn from observing the two-turn defused conflict, or "compliance exchange." Observing these undeveloped conflicts may help us understand why and how children can avoid potentially destructive confrontations with their peers.

IMPLICATIONS FOR TEACHERS: USING WHAT WE KNOW

What we know about children's conflicts with their peers suggests ways that teachers can help children create positive resolutions. By observing and evaluating children's disputes with the tools we discussed in Chapter 3, teachers can decide when to offer appropriate guidance. In many cases, children are capable of resolving conflicts on their own. Teachers can also provide a supportive physical and social environment. Thinking of conflict resolution ability as a developmental process may make teachers more comfortable with children's early efforts.

By observing the issues of children's conflicts, teachers may decide whether to intervene. Disagreements about play decisions and other issues of control over the social environment are more likely to end agreeably than arguments about possession issues. Conflict strategies may provide another clue for teachers. Children who use reasoning and explain their actions to each other are likely to create their own solutions. Physical strategies and simple verbal opposition are less effective. In these conflicts, teachers can help children find more words to use.

The context of friendship and playing together suggests another key question for teachers to ask: "Were the children playing together before the conflict?" Prior interaction and friendship provide motivation for children to resolve disputes on their own and continue to play afterwards.

We can now begin to develop our checklists and other observation tools based on what we know about conflict issues, strategies, and outcomes. We can record information about who is involved, the language used, and how long conflicts last. The Appendix will include some tools for you to use, and you can develop your own by putting together what you've learned in Chapters 3 and 4.

Teachers can encourage using words and listening among children in their classrooms. Encouraging children to use shared words and phrases will help them solve or minimize conflicts. Words like "Sorry," "Thank you," and "Can I help you fix it?" de-escalate potential conflicts. "It's okay to do that" or "It's not okay to do that" give children words that define the boundaries of expected behaviors and social rules. "Use your words" reminds children to use verbal, not physical, strategies. "Listen to her words" promotes perspective-taking and provides a basis for understanding and reasoning as children create mutually agreeable resolutions.

This last recommendation has immediate and far-reaching implications for practice. Teachers frequently encourage children to "use words," but they rarely emphasize *listening* to each other's words in order to develop a genuine dialogue. Taken together, these implications suggest that teachers can work toward creating a classroom context for peer mediation, conciliation, and mutually agreeable, child-generated resolutions.

>>

SUMMARY

Looking closely at children's conflicts, we can see the complexity of these social interactions. Peer conflicts are not random or wanton behaviors. They are structured events among children. As conflicts develop, children respond according to their understanding of the words and actions of their peers. They are both creating and responding to their notion of a social order. While there is no such thing as a "typical" conflict, teachers and caregivers can learn a great deal through close observation of the structural and contextual characteristics of children's conflicts, and especially of those conflicts that result in mutually agreeable solutions. We will be able to use this information to guide children as they grow in understanding and managing conflicts with their peers.

SUPPLEMENTARY MATERIALS FOR CHAPTER 4

Research Focus

In a recent study, the number of full, three-turn conflicts was less than might have been expected based on previous research. Researchers have reported an overall rate across studies of 5 conflicts per hour using event sampling (ranging from 2 to 23). The 75 conflicts in this research were observed during 27.5 hours of videotape data collection, a rate of approximately 2.7 per hour (Wheeler, 1997). The large number of compliance exchanges is interesting because it represents many more of these "emergent" or "defused" conflicts than in previous research. Laursen and Hartup (1989) reported that only 30%, or 46, of their interactions were two-turn exchanges, and 70%, or 108, were three-turn exchanges. In this study, the 79 compliance exchanges represent 51%, more than half of the oppositions, that ended before escalating into full conflicts. A new question emerges: "Why did these interactions fail to develop into conflicts?" Can you suggest some reasons?

APPLICATION EXERCISES

1. Answer these discussion questions that reflect an integrated approach to understanding children's conflicts:
   - Can children's conflicts be described in typical categories?
   - What kinds of conflict issues, strategies, and outcomes do you see in your setting?
2. Using the observation tools from Chapter 3, develop, try out, and revise your own observation tools to learn about the aspects of children's conflicts discussed in this chapter.
3. Explore the children's understanding of conflicts of their own conflicts. What would the children in your setting say if you ask them about their disagreements or "problems" with friends?

THINKING ABOUT ALL CHILDREN

1. Observing children's interactions, do you see commonalities and differences in the play of girls and boys?
2. Do you see differences in their conflicts and the way the children manage them?
3. Do you see differences in the way adults respond to the children's conflicts?

5

Cognitive-Developmental, Sociomoral, and Sociocultural Perspectives

"But sometimes you just don't solve things, so you do something else."

Chapter 5 Objectives: Chapters 5 and 6 present peer conflict from several theoretical perspectives of children's development and learning. Unlike in many books, connections to theory were not presented in the first chapter. Now that we have established a framework for a discussion of children's conflicts, aspects of theories about children and their development are introduced. In this way, the theories may make more sense as we make connections to real life. The purpose of theory to explain or predict behavior is now more relevant and meaningful, and it engages us in critical thinking, asking, "How much does this theory explain about what we observe in children's conflicts?" and "What can we expect children to say or do?" The cognitive-developmental and sociocultural theories in Chapter 5 are both related to constructivism. Our understanding is also strongly influenced by ecological systems theory. Observation activities encourage students to connect children's conflict interactions to what we know about how children learn and grow in all areas: cognitive, linguistic, social, emotional, and cultural.

Chapter Outline

A CONFLICT AT CLEAN-UP TIME

Children (all $3\frac{1}{2}$) have been using masking tape on the floor, making roads during center time. It is now clean-up time. Maria is pulling up tape. Stefan approaches and begins to pull up tape.

Maria: No, I'm doing it.

Stefan continues to pull tape.

Maria: No, Stefan, stop!

Maria pushes Stefan away. They fall and are rolling on the floor together. Nicole is standing a few feet away, near more tape on the floor.

Nicole: Stefan, here's some over here. She was doing it first.

Nicole stands with tape stuck to her fingers. All three giggle. Maria and Stefan both pull up tape in different spots.

Maria: Stefan, do this part.

Maria, Stefan, and Nicole finish up on the same area of tape.

PEER CONFLICT AND CHILDREN'S DEVELOPMENT

A number of theoretical perspectives have described the contribution of peer conflicts to children's development. These theories examine growth within a child (*intrapsychological*) and between people (*interpsychological*). Cognitive developmental psychologists, sociomoral and sociocultural theorists, sociologists, and sociolinguists have all supported the value of children's peer conflicts within their own disciplines' frameworks. For cognitive-developmentalists, peer conflict leads to internal cognitive growth (Piaget, 1962). Sociomoral theorists give us a framework for children's moral decision-making in conflicts with peers. In sociocultural theory, conflict is a social event or practical activity (Vygotsky, 1978). Sociologists have described children's conflicts as vehicles for social organization (Maynard,

1985b; Strauss, 2002). Sociolinguists discuss conflict talk, or arguing, as a speech event or discourse phenomenon (Brenneis & Lein, 1977). Considering all these different ways to explain children's conflicts, an interdisciplinary approach to the study of peer conflicts will help provide a clear understanding of this aspect of children's lives (Shantz & Hartup, 1992).

COGNITIVE-DEVELOPMENTAL PERSPECTIVES

Much of our recent understanding of children's peer conflicts has been based on cognitive-developmental theory. This perspective describes peer conflict as a process that encourages cognitive growth, logical thinking, and perspective-taking among young children (Piaget, 1962).

PIAGET

Cognitive Growth

Peer conflict creates cognitive conflict, which in turn fosters individual cognitive development. In Piaget's theory, peer conflict contributes to this development in three ways. First, peer interaction creates *cognitive conflict*, a state of disequilibrium in which children's own cognitive structures are at odds with the environment. The conflict is resolved through a process of accommodation as children restructure their thinking and, as a result, experience internal cognitive growth (Arcaro-McPhee et al., 2002; Forman & Kraker, 1985; DeVries & Zan, 1994).

Second, peer interaction is qualitatively different from adult-child interaction. In a conflict situation, children are more likely to comply behaviorally with an adult without making any internal cognitive adjustments, but will challenge their peers. Confrontation with peers can be more powerful in children's cognitive growth than imitation of adults (Bell et al., 1985; Vespo et al., 1995).

Piaget's third point is that cognitive development results from social coordination as children build consensus. In this process, children work together and actively construct solutions to their problems, as we see Maria, Stefan, and Nicole do in our example.

A typical conflict between young children, an argument over a toy, illustrates these points. First, in the *schema*, or cognitive structure, of the very young child, a toy in one's possession may mean permanent ownership. The idea that someone else may have a right of possession is a new concept that must be accommodated. Following Piaget's second point, because children are less likely to comply in handing over the toy to another child than to an adult, they will offer opposition and perhaps argument. Finally, older children may experience cognitive development as they find a solution to the dispute.

Logical Thinking

Young children develop logical thinking as they present arguments to others. As they become aware that others do not share their thinking, children must try to convince their audience of their views, listen to opposing positions, integrate various arguments, and arrive at a consensus. Studies of children's cognitive processes in conflicts suggest that there is a developmental pattern in preschoolers' ability to negotiate and to persuade their peers (DeVries & Zan, 1994; Laursen & Hartup, 1989; Lubin & Forbes, 1984).

The following example illustrates children's explicit understanding of persuasion in peer interactions. An adult interviewer is asking April about her understanding of conflicts and her approach to resolving them through persuasion.

Interviewer: I'd like to know how people solve their problems when they have arguments. What if someone wanted to play and you didn't want them?

April (age 4):   I would tell them I wanted to play with Natalie and Mary Peyton and they should change their minds and they probably would.

Perspective-Taking

Young children increase their perspective-taking, the ability to see things as others see them, through conflicts with their peers. As they experience opposing viewpoints in social interaction, children become aware that other points of view exist, and they begin to understand, if not agree with, what others say and think. Children's understanding of their peers and their conception of social rules are related to conflict resolution strategies (Malloy & McMurray, 1996; Shantz & Shantz, 1985). In the clean-up time conflict in this chapter, Maria has broadened her perspective to include Stefan's claim to the "tape-pulling." April's words about persuasion, although not empathetic, suggest that she is aware that others have their own perspectives that are different from hers.

Post-Piagetian Cognitive Theories

Further discussion about children's development continues to support the idea that cognitive conflict is necessary for cognitive development. However, children may not be able to "fully benefit from cognitive conflict until they reach a level of development sufficient for comprehending the conflict itself" (Chapman & McBride, 1992, p. 58). Answers to this question may be found if we consider the effects of factors such as socioeconomic status, social dominance, home language and culture, and specific individual differences among children. Researchers have identified a need to extend the boundaries of our study of children's conflicts to combine both children's social understanding and their cognitive growth (Corsaro, 1986; DeVries & Zahn, 1994; Dunn & Cutting, 1999; Musatti, 1986; Shantz, 1987; Tobin et al., 1989). This movement toward a sociocognitive framework draws on the perspectives of sociocultural, sociolinguistic, and sociological theory that we will explore in this book.

New theories are emerging to explain young children's thinking and development. We continue to ask whether these new theories will provide insight into children's conflicts. *Information processing theory* presents cognitive development as a continuous process. Using a model similar to computer processing, this perspective tells us that the mind codes, transforms, and organizes sensory input into behavioral output. Mostly applied in academic learning situations, this theory has had little application to date in understanding children's social, emotional, and moral development (Klahr & MacWhinney, 1998; Siegler, 1998). However, *information processing* is a growing theory that may at some point add to our understanding of the way children reason and negotiate in their conflicts.

SOCIOMORAL PERSPECTIVES

Theories of moral development also give us a clear framework for understanding children's conflicts (see Figure 5–1). As children develop moral understanding, they are able to distinguish right from wrong, recognize standards of behavior toward others, and resolve moral dilemmas based on ideals of justice, fairness, or caring.

Children develop perspective-taking and problem-solving through constructive conflicts with peers.

Piaget	Kohlberg	Damon	Gilligan
According to Piaget, stages of children's moral development align with his stages of cognitive development.	Kohlberg expanded on Piaget's theory with additional stages that extend into the highest level of adult reasoning.	Damon developed earlier stages that extend Kohlberg's in order to describe very young children's moral reasoning and offer greater complexity to children's early moral thinking about distribution.	Gilligan does not present stages but describes different perspectives that guide moral reasoning that are more aligned with gender than with age.
Premoral: Young children invent their own rules and change them as they play and make decisions.	Preconventional/Premoral reasoning: Stage 1: Punishment and obedience orientation: Decisions conform with adult authority to avoid punishment.	Stage 0A: Undifferentiated reasoning based on self orientation. Own wishes and needs are satisfied.	Abstract justice and fairness/individual orientation
Moral realism/ heteronomous morality: Children make decisions by following rules as determined by others without questioning authority.	Stage 2: Naïve instrumental hedonism: Decisions are based on rewards and self-interest.	Stage 0B: Undifferentiated reasoning based on strict equality. The same for all.	Versus
Moral relativism/ autonomous morality: Children consider aspects of the situation, such as intention, when making decisions.	Conventional reasoning: Stage 3: Conformity and approval: Good boy/good girl decisions made to please others.	Stage 1A: Differentiated reasoning based on merit. Hard workers deserve more.	Relationships and caring/ other or interpersonal orientation
	Stage 4: Conformity to social order: Decisions follow society's laws and rules.	Stage 1B: Differentiated reasoning based on need with some consideration of merit and reciprocity.	
	Post-conventional reasoning: Stage 5: Law as social contract: Laws are made by people who can agree to change them.		
	Stage 6: Universal ethical principals: Respect for human dignity guides all decision-making.		

Figure 5–1
Comparison of theories of moral reasoning.

Stage Theories: Kohlberg, Piaget, and Damon

Piaget and Kohlberg explained children's moral development in the context of stages of cognitive development. Young children experience what Piaget calls *moral realism*, which is described as a *morality of constraint* guided by deference to adults and avoidance of negative consequences. Similarly, Kohlberg places children in *preconventional* stages of morality, with decision-making based on obedience to authority, concern for rewards and punishment, and pragmatic concerns for one's needs and interests.

Extending Kohlberg's six well-known stages, William Damon (1977) describes additional stages for younger children's moral reasoning. His stages are based on children's emerging understanding of adult desires as independent from their own and on their increasing ability to take the perspectives of others. An important point for adults to remember is that, with guidance, children may understand or follow a model of reasoning at a higher stage than their own. Providing opportunities for children to imitate and practice thinking at higher stages will help them further develop their moral reasoning (Upright, 2002).

Teachers Talk About Learning Moral Decision-Making

The teacher in this kindergarten classroom encourages children to be generous and conciliatory when conflicts arise. She uses the phrase "being the bigger person" to mean being someone who is willing to walk away from an issue, rather than someone who persists and continues to fight. This context for moral decision-making provides children with an opportunity to practice this higher-level thinking.

At the beginning of Drop-Everything-and-Read Time, Robert and DeShaun grab the same yellow chair at the same time. (The yellow chairs are larger and therefore preferred.)

DeShaun:	This is my chair, Robert.
Robert:	No, it's not. It's my chair.

They pull the chair back and forth between them.

DeShaun:	Get off, Robert. It's my chair.
Robert:	I was sitting in this chair. It goes to my desk.
DeShaun:	Mrs. Stone, Mrs. Stone, tell Robert to give me my chair.
Mrs. Stone:	What is the problem, children? There are 10 chairs just like this one in this class. You need to think of a way to solve this problem without creating a problem for yourself. Who can be the bigger person?

The two boys stare at each other as if to see who is going to be the bigger person.

DeShaun (shrugs): That's all right. I'll get another one.

Limitations of Stage Theories

Early childhood professionals may intuitively feel that children have a greater moral competence than stage theorists have suggested. Critical perspectives in early childhood education suggest that there are limitations to the idea of development in stages and that children are more capable and learn in less rigid patterns than stage theories imply (Donaldson, 1978; Graue & Walsh, 1998; Soto, 2000). Young children have demonstrated awareness of the distinction between moral rules and social conventions (Arcaro-McPhee et al., 2002; Nucci, 1985; Turiel, 1983). Children's moral decision-making may be domain-specific. In other words, children may exhibit more advanced moral reasoning in some situations than in others. In their conflicts, they see a difference between moral issues, such as hurting one another or taking toys, and social rules and routines, such as breaking in line or not cleaning up.

Relationships and Caring: Gilligan and Noddings

Young children have also exhibited evidence of empathy, caring, and prosocial behavior to a greater degree than the long-accepted stages of Piaget and Kohlberg would indicate. Carol Gilligan's landmark work, *In a Different Voice* (1982), created a new understanding of moral thinking, theorizing that women and men, adolescents and adults, may make moral decisions in different but equally valid ways. Gilligan's theory does not focus on stages but describes a contrast in the basis for one's reasoning, according to varying standards of what is important in the moral decision. Varying standards can be 1) a sense of abstract justice and fairness, or 2) a concern for connectedness in human relationships and caring. These basic contrasts in moral understanding can be found in the causes of conflicts, as well as in the strategies that children and adults use to resolve them.

Additional concern for an ethic or care, and for altruism and empathy, give us a new framework for what we see in children's interactions with peers (Thurston & Berkeley, 2003). Children's prosocial behaviors are as natural and frequent as the antisocial behaviors that attract adult notice (Gilligan, 1982; Goldstein, 1998; Kohn, 1991; Noddings, 1995). Nel Noddings gives us a new view on the idea of caring. She describes care as an active and intentional interaction between the one who gives and the one who receives. An environment of active caring provides students with both the tools and the motivation to resolve their conflicts. As one child explained, in a conflict, "Because you're friends, you work it out."

In a classroom setting, an ethic of care can be supported by a curriculum centered on themes of caring. Teachers may design a curriculum for young children centered on themes of caring, such as helping others, kindness, or food and hunger. Caring for the environment is a theme that is easily understood and leads children to thinking about caring for something beyond themselves, something that they share with the whole world (Ramsey, 1998). We will explore applications of themes of caring in greater detail in our later chapters on creating classrooms for caring and conflict resolution (Chapter 7).

Four Examples of Caring Behaviors Among Young Children

Children demonstrated caring through the helping behaviors and prosocial words in these four examples, observed in an early childhood program:

Children are playing outside on the blacktop. J. C. (age 4) has a plastic hockey stick and ball. Casey (age 3) also wants one. J. C. goes to the shed and gets him one.

Tomas (age 5) wants to paint a cardboard tube and asks the girls (age 5) at the table for paint.

Janie: It's alright, Tomas. You can use mine.

Heidi also offers him her paint.

Carla (age 4) slips and falls on the waffle blocks, a little bit away from Heidi and Meg (both age 5). Heidi goes to help her up.

Heidi to Carla: Are you okay, Carla?

Meg (age 5) is looking sad as she stands alone in the hallway. Jonah (age 5) asks her what is wrong and offers to play with her.

TEACHERS TALK ABOUT CARING IN AN INCLUSIVE CLASSROOM

"My students treat those with noticeable special needs by being more helpful, more caring, and more understanding with the same conflicts that they might have with a non-special education student. I had a child with autism last year and have a child with Downs this year, and it is amazing how wonderfully the students treat this child. They are excited to see him, ask where he is when he is absent, and call out good-bye when he leaves. He causes a lot of conflict in my class too, but the other children blow it off more easily with him than with the other students."

SOCIOCULTURAL PERSPECTIVES

Sociocultural theory describes peer conflict as a problem-solving activity in which children not only develop cognitively, but also create and conserve cultural systems through social interaction with their peers. This perspective has its roots in the work of Soviet psychologist Lev Vygotsky (1978). In his study of human development and socialization, Vygotsky proposed that social interaction "provides children with systems of signs and cultural meanings," and that "historically determined culture becomes the very driving force of development via the educational process" (Musatti, 1986, p. 32). Vygotsky's work has significant and direct applications in many areas of teaching and learning. In the following sections, we will see how his theories help explain children's conflicts.

VYGOTSKY

Process and Change

Four themes in Vygotsky's theory are relevant to children's peer conflicts. The first is his emphasis on process and change. Vygotsky believed that "the key motivating factor for development and change is conflict and problem-solving" (Corsaro 1985, p. 58). Higher functions of thought occur in argument than in reflection (Cazden, 1988). Peer play is necessary for children to develop social knowledge and interaction skills. Children's shared peer culture includes rules and rituals governing issues such as group entry disputes and roleplay decisions (Corsaro, 1985).

Practical Activity

A second theme is the idea of a relationship between practical activity and human development. Coping with the demands of change is a practical activity that leads to social and psychological development. Practical activities "develop from the child's attempts to deal with everyday problems or difficulties" (Corsaro, 1985, p. 59). Conflict is a social event leading to practical activities, and eventually to internalizing these activities. Corsaro provides additional support for this idea from his studies of the peer culture of preschoolers, citing children's efforts to gain control over their lives and to establish shared social activities with their peers.

Internalization

A third principle of Vygotsky's theory is his concept of the internalization of human society and culture: "Every function in the child's development appears twice: first on the social level, and later on the individual level; first, between people (interpsychological), and then inside the child (intrapsychological)" (Vygotsky, 1978, p. 102). Vygotsky's illustration of internalization describes the gesture of pointing. A child extends an arm in an unsuccessful attempt to grasp an object. The mother responds by pointing to the object. Thus the child learns the gesture of pointing, not from direct experience with the object but from another person.

This concept of initial social learning, or "internal reproduction of external operations," provides a contrast to Piagetian theory in the locus of development (Vygotsky, 1978). For Piaget, development is internally driven and precedes learning. For Vygotsky, development is socially driven, in the context of culture and history, and precedes development. This process of internalization occurs gradually, the transformation taking place over time. Peer interaction and social conflict provide a context for this interpsychological phase of children's development. With the emphasis on the social level of learning, a Vygotskian approach calls for the inclusion of aspects such as gender, race and ethnicity, family structures, socioeconomic status, political environment, and peer culture in understanding children's development (Bronfenbrenner, 1979; Tobin et al., 1989).

Zone of Proximal Development

The final piece of Vygotsky's theory is the zone of proximal development. This term describes the child's mental ability as emerging competence rather than as a measure of past achievement; what children are able to do with help rather than on their own. "It is the distance between the actual developmental level as determined by independent problem-solving and the level of potential development as determined through problem-solving under adult guidance or in collaboration with more capable peers" (Vygotsky, 1978, p. 86). Vygotsky's own metaphor describes the zone of proximal development as the "buds" or "flowers" of development, rather than its "fruits" (p. 86). According to Vygotsky, two 8-year-olds may both be able to solve a problem individually with the ability of an 8-year-old. If, however, with adult guidance, one is able to solve problems at the level of a 9-year-old and the other at the level of a 12-year-old, their abilities are not the same.

Children are capable of functioning at a higher level of development with assistance from an adult or a more mature peer than when they function on their own. An example of this concept occurs in children's play with peers. A dispute or conflict situation with more capable peers provides an opportunity for children to engage in more advanced negotiation strategies.

A Conflict in the Art Room

Tomas is trying out a number of ways to deal with this everyday difficulty, learning first on a social level what will work in this situation with Daniel. The teacher, without intervening in a directive manner, provides some scaffolding to both boys about the effects of their words on one another.

Daniel (age 5) has made a large paper mask for Tomas (age 5), who is now coloring it. Daniel stands beside him at the table.

Daniel (with some frustration): I'm trying to help you.

Tomas continues to color, ignoring him.

Daniel (now crying): You're making me mad.

Teacher is also sitting at the table, fixing her glasses as she listens.

Daniel: Have patience with me.

Tomas: You don't color very good.

Daniel: I'm trying my best.

Tomas: But you go like this (demonstrates scribbling) and then it's not all blue.

Daniel: Let me help!

Tomas: I'm not going to let you come to my house.

Daniel cries.

Teacher: He probably doesn't mean forever. Work it out. Tomas, look at his face.

Daniel offers to help Tomas put the mask on. Clean-up bell rings.

Daniel: You should have let me help. I'll color everything blue.

(He colors while Tomas goes to get a streamer for the mask.)

Daniel (showing the mask to Tomas): Is this good?

TEACHERS TALK ABOUT CHILDREN ACTING AS MORE CAPABLE PEERS

"Some of my children try to resolve their conflicts by talking it out. I can tell by their conversations with me when they come to me after their attempts have not worked. I do believe these strategies work better when they are interacting with someone who is younger than them, but not a peer or older child. They're only 6 years old."

Building on Vygotsky's Work

Neo-Vygotskians have extended his concepts of peer interaction to the idea of collaboration that may be implied or non-verbal as children approach a problem. Children may begin without a clear idea of what the problem is or how to solve it. Cognition is described as shared activity, not something that "operates exclusively in people's heads" (Forman & Kraker, 1985, p. 29). Peer collaboration studies have involved observations of children's problem-solving activities (Bell et al., 1985; Forman & Kraker, 1985). In collaboration, children demonstrated a higher level of reasoning than in individual thinking. Similarly, in a study of first-graders' friendship development, Rizzo (1989) suggests that children's observed behaviors in conflicts with friends demonstrated concepts such as loyalty, acceptance, and sharing, although these concepts were not evident in interviews with the children. Following Vygotsky's theory, this "raw material" of practical activity may later develop into reflective thought (p. 70).

The conflict at clean-up time provides examples of Vygotsky's principles: Maria's internalization and Nicole's role as the more capable peer. Nicole voices the understood prominence of the rule of prior ownership/space/participation, "She was doing it first," but she generates an alternate solution that allows Stefan to join the activity.

Interpretivist Perspective

Writers and thinkers have worked to reconcile the theories of Piaget and Vygotsky where they do not agree. Corsaro and Eder (1990) propose that Vygotsky's *interpsychological* perspective extends and complements the *intrapsychological* view of cognitive-developmental theory. Combining Vygotskian and Piagetian constructivist theories, Corsaro offers an *interpretive* approach, which contends that "children discover a world endowed with meaning and help to shape and share in their own developmental experiences through participation in everyday cultural routines" (Corsaro & Eder, 1990, p. 199). In an analysis of Italian preschoolers' conversational disputes, Corsaro and Rizzo (1988) demonstrate that children produce their own social world and collectively reproduce, or appropriate, the adult world. Studying children's arguing is another means of integrating the perspectives of Piaget and Vygotsky (Chapman & McBride, 1992).

Figure 5–2
Bronfenbrenner's ecological systems.

ECOLOGICAL SYSTEMS THEORY

Bronfenbrenner (1979) offers a similar view of children's "development-in-context" within nested cultural-ecological systems (see Figure 5–2). As we have seen in Chapter 1, all the ecological systems play a powerful role in children's development. Their peer conflicts take place in the *microsystem* of the child's peer culture and the early childhood program setting. Interacting and negotiating with age-mates, children learn their roles as children within their first peer culture. Later, they begin to develop skills and knowledge needed for their later roles in an adult peer culture. An example of children's conflicts found in cross-cultural work contrasts disputes between preschoolers in Japan and the United States. Japanese children were expected to work out their differences on their own, while teachers in the American preschool mediated conflicts with children (Tobin et al., 1989). Children's everyday lives, and the way they experience and resolve conflicts, are affected directly and indirectly by what is happening in each of the systems. Throughout this book, we will see how school and center, family, community, the media, effects of the economy, and world events all play a part in children's development and provide a framework for conflicts and conflict resolution.

TEACHERS TALK

> "Conflicts are a necessary part of growing up. Children need to learn to work things out in order to survive in the real world. Childhood is a time to build those skills necessary to get along with other people, and resolve conflicts appropriately. I think children learn more on the playground about making it in life than we could ever teach them in the classroom."

IMPLICATIONS FOR TEACHERS: LINKING THEORY AND PRACTICE

Conflict and Children's Development: The Hundred Languages of Children

The educators in the municipal schools of Reggio Emilia, Italy, have drawn on the works of Dewey, Piaget, and Vygotsky to create powerful learning communities for young children. The following discussion of children's conflicts supports the view of conflict as a natural and valuable part of children's development.

> Conflicts and the recognition of differences are essential, in our view. Conflict transforms the relationship a child has with peers—opposition, negotiation, listening to the other's point of view and deciding whether or not to adopt it, and reformulating an initial premise are part of the processes of assimilation and accommodation into the group. We see these dynamics, until a short time ago considered only as part of the socialization process, also to be substantially cognitive procedures, and they are an essential element of democracy (Rinaldi, 1998, p. 115–118).

Adult Intervention and Guidance

From our new understanding about children's learning in terms of *cognitive development*, we now know that teachers can support children's learning by giving them space to engage in non-destructive conflict. Listening to their reasoning on their own and in *collaboration* with others can be a way of assessing their cognitive and language development, as well as their social and emotional development. Teachers, as well as *more capable peers*, can provide *scaffolding* to children, guiding them within their *zone of proximal development* through more advanced conflict resolution skills, developing greater perspective-taking, generating alternative solutions, and perceiving cause-and-effect. This scaffolding is based on meaningful learning, not on an ineffective directive to "tell him you are sorry." The idea of learning from a

---

WORKING WITH CHILDREN: A PREVIEW

Project Work

In Part 3 of this book, we will concentrate on what teachers can do in classrooms, but here is a preview. One strategy that we can introduce at this point is the idea of *project work*, as described as the Project Approach (Katz & Chard, 1989) and, in Reggio Emilia, as *progettazione*. From a Reggio Emilia perspective, Carla Rinaldi describes children's learning through conflicts and negotiation that naturally arise as children work together. Project work, or *progettazione*, provides a vehicle for this learning.

> "Now you can see the issues in their full richness but also in their complexity. The adults' difficulty is to initiate and nurture situations that stimulate this kind of learning process, where conflict and negotiation appear as the driving force for growth. *Progettazione* allows for this social constructivist process to develop" (Rinaldi, 1998, p. 118).

In Chapter 8, we will investigate project work in further detail.

---

more capable peer also plays out as children spontaneously assume the role of peer mediator on behalf of others in conflict situations. The implication again is for the adult to allow children, both those engaged in conflicts and those who may join as mediators, the time and space to arrive at a positive resolution of the conflict. Look for more on adult intervention in Chapter 10.

PUTTING THE PIECES TOGETHER

We can begin to bring together the topics of the preceding chapters, observing and listening to children (Chapter 3) and recognizing the characteristics and anatomy of conflicts (Chapter 4) with understanding the perspective from the theoretical knowledge of the role of conflict in children's development (Chapters 5 and 6). Linking this knowledge will guide teachers in deciding when to intervene and how to support a learning and social environment to foster the development of conflict resolution skills. We will find more specific strategies for teaching and learning in Part 3.

>>

SUMMARY

As we work toward our goals of helping children understand, manage, and resolve their conflicts, we will place these particular interactions in the context of our knowledge of their development. In later chapters, we will consider observation and analysis of conflicts. We will look closely at mutually agreeable conflict outcomes, with active and child-constructed resolutions, as children in a dispute work

Observing children and understanding the nature of peer conflicts will guide teachers in deciding when to intervene.

to successfully solve the problem. This type of outcome reflects the cognitive-developmental emphasis on learning in conflict and perspective-taking, as well as elements of sociomoral and sociocultural theory.

Varying theoretical perspectives (cognitive-developmental, sociomoral, and sociocultural) explain the contributions of children's constructive peer conflicts to their development. This discussion of theory leads (in the next chapter) to an examination of how sociological theory may continue to extend our understanding of children's conflicts beyond their individual development into their social organization and social knowledge, and how sociolingistics give us new insights into the rich and varied language of children's arguments.

SUPPLEMENTARY MATERIALS FOR CHAPTER 5

Research Focus/Teacher as Researcher

An article on preschool children's abilities to recognize diversity diversify classifications reported that a multicultural curriculum project was effective in helping children identify others according to more than one physical attribute (gender, skin color, size, and so on). How do the children in your setting classify other people?

(Bernstein, J., Zimmerman, T. S., Werner-Wilson, R. J., & Vosburg, J. (2000). Preschool children's classification skills in a multicultural education intervention to promote acceptance of ethnic diversity. Journal of Research in Childhood Education, 14, 181–192.)

APPLICATION EXERCISES

1. Question for discussion: Review various elements of Piaget and Vygotsky's theories. How do these theories help explain what children do and say in your setting?

2. Working in a small group, illustrate one or more points of the theories from the chapter using examples of children's conflicts, from your actual experience, or from something invented. (Role play works well here.)

3. Can you think of implications for your current or future practice based on what you have learned so far about children's conflicts?

4. Writing application: Use this discussion starter. "Children's conflicts, like other aspects of behavior and development, are …"

THINKING ABOUT ALL CHILDREN

1. We have mentioned culture and home language in this chapter in the context of our theories. How much do the theories in this chapter explain the peaceful peer interactions and conflicts between children with varying abilities and developmental levels?

6

Sociological, Sociolinguistic, and Social Learning Perspectives

"You fruity-head!"
"You tooty-head!"
"You're a bagel-head!"
"We'll you're a ... a ... bacon-head!!!"
"I'm not playing with you. I'm playing with Ryan!"
"Nuh-unh! You got to play with everybody. Ms L. says so."

>> >

Chapter 6 Objectives: Chapter 6 presents children's conflict interaction as a process for learning about the social and political world, and the sociological notions of groups, allies, roles, and negotiations. The rich language of children's arguments and wordplay is explained in sociolinguistic theory. Connecting theory with practice, we will return to the question posed in Chapter 3: "What do children really mean?" And we will explore more ways of understanding and learning about the world as children do.

Chapter Outline
Sociological Perspectives
    The Positive Functions of Conflict
    Shared Understandings in Children's Peer Culture: Interpretivism
    Implications for Practice: Children's Group Structures
Sociolinguistic Perspectives
    Children's Arguments
    Verbal Rough-and-Tumble Play
    Name-Calling
    Implications for Practice: Understanding Arguing and Name-Calling
Social Learning Perspectives
    Social Learning and Social Cognition
    Behaviorism
    Implications for Practice
Summary

Negotiating in the Hallway

Meg and Heidi (age 5) discuss arrangements for play partners during activity time.

Meg: No, I can't play with you, 'cause Penelope just wants to play with me.

Heidi: You can play with me on the playground.

Forming Alliances at Recess

On the playground, three first-grade boys have a more complex negotiation.

Dantay to Geoffrey: I won't play with you unless you obey me.

J. C. to Dantay: I'll play with you, Dantay.

Geoffrey: If J. C. is playing with you, then I'll play.

SOCIOLOGICAL PERSPECTIVES

What would a sociologist see in the interactions between Meg and Heidi, and between Dantay and J. C.? There are many interesting things going on in children's conflicts. Friendships and alliances form and fall apart. Children negotiate and threaten. They tease, laugh, and squabble. Can we find more explanations in other disciplines and theories?

We may think of sociology, in part, as the study of groups of people in organizations or cultures defined by shared beliefs and practices. A sociological perspective describes conflict as a vehicle for social organization. Conflict is one of the ways by which we organize our social world. Although research in sociology that directly addresses children's peer conflict is limited, there is extensive writing in the field, both on conflict in general and on children's socialization. Watching children define play groups through negotiation and argument, Early Childhood professionals can understand how sociology may help us explain what is happening in children's conflicts. Aspects of children's conflicts that seem to make sense from a sociological perspective include group entry issues and resolutions mediated by peers. We can see children in play forming alliances and "making treaties" with all the seriousness of diplomats.

Within the field of contemporary sociology, four major perspectives are dominant in the United States, and there is an active dialogue in the field about the merits of each. To add to the other theories in Chapters 5 and 6, we will look at children's conflicts through the lenses of structural-functionalism and conflict theory (Strauss, 2002).

The Positive Functions of Conflict

Writers in 20th-century sociology explained the positive functions of conflict and described conflict as constructive rather than destructive. Conflict establishes and maintains the boundaries and identity of societies and groups. From a sociological perspective, there are two types of conflicts: *realistic* conflicts, which involve alternative goals and means, and *unrealistic* conflicts, which provide release of aggressive tension due to frustration. This is according to Lewis Coser, an early writer in the field of conflict theory (1956).

Coser (1956) uses the example of children's conflicts to illustrate his theory of conflict as a unifier, an experience through which we can get to know another person. Previously unacquainted children who argue over a toy and subsequently play together cooperatively demonstrate that conflict can be "a means of acquiring knowledge about an initially unknown person, and of establishing basis for other forms of interaction" (p. 122).

Social conflict among children plays several functions (Maynard, 1985b). Children "acquire a sense of social structure through conflict" (p. 207). The primary, or manifest, function of conflict is the production of children's small-group society, which occurs in three ways. First, children create a social organization defined by an orderly process of dispute. Next, through in-group disputes, children create political or partisan alignments. Finally, the social organization of conflict is momentary and practical, and alliances change as issues are resolved or changed.

The secondary, or latent, functions of children's peer conflict help children acquire a sense of social structure through experience with social organization within conflict episodes, and help them develop relationships of authority and friendships, which extend beyond particular conflict encounters (Dunn & Cutting, 1999; Strauss, 2002; Vespo et al., 1995).

In the following examples, we can see how children define groups, form alliances, and apply shared rules of organization.

Gender Group Identity in the Box City

The multiage K-first class is developing a "box city" in the classroom with large cardboard boxes.

Daniel (age 5) and Todd (age 5) are "attacking" the cardboard box tent occupied by April and Mary Peyton (both age 5).

Mary Peyton: Get out of here! (They charge the girls' tent.) No boys in our tent! Close the door so they don't see us! Get out of here, you dummies!

The boys have retreated to make a new plan.

YOUR CHILDHOOD MEMORIES

Do you remember being 6 or 7 years old? Think about the rules of your play group, who was in and who was out. Based on that memory, can you describe exactly what happens when three children play together, as opposed to two or four or more?

Forming Alliances on the Playground

On the playground, three boys negotiate about who will play together.

Daniel (age 5) to Benjamin (age 4):	I won't play with you unless you obey me.
J. C. (age 4) to Daniel:	I'll play with you, Daniel.
Benjamin:	If J. C. is playing with you, then I'll play.

Shared Understandings in Children's Peer Culture: Interpretivism

Sociology focuses on children's "anticipatory socialization," the process by which children learn to take their places in their society as adults. In contrast, an interpretivist explores children's socialization in their own world of childhood, a phenomenon that takes place in children's interactions with other children (Cicourel, 1970; Corsaro, 1985; Corsaro & Eder, 1990; Corsaro & Schwartz, 1991; Gruae & Walsh, 1998). Instead of individual social development, "childhood socialization should be understood as a collective and social process" (Corsaro & Schwartz, 1991, p. 234). "It is not just that the child must make his knowledge his own, but that he must make it known in a community of those who share his sense of belonging to a culture" (Bruner, 1986, p. 127). "Children enter into social systems and, by interacting and negotiating with others, establish shared understandings that become fundamental social knowledge on which they continually build" (Corsaro & Schwartz, 1991. p. 235).

We have already explored the idea of the peer culture defined by children as a way of observing children, in Chapter 3. An *interpretivist* view provides a context for the investigation of children's peer conflicts. In his ethnographic study of preschoolers' peer culture, Corsaro (1985) offers evidence of children's shared understanding of the rules of their social organization. Observing children as they deal with everyday life, including conflicts over entry into ongoing group play, Corsaro concludes that "children attempt to gain control over their lives through communal production and sharing of social activities with peers" (p. 272).

Children learn rules of social regulation from interaction with their peers. Making a further connection to what we know, we can look again at the rules of social organization that guide children's conflicts. In possession conflicts, toddlers are most often guided by a rule of dominance of a more powerful peer over a subordinate. Preschoolers, however, follow the rule of prior possession (Bakeman & Brownlee, 1982; Singer & Hannikainen, 2002). Sociological theory also helps us understand children's conflicts as we observe examples of their alliances, partnerships, and interventions in disputes by a third child. In the preschool peer culture, children learn the rules of groups and social structure (Corsaro, 1985; Dunn & Cutting, 1999; Maynard, 1985a, 1985b).

The following is an example of children's social negotiation.

Defining a Group in the Box City

The multiage K-first grade is developing a box city in the classroom with large cardboard boxes. Natalie and Aline are building a house in the box city. Monique and Carla come to join them. A group entry issue follows.

Natalie: We'll build another house for you.

Monique: This house isn't as big as yours.

Aline: Well, you can't build with us.

Natalie to Aline: Come on, Aline. Let's build somewhere else.

Implications for Practice: Children's Group Structures

• Teachers need to be aware of the peer group structures, alliances and partnerships that exist in the class and try to observe and understand these group processes.
• Building on class routines and decision-making structures, teachers can provide models that children can internalize and apply in their peer group processes.
• Class meetings can include explicit discussions about the meaning of democracy and consensus-building in your classroom.
• Teachers can also observe closely and ask themselves, "What roles and organizational abilities do I see in these child social organizations that suggest capabilities I may not have seen before? How have children defined membership in the group? Is it exclusionary on the basis of harmful bias or prejudice? Is this a positive peer organization or an exploitive one?"

Sociology, with its rich literature of conflict and socialization, provides a valuable basis for the study of children's peer conflicts and contributes to our understanding of the development of children's social organization and cultural knowledge. Looking at conflicts as a shared dimension of children's peer organization leads to a discussion of arguments, or how children use language in conflict. In the next section, sociolinguistic theory addresses this issue.

SOCIOLINGUISTIC PERSPECTIVES

Listening to children talk to themselves, we hear some remarkable things. We hear imaginative, descriptive language that is a window into their understanding. When children talk together, their social language is equally rich. In their conflicts, we hear wonderful negotiating and skillful bargaining, but also arguments, and name calling and many different ways for children to communicate in a shared language encounter.

Listening to children's conversations, we hear rich and varied social language.

WORKING WITH CHILDREN: A PREVIEW

Cooperative Learning Groups in Primary Classrooms

Cooperative learning groups are planned so that children of different abilities and characteristics will work together collaboratively. A number of theories that we have discussed help explain why cooperative learning can be effective. Can you explain how these theories work in cooperative learning? Can you think of other theories that apply as well?

Cognitive-developmental theory: Through collaboration, children gain cognitively through cognitive conflict, hearing the viewpoints of others, and the co-construction of knowledge.

Sociocultural theory: Children work with more capable peers and are able to function within their zone of proximal development. Peers provide scaffolding for learning and an opportunity for children to learn on a social plane before learning within themselves.

Sociological theory: Cooperative learning emphasizes effective small-group processes and results in the development of group definition and cohesion.

In Chapter 9, we will focus on teaching and learning in classrooms for peacemaking and conflict resolution for primary-grade children from age 6 to 8, including more on cooperative learning.

This brings us to the question, "What is sociolinguistic theory, and what does it tell us about children's peer conflicts?" This multi-disciplinary approach to discourse analysis combines, most notably, aspects of sociology and linguistics, and it also draws on anthropology, ethnography, and psychology (Cazden, 1988; Grimshaw, 1990; Sheldon, 1993). Sociolinguists concern themselves with language as an important element in social interaction. "Talk used to build social organization within face-to-face interaction" is the basis for Goodwin's 1990 study of the ways that urban African-American children create their social world. Studying the conversations of Italian preschoolers, Corsaro and Rizzo (1988) demonstrated that children's culture both depends on and contributes to children's ability to communicate with each other.

Children's Arguments

What about arguing? The study of arguments within sociolinguistics offers a significant contribution to the literature on children's conflicts. Grimshaw (1990) points out that both discourse and conflict are "pervasive" and "ubiquitous" within the human condition, and that the study of "conflict talk" offers insight into the nature of social conflict. From a sociolinguistic point of view, conflict is defined in terms of discourse phenomena as "mutual verbal opposition" (Garvey & Shantz, 1992, p. 113). Conflict, or argument, is a "speech event" with characteristic patterns of structure and content (Brenneis & Lein, 1977). Eisenberg and Garvey define "adversarial episodes" of peer interaction in their research with preschool children, with a definite structure: "Beginning with the first instance of opposition and ending when (1) an obvious settlement was reached, (2) one child left the scene of interaction and was not pursued, and (3) the discourse topic [was] altered and not resumed for a period of one minute" (Corsaro & Rizzo, 1990, p. 23).

A Pencil Conflict

The "conflict talk" in this example of a common possession dispute follows the discourse patterns described previously: an initial act, statements of mutual opposition, elaboration, and reasoning, and finally a negotiation of an agreeable settlement.

Takisha: That's my pencil.

George: I got it from the basket.

Takisha: Give it to me. It's my pencil.

George: No, I got it from the basket.

Takisha: Give it to me now!

George: No, I got it from the basket. There are other pencils in the basket. Get one of those.

Takisha: Here is a pencil from the basket. It has a point and an eraser. Can you use this one and give me my pencil back?

George: Okay. [gives the pencil back]

"Sociolinguistics describes the value of verbal conflict, or arguments, for children. Arguments provide occasions for children to assume specific social identities, as they exercise a 'rich set of voices'" (Goodwin, 1990, p. 239). In their disputes, children are required to understand and strategically apply rules of discourse (Brenneis & Lein, 1977). According to Goodwin and Goodwin (1987), "Arguing provides children with a rich arena for development of proficiency in language, syntax, and social organization" (p. 200). This research on the activity of arguing presented an analysis of the structure and procedures used to construct an argument. "Argumentation, rather than being disorderly, gives children an opportunity to explore through production use the natural structures of their language"
(p. 226). This evaluation of arguing as a phenomenon that is both natural and orderly is echoed by Corsaro and Rizzo (1990). As positive experiences, verbal disputes contribute to children's communication ability and social knowledge. Corsaro & Rizzo (1988) describe the structure of Italian children's lively debates, or *discussioni*. These debates include claims and counterclaims, stylized aggravation of disagreements, and dramatization of evidence supporting their claims.

Through arguments, children learn rules of behavior, increase their verbal skills, and identify the boundaries and expectations of their social world. As a group, children produce their own rules and boundaries within their peer culture (Corsaro, 1985; Corsaro & Rizzo, 1990). "Conflict is a special aspect of communicative competence and, thereby, social competence" (Garvey & Shantz, 1992, p. 117).

TEACHERS TALK ABOUT ARGUING

"I find day-to-day successes in the times I sit down near kids and listen to what they have to say and watch them talk to each other and successfully work out a conflict. I also enjoy watching two friends argue over an issue without getting physical and allowing them to argue through it independently and successfully, and to watch them walk away as friends."

Consistent with Vygotsky's perspective, sociolinguists view children's conflicts as a process that constructs and maintains culture. A strength of sociolinguistic theory is its emphasis on the relationship between culture and language (Goodwin, 1990; D'Amato, 1989; Corsaro & Rizzo, 1988, 1990). Corsaro and Rizzo (1990) compared the disputes of Italian and American preschoolers. In both groups, conflicts were part of the children's peer culture and involved similar issues related to play. A major difference was the importance of verbal routines in the disputes of the Italian children. Although these discussions are generated through the peer group, they replicate the conversational style of Italian adults (Corsaro & Rizzo, 1988, 1990). In D'Amato's (1989) study of rivalry, Hawaiian boys demonstrated cultural

Can you imagine what these children are talking about?

values and expectations explicitly referring to Hawaiian characteristics in play-ground arguments.

Verbal Rough-and-Tumble Play

Parent (in kitchen):   "Stop arguing, you two!"

Children (together in another room):   "We're not arguing! We're just playing!"

As we suggested in Chapter 3, children have different basic purposes for argu-ing. The objective may be to achieve resolution, or it may be to sustain the argu-ment. Although much attention has been given to resolution, very often conflicts among children are not resolved. The argument is an end in itself. These argu-ments are carried on through understood formulas, such as those described as the "contradictory routines" of part-Hawaiian children (Watson-Gegeo & Boggs, 1977), "he-said-she-said" among urban African-American girls (Goodwin, 1990), or *discussioni* (Corsaro & Rizzo, 1988). Whether seeking resolution to a dispute or engaging in playful discourse routines, mutual understanding is a necessary framework for conflict talk. "Even young children's conflict talk can be surpris-ingly diverse and versatile" (Garvey & Shantz, 1992, p. 117). Sociolinguistic theory provides a framework for understanding the strength of children's verbal strate-gies and their use of recurring phrases in solving conflicts (Brenneis & Lein, 1977;

Eisenberg & Garvey, 1981). Ritual conflicts are arguments that follow a formula. Frequently observed ritual conflicts involve superiority and rivalries between "the boys and the girls."

There are a variety of dimensions of conflict, according to this sociolinguistic perspective:

1. Serious and non-serious conflicts are distinguished by the intention of the participants, either earnest or playful (a dispute over an object or the verbal rough-and-tumble teasing over a girlfriend).

2. Ritual conflicts, either serious or playful, follow a specific format. There is usually a winner and a loser; performances may be evaluated by an audience.

3. Pretend conflicts occur in the context, or frame, of pretend play (the good guys against the bad guys).

4. Mitigated and aggravated conflicts involve differences in tone (good-natured or hostile) and in direction as the dispute diminishes or escalates (Garvey & Shantz, 1992).

An Argument in the Book Center

An episode among the 5-year-olds in the reading area suggests this ritualistic superiority debate. Jennifer, Heidi, Meg, Janie, Penelope, and Daniel all have books.

Jennifer to Daniel:	You can't even read.
Daniel:	I can read this. [holds up a book]
Jennifer:	No, you can't. You skip pages.
Heidi:	Daniel's playing a trick on you, girl!
Jennifer (after a pause):	I already know how to tell time without a watch!

Name-Calling

Name-calling is often an occasion for "playing with words," such as the 3-year-olds at the beginning of the chapter enjoying the rhyme of "fruity-head" and "tooty-head" and the 5-year-olds in a name-calling exchange saying "bagel-head" and "bacon-head." This way of looking at conflicts reminds observers to be aware of children's intentions in ritual disputes and in pretend conflicts. Name-calling can either be the instigating issue of a conflict or a form of verbal strategy. As you will recall from Chapter 4, verbal strategies, including name-calling, can be either non-aggressive or aggressive and hostile. Hurtful name-calling may be based on physical characteristics (size or other aspects of appearance), family, culture or language group, ability, or what a child's name sounds like. Another cue: What is the other child's response? Does he/she return with more name-calling that is some equivalent or is there hurt silence, tears, or a physical retaliation? None of these are positive responses. A teacher's response in this situation, as with harmful physical aggression, is to keep children from physical or psychological harm. (See the NAEYC Code of Ethical Conduct, available full text online at *http://www.naeyc.org/ resources/position_statements/pseth98.htm.*)

Implications for Practice: Understanding Arguing and Name-Calling

- Listening to children's arguments provides an opportunity to assess children's language in a different context. (You may be surprised at children's eloquence when trying to persuade other children to their viewpoints!)
- Hearing cultural uses of language provides another window into children's worldview.
- Hearing children's strategies in conflict helps teachers determine whether to intervene and how to plan the curriculum and learning environment to give children the verbal tools to resolve or defuse conflicts.
- Children's arguing will help teachers gauge whether language is hurtful teasing or wordplay. It also helps them assess the intensity and degree of escalation in order to decide on intervention.
- Implications of name-calling include whether the understood intent of the name-calling is affectionate and playful or hurtful and damaging.

SOCIAL LEARNING PERSPECTIVES

Behaviorism and social learning theory have a limited application to our topic of helping children understand, manage, and resolve their conflicts. However, this perspective warrants our attention as we examine characteristics of a caring classroom in Chapter 7 and criteria for program models in Chapter 12. Traditional *behaviorism* defines learning not as development, but as an accumulation of behaviors acquired through a dual process of stimulus and response. Learning occurs through conditioning as a result of the extrinsic motivators of reward, or reinforcement, and punishment. Proponents of behaviorism include Locke, Pavlov, Hull, Skinner, and Watson.

Social Learning and Social Cognition

This theory moves beyond traditional behaviorism to stress the importance of adult role models in children's learning. Children learn and imitate behaviors by observing adults. Albert Bandura first introduced the idea of applying behaviorism to children's social learning. In his later work, he moved from social learning to a *social-cognitive* perspective to account more for children's awareness of their behaviors. In Bandura's triadic theory of social cognition, children learn through three integrated processes: personal, environmental, and behavioral. In the classroom, teachers' verbal and nonverbal messages provide powerful social learning models for children (Stanulis & Manning, 2002).

Behaviorism

Elements of behaviorist practices are widespread in schools and classrooms and in families. Often they have the desired immediate effect, but perhaps less so over time. For example, a program designed to stimulate interest in reading rewards children with pizza after they have read a certain number of books. The response could be, "I read all those books to get the pizza and found out that I really like to read!" Or the response could be, "I read enough books to get the pizza, so I don't have to read anymore, right?" In our context, the behaviorist approach of using extrinsic motivators to achieve quiet and non-disruptive classrooms is not consistent with other theories that emphasize the contributions of constructive conflict to children's cognitive development, intrinsic motivation, and empathy and caring.

Implications for Practice

Implications of social learning theory and behaviorism include these considerations:

1. In cases where children exhibit exceptional behaviors, such as persistent aggression and chronic lack of response to social cues, teachers may work with related-service providers in programs based on applied behavior analysis.
2. Social learning theory brings an awareness of the power of the actions and reactions of adults. It provides an important reminder to teachers to consider inappropriate but all-too-human reactions to undesirable behaviors.
3. Rewards can be effective in the short term, and most adults use them sometimes, but it is important to understand the limitations and even, as Alfie Kohn (2001) writes, "the risks of rewards." We will address these issues of intrinsic and extrinsic motivation in Part 3.

>>>

SUMMARY

The preceding chapter has presented a broad range of theoretical perspectives that can help us understand children's conflicts. The importance of an interdisciplinary framework is certain. Children's conflicts offer an avenue for investigating their individual development, as well as their growing awareness of themselves, each other, and their social environment. Conflict helps children define their peer groups and understand their social world. Furthermore, argument expands children's perspective-taking and enriches their verbal expression. As we will see in the next chapter, resolving conflicts helps to maintain friendships and keep the peer group intact.

How much does it explain? The theories in chapter 5 addressed developmental change. In the sociological, sociolinguistic, and social learning theories in this chapter, the emphasis is instead on social interaction, role relationships, and cultural features (Garvey & Shantz, 1992). Unlike much of psychological and cognitive-developmental research, sociolinguistic writing includes numerous studies of different cultures and their approaches to disputes. There is concern for understanding culturally driven behaviors and activities. The differences in these theories suggest that a full understanding of children's peer conflicts will only be provided by a study of multiple perspectives.

>>>

SUPPLEMENTARY MATERIALS FOR CHAPTER 6

Research Focus/Teacher Research

Are there standard formulas of speech or speech protocols that children use as conflict strategies? Look for these types or others in your classroom:

1. The insistence exchange
2. The begging "puh-leeze!"
3. The promise, "I'll be you best friend forever ...!"

>>>

APPLICATION EXERCISES

Observe types of conflicts among the children in your setting, using anecdotal records or a checklist. Develop your own way of capturing your observations. Analyze what you have observed.

1. Serious and non-serious conflicts are distinguished by the intention of the participants, either earnest or playful (a dispute over an object or the verbal rough-and-tumble teasing over a girlfriend).
2. Ritual conflicts, either serious or playful, follow a specific format. There is usually a winner and a loser; performances may be evaluated by an audience.
3. Pretend conflicts occur in the context, or frame, of pretend play (the good guys against the bad guys).
4. Mitigated and aggravated conflicts involve differences in tone (good-natured or hostile) and in direction as the dispute diminishes or escalates (Garvey & Shantz, 1992).

>>

THINKING ABOUT ALL CHILDREN

The work of Shirley Brice Heath (1983) on children's family communication styles provides an important perspective on the use of language at home and at school. In *Preschool in Three Cultures*, the research team found that Japanese children learn to go back and forth from formal Japanese to informal speaking (Tobin et al., 1989). Do you notice different peer-defined language styles when children talk together?

III

Helping Children Understand, Manage, and Resolve Conflicts: "A Three-Layer Cake"

Part 3—Introduction: These chapters address practical implications for current and future practitioners in settings for early care and education. The model of the "Three-Layer Cake" describes how teachers and caregivers can create learning environments for prosocial interaction and conflict resolution. The bottom layer is the caring classroom environment. The middle layer includes curriculum and learning experiences that support children's conflict resolution and peacemaking. The top layer includes adult intervention when conflicts inevitably arise. The cake image is completed by the connection with family and community as the icing all around.

7

Creating a Caring Classroom

A teacher of threes:

"There are very few rules in the threes class, and they are created with the children each semester. The rules are 'Be gentle with your body, your toys, and your words,' 'Treat others well,' and 'Ask permission before touching your friends.' These are logical rules for children, and therefore, conflicts rarely arise due to the rules."

Chapter 7 Objectives: Chapter 7 introduces the image of the "cake" and presents the "bottom layer," the foundation of commitment to a caring community, as children and teachers alike develop a view of themselves as kind and caring individuals in a caring, inclusive community. Teachers communicate their commitment explicitly in their words and implicitly in the physical and social environment they create in the classroom.

Chapter Outline

THE THREE-LAYER CAKE

Building an Early Childhood Setting
for Peace and Conflict Resolution

We have seen that conflicts, arguments, disputes, quarrels, and even fights occur naturally and frequently among young children as they interact in an early childhood classroom. As Early Childhood educators, we want to provide a safe, happy environment for children, one that is peaceful and harmonious, where effective learning can take place. We also need to develop appropriate expectations of children's conflict behaviors and create ways to facilitate independent, positive resolutions through the physical and social environment by creating a caring group environment, valuing the role of play, and offering guidance at appropriate times. Our goal is to help all young children to become peacemakers in what is an often troubled world:

> "Peace is not the absence of conflict. Conflict is an inevitable fact of daily life—internal, interpersonal, intergroup and international conflict. Peace consists in creatively dealing with conflict. Peace is the process of working to resolve conflicts in such a way that both sides win, with increased harmony as the outcome of the conflict and its resolution. The resolution is peaceful if the participants come to want to cooperate more fully and find themselves enabled to do so." (McGinnis & McGinnis in Wichert, 1989, p. xi).

The preceding quotation describes two basic conditions for peace: the *desire* to resolve conflicts agreeably, and the *tools* to do so. We found evidence of these conditions when we examined characteristics of children's conflicts that end with mutually agreeable outcomes. First we found that children playing together before conflict, those who are friends, end conflicts peacefully because they have the *desire* or motivation. We also found that those who use words of reason and negotiation are able to resolve conflicts because they have the *tools* to do so. Beyond the motivation inspired by friendship, children my also be motivated to resolve and even to defuse conflicts because of a more general desire for peace and a caring for others. Creating that environment of caring is the focus of this chapter and will become, as we are about to see, the bottom layer of our cake.

We will work with an image of how to achieve this goal: a three-layer cake with icing (see Figure 7–1). The bottom layer is the caring environment that is the context for all the interactions among the children and adults in your setting. The middle layer includes curriculum ideas and activities to encourage social development and conflict management ability. The top layer involves your decision-making when conflicts inevitably arise, including when and how to intervene. Finally, the icing that surrounds the layers on the top and sides of the cake is the connection with family and community.

Figure 7–1
Three-layer cake: Commitment to a peaceful classroom.

The Bottom Layer: A Caring Classroom Environment

In the bottom layer, we will look at ways to create a positive classroom environment, beginning with your purposeful and explicit commitment to a caring classroom. In your caring classroom, the physical and social environment will encourage children's perspective-taking and empathy, and support them with tools for resolving conflicts peacefully and constructively. As noted in the McGinnis quote, children in a caring classroom sincerely desire to resolve conflicts with others. We will now look closely at this important first layer.

A CARING CLASSROOM ENVIRONMENT

What Is Caring?

In Early Childhood education, the words "caring" and "caring classrooms" are heard frequently. What are we saying with the word "caring?" Does it mean that we feel warmly toward children and that we provide what we envision as a nurturing environment, a place that children want to be because they know that someone loves them? We can certainly agree upon these as goals that we share

(Goldstein, 1998). But there is another way to consider "caring." First of all, we can see "caring" not as an adjective but as an action word. Second, we can create a classroom where not only the adults but also the children do the caring.

"Caring" can be used as an adjective that describes a personal quality or a frame of mind, or as a verb form that defines an action, something that you do for another or yourself. Noddings (1984, 1992) defines "to care" and "to be cared for" as basic human needs. The act of caring is a mutual encounter in a relationship between two people, the one doing the caring and the one who is cared for. The caring classroom is one where mutual caring encounters happen. The teacher builds opportunities for caring encounters, and provides opportunities for all children to both give and receive care.

In this way, it is important for children as well as the teacher to recognize themselves as those who "*care for*." In everyday life in centers and schools, children engage in acts of caring toward one another, such as offering to share toys and materials, making a space for others in play or in line, and offering comfort to those who are hurt or sad. In keeping with the idea of children's peer culture, sometimes children's acts of mutual caring are not apparent to adults. The ways that adults encourage and recognize children's acts of caring may not be the same as the ways that children define and understand caring in the culture of peers or siblings, such as affectionate "teasing," the verbal rough-and-tumble play that signals inclusion within the group. Even physical rough-and-tumble play may be an expression of caring among boys, who may feel that methods of communicating caring, such as hugs, are not available to them (Pollack, 1998). Reed and Brown (2000) suggest that adults should "reconsider the importance of rough and tumble play as one way boys express care, fondness, and friendships toward each other" (p. 104).

TEACHERS TALK ABOUT THE NEW CHILD IN THE CLASS

"John came in with some behavior issues and was testing the waters when he joined us in March. What helped, I think, was the sense of community that we had already established in the classroom. I enlisted the aid of peers to help him remember the rules. Alternately, he has setbacks and makes progress. Today, he hit a child in the face. It was more of a token hit than an injuring one, so water, not ice was indicated for treatment. After my initial suggestion, he took the injured child to the bathroom to get some water, comforted him on the bench, and then walked hand-in-hand with him on the playground, saying, 'It's all right.' The other child seemed content."

TEACHERS TALK ABOUT ACTS OF CARING

"When Celia (a 4-year-old) sees someone begin to cry, she goes ups to them and, without knowing what the problem is, she puts an arm around them and tells them, 'Don't cry. Mrs. Lewis can fix it or you can have your mommy make it better.' She then takes the child by the hand and engages them in an activity with her."

Friendship in a caring classroom.

DISCUSSION AND APPLICATION

Have you seen active caring among children or adults in the way that Noddings describes? Please add an example.

Communicating Your Commitment to a Caring Community

The first step in creating your caring community is in demonstrating your own commitment to a peaceful, prosocial environment. Be explicit about your commitment and what you believe is important, first to yourself and then to others, beginning with the children in your class or center. Let children know what you care about. Being clear and explicit with children demonstrates your respect for them and provides a model for putting their own commitment into words.

Two things that you may feel strongly about and hope to communicate to children are that prosocial behavior is as natural for children as antisocial behavior (Kohn, 1991), and that justice, fairness, safety, empathy, caring, or other values are important to you.

What can you do and say to communicate your commitment? To demonstrate your commitment, it is important to use respectful and positive words when speaking to both children and adults: "Please," "Thank you," "Can I help?" Adult modeling is powerful, and children notice if adults speak to other adults differently (either more kindly and respectfully, or less!) than they speak to children.

The words you choose should be your own in order to be authentic and meaningful. You can express what is important to you while being open to what is important to others as well, hearing "different voices" (Gilligan, 1982). Providing an authentic and sincere demonstration of your commitment leads to children valuing the idea of being committed to an ideal or to a philosophy, not "do as I say, not as I do."

Being explicit about your way of understanding provides *scaffolding* to children to help them construct and internalize their own understanding, an example of the sociocultural theory we explored in Chapter 5. As you will recall, scaffolding is the approach to guiding children in ways of thinking that they are not ready to do independently. Through scaffolding, the adult or more capable peer helps children climb up a rung or two into that *zone of proximal development*, where they are capable of thinking with some help (Vygotsky, 1978).

Developing Perspective-Taking and Empathy in a Caring Classroom

A critical component of children's participation in caring encounters is their ability to see the world as others see it. In the next few chapters, we will talk about specific curriculum activities to help children develop perspective-taking. Empathy, seemingly innate in some children, can be modeled and learned by others as well. Here are a few ways that adults can help build those qualities in a caring classroom.

If children enjoy the emotional freedom and security that their own needs will be met, they will then be able to turn their attention to helping meet the needs of others. Adults in the caring classroom will reassure children that they will receive attention, materials, space, or opportunities for special or routine activities.

In the caring classroom, adults help children become aware of each other's feelings and of the results of their actions, both positive and negative. "How do you think she will feel if you don't …?" or "Look how happy he is when you…." Adults often only take these steps when a grievance has occurred, but it is equally important for children to observe the positive effects of their prosocial actions on others. In either case, here are some steps to help children become actively aware of others' feelings.

First, help children recognize and understand what is happening by noticing and listening. Guide them with these prompts:

"Look at her face or body."

"Listen to what she is saying or doing."

"Ask her how she feels."

Then, help the child describe and label the response of the other child. In this way, both children may create shared language to call on in future situations. This process incorporates both the Vygotskian model of *scaffolding* and the concept of language as a tool for practical activity.

STRATEGIES FOR ENCOURAGING PERSPECTIVE-TAKING AND EMPATHY

In an image similar to the three-layer cake, teachers encourage perspective-taking and empathy in three contexts:

- *Modeling* perspective-talking and empathic adult-to-child and child-to-adult interactions in day-to-day life in the classroom.
  - *Learning and practicing* perspective-taking and empathy as a planned part of the curriculum.
  - *Scaffolding* to guide children when an occasion arises that calls for perspective-taking.

In Chapters 8 and 9, we will explore learning activities that incorporate these and other tools that children need for conflict resolution and peacemaking.

FOR DISCUSSION AND FURTHER READING

If you have observed young children demonstrating perspective-taking and empathy, how do your observations fit with the various theories of children's cognitive and sociomoral development that we explored in Chapters 5 and 6 (Piaget, Kohlberg, Damon, Gilligan)? You may want to read what others have written (Lilian Katz, David Elkind, Alfie Kohn, Margaret Donaldson).

Defining Democracy in the Classroom

Teachers may use a democratic approach to classroom decision-making as a way to practice perspective-taking and consensus-building. In class meetings, children have an opportunity to hear and consider varying ideas and points of view in order to make a decision agreed upon by all. Examples include generating classroom rules, choosing the name of a class pet, deciding names for learning groups, or solving a problem that has come up.

What exactly does "democracy" mean in the classroom? Is it respect for the rights of all members of the group and participation in decision-making or is the emphasis on voting and the "majority rule"? Does "democracy" mean "We all vote and, if your side gets fewer votes, you lose"? Or does it mean that all sides have a voice and all members are heard, with the idea of reaching consensus? (You could do some research on the early Greek version of democracy, rather than the representative democracy in a republic.) Young children may see voting as competition with winners and losers, rather than a way to come to a decision if there is no consensus. Teachers in a caring classroom with young children may prefer the consensus-building form of democracy, in which generating universally agreeable alternatives may substitute for voting.

APPLICATIONS IN PRACTICE

Think about how children construct an idea of democracy with their experiences in an Early Child-hood setting, and in their homes and neighborhoods:

• How does decision-making happen in your classroom?

• What approaches to decision-making do children see and experience outside the classroom?

TEACHERS TALK ABOUT A CARING THIRD-GRADE CLASSROOM

"In the beginning of the year, we discuss the importance of respect and allowing all students the right to learn. We generate a list of rules as a class, and they take ownership by creating and signing them. I have my students learn to cooperate by working together, trusting, helping, sharing with each other. I feel it is vital to get to know the students on a personal level. Every Monday morning, we take 20 minutes to go around the room and tell about our weekend. This allows me to find out what is going on in their lives, and I can refer to those experiences in the future. I always tell them about my weekend as well, so they feel that closeness to me and can relate to me on another level."

CLASSROOM ENVIRONMENTS FOR PEACEMAKING AND CONFLICT RESOLUTION

The decisions that teachers make about the classroom environment play an important part in creating a caring classroom. Everyday life in a classroom is affected by aspects of the social environment: grouping, schedules, balance of activities, classroom rules, role assignments, numbers of children and adults in the room, and expectations for inclusion in play and other groups. The physical environment also plays a part, including room arrangement, traffic patterns, number and type of materials, noise level, community and individual spaces, colors and light, and wall spaces. We will look more at age-specific environments in Chapters 8 and 9.

Evaluating the Physical and Social Environment

The following are some considerations in evaluating the classroom environment for caring and peacemaking. These items can be made into a checklist for an evaluation of your classroom. In Chapters 8 and 9, we will look at specifics of the environment for different age groups.

1. Check for recurring conflicts to see whether there are certain areas, times of day, or types of activities that seem to bring on frequent conflicts. Observe closely to see what it is about the situation or setting that seems to be contributing to conflict.

TWO CLASSROOMS: GROUPING CHILDREN

Classroom Number 1: An observer reports, "The students in this classroom are always next to the same one or two people, which provides them with minimal interaction. When these children are asked to work together, there is a great deal of conflict."

Classroom Number 2: "I group the students in my class in a variety of ways that change often. Each month, I change seating assignments, which gives the students a chance to sit at a different table, and with different children throughout the year. I also assign partners for my students each week. Their partner is the person they walk with in line, sit with on the bus if we have a field trip, and pair up with for cooperative games. Because these partners change so often, and everyone eventually is everyone's partner, the class is a very unified group. They develop relationships with each other that may not have had the chance to develop, and they learn to work with all different kinds of personalities. Monday morning, when my students walk in the door, the first thing they do is to run up to the board to check out who their partner is for the week. Girls and boys, high and low students, shy and outgoing personalities are mixed up every week so a unique dynamic takes place. Although this system takes extra time on my part, the benefits are well worth the effort."

---

   2. Determine the trends and patterns for conflicts and make changes in order to prevent persistent, non-constructive conflicts.

   3. Consider age-appropriate and culturally responsive expectations for children's ability to negotiate in sharing materials and space.

   4. Observe whether time and transitions cause stress.

Observing and Making Changes: Teachers Take a Closer Look

In addition to developing a positive social environment, teachers can create physical environments to promote peaceful interactions among children. A group of teachers and Early Childhood professionals recently spent time observing children and closely examining aspects of the physical environment in their classrooms. They found some areas that sparked conflicts, and others that encouraged peaceful encounters. The following suggestions are based on their observations and some of the changes they made.

Arranging Classrooms for Peace

Traffic Flow: The room arrangement gives children space to move about the room without bumping elbows and desks, and space to line up without crowding or jostling.

   Face-to-Face Seating: Children have an opportunity to fully attend to one another and to collaborate more naturally, developing mini-communities in table or desk groupings.

Location for Distracting Activities: Centers where movement and sounds may distract others are placed around the walls away from the central table groupings of the learning community, or in a suitable non-distracting arrangement. Children are purposeful in respecting others as they work.

Collaborative Learning Centers: Children practice collaborating, problem-solving, and perspective-taking in centers designed for learning and working together. An integral part of curricular learning objectives, these centers are not "something to do when (or if) you finish your work."

Places for Peacemaking: A Peace Table or Peace Corner is a valued place where children develop peacemaking and conflict resolution skills to use in the classroom and beyond.

Suggestions for Making Changes

- Evaluate classroom activities, including routines and use of materials. Do the activities encourage competition or collaboration?
- Engage children in decision-making about room arrangement, seating assignments, and transitions.
- Allow children more time for completing work, or just for thinking about things. Find creative ways to reduce this source of stress and friction among children.
- Reassure children that their needs will be met so that they will then be free to notice and help to meet the needs of others.

TEACHERS TALK ABOUT PROBLEM TIMES AND A SOLUTION

"Many of our troubles in kindergarten seem to occur during transition times, especially when cleaning the block area, where quarters are close and tempers flare. We also were having problems during unstructured periods after breakfast and lunch. Although some of this was unavoidable, as some children eat much faster than others, there were some workable solutions. I added more music and movement time after breakfast, and this new approach has worked wonders."

In Spite of It All

In a crowded environment, there can be evidence of children's persistently prosocial nature. Caring often thrives among children in spite of environments that are not conducive to caring and conflict resolution. An observer reports of one classroom: "Space is provided at play stations; however, there is not enough room for every child in the classroom at each station, and there is pushing and shoving and there are frequent conflicts. Therefore, the teacher selects children for play stations. Today, at the rice table, only four have been selected. While everyone else is playing, a little boy is lying on the floor. The other children just walk around him. When one girl finishes at the rice table, she goes to him and tells him, 'You can take my place.' He then gets up. The girl goes to building blocks and sits beside another girl who has been playing by herself. Following [that], another girl comes over to play with the girl who was playing by herself."

RESOURCE FOR THE VISUAL ENVIRONMENT IN A CARING CLASSROOM

In addition to child-generated creations, poster art on the walls can remind children and adults alike about caring, respect, and inclusiveness. The Teaching Tolerance Project offers its One World Poster Set (free as of this writing) to teachers. (Teaching Tolerance, 40 Washington Avenue, Montgomery, AL 36104. Information available at www.teachingtolerance.org)

AN INCLUSIVE COMMUNITY FOR ALL CHILDREN

A Culturally Responsive Classroom

As we have mentioned throughout this book, there is increasing diversity in classrooms and other Early Childhood settings. This diversity takes the form of differences in ability, color, ethnicity, language, culture, religion, family income, family structure, and more. In a culturally responsive classroom, the physical, social, and learning environment welcomes and includes all children. In a culturally responsive and inclusive classroom, all children have a feeling of belonging.

An actively caring classroom is a safe and inclusive community for all children. Teachers will realize that the positive effects of a caring classroom in which there is diversity among children will work in two directions. By interacting in shared experiences with children who are different in some way from themselves, children can learn perspective-taking, seeing the world in a different way. This awareness will contribute to active caring in the community. At the same time, in the welcoming environment of a caring classroom, understanding and friendships among diverse children are more apt to flourish.

Here are some ways to make that caring classroom an inclusive one as well. In the following section, there are references to helpful resources, such as *Roots and Wing* by Stacey York, *Starting Small* by the Teaching Tolerance Project, and *The Anti-Bias Curriculum* by Louise Derman-Sparks and the A.B.C. Task Force. Teachers and adults in a caring classroom will find thorough presentations about culturally responsive teaching and learning in a number of valuable books, some of which are listed at the end of this chapter. What follows is a brief overview.

It All Starts with You

1. Teachers need to begin by defining our own cultural identity and discovering our multiple cultural lenses. We must identify our own worldview before hoping to understand the worldviews of others.

2. Teachers need to reflect continually on our own biases, assumptions, goals, and behaviors.

Fostering Respect for Differences

1. Teachers can encourage children to notice and appreciate their own physical traits and those of others to help affirm identity. Use mirrors, self-portraits, "Who Am I?" guessing games using photos of children's hands or backs of heads, or People Color paints (Teaching Tolerance Project, 1997). Children are aware of differences in color and ability earlier than adults might suppose (Ramsey, 1998; Van Ausdale & Feagin, 2001; York, 1992).

2. Teachers should create opportunities for children and adults to process diversity-related information. Point out relevant special facts, such as the ability to speak two languages, beautiful skin color, and unique cultural traditions. Guide these discussions and openly value diversity (Teaching Tolerance Project, 1997).

3. Teachers must build cultural continuity between home and school, supporting the home language and providing workshops for families on meaningful topics. Invite families to share.

4. Teachers need to be aware of gender bias in seating arrangements, groupings, or teams. Ensure that classroom materials are non-sexist, do not allow exclusion or derision based on gender, and use non-sexist language (Pollack, 1998; Ramsey, 1998; Teaching Tolerance Project, 1997).

5. Teachers should evaluate curriculum, activities, books, and other materials for evidence of diversity. Critically evaluate books and materials for bias and stereotypes (Derman-Sparks, 1989; Ramsey, 1998; York, 1992).

Well-chosen children's literature can support respect for differences.

Confronting Prejudice and Discrimination

1. Teachers should take an active role against hurtful situations that occur in their classrooms. They should intervene when children are excluded because of race, gender, culture, class, disability, or language. Address misunderstandings; when a child uses a racial epithet, determine the child's understanding of the term and explain that the word is hurtful (Ramsey, 1998; Teaching Tolerance Project, 1997; Van Ausdale & Feagin, 2001).

2. Teachers need to respond to children's questions about differences instead of avoiding the discussion (York, 1992).

3. Teachers may engage in activism with young children (Derman-Sparks, 1989; Roberts, 2002). The Teaching Tolerance Project describes this as "nurturing justice" (1997) and suggests projects that are meaningful for school or community such as adopting a local nursing home or homeless shelter.

PEOPLE COLORS FOR COMMUNITY-BUILDING AND AFFIRMATION

The Video: A favorite learning experience for adults and children is using multicultural skin tone paints to find out what color our skin is. The *Starting Small* video (Teaching Tolerance Project, 1997) includes a segment about children who learn that there are no "white" or "black" children in their class. Together, they delight in finding their colors by mixing and matching People Color paints. Some are "peach," while others are perhaps a mix of "fawn" and "toast" or "amber" and "mahogany."

Teachers Learn: After watching the video, a group of teachers is thrilled to try it themselves. As with the children, the group shares the experience as a group, shattering old notions and linked labels, affirming for themselves and each other what is unique about them, and celebrating their differences and commonalities.

Children Learn: After her own People Colors paint experiences in the teacher group, Mrs. H. brings the activity into her kindergarten classroom. She has started to read her children a picture book about Rosa Parks. The children correct Mrs. H., instructing her not to read the words "black" and "white" but instead decide to use the words "creamy people" and "brown-skinned people."

Teachers Learn from Children: Mrs. H. returns to the teacher group the following week with her story. Following the children's example, the teachers adopt the new language for their discussions. They discover that "creamy" and "brown-skinned" not only seem more accurate, but also leave behind the baggage of stereotype and bias that accompany the old labels.

"Caring For" and "Caring By" Children with Special Needs

In the caring classroom, all children participate in encounters as both those "caring for" and those "being cared for." We have seen that children who are developing typically have opportunities to act as "carers" toward children with special needs.

Inclusive classrooms are settings where children can develop nurturing and awareness of the needs of others.

A TEACHER'S OBSERVATIONS

"The children with Down's Syndrome participate in all the preschool play and routine activities. The other children seem to be especially patient and helpful with them.

"For example, the children themselves are usually are very strict about our rule of four children in the loft. But when Catherine, a 4-year-old with Down's Syndrome, climbs up and joins four others, they allow her to remain. One day, in the loft, she was putting a sun visor on Natalie's head. Natalie just took it off without saying anything. Catherine put the visor back on her head two more times. Each time, Natalie simply took it off again without a word. Other times, children help and care for other classmates with Down's Syndrome. Christopher often sits near Catherine at story time and accompanies her to the bathroom. In another classroom, Jonah brings Kelly (a child with Down's Syndrome) a doll, and Heidi offers her a lap during story time.

"By the same token, children with special needs, delays, and disabilities may also have opportunities to assume the 'caring for' role. Stressing ability over disability, teachers can work to find ways that are appropriate for each child to engage in caring encounters. Perhaps it is even more important for teachers to facilitate active 'caring for' among children who spend much of their experience in the more passive role of receiving care from others.

STRATEGIES FOR CARING ENCOUNTERS IN AN INCLUSIVE CLASSROOM

Each person has an opportunity to help and to receive help from others. To facilitate children's awareness of ways that each child can be part of a caring encounter, teachers can use this strategy:

Each child lists (or dictates) the following four items. Use pictures or symbols for non-verbal or pre-verbal children. Post the lists in the classroom for all to see.

- Something I am good at
- Something I may need help with
- Ways I can help others
- Ways to ask others for help

And always, children and adults use a shared language that communicates inclusiveness: "In our classroom, we ..."

What Does It Mean to Be a Friend in a Caring Classroom?

In many Early Childhood settings, adults say "we are all friends here." In the sense that all children will respect and care for each other in a caring classroom, as friends do, that statement is true. Like adults, however, children do have preferred playmates who they consider to be friends. In a caring classroom, of course, there are children who are friends and others who are non-friend peers. In Chapter 9, we will explore further the issues related to peer acceptance and rejection.

At the beginning of this chapter, we found two conditions for peaceful resolution of conflict. The first condition is the desire for peaceful resolution. This is easy, natural, and likely among friends and natural allies in the peer culture. But what about non-friend peers and other children who are not natural allies, who may be in some way different from each other? We hope that, in a culturally responsive and inclusive classroom, children will act as *caring* individuals toward *all* children. We hope that children will act from a sense of themselves as *caring people* and as members of a *caring community* (Kohn, 1991).

HELPING CHILDREN SEE THEMSELVES AS PEACEMAKERS

We have discussed the goal that children will see themselves as kind and caring individuals, part of an inclusive classroom community. When children see themselves as kind and caring, sharing is a natural and normal act, not a means to an

Like these children, friends can build and play together in a caring classroom.

end such as earning praise for sharing or getting something in return (actually bartering). Avoid promoting the "what's in it for me" rationale for sharing or helping: "If you give him the pencil, then you can get the marker." Rather, the empathic response from a child for whom sharing is a natural thing to do would be, "I can see you need the pencil. Here it is." Share your expectation that all children can be, and should be, peacemakers. This is an inclusionary, non-elitist approach that implies a shared responsibility of the class as a community to support conflict resolution and peacemaking.

SUMMARY

As we have seen, teachers can help set the stage for a culture of caring and peacemaking by providing children with a shared language as atool for defusing and resolving conflicts. In the context of an Early Childhood classroom, we ask the question, "Can we create an environment of caring where, as in the McGinnis quote in this chapter, children have the desire and the tools for resolving conflicts and assuming roles as peacemakers?"

SUPPLEMENTARY MATERIALS FOR CHAPTER 7

Research Focus/Teacher as Researcher

You may be interested in reading Lisa Goldstein's 1998 article, "More than Gentle Smiles and Warm Hugs," and begin to observe and record evidence of children *caring for* one another and *being cared for* by another. You may even design an action research plan to investigate whether children's acts of caring will be more frequent and intentional if you have class meetings about caring, or if you read and discuss stories where caring takes place.

Goldstein, L. S. (1998). More than gentle smiles and warm hugs: Applying the ethic of care to early childhood education. *Journal of Research in Childhood Education*, 12, 244–261.

APPLICATION EXERCISES

1. In pairs, think about strategies for helping children to see themselves as caring individuals. What can you do in your setting?
2. What respectful words and phrases do you use in your classroom? (Example

from Chapter 6: The teacher says, "Be the bigger person. It takes a big person to do that.")
3. Now that we have looked at all the layers, do you think that the cake should be

three equal layers (all the same size) or tiered with the bottom layer larger than the middle and the middle layer larger than the top?

4. Can you think of another image instead of the three-layer cake? Some suggestions have included concentric circles, as in the nested ecological systems, or a triangle, as in Maslow, or an inverted triangle. Do these images resonate with a particular theoretical perspective?

5. List aspects of the environment that contribute to a prosocial, caring community in your classroom (the positive aspects) and those aspects that may add to the likelihood of conflict (the negative aspects). Do you see patterns or trends?

THINKING ABOUT ALL CHILDREN

1. The *Starting Small* video shows children and teachers using People Colors for classroom community and building a ramp for wheelchair accessibility to their school. How "doable" are activities like these in your setting? What can you do to make these activities possible?

2. Inclusion and Ability: Return to the examination of your environment. Are there barriers (physical or otherwise) to the inclusion of all children?

3. Children receive social cues from the environment and from others. In your setting, try to help the children understand social cues that they give and receive. Ask the children to explain to one another what they are seeing in their interactions with each other.

WEB SITES FOR PEACEMAKING AND CARING

Responsive Classroom, Northeast Foundation for Children: *www.responsiveclassoom.org*

Teaching Tolerance Project of the Southern Poverty Law Center: *www.teachingtolerance.org*

Teachers Resisting Unhealthy Children's Entertainment: *truceteachers.org*

Culture of Peace Initiative *www.unesco.org*

Connect for Kids: *www.connect4kids.org*

League of Peaceful Schools, Nova Scotia: *http://www.leagueofpeacefulschools.ns.ca*

Neveh Shalom (School for Israeli and Palestinian Children): *http://www.nswas.com*

Teach Peace (Materials for Pre-K children and teachers): *http://www.come.to/Rose4Peace*

World PeaceProject for Children: *http://www.sadako.org*

>>>

RESOURCES FOR UNDERSTANDING AND TEACHING DIVERSITY

Byrnes, D. A., & Kiger, G. (Eds.) (1992). *Common bonds: Anti-bias teaching in a diverse society*. Olney, MD: Association for Childhood Education International.

DeGaetano, Y., Williams, L. R., & Volk, D. (1998). *Kaleidoscope: A multicultural approach for the primary school classroom*. Upper Saddle River, NJ: Merrill/Prentice Hall.

Delpit, L. (1995). *Other people's children: Cultural conflict in the classroom*. New York: The New Press.

Derman-Sparks, L. (1989). *Anti-bias curriculum: Tools for empowering young children*. Washington, DC: National Association for the Education of Young Children.

Kozol, J. (1995). *Amazing grace: The lives of children and the conscience of a nation*. New York: Crown.

Ladson-Billings, G. (1994). *The dreamkeepers: Successful teachers of African-American children*. San Francisco: Jossey-Bass.

Lynch, E. W., & Hanson, M. J. (1992). *Developing cross-cultural competence: A guide to working with young children and their families*. Baltimore, MD: Paul H. Brookes.

Neugebauer, B. (Ed.). (1992). *Alike and different: Exploring our humanity with young children*. Washington, DC: National Association for the Education of Young Children.

Swiniarski, L. A., Breitborde, M., Murphy, J. (1999). *Educating the global village: Including the young child in the world*. Upper Saddle River, NJ: Merrill/Prentice Hall.

Teaching Tolerance Project. (1997). Starting small: *Teaching tolerance in preschool and the early grades*. Montgomery, AL: Southern Poverty Law Center.

York, S. (1992). *Roots and wings: Affirming culture in early childhood programs*. St.Paul, MN: Redleaf Press.

Note: *Teaching Tolerance* is mailed twice a year at no cost to educators by the Southern Poverty Law Center, 400 Washington Ave., Montgomery, AL 36104 (FAX: 205–264–3121). Ask about the Starting Small Teaching Kit and other free resources for teachers listed on the web site.

Curriculum for Caring and Conflict Resolution: Preschool and Kindergarten

"Helping others is a constant theme in our classroom."

Chapter 8 Objectives: As we continue to build the "Three-Layer Cake," we will see how teachers and caregivers can create learning environments for prosocial interaction and conflict resolution. Chapters 8 and 9 describe the middle layer of the cake, the curriculum activities, materials, and routines through which children learn awareness, strategies and behaviors to avoid destructive conflicts and to resolve their constructive conflicts. Chapter 8 addresses developmental needs and characteristics, and appropriate curriculum for young children in two age groups in the preschool years: twos and threes, and fours and fives. Chapter 9 will focus on 6- to 8-year-olds in the primary years. An important concern in each chapter will be curriculum that is culturally responsive and meets the needs of children with special needs,

145

developmental delays, and disabilities. Curriculum connections for families will be expanded in Chapter 11.

Chapter Outline

UNDERSTANDING CHILDREN AND HELPING THEM LEARN

Children's Development Related to Conflict Resolution

What do we know about 2- and 3-year-olds and 4- and 5-year-olds to help us understand and guide them in the development of their ability to resolve conflicts?

Conflict resolution is connected to all areas of development. At this point, we will explore how certain aspects of development are related to children's growing capacity for conflict resolution and peacemaking. This book does not attempt to provide a comprehensive review of the development of young children, which is available in many other books. As Early Childhood professionals, we are challenged to apply what we know about children from our study and experiences and to carefully consider individual developmental and temperament differences in children as we guide them in their growing ability to resolve conflicts.

What Do Children Need for Conflict Resolution?

As we prepare environments and curricula for children, what do we hope to accomplish in order for children to develop conflict resolution and peacemaking ability? We have seen in earlier chapters that, in order to resolve conflicts, children need to develop attributes such as the following:

Empathy and perspective-taking

Ability to generate alternative solutions

Capacity for authentic communication

Self-control

Kindness and compassion

Collaboration and cooperation

How Can Classroom Decisions Make a Difference?

How do our classroom decisions make a difference? Classroom environments and curriculum for conflict resolution can facilitate the development of the preceding attributes. Within both the planned curriculum and the "hidden" curriculum, there are opportunities for teachers to bring conflict resolution learning into the classroom. Early Childhood professionals have a vast number of strategies already in place, or nearly in place. Many teachers and caregivers are doing exactly what will be described in this book. Some are doing what is described, but may want to fine-tune or make adaptations. Others may want to add whole new strategies. It is important for teachers to make explicit to children exactly what sorts of prosocial skills are part of these everyday school experiences.

As an example, tracing children's bodies on butcher paper for life-sized self-portaits is an activity that teachers often do early in the school year. Instead of having a teacher draw each child, one at a time, try having children trace each other and coloring together, noticing each other's appearance closely. Displaying these life-sized portaits around the room, even using a single long sheet of paper if there is space, is a demonstrable community-builder. Following the collaborative activity, children and teachers celebrate this visual representation of the classroom community.

These two chapters will provide a number of ideas, but they will only begin to scratch the surface of what can be done. You will recognize many of these strategies as part of your own repertoire, although you perhaps may not have realized the aspects of conflict resolution that are embedded. Many games and activities will be familiar from your own experiences in school, neighborhood, scouts, camp, church groups, and, in some cases, from trust-building and team-building sessions in the adult workplace. Of course, there are numerous variations of these activities.

In some cases, where the game or activity has come from a specific source, that source will be included.

In order to expand your repertoire, first look at what you are doing and consider how your present activities can be refocused for conflict resolution and peacemaking. Then add new strategies from helpful books full of activities. (Several are listed in the Appendix.)

How Do Games Help?

Children can learn much from appropriate and well-planned games. Objectives for games include the following:

1. Cooperation
2. Communication skills
3. Body awareness
4. Self-esteem/affirmation
5. Altruistic behavior
6. Consensus building
7. Generating alternatives
8. Perspective-taking
9. Fun

How to Adapt Competitive Games

Many adults remember playing competitive games as children. Those games, like Dodge Ball and Red Rover, clearly do not meet the preceding objectives. Competition and demonstrating physical superiority were very much part of the "old" games. In some cases, teachers may decide that games like Red Rover and Dodge Ball simply do not have a place in their classes. In other cases, existing games may be adapted to become prosocial games. A well-known example is Cooperative Musical Chairs, in which the object of the game is to keep everyone in the dwindling number of chairs, rather than a physical contest to exclude children one by one.

Using the list of objectives, teachers can ask how a game can be changed so that children work together to achieve a shared goal. In a timed event, the goal can be to race against the clock instead of one another. Add a creative twist: how many different ways can the class think of to get across the finish line? In an event with points, how quickly can the whole class get to 100? Make sure that games do not always reward children's size or physical prowess and that the outcome is not necessarily an extrinsic reward.

TWO- AND THREE-YEAR-OLDS

Developmental Characteristics of Twos and Threes

Finding Their Place in the World

What do we know about 2- and 3-year-olds that can help us understand and guide them in the development of their ability to resolve conflicts? We begin these chapters with 2-year-olds, as interaction with peers begins to play a part in their lives. In this section, we will explore the early preschool years, ages 2 to 3, where there is a wide developmental range with rapid development. At this age, young children experience tremendous growth in all areas, growing from toddlerhood to preschoolers with the energy and coordination to take on the world.

The main developmental characteristic that concerns our study of twos and threes and their conflict resolution is this rapid growth of understanding of the self and others, and of the ability to relate to others and communicate with them. Our plans for teaching, learning, and caring support these developmental concerns. Therefore, observing children to understand where they are developmentally from day to day is critical. (Here is another opportunity to practice the observational tools you learned in Chapter 3.) Knowing each child is a more critical factor than age-related interpretation of development or any other guidelines.

Cognitive/Language Development

Between the ages of 2 and 4, children demonstrate greatly increasing language competence. Children's vocabulary develops from about 40 to 50 words at 20 months to perhaps 14,000 by age 6 (Puckett & Black, 2001). Children need to develop both *expressive* language, in order to make their needs and preferences known, and *receptive* language, to understand what adults and children are saying. In increasingly complex interactive contexts, 2-year-olds and young threes may still rely on non-verbal communication in interaction with peers. Children are learning through social interaction, developing an understanding of causes and consequences. At age 2, they are engaging in early symbolic play, with simple representation of objects and symbolic actions using realistic toys and props. More complex imaginative play emerges among threes.

Physical/Motor Development

Both small and large motor development are increasing rapidly, and children have more opportunities to encounter their surroundings. Coordination grows and, from age 2 to 4, lack of control over physical movement and accidental bumps lessen. In physical play, twos can jump, throw a ball in a non-directed fashion, and stop a rolling ball. As threes, they are able to throw a ball in a directed way, avoid obstacles, and stop walking or running readily (Puckett & Black, 2001).

Playing close to each other, these two are demonstrating their growing physical/motor development and their awareness for others.

Social/Emotional/Moral Development

Social competence is also emerging in these early preschool years. Children are developing greater social cognition, which includes knowledge of self, knowledge of others, and knowledge of self in relation to others (Weiser, 1991). Knowledge of self includes gender identity as male or female, which develops around age 3 or 4 (Edwards, 1986; Puckett & Black, 2001; Ramsey, 1998). As early as age 2 or 3, children begin to develop sex-role knowledge, and gradually they develop preferences for activities labeled "male" or "female" by media, adults, and peers. An early awareness of self and others, of likenesses and differences, include an awareness of differences in color, gender, and ability. There is evidence, even in these early preschool years, of the development of negative bias against children with disabilities (Edwards, 1986; Van Ausdale & Feagin, 2001).

Children at age 3 form friendships and begin to show evidence of moral decisions based on their understanding of right and wrong, as we could see in Chapter 4. (Jonathan tells Billy, "You can't use your bodies! It's not okay. Use your words.") As we learn more about children's social development, we see evidence of empathy and caring among 2- and 3-year-olds. Self-control emerges at age 2, and delayed gratification develops by age 3 (Puckett & Black, 2001). At age 2, children's social play is solitary and on looking; among threes, there is parallel and associative play.

HOW MUCH DO THEORIES EXPLAIN?

Review these theories in the context of children's conflict issues and strategies:

Erikson's and Psychosocial Development:
   Autonomy versus shame and doubt, ages 1–3
   Initiative versus guilt, ages 3–6
   Industry versus inferiority, ages 6–11
Piaget's Cognitive Development:
   Sensorimotor, 2
   Preoperational, 3–7
   Concrete operational, 8–11
Piaget and Moral Development:
   Premoral (younger than 6)
   Moral realism (begins around age 6)
   Moral relativism (around 10)

We have previously mentioned limitations of stage theories. Try thinking about the theories of Vygotsky, Bronfenbrenner, Gilligan, and Maslow to help explain aspects of children's development in conflict resolution that will guide us in creating curricula for caring and conflict resolution.

What Do Twos and Threes Fight About, and How?

Conflict Issues

As we found in Chapter 4, possession issues dominate children's conflicts in this age group. Object issues are more frequent than disputes over space or rules. In addition, there are conflicts as a result of inadvertent annoyance, especially among twos, as they are busy exploring and touching people as well as objects. Bumping into things and knocking things down may spark a protest and then evoke a response to the initial action. Without a specific issue to pursue, accidental annoyance conflict among twos and young threes does not often continue. Among older threes, who may be in a larger group setting, opportunities for social conflicts increase. In play centers and routine times, there may be conflicts about school rules and norms and about aspects of social play. With rapid growth in all areas, developmental mismatches among age-peers may challenge children's perspective-taking ability.

Strategies That Twos and Threes Use

The most common strategies among twos and younger threes are simple verbal insistence or non-aggressive physical strategies. As children's ability to verbalize increases, so does their repertoire of strategies. The closeness of adult supervision frequently found in groups of twos and young threes means that adults will often step in to end conflicts, not by guiding children to resolution, but by distracting or removing children or providing duplicate or substitute toys. We will explore adult intervention in Chapter 10, with ways to provide appropriate scaffolding and modeling for children.

TEACHERS TALK: LEARNING TO SHARE AND CONSERVE

Ms. C, a teacher of threes: "I have an ample, albeit old, supply of materials in the class-room for the children to work with at all times. During worktimes, the children have nine areas full of supplies to use. The areas are art, sensory, play dough, blocks, manipula-tives, writing, science, dramatic play, books/quiet area. I do not provide an excessive amount of supplies because I feel that it is important for the children to understand that supplies are limited and that conservation is important. This also allows each child ample opportunity to be creative with supplies, recycle supplies, and to have practice sharing and negotiating with peers."

Classroom Environments for Cooperation

In planning for children's environments to promote conflict resolution and peace-making, teachers incorporate elements of a caring classroom (Chapter 7) and con-cerns for children's needs (and are reminded of Maslow's hierarchy), as well as developmental and learning considerations. They plan for both the physical and social environments in the classroom setting.

Physical Environment for Twos and Threes

Room arrangement can make a difference. Young children need clear pathways and space to move without bumping into each other, and places to play together or beside each other in an inviting but not overstimulating or cluttered physical environment. The idea is that they are coming to the classroom to play with other *children*, not coming to play with *toys*. Visual displays should be welcoming, but again not overwhelming, reflecting diverse children at play, multilingual labels and posters, and pictures of and by children in the group.

Materials in the classroom for twos and threes should include realistic toys and props for emerging representation in their imaginative play, real and tangible objects for exploring, dolls and stuffed animals for caring, and toys and materials for small and large motor development. Materials and activities to support chil-dren developing awareness of others and opportunities for interaction include mirrors, musical instruments, balls, dolls, and house play. Threes will also enjoy playing alongside their peers with sand and water, construction toys, and other activities that lend themselves to more social play among children. Environments for young children need to include materials and spaces for children with sensory integration needs.

Technology, both assistive/adaptive and mainstream, can provide valuable interactive materials for twos and threes. Materials need to be sturdy and safe to minimize constant adult monitoring of every activity. Close observing of children's play will guide decisions about how many duplicate toys and materials to have. Too few toys will stretch the limits of children's emerging ability to share and take turns, but fewer toys may give children early opportunities for guided sharing and thinking of others. Pets and plants can also provide caring opportunities for twos and threes, as well as older children.

Social Environment for Twos and Threes

Routine times and transitions match children's developmental levels, and they provide powerful opportunities for observing adult models and practicing peaceful and caring language and behaviors. Routine times include circle times, snack and meal times, arriving, and leaving. Responding to signals from children, being flexible, and having reasonable expectations reduces frustration and uncertainty, which gives children a comfort level in noticing and interacting with their peers (Collins & McGaha, 2000).

Scheduling is critical for twos and threes. The pacing of the day should be balanced and include "down time needed." The timetable should match the daily rhythms of the children and not the adults.

Grouping for twos and some young threes is different from that for older children. Standard room configurations are usually for groups of four. Younger twos interact more successfully with one other child at a time. Groups of two, not four, will work better with these very young preschoolers.

Adults in the setting should be close by to observe and guide children. Especially with the very young, recommended adult-child ratios in the United States call for many adults. Although this is important for children's safety and care, it is equally important that adult-child interactions do not preclude opportunities for meaningful child-child interactions.

Language is part of the children's environment. Words that promote awareness of people and objects are incorporated into planned learning activities, as well as into everyday activities. Words are used to label not only objects but actions and feelings, and children hear and learn a language of kindness and caring. Language includes signing and multilingual vocabulary in songs, stories, and routine times.

Teaching and Learning: Curriculum Models and Activities

Curriculum Models

Programs for twos and threes may be guided by developmentally appropriate practices published by NAEYC, with specific day-to-day and long-range planning by the staff of the center. Other programs may follow published curricula, such as High Scope, the Creative Curriculum, and others. Regardless of the particular choice, a curriculum for conflict resolution and peacemaking should include dimensions of best practices for young children and instruction grounded in the children's experiences, with multiple concrete opportunities for learning through touching, looking, and active caring.

Group Activities for Learning Conflict Resolution

Introducing Thinking Games   Children learn when they are engaged in a meaningful topic in an authentic context and can explore possibilities in a safe and accepting environment. In *Promoting Social and Moral Development in Young Children*, Edwards (1986) presents the idea of *thinking games*, which help teachers provide just such opportunities. What *thinking games* are and how to use them are described below. Edwards frames the idea of thinking games in terms of Piagetian questioning, but we can extend the theoretical frame to include the Vygotskian ideas of scaffolding and internalization. (Remember Chapter 5.) Thinking games are described below.

Getting Ready for Thinking Games with Twos   Edwards (1986) recommends thinking games for children from ages 3 to 6. For our 2-year-olds, we can get ready for thinking games. A teacher uses a book, a picture, or puppets to provide a clear and concrete situation that is within the experience of the children. The teacher may ask what a character may say or do next. Children may respond verbally or non-verbally by pointing to pictures or with facial expressions or movements.

Puppets can be used for thinking games with three's.

Thinking Games with Threes   Teachers conduct thinking games at circle time, or when the group is gathered, after the children have already greeted each other and socialized but are not too tired for the focus and mental energy that a thinking game may require. In these examples, the teacher uses puppets or dolls to present a conflict over possession of a toy. To help children practice generating alternatives, the thinking game question might be, "What Might They Do?", or, to explore consequences, "The Why Game" (Crary, 1984).

Another thinking game suitable for threes encourages children to practice perspective-taking. In "The Birthday Store," children are asked to select, from a variety of items something that would be a good birthday present for a grandfather, baby sister, aunt, or others (Edwards, 1986).

THINKING GAMES

A thinking game is a "story situation presented to children for discussion" (Edwards, 1986, p. 23). The story presents children with a social-cognitive problem, or cognitive conflict, to which they are invited to take a stand or say what they think. In a safe and accepting environment, children have an opportunity to confront an internal dilemma or an interpersonal situation. They identify the conflict issue, suggest solutions, and explain the reasons for the solutions suggested. Teachers may prompt children to explore more aspects, effects, and possibilities in the situation. Children's responses to conflict story situations will vary with age, development, and experience.

Conducting Thinking Games

Begin with a question that frames the problem. Continue with an encouraging "why" question as children explain their initial response to the problem. Follow up with probes to clarify, explore more issues, or extend the issue to another situation.

The story may be presented in different ways:

- Skits, puppets, simple props
- Interviews with children

Story ideas may come from anywhere:

- Research: Piaget's story of the broken cups
- Real or imagined stories (What is friendship? Who is a friend?)
- Books: The protagonist in *The Messy Rabbit* faces a series of conflicts

---

Cooperative Games and Activities

Many activities in the classroom for twos and threes are opportunities for cooperation and community-building. Songs and fingerplays using children's names create affirmation and other awareness, as well as a sense of shared activity. Language games and simple paired games work well with twos. Drama in the classroom for young preschoolers involves simultaneous solo play, as children respond in their unique ways to activities such as showing what "happy" or "sad" might look like, showing feelings with facial expressions, or using mirrors. At the end of the chapter is a list of games to start you off.

Caring and Social Action

As we recall children's growing capacity for empathy, we can also model and suggest to children actions that they may take on behalf of others. The first and most basic form of social action is to insist on kindness and caring, on the part of other-sand to confront unkindness and bias. Children are engaging in social actions if they are able to stick up for others by saying, "It's not nice to call names" or, as in Vivian Paley's words (1992), "You can't say you can't play."

FOUR- AND FIVE-YEAR-OLDS

Developmental Characteristics of Fours and Fives

Growing Peer Orientation and Social Interaction

What do we know about 4- and 5-year olds that can help us understand and guide them in the development of their ability to resolve conflicts? In this section, we move to the older preschoolers and kindergarteners, ages 4 and 5. At this age, young children continue to experience remarkable growth, especially in their orientation toward peers, in a more clearly defined understanding of self in relation to others, and in their energetic engagement in imagination and play. Friendship and social competence are important in these later preschool and kindergarten years. Teachers and caregivers should plan for teaching, learning, and caring with these newer developmental concerns in mind.

Cognitive/Language Development

With increasing cognitive development, fours and fives are better able to understand others, anticipate cause and effect, and consider alternative viewpoints. With greater communicative competence and expanding vocabulary, they are able to

---

READY FOR ACTION?

Caring and social action must be meaningful, appropriate, and doable for children.

As a teen volunteer, Alice is working with a group of threes in a summer camp session. The organizers have decided that all age groups will use the theme of "The Rainforest." Sitting on the floor with the children, Alice tells them about the threats to the ecology of the rainforest. All of a sudden, the threes are on their feet, heading toward the door. "Where is everybody going?" asks Alice. With great urgency, they reply, "We've got to save the rainforest!" These threes are ready for action, but they need to connect with something more meaningful and doable than saving the rainforest. What would you suggest?

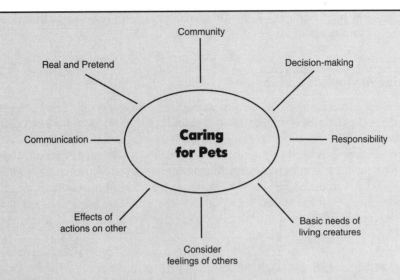

Community: We can all love and care for him.

Decision-making: We need to agree on a name for the pet and decide a schedule for feeding, cage-cleaning, and weekend home visits.

Responsibility: We need to remember his needs every day.

Basic needs of living creatures: Shelter, food, water, safety, love.

Considering the feelings of others: What might make him feel frightened? We need to handle him carefully or he will feel pain. Developing a capacity for nurturing: he is small and needs our care.

Effects of actions on others: What will happen if we do not feed him or treat him with care?

Communication: How can he tell us what he needs? How can we show that we love him?

Real and pretend: This is not a stuffed animal.

Then there is the science, math, and literacy learning that can be integrated into having and caring for a class pet.

make themselves understood as well. Sociodramatic play, with its major contributions to all areas of development, flourishes in these years.

Physical/Motor Development

In the areas of physical/motor development, children enjoy greater coordination and dexterity, and display a great deal of energy. Increased spatial and body awareness allows children to run through a play area without accidentally bumping into things. On the playground, they are adept at riding toys and can climb, throw, and catch. They enjoy non-competitive games and creative responses to music. Small motor skills include using crayons and markers, scissors, small construction toys, and manipulatives. They have developed many self-help skills, which sometimes leads to conflicts over wanting to do things themselves, without help from peers or adults (Puckett & Black, 2001).

Social/Emotional/Moral Development

Fours and fives experience a growing social competence. They are more aware of the effect of their words and actions on others. Gender constancy develops between the ages of five and seven. Familiarity with gender roles and gender stereotypes, as well as prejudice and stereotypes learned from adults, may lead to name-calling and exclusion. Children develop social preferences and friendships based on shared likes and dislikes, and on a mutual comfort level and understanding. Children learn both positive and negative behaviors from peers. At this age, children's peer culture develops in the preschool and kindergarten. Cooperative play thrives.

As we have seen in earlier chapters, children's moral decision-making may be based on the ideas of right and wrong, justice, and fairness. They are close to developing moral realism, the idea of rules and consequences but not intentionality. Moral relativism develops later, in a Piagetian view. There may be another way to look at children's moral reasoning, based on the writing of Carol Gilligan (1982) and on evidence of empathy among young children.

PEER-RELATED SOCIAL COMPETENCE

Defined by three general abilities:

Peer group entry:

    Strategies for successful group entry:

        Knowing how to communicate with host children

        Maintaining proximity

        Figuring out the rules

        Joining ongoing play without redirecting

Conflict resolution

    Strategies for conflict resolution coincide with use of reason and negotiation

Maintaining play

    Strategies for conflict resolution:

        Maintaining roles

        Managing the ongoing interaction

(Guralnick, 1994, p. 48)

What Do Fours and Fives Fight About, and How?

Conflict Issues for Fours and Fives

Fours and fives engage in a full range of conflicts: not only possession of objects and space, but also issues related to the social environment. With more complex peer play, there are issues about group entry, rules, friendship, superiority, and social conventions. Conflicts are also part of the play as children engage in both pretend and real disputes (Malloy, 2002). In making sense of the world through play, teachers observe play themes that involve violence and fighting. See the following text for more on what Levin has called "The War Play Dilemma."

Strategies That Fours and Fives Use

Older preschoolers and kindergarteners, with their greater communication skills and other-awareness, use more verbal strategies, including reasoning, negotiation, and persuasion. A powerful tool at this age is the "friendship threat." Children's strategies now include generating alternative solutions, waiting for turns, and calling on adults for intervention. Strategies may include aggression as children learn that it can be a powerful response. As discussed earlier, aggression may either be instrumental or hostile. Other categories of aggression have been suggested (accidental, reactive, and bullying), but all include some degree of intentional harm.

CHILDREN'S VIOLENT PLAY

When playing out violent themes and replaying plots of television shows, children rarely intend to harm one another. Although accidents do happen, the main concern among adults is that children learn through play how the world works and begin to define their role in the world. Do adults want children to practice through play to become violent people, or to begin to see violence as a normal and accepted way of interacting with others?

In Chapter 1, we considered sources of violence in children's lives. The media, especially television, is a constant presence. Levin (1998) points out that television is gradually presenting violence in increasingly realistic ways, moving from cartoon-animal violence to human actors in realistic roles. Teachers can choose to eliminate all violent play, to restrict violent play, or to allow children to enact whatever they wish. In all three choices, teachers wisely provide alternatives for children's play themes. In her book *Under Deadman's Skin*, Janet Katch (2001) describes the rules, generated with children, for violent play, stories, and enactments in her kindergarten class: "No blood, no cutting off body parts, and no guts spilled." What happens in your setting?

Classroom Environments for Cooperation

The preschool/kindergarten setting has many naturally occurring opportunities for developing cooperation and community-building. Taking full advantage of these opportunities will add to children's conflict resolution and peacemaking. (In

Chapter 7, we explored elements of the caring classroom environment, and in Chapter 3, we considered ways to observe your setting.)

Physical Environment for Fours and Fives

Fours and fives need space to accommodate their growing physical size and energy level and their group play. The room arrangement needs to allow for unencumbered traffic flow, spaces for children both alone and in groups, access to materials, and entry in and out of play and work areas. Children need to be able to find quiet places for "down time." The room should be accessible to children with special needs, to increase their independence and reduce frustration that may lead to conflict with their peers. In kindergarten classrooms, as in preschool or prekindergarten classrooms, floor space is as valuable as table space.

Materials for fours and fives include unrealistic props for imaginative play. Teachers may create situations for cooperation and collaboration by having shared materials and community property. Shared play spaces include tire swings for two, easels side by side, and three chairs in front of the computer. The key words to describe an environment for cooperation are "working together." Adaptive equipment, including computers, will facilitate play and interaction among all children in an inclusive setting. Teachers must carefully evaluate and choose non-biased toys, books, art materials, computer software, and visual displays that reinforce themes of caring and cooperation.

TEACHERS TALK: WHERE CONFLICTS HAPPEN

"I am privileged to have a large classroom with all the necessary areas for a creative kindergarten environment. Housekeeping, dress-ups, blocks, easels, woodworking, computers, just to name a few. This week, all of the conflict occurred on one side of the room. The housekeeping/dramatic play side did not have any conflicts, while computer, Lego, and blocks had several. When thinking about the nature of the conflicts, however, they almost all involved sharing something. With the computer, it was time that was most often argued about. With the Legos, it was the prime Lego pieces that helped create the coolest objects that were fought over, and the conflicts in blocks involved the wreckage of a masterpiece by a student who was not involved in the building of it. There were fewer students in the side of the room with the conflicts, but more issues to fight about. The activities going on in the other half of the room involved playing house, putting on puppet shows, and dressing up. I think the nature of these events naturally led to cooperation, and the amounts of materials available are extensive. We have enough dress-up clothes for all three classrooms, and enough play food and kitchen items for an entire army. I think this surplus of supplies my help alleviate many conflicts, and the natural love for pretend play helps as well."

Discussion Question: Compare this teacher's approach to Ms. C's we read about earlier. How many materials should children have available to them?

Social Environment for Fours and Fives

Routine times in classrooms for fours and fives make a powerful contribution to the environment for conflict resolution and peacemaking. The daily routine includes a "good morning" by name for each child from the teacher and other children. Each child says hello to others, beginning the day by recognizing others and being recognized. These sincere morning greetings are a form of mutual caring encounters (as in Noddings) and reinforce the sense of the class as a community. This phenomenon is repeated throughout the day, with a pervasive "other" orientation in sharing and cooperation during routine times: meals, clean-up time, taking off and putting on coats, and so forth.

MAILBOXES IN REGGIO EMILIA

Children in the municipal schools in Reggio Emilia use mailboxes for daily communication and expressions of friendship and caring. Children routinely give each other pictures and messages, delivering them to each other's mailboxes. The objective is community-building and caring, and the outcome easily supports children's emerging literacy.

Rules, routines, and expectations for children are clear, consistent, and meaningful, expressed in language shared by children and adults. Daily schedules and transitions are planned with respect for children and their physical, social, and emotional needs. Time for fully developed play supports growing social competence and allows for more productive and fully engaged play.

Class meetings are another way to support conflict resolution and peacemaking, and to strengthen the classroom community. Children and teachers share adventures and plan the day, but perhaps more importantly, they use class meetings to make classroom decisions, agree upon class rules, and solve problems (Charles, 2000; Charney, 1992, 2002). Katch's kindergarteners used a class meeting to confront the issue of violent play (2001). The rules they generated represented a negotiation between children and teacher and were respected by all.

TEACHERS TALK: ESTABLISHING RULES AND ROUTINES

"The rules and routines are established by the class in morning meetings. We have a set of rules based on the idea of respecting others. We recently discussed the question, 'What do we need to be safe?' We revisit the rules as a class when there is a need. We will then discuss the question, 'Do we need to make changes or add something?'"

With higher adult-to-child ratios, adults in the preschool and kindergarten are a less immediate and constant presence than with twos and threes, and there is more peer interaction. Opportunities for one-on-one and small-group interaction are important, however, and can allow teachers to access children's ideas through their drawing, block building, and other play. These conversations offer a way to hear what is important to children and learn more about their social knowledge and emotional needs.

BEING AVAILABLE

Adults need to be available to help children individually and as a group, especially in times of crisis and uncertainty. These times may be a result of a widespread tragedy or something happening in the life of the individual child. Teachers should help give children ways to feel safe, ways to make things make sense, and reassurance that someone will be there to listen.

The social environment includes the language of the community, characterized by the inclusive "we" and language of caring and other-awareness. As with twos and threes, children practice and share language that helps with conflict resolution and peacemaking. Teachers can help children learn how to talk through conflicts before they occur. Key words and phrases are incorporated into the culture of the classroom (positive action phrases and invitations to listen) to help children communicate with each other directly. There will be further suggestions about language for conflict resolution in Chapter 10. (Note that "Implications for Teachers" in Chapter 4 mentioned encouraging words and listening, and communicating shared values and practices through a shared vocabulary to help children solve or minimize conflicts.)

Learning Centers and Play Spaces

In many settings, centers (learning, play, or activity centers) are where the main business of the day occurs. Even in kindergarten schedules with less choice time, these activities can play a valuable role in all areas of development, including children's conflict resolution. Places for cooperation and conflict management skills include the following:

• *Dramatic play:* Children engage in fantasy and reality, use open-ended materials, adopt multiple roles and cultures, and, in sociodramatic play, experience joint decision-making and negotiating. As we have seen, dramatic play is a safe and powerful way for children to practice social skills.

• *Blocks:* This area should not become gender-segregated. "Traffic" and territory need to be negotiated, building decisions made. Accessories extend the play. Dictate signs to demonstrate value for collaborative block-building efforts.

• *Table Toys and Manipulatives:* Having multiple-child rather than single-child toys and materials encourages associative and cooperative play and shared problem-solving.

Blocks like these provide wonderful opportunities for collaborative problem-solving.

- *Art:* Children experience conversation at the art table or using Play-Doh. They enjoy collaborative and cooperative art, such as a group mural or sculpture. They share materials (both using them and sharing responsibility for cleaning and care). Inspiring examples are found in the *ateliers* and classrooms in Reggio Emilia schools.
- *Books:* Children may conduct an internal dialogue with characters or situations in books. This dialogue can be a starting place for a discussion with adults or other children. In the library center or book corner, children enjoy books alone, make comments about what they are reading, or even share standard-sized books and Big Books.
- *Computer Center:* Increasingly available but not universal, computers with high-quality software can provide for negotiating, turn-taking, and problem-solving. Computers can provide play experiences for children with special needs, and can address equity issues for girls and others.
- *Outdoor Play:* Children have even more peer culture autonomy, with more distant adult presence, and have opportunities for negotiation and cooperation. Not to be overlooked is outdoor pretend play, in its own way often as complex as indoor dramatic play. Teachers should also consider issues of violent and non-violent play, inclusion and exclusion from play, possession of territory and objects, and teasing and superiority of size and physical ability.

Teaching and Learning: Curriculum Models and Activities

Curriculum Models

Curriculum based on developmentally appropriate practices support children's conflict resolution and peacemaking. Of particular interest in this context are models with a basic premise of working together in authentic collaboration.

Project Approach   The Project Approach, developed by Lilian Katz and Sylvia Chard (1995), is a way of teaching and learning that involves children's active participation in an in-depth investigation of a topic that is meaningful to them. Together with adult guidance, children generate questions to explore about the topic and develop ways to find answers. Children not only learn about the topic, but develop skills and dispositions for learning and working collaboratively. Project work, with its multiple ways of investigating a topic, welcomes divergent perspectives and allows children with different strengths and abilities to contribute.

Reggio Emilia   Early childhood programs inspired by the municipal schools of Reggio Emilia share this project-based learning. Furthermore, the guiding principles of Reggio-inspired programs provide a powerful context for conflict resolution and peacemaking. Values in these programs are a sense of community within the school, and of the school within the community; of collaboration among children, among children and teachers, and among teachers and families; and the image of the child as capable. In the narration of a video about a project on making a portrait of a lion, we are told that "children learn that working together is a beautiful thing" (from the Reggio Children video, *To Make a Portrait of a Lion*, 1987.)

Conflict Resolution Activities for Groups

Thinking Games   Thinking games for fours and fives can be more complex than those for threes. Experiencing a thinking game with other children requires perspective-taking, listening, and presenting a logical argument. They learn that what they do or say is connected with what others do or say. Using a favorite story, children confront the dilemma of *The Messy Rabbit*, who may miss seeing the clown at the circus because he has not cleaned his room. (Nivola, C. A. [1978]. *The messy rabbit*. New York: Knopf Publishing Group, New York). Another thinking game is based on the familiar Piagetian example of the broken cups (Edwards, 1986; Crary, 1984). One child breaks several cups accidentally while trying to be helpful; another child breaks one cup on purpose. The question is which situation was worse, and what should be the consequence for each child.

Engaging Our Imaginations   Fours and fives, being more experienced in imaginative play, use puppets and role-playing to explore social issues in a safe environment. Books, pictures, and photographs can also be used as discussion prompts. The arts, and particularly drama, can help children express their own feelings and "try on" the feelings of others. In story drama, children create reenactments of stories, building, retelling, and sometimes redirecting the storyline or creating new roles. In a simple story drama, children retell "Caps for Sale," portraying with few words the gleeful mischief of the monkeys and the weariness, surprise, anger, frustration, and resignation of the peddler. In a more complex story drama about Rumplestiltskin, children become the king's advisors faced with a perplexing dilemma.

Story drama is particularly effective in engaging children with special needs through the freedom of being someone different, as well as the focus on individual creative interpretation and improvisation. Story drama also draws on situations and stories from many cultures and welcomes many voices (Brown & Pleydell, 1999; Carroll, personal communication, 2002; Saldana, 1995).

TEACHERS TALK: LEARNING HOW WORDS CAN HURT

A kindergarten teacher talks about Scrunchy Sam: "This is a way to visibly show how our words can hurt. Introduce your class to Sam, who is a life-sized person made out of bulletin board paper. Tell them that Sam is here to teach us how words can hurt. Next, brainstorm with the class some things that someone has said to them that made them feel angry, hurt, sad, or put down. (Do not use names.) We call these words wrinkle words, and as they are written down, that child should come up and scrunch up a part of Sam. By the time everyone gets a turn, poor Sam is wrinkled up into a tight little ball. We then discuss how Sam feels now. After that, we ask what could make Sam feel better. Each child then comes up with a 'smooth' word to help Sam feel better, and smooths out some of the wrinkles as he does. When we have all smoothed Sam out, we discuss whether he looks like he did when we started. Of course he doesn't, because we can never take back the hurt those words caused, we can only smooth them over. Each one of the wrinkles leaves its mark, even after we try to fix it. Our conclusion is to rip up and throw away the wrinkle words and to save the smooth words."

Cooperative Games and Activities

Music: Singing, Moving, Playing   How many games and activities happen in your class that promote cooperation, caring, and peacemaking? Have you considered dance, movement and music, and even cooking as well as games? The act of singing and making music together with rhythm instruments is such an activity. Children may choose to sing, play, move, or clap as part of the musical *ensemble*. Together, we enjoy the sounds of our own voices and instruments, and we hear and celebrate the music that is the sound we make all together. Sometimes, the song may even be about others, feelings, and peacemaking. (You may find ideas in song books, recordings, and peacemaking/conflict resolution curriculum resources.) A few examples:

Peacemakers (and others from *Songs for Peacemakers*, Educational Activities, Inc.)

I Love You, There's No Doubt About It

If You're Happy and You Know It (for this old song, use facial expressions for a variety of feelings)

Free to Be You and Me

Music Works Wonders/Maravillas Musicales (Sesame Workshop: a dual-language video)

Multicultural Children's Songs, by Ella Jenkins

Music Web Sites
Music resources: *www.amc_music.org*
Music Works Wonders (see *sesamestreet.com*)

Games for Fours and Fives   Preschool and kindergarten children enjoy active games that are cooperative rather than competitive. Games for fours and fives allow children to encourage and engage with peers in a common effort. Parachute play (described below) is an example of an activity that simply will not work without a cohesive group effort. For many of these physical games, children develop trust and engage in physical problem-solving.

Here are a few games that may be familiar: spider web with a ball of string, Twister, Hot and Cold, cooperative musical chairs, variations on three-legged racing, back-to-back lifts. Examples of games that may be new: Wrap a Friend, This Ain't No Piano, and Gyrating Reptile. Details of these games and their sources are provided at the end of the chapter (Wichert, 1989; Luvmour & Luvmour, 1990; Prutzman et al., 1988).

Caring and Social Action

Social action for fours and fives may mean standing up for another person. This action is an important first step as children begin to see themselves as kind and caring. Teachers also bring social action into the group experience so that children begin to see themselves as a kind and caring community.

Teaching and learning in the preschool and kindergarten classroom are often organized around themes. Caring and social action can guide these themes and activities, and can incorporate concepts of friendship, cooperation, kindness, and compassion (Noddings, 1995). A caring variation of the theme "Community Helpers" could be along the lines of "How We Help Others," involving thinking games; noticing examples of helping in books, stories, and everyday life; caring roles in dramatic play, such as a veterinarian's office; and class meetings about ways that children and adults provide help to others.

As mentioned in Chapter 5, the environment is another theme of caring that is accessible and meaningful to adults, and it can be within children's direct experience. Without venturing into global warming and the ozone layer, children can find significance in maintaining a clean environment, providing a safe home for animals, protecting plants, and conserving resources by recycling and only using what they need. Children can take the next step into social action with a doable environmental project at school or at home.

More examples and suggestions for caring: As an alternative to the usual "All About Me" theme, children and teachers may begin the year with an "All About

Us" theme, with the emphasis on the classroom community. The theme affirms each child, encourages connections among children, and defines the community. Intergenerational activities provide rich opportunities for mutual caring encounters between young children and older adults. For example, in a school in Reggio Emilia, older preschoolers created a book to welcome new children coming to the school.

CARING ACTIONS THAT ARE MEANINGFUL TO CHILDREN: THE CANNED FOOD DRIVE?

"Here's the can of peas my mom gave me to bring in." Providing for those in need is an important social action. In a caring classroom, children are connected to the meaning and importance of what they are doing and are active participants.

THREE TEACHERS TALK ABOUT HELPING OTHERS

"One of the things we do each year at Thanksgiving is make a hand with each child's name on it, and write something they are thankful for on it. Then they each take their hand off the tree when they bring in a pair of mittens for a needy child. These then get donated to various organizations. Our hand tree becomes a mitten tree by Christmas. It is a little way in which to help others in what is often an over looked item."

"We develop a monthly Sharing with Others project, starting with a box of pencils for the first month. We label the box 'Pencils to Share' and explain to the children that the boxes are for those in need. Each month we do a different item, and by the end of the year, we start an outreach project for the school and community. The children come up with a project that they think will help others."

"I think whether we realize it or not, our students are going to remember making a difference in someone's life by donating food, toys, etc. I think we all have the right idea, but the key is for us to continue modeling the things we want children to do, then let them practice it over and over again. Maybe it will become ingrained! And maybe they will pass on what they know to a friend or a family member!"

ALL CHILDREN

Culture and Language

A classroom environment that is culturally diverse helps create an environment for conflict resolution, and by the same token, a caring classroom environment that is conducive to conflict resolution helps create an environment that is responsive to diversity. Throughout this chapter, we have mentioned awareness of culture and ability in the curriculum for caring conflict resolution. Further considerations for a culturally responsive curriculum follow.

Extend diversity into all elements of play and curriculum—dramatic play, blocks, table toys, art, music, books, and outdoor plays—by actively incorporating what is familiar and experienced by all children. Ask yourself whether the curriculum in your classroom is "a mirror or a wall" (King, et al). Evaluate your curriculum and activities for diversity; evaluate books for bias and stereotypes. Resources for evaluation tools and checklists are in Ramsey (1998), York (1992), and Derman-Sparks (1989).

Provide talking and sharing time for all children in a psychologically safe environment. Encourage in all children the habit of respectful listening to one other, being aware that there are different but equally valid ways of speaking. Develop communication skills for talking to children about differences and provide children with appropriate ways to talk about differences as well. Model this understanding of linguistic diversity and incorporate elements of children's home languages into the classroom environment.

Ability

We have mentioned the importance of including all children in the classroom environment and of including children with special needs in the context of mutually caring encounters. Playing with peers is valuable for children with special needs, although difficulties may arise due to issues such as difficulty in communicating with peers, lack of understanding of cause and effect, or self-control that is not as developed as that of age-mates. (Remember that not all children with special needs will experience the same issues. Each child has individual abilities.)

Consider aspects of the physical and social environment that support children with special needs and areas of the environment and curriculum that may be adapted to facilitate conflict-free play and learning with peers. Children with special needs, developmental delays, atypical development, and medically diagnosed conditions may need additional support for developing social competence, including intervention to support their play processes. Teachers should work with families and transdisciplinary teams to determine specific support strategies for each child. The goal of the adult in facilitating play is that ultimately the play itself will begin to facilitate children's social and cognitive development (Campbell, McGregor, & Nasik, 1994; Guralnick, 1994; Linder, 1994; Puckett & Black, 2001).

RESOURCES FOR THE CARING CLASSROOM

Finding, Evaluating, and Adapting Materials

There are numerous resources for teachers and children that specifically address conflict resolution and peacemaking. A number of book titles and web sites are listed in this book, and others can be located easily. As with all materials for teaching and learning, teachers should evaluate resources for appropriateness for the age and

development of all children in an inclusive setting, for degree of cultural responsiveness, and for practicality. Chapter 12 of this book will offer an overview of conflict resolution programs and suggest specific criteria for evaluating and adapting
them. The evaluation criteria for bias and stereotype in the preceding resources are
also helpful in evaluating materials in the context of conflict resolution.

Teachers may also find existing materials that support conflict resolution and
peacemaking, or that can be adapted. In adapting a book or activity, teachers
should ask, "What is it about this material that does not fit with the caring classroom (empathy, solving conflicts positively, etc.)? What about this material can be
changed to make it fit into a caring classroom framework?" Teachers may even
involve children in the adaptation. "I really like this story, except for the part when
the wolf is unkind to the grandmother. What do you think? How do you think we
can make the story different?"

Books for Children

Books can be used to illustrate and reinforce specific attributes of conflict resolution and peacemaking, listed at the beginning of this chapter. High-quality children's literature in which the main character demonstrates these attributes
(*Swimmy*, Lionni) or confronts a conflict (*Peter's Chair*, Keats) provides powerful
learning for children. You may find that certain authors, such as Leo Lionni, have
written many books with social themes that are read over and over and have been
enjoyed by many children and adults. A number of books, both those recently written and old favorites, are listed in the Appendix in categories such as perspective-
taking, caring, cooperation, problem-solving, feelings, friendship, and kindness.
Some books are specifically on the topic of children's conflicts. *The Best Day of the
Week* is an example of a book about children in conflict, to be used in conjunction
with a teacher's curriculum guide, *When Push Comes Before Shove: Building Conflict
Resolution Skills with Children*, by Nancy Carlsson-Paige and Diane Levin (1998).

More Games and Activities for a Caring Classroom

Sources

The games and activities described here and in the table that follows have been collected, invented, and adapted over a long period of time. Some have appeared in
multiple sources, and many are part of the familiar "handed-down" repertoire of
many adults who work with young children. The following resources were the
inspiration for a number of the activities in this book (Chapters 8 and 9). *Everybody
Wins* provided the model for adding the very useful activity level information.

Crary, E. (1984). *Kids can cooperate*. Seattle: Parenting Press.
Edwards, C. P. (1986). *Promoting social and moral development in young children: Creative approaches for the classroom*. New York: Teachers College Press.

Luvmour, S., & Luvmour, J. (1990). *Everybody wins*. Philadelphia: New Society Publishers.

Prutzman, P., Stern, L., Burger, M. L., Bodenhamer, G. (1988). *The friendly classroom for a small planet*. Philadelphia: New Society Publishers.

Wichert, S. (1989). *Keeping the peace: Practicing cooperation and conflict resolution*. Philadelphia: New Society Publishers.

Collaborative Activities

Collaborating for Peace: There are many variations of collaborative projects in which children add their own representations and expressions of what peace means to them: peace quilts, peace murals, peace poles, peace web sites, or a mountain of peace pebbles.

Group Recordings: Extend the idea of making music or acting to making audio or video recordings of class activities. Every day there are more ways to use technology to capture what is going on in sound, slide shows, and movies. Children can record singing, sound effects, and group storytelling, as well as dance and drama. Then they can play it over and over, enjoying their community efforts.

Cooperation Fruit Salad/Friendship Soup: Everyone adds something to the bowl or pot, and we all enjoy.

Games

Human Jigsaw Puzzle: Children lie down flat on the floor with their arms and legs in interlocking positions. They get up, walk around, come back, and try to make the same puzzle again (Prutzman et al., 1988).

Rainstorm: This is an old favorite. The rain sounds begin by rubbing hands together, patting legs, stomping feet. The noise grows until the storm begins to subside, and the sounds gradually drop off again. Noises can grow by having the whole group add sounds or by adding people with different sounds.

Scavenger Hunt: This is another old one with many variations. Groups go around the classroom or school to round up easy-to-find or harder-to-find items. This game can be made minimally competitive among groups by having different items and not making it a race. Groups that have found all their items can join others who are still hunting.

Zoom: Players send the word "zoom" around the circle by turning their heads to look at the person on the right. Change directions and send "eek" to the person on the left. After everyone has "zoomed" and "eeked" once, players may change direction (and words) spontaneously. Try to keep from forgetting which word to say! (Prutzman et al.)

Parachute Play

Here are two parachute activities to add to your repertoire. Although a round shape works best for Tornado, you can try these with a large sheet if you do not have a parachute.

Tornado   (Ages 3 to 5): Place three children in the center of the parachute, back to back. They should hook elbows and sit with legs crossed. Everyone holding the parachute walks around almost twice, keeping the parachute taut. On the count of three, everyone takes a couple of steps back, pulling the parachute toward themselves. The children sitting in the "eye of the tornado" will spin around.

(Ages 6–8): Same procedure, but only two children should be allowed in the center at a time. They should assume the same position, locking arms back to back, with legs crossed. (Over age 8: Bigger people can anchor the parachute with their own weight. Therefore, only one individual should assume the center position with legs crossed.)

Alligator   Everyone sits on the ground with legs out straight, holding the parachute at chin level. Someone chosen to be the "alligator" goes into his/her "swamp" under the parachute. Slowly, the alligator moves about the swamp and taps the feet of another "alligator," who then goes under the parachute. The "alligator" continues to tap feet until everyone is under the parachute. This game can be played with eyes open or closed, depending on the age group.

SUMMARY

Creating a caring classroom community for young children starts with an understanding of what is it like to be two to three or four to five. Twos and threes are finding their place in the world, with an increasing ability to get around on their own. They are discovering a new world that they now share with peers and playmates. Fours and fives in preschool and kindergarten are even more interested in their peers and have even more energy, ways to communicate, and interests in playing together and pretending. Teachers can arrange the social and physical environment to encourage conflict resolution and peacemaking in a caring classroom community.

SUPPLEMENTARY MATERIALS FOR CHAPTER 8

Research Focus:

How can we determine what actually works in helping children develop social skills? The following article presents research on the effectiveness of a social skills intervention program, the Play Time Social Time Curriculum. Locate and read this article to learn more about ways to evaluate programs and apply research findings to your practice.

Kamps, D. M., Tankersly, M., and Ellis, C. (2000). Social skills interventions for young at-risk students: A 2-year follow-up study. *Behavioral Disorders, 25*(4), 310–324.

Head Start children received a social skills intervention consisting of affection activities (games [see Table 8–1] and songs that incorporated hugs, pats on the back, and high fives); social skills lessons; modeling and role-playing acts of sharing, agreeing, and helping; reciprocal peer mentoring; and parent support. Researchers found positive effects on aggression, out-of-seat behaviors, and negative verbal statements and increased compliance behaviors and prosocial peer interactions.

>>

APPLICATION EXERCISES

1. Expanding your repertoire of activities and games:
   a. Look for a conflict-resolution activity book that is suitable for the children in your setting and find new games and activities.
   b. Think about games and activities that you are already using and analyze them for what children are learning. Are they cooperative or competitive? Do they require children to use perspective-taking, collaborating, generating alternative solutions, and working together?
   c. Are there games or activities that you can change or adapt to incorporate aspects of conflict resolution and peacemaking? Make changes and see what happens.
2. Choose some of the games suggested in this chapter and discuss ways in which they help children learn conflict resolution and peacemaking.
3. Make a floor plan of your setting and analyze traffic flow, spaces for children alone and in groups, access to materials, and entry in and out of play and work areas.
4. Investigate intergenerational programs or organizations in your community. Pilot a program in your classroom that will bring young children and older people together.

>>

THINKING ABOUT ALL CHILDREN

We have mentioned that "curriculum should be a mirror not a wall" (King et al., 1994). Evaluate your classroom materials and learning experiences with the eyes of each child in your class. Do you see a mirror or a wall? You may also use the evaluation checklists in the Anti-Bias Curriculum and other sources.

TABLE 8–1 GAMES AND ACTIVITIES FOR PEACE-MAKING AND COMMUNITY-BUILDING: PRESCHOOL AND KINDERGARTEN
(DETAILS OF HOW TO PLAY THE GAMES ARE FOUND IN THE APPENDIX.)

Game	Ages	Group Size	Materials	Activity Level (1=most active)
Lemonade: team pantomime (Luvmour)	4+	8+	None	2
Popcorn Balls: all "pop" and form one big ball (Luvmour)	3+	7+	None	2
Rolling Along: pairs roll with feet touching (Luvmour)	3+	pairs	None	2
Cooperative Musical Chairs: no one leaves; all pile on each other on remaining chairs	3+	6+	Music, pillows or chairs	2
Find Your Animal Mate: act out an animal and find your mate (Luvmour)	3+	8+	Slips of paper with animal names or pictures	3
Animal Acting: animal pantomimes (Luvmour)	3+	5+	None	3
Gyrating Reptile: one long snake moves by "tummy power" (Luvmour)	4+	5+	None	3
Cooperative Story Telling: everyone adds a part	3+	5+	None (props optional)	5
Cooperative Spider Web #1: make a web by rolling a ball of yarn back and forth across a circle	3+	5–10	Ball of yarn or string	5
Body Sculpture: create with bodies in pairs or teams (Wichert)	4+	5–18	None	4
Tracing a Friend: trace on paper; adapt this for all ages (Wichert)	3+	up to 10	Large paper, crayons	4
Hot and Cold: group feedback to find object	3+	5–15	None	5
This Ain't No Piano: everyone has a unique sound, played together (Wichert)	4+	5–12	None	4
Wrap a Friend: team effort with paper or toilet paper; wrappee breaks out at end (Wichert)	4+	Adult: child =1:8	Large newsprint, masking tape	4
Blanket Toss and Catch: everyone holds on to toss balls; many other ideas; parachute play	3+	6–10	Blanket or sheet, ball	3
Cooperative Spider Web #2: all untangle separate strings with treat or prize at the end of each	5+	6+	Lots of yarn or string, treat for each	2
Favorite Things Chart: a group list of everyone's favorites; find out how alike and different our favorites are	3+	Any size class or group	Paper or card-board for chart, markers	5

9   Curriculum for Conflict Resolution: Primary Grades

"At the beginning of the year we do team building and discuss the concept of a team and how teammates help each other. The class then generates a team name to go by for the rest of the year. It is a complimentary adjective and an animal. They are the 'Fantastic Frogs' instead of Mrs. Emmett's class. When I call them to come in at recess, I use this name and the children chant, 'Let's go, Frogs!' This helps the class bond as a team with a common trait that they all share."

Chapter 9 Objectives: This chapter continues to build the middle layer of the "Three-Layer Cake" with learning environments for conflict resolution and peacemaking among 6- to 8-year old children, typically in the primary grades. We will explore curriculum activities, materials, and routines to help children of this age further develop ways to understand, manage, and resolve conflicts. We will continue to emphasize curriculum and materials that are culturally responsive and meet the needs of children with special needs, developmental delays, and disabilities.

Chapter 9 Outline
Understanding Children and Helping Them Learn
    Children in the Primary Years: Six-, Seven-, and Eight-Year-Olds
Developmental Characteristics of Primary Age Children

UNDERSTANDING CHILDREN AND HELPING THEM LEARN

Children in the Primary Years: Six-, Seven-, and Eight-Year-Olds

As in the preceding chapter, we will now think about how our understanding of 6-, 7-, and 8-year-old children will guide us in supporting their growing ability to resolve conflicts with their peers. Again, we will choose only a few pieces of children's development to discuss as a complement to a more complete study. What we will see are areas that are different from what has been happening with younger children, and what is happening that relates to peer interaction and conflict resolution. Looking at the developmental characteristics of primary age children, we will also ask the question, "What's important now in children's lives?"

DEVELOPMENTAL CHARACTERISTICS OF PRIMARY AGE CHILDREN

Being Friends and Making Things Work

In the years from ages 6 to 8, children find their world enlarging beyond the family to include more children and adults, with new places to go and things to do. Two important themes have emerged for this age group: "being friends" and "making things work." Making friends and being part of a circle of friends is an important part of life. Children are also finding expanded physical and cognitive ability and enjoy making things work. They enjoy the sense of accomplishment they get from making plans and carrying them out.

Friendship and Peer Group Affiliation

Being friends with others is closely linked to peer group affiliation. We will discuss peer affiliation and also friendship, a special type of affiliation, as well as group acceptance and rejection and different aspects of children's social relationships. A sense of belonging, beyond belonging in the family setting, is becoming more important to primary age children. Among basic needs in Maslow's hierarchy is a sense of belonging (see Figure 9–1). At this age, that need becomes important. In Chapter 3, we discussed the idea of children's peer culture. Affiliating with particular peers goes further in helping children establish a sense of self, try on roles, and practice ways of relating to others and to the world. Children choose peer affiliations by asking, "Who is like me?", "Who likes the same things that I like?", "Who does the same things?", or perhaps even, "Who looks like me?"

How do children define friendships? Diane Levin suggests that children begin with commonalities of gender, race, class, and ability, and then "move to another level" in the basis of friendship where loyalty, shared history of friendship, and

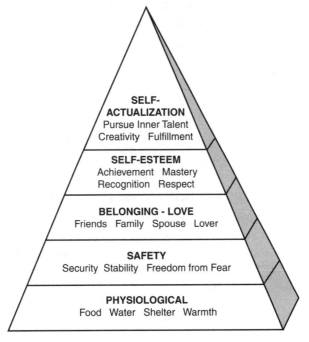

Figure 9–1
Maslow's Hierarchy of Needs.

empathy develop. Children's friendship patterns are "always developing and changing" (personal communication, November, 2002).

Basic needs: Physiological (food, drink)

Safety (security, psychological safety)

Belongingness and love (affiliation, acceptance, affection)

Esteem (competence, approval, recognition)

Meta needs: Cognitive

Aesthetic

Self-actualization (Puckett & Black, 2001, p. 426–427)

Building on this need for affiliation, Ms. Emmett inspires a sense of belonging with her class's identity as "Fantastic Frogs." Affiliation can also develop through activities that are now age-appropriate, such as scouts, sports, or other clubs. Children are drawn together as they share interests such as hobbies or collections. Affiliation also occurs because of proximity or availability, as well as common interests.

Peer group affiliation is positive and is a needed part of primary children's development. However, affiliations formed at this age can also be detrimental if the groups are exclusionary and have arbitrary membership parameters such as gender, race, ability, or socioeconomic status. In this case, children are encountering classism, racism, sexism, and discrimination based on ability or appearance. This leads to greater potential for conflicts (King et al, 1994; Van Ausdale & Feagin, 2001). As we will see later, gender identity and gender role behaviors are becoming more clearly defined and increasingly determine peer group affiliation.

Discussion Question

When is gender affiliation an appropriate part of the development of gender identity, and when is it inappropriate? How do you react to "No girls allowed" or "No boys allowed"?

Feeling Capable: Erikson's Industry Versus Inferiority

An important part of being ages 6, 7, or 8 is an increasing need to feel competent. Children are intentional and want to accomplish what they set out to do; in other words, they have a sense of productivity with intentionality. In this way, Erikson's psychosocial stage of Industry versus Inferiority describes primary-age children well. Physical and cognitive development support this capability now. Children are better able to plan ahead and have the physical ability to carry out their plans. Part of feeling capable and also belonging is knowing the rules in a particular setting. These developmental dimensions, a need for industry and accomplishment and a need to belong, have clear implications for social interaction, conflict issues, and ways of managing and resolving conflicts.

Cognitive/Language Development

Cognitive development increases among 6- to 8-year-olds as they begin to progress from Piaget's pre-operational thought to concrete operational thought. Memory, perspective-taking, and concept acquisition are becoming stronger in the transition to concrete operations. Information processing theory describes children's conflict resolution ability in terms of greater memory and more reflection. Among the areas of cognitive growth are increased logical-mathematical thinking; the ability to conserve, which leads to more flexibility and logic; and reversibility, which helps children generate alternative ways to solve problems. In general, children have a growing understanding of the social world. At this age, peers contribute to cognitive development as well as to social and emotional development. Children's understanding of games, pretend play, and rules is becoming more cognitively complex. Games offer the opportunity to enjoy and further develop problem-solving. Children from ages 6 to 8 grow and develop on different timetables, and their responses to others are affected by the context of culture and home language. Differential development among children may lead to conflict. All these factors clearly relate to new issues, as we will see, and new capabilities in conflict strategies and resolutions.

Language development is marked by emerging use of figures of speech, humor (remember those grape and elephant jokes?), and the ability to lie (Puckett & Black, 2001). Children are able to express themselves more clearly in a discussion or argument and can better understand other points of view. Our theoretical connection here is to Vygotsky and the idea of language as a tool. In their conversation with others, children understand more subtle cues, shades of meaning, and registers of language that indicate affect and emotion. They also demonstrate metalinguistic awareness, the ability to think about forms and meanings of language. Vocabulary is more accurate, more precise, and follows conventional usages. Rules of language and figures of speech, however, are culture-specific and can help define both peer and family culture. Children at primary age (and younger children as well) understand the power of hurtful words.

Physical/Motor Development

Large motor development among 6- to 8-year-olds includes gaining fundamental skills needed for physical games and sports (catching, jumping, kicking, throwing). Greater perceptual motor development and the ability to adjust their bodies to a space helps in games and sports. Games with rules and organized sports can contribute to positive aspects of children's development, self-esteem, greater social competence, and a source of group affiliation. With a strong relationship between the physical and psychosocial, now is the time for adults to stress cooperation in games and offer alternatives to competition. Children at this age may be physically vulnerable due to fatigue or hunger (Fallin et al, 2001).

Issues for families and teachers about sports include knowing what is appropriate and what is not. Are team sports right for a particular child? Physical developmental rates are variable. Concerns include coaches and even families who value winning, and children being embarrassed by failure. Is there an expectation of competence and an emphasis on competition, and how does the child respond? It is important to understand differences in children's abilities, in their awareness of physical competence, and the importance they place on physical competence and ability. Is playing on a team with a friend and the sense of affiliation of team membership a strong and positive motivation? These are important considerations for choosing activities with children wisely and inclusively.

Example

Bill, age 6, is in his first year on the swim team. At a developmental meet, he finishes fifth in his race across the pool. Looking around him at the finish, he climbs out of the pool, announcing with satisfaction and sincere conviction, "Hey! I tied for second with my best friend Kevin!"

The idea that all children can enjoy sports has led to opportunities through Special Olympics, Challengers baseball, and gymnastics classes for children with disabilities. There are positive aspects of team sports for children when they are appropriate for children's physical, cognitive, and social/emotional development.

Small motor ability among typically developing children of this age includes using pencils, tools, and game pieces. Problem-solving along with motor development leads to independence and self-confidence. As children engage in other games, building activities, and creative constructions, they will benefit from classrooms where all learning styles and individual interests are valued. Third grade is also a critical year in children's interest in school. During this potential "turn-off" age for school interest, meaningful ways to connect with learning can make a crucial difference.

Social/Emotional Development

A question for primary children is, "Who am I in relation to others?" During these years, children experience a cycle of emotional equilibrium and disequilibrium. There are boisterous, active sixes and introspective sevens and eights who are regrouping and feeling more "together" again. As with any set of developmental characteristics, there is not a precise timetable. Children deal with fears about attachment to family and friends and continue to develop a concept of self. There are worries about rejection by peers and family, scolding, embarrassment, and not doing well. Fortunately for adults who care about them, they are able to name emotions (Puckett & Black, 2001).

Children continue to grow in awareness of diversity. Aboud (1988) has described the development of racial awareness, and more recent research confirms and extends children's early awareness and understanding (Ramsey, 1998; Van Ausdale & Feagin, 2001). Gender differences play a greater role in children's affiliation. A note about gender identity: Sex is biologically determined; gender is psy-

Friendships and enjoying the same activities are important for six- to eight-year-olds.

chologically, socially, and culturally constructed. As we will see, friendships are less transient and situational, and more selective. Children are also aware of being offensive in their interactions with others.

Gender issues have gained greater prominence in recent years as researchers have explored the hazards of growing up as a boy and as a girl in the United States. William Pollack (1998) describes the Boy Code, an internalized sense of isolation, disconnectedness, and unrealistic expectations that, by adolescence, may result in violence or withdrawal from others. Mary Pipher (1994) draws a picture of the adolescent girl that is no less disturbing. A clue in understanding these growing-up issues is offered by Carol Gilligan (2001), who explains that the critical time for forming relationships and capturing a sense of self for boys is around age 5 to 7 and for girls around age 15. All children are at risk for some form of gender bias, and the implications for adults in the role of the caring "other" are clear and compelling.

Moral Development

Moral development has been described by Piaget in stages as well, although we could think of these as moral orientations that are not related to ages or stages. First, moral realism is characterized by rule-bound thinking and behaving, a view of rules as important and unalterable. There is an obedience/punishment orientation. The rule-bound nature of children's moral decision-making is consistent with

---

DEVELOPMENT OF FRIENDSHIPS

Selman describes children's levels of friendship and social perspectives (Ramsey, 1991). We should view any delineation of stages with some caution, knowing that there is clear overlap across levels, and differences in children and situations. How does this match your observations of children?

Level 0, ages 3–7: Undifferentiated perspective ("We all think alike").

Level 1, ages 4–9: Differentiated perspective ("We don't think the same way").

Level 2, ages 6–12: Reciprocal ("I am aware of what others are thinking about me").

---

other characteristics of the period that we have discussed. Earlier, we looked at stages of children's moral reasoning. (Please refer to the chart in Chapter 5.) Damon's stages of moral decision-making correspond closely to Selman's stages of friendship (Ramsey, 1991).

It is important to ask how much these explanations of children's moral understanding explain contemporary children's thinking. Is this view current and reflective of cultural differences?

WHAT DO SIXES TO EIGHTS FIGHT ABOUT, AND HOW?

Conflict Issues for Sixes to Eights

New Issues to Deal with

New issues facing primary age children related to conflict include friendship and group membership, interpretation of rules, choosing sides in games, loyalty, and establishing competence or superiority. These issues are clearly interrelated. They may be demonstrated in instigating actions and behaviors such as aggression, teasing, put-downs, possession, and exclusion/friendship. The basic issues described in Chapter 4 (control of social and physical environment) persist, but new ones have developed among these older children.

PRIMARY CHILDREN: MOVING OUT INTO THE WORLD

In addition to the theorists we have mentioned, we can explore Bronfenbrenner's (1979) ecological systems theory. The world of the primary child moves from the *microsystem* into the *mesosytem* between school and home, and is even more greatly influenced by the *exosystem* and the *macrosystem*. Can you see how the media, popular books and games, societal issues about health and the environment, and testing and accountability in school fit into these systems?

How do new aspects of development affect the conflicts that 6- to 8-year-olds experience? Reactive conflicts occur in response to physical or verbal aggression. Cultural conflicts are also part of the conflict arena (Van Ausdale & Feagin, 2001), as are issues of group boundaries and exclusion. Violence can be a means of exclusion (Katch, 2001).

TEACHERS TALK ABOUT PRIMARY CONFLICT ISSUES

A third-grade teacher: *"Conflict among girls is so ... personal!!"*

Reading resource teacher: *"The issues I see are territory, dominance, self-esteem, ego, material possessions, and cultural and religious conflicts."*

Physical and possession issues now include school materials (pencils, markers) and computer time. Object conflicts may actually be annoyances, such as taking a hat to bother someone. Social issues revolve even more around peers and friendships, with new emphasis on role and status within the peer group. Issues are related to superiority, accomplishment, achievement, and products. Competition also emerges as an issue. Being right, doing the right thing, and following rules and social conventions are important. Computer conflicts occur as a result of sharing time and equipment, as well as superiority, rules, and competitive games. A few of these conflict areas for primary children are highlighted in the following sections: *peer status and friendship issues, competition and team play,* and *bullying.*

Peer Group Status: Acceptance or Rejection   What children think of their peers is an important factor in children's conflicts. Children experience different types of status among peers. There are popular, accepted, rejected, neglected, and controversial children (Ramsey, 1991; others more recent). Popular and socially accepted children have high self-esteem and self-confidence, enjoy the company of others, and have mutual loyalty, respect, trust, and support. Children who are rejected by peers are disliked. Neglected children are ignored. Controversial children may not be well-liked, but they do arouse interest and are influential in the group. Some of the qualities that lead to acceptance or rejection have an impact on how children deal with conflict. Accepted children demonstrate social competence, such as knowing how to enter a group and read social cues, and are able to negotiate conflict. Rejected children are perceived to be aggressive in peer interactions and demonstrate inappropriate social responses.

Peer status has further implications for creating a caring classroom for conflict resolution. The effects on children who are rejected are powerful, and the effects on children who reject others are harmful as well. These effects are minimized in a classroom community where children demonstrate caring, inclusiveness, empathy, and other-awareness. If children are rejected or excluded because of prejudice, teachers must work to eliminate bias. Teachers can help children, especially rejected and neglected children, develop greater social competence.

Friendship Issues Being friends is important to primary-age children. Conflict among friends is related to maintaining friendships. Hartup (1991) reminds us that not all friendships are alike. Some are rocky and others are steady as a rock. In either case, there are more conflicts, as well as more cooperation, among friends than among non-friend peers. Conflicts between friends last longer as children work toward a conciliatory outcome. Issues are similar to those among non-friends, although conflicts do arise as friendships are formed or realigned. Friends see themselves as equal partners in the relationship. Friendships are formed through affiliation and common interests, with shared activities and clearly understood reciprocity. Friends spend time with each other and enjoy each other's company. These factors provide the motivation for friends to persevere in working to resolve conflicts.

Competition and Team Play As we mentioned earlier, primary-age children are physically ready for certain sports and physical activities. They are interested in being part of a group and enjoy demonstrating competence. What types of conflicts may arise in team play? There may be arguments over rules, superiority, exclusion, put-downs, or exclusionary cliques within the team. What should adults do about these conflicts? Adult team leaders and coaches have roles with the team, similar in a way to the teacher's role in the classroom, in guiding players to develop a sense of community within the team that is supportive of all members.

Contrasting examples from children and adults about team sports:
Child talks about team sports: "Don't say, 'Ha, ha! You're a loser!'"
Child talks about team sports: "You shouldn't be mean to people. It's only a game."
Parent to child on the soccer field during a game: "What are you doing, Danny? Do you think you're out there just to have fun!!?"

Sportsmanship in team sports and playground sports can be positive social learning experiences for children. However, competition is built into team and individual sports. Is it appropriate for young children? Researchers have suggested that children do not demonstrate a sense of competition until around age 8, and earlier interest in participation may be the result of a desire to meet parents' expectations (American Academy of Pediatrics, 2001). It is important to avoid pushing children beyond their physical developmental level, and to give them time to try things out until they begin to make choices about their own interests. Outside of school, after-school programs, boys and girls clubs, scouts, and other non-sports activities have the potential to provide positive experiences.

DISCUSSION QUESTION

What are the positives and negatives of team sports, playground sports, and rough-and-tumble play?

Many primary-age children enjoy games and team sports with friends.

DISCUSSION QUESTION ABOUT ORGANIZED ACTIVITIES

There are two more questions to consider. One is about the "over-programmed child." Do children have any unstructured play time after school? Another question is about equity and access. Are sports and other activities available to all children, or only to those from middle- and upper-income families?

Bullying in the Classroom   Bullying is a physical or psychological intimidation, done repeatedly over time, that is unprovoked and harmful. Unlike a conflict in which peers disagree over an issue, bullying by definition is an unequal interaction, with an imbalance of power between bully and victim, without an authentic issue. Bullying can be direct actions that cause verbal or physical harm or indirect actions, such as exclusion or rejection. Bullying is different from conflict between peers seeking to resolve an issue. In an instance of bullying, there is no issue to be resolved, and the unbalanced relationship between bully and victim does not suggest that the children are peers.

What causes bullying? Bullying is a result of an attempt to establish superiority and to exclude others, especially due to differences in color, language, class, or physical differences including size and disability. Victims are those perceived as less powerful and those not physically, emotionally, or cognitively able to resist, confront, or retaliate.

More boys than girls are reported to act as bullies. Bullying has been identified as a gender issue, with boys as bullies and girls and smaller boys as victims, although girls can be bullies, especially in single-sex settings (Froschl & Sprung, 1999). Newer research has shown what many teachers have known intuitively: Girls can be bullies, but in a different way than boys. Preschool girls engage in more "relationally aggressive" behaviors, as opposed to the overtly aggressive behaviors of boys (Crick et al, 1997). *Relationally aggressive* behavior causes hurt to children's peer relationships, such as through social exclusion or spreading rumors. Boys' *overt aggression* involves bodily harm or threat of harm. Bullies behave in the way that will do the most damage to their victims. If girls value their social relationships, this relationally aggressive bullying behavior is a powerful strategy.

Bullying is everyone's problem (Froschl & Gropper, 1999). It is pervasive. The statistics vary depending on the source, but they are compelling in all cases. In a study of 15,686 students, the National Institute of Child Health and Human Development reported that at least 30% of school children are victims of bullying (Okie, 2001). The National Center for Education Statistics (1993) reports similar findings. Not only is bullying pervasive, but all parties are affected: the victims, the bullies themselves, and the onlookers in the environment. Bullying is usually observed in elementary school, growing through high school and perhaps at its most prevalent in the middle-school years. Recent research has found clear evidence of bullying behaviors in children as young as 4 (Danby & Baker, 2001), as well as among kindergarten- and primary-age children (Froschl & Gropper, 1999).

The effects on bullies, victims, and onlookers are powerful. Although being bullied is a painful adult memory, many adults see it as a childhood rite of passage. The effects of bullying include self-esteem issues for victims. Bullies practice inappropriate social actions, acquire misconceptions about power, and ultimately experience peer rejection. Victims are afraid to tell adults, fearing retaliation. Children who are onlookers may also develop a misunderstanding of power and feelings of helplessness unless they learn to stand up for victims (Garbarino, 1995).

Bullying that is not stopped undermines the idea of school as a safe place for children. Intervention is needed, both for bully and victim. Bullying does not thrive in a truly caring community, where each person looks out for others (Chapter 7 ideas relate here). Adult intervention is needed when bullying occurs (Chapter 10).

The implications for teachers are clear. Additional classroom strategies create a climate that allows others to diminish the occurrence of bullying. Examples include worry boxes and class meetings to discuss bullying and what onlookers can do. Curricula that help include the project approach, where children work together on activities. There are published programs that address bullying (Chapter 12) and provide intervention for bullies, as well as ways for victims to respond to bullies and ways for onlookers to find the courage to act on behalf of the victim. One example is *Quit It!*, a program from Educational Equity Concepts. Children's literature can be used to bring up a situation like bullying that seeks to thrive below the radar of adult authority. (For books about discussing bullying with children, see the Appendix.) Teachers need to do the following:

- Listen to children and *know* what is going on in the classroom.
- Be alert to symptoms of bullying, such as changed behaviors, passivity, and withdrawal from group activities.
- Understand the nature of both overt and relationally aggressive bullying.
- Realize that bullying is a class-wide problem. None of us can allow it to happen in our classroom community.
- Make explicit your commitment to children that bullying is something that "we do not want in our classroom."
- Assure children that you will intervene.
- Help children learn how to make friends and be a friend.
- Give yourself a break and read Vivian Paley's (1999) *The Kindness of Children*.

For on-line information about bullying, go to the National Crime Prevention Council Web site, www.ncpc.org. This site has several links with articles, fact sheets, and activities about bullying, as well as about safe communities and crime prevention.

TEACHERS TALK: THE "WANDERING BULLY"

"I was finally able to take time to really observe our 'wandering bully' in action. We knew that J seemed to have a penchant for annoying his peers because of the various protests that would arise from one aggravated party or another. Sitting and watching him play for several days after lunch showed me the magnitude of the problem. He would tease a child about a puzzle, perhaps withholding the last piece deliberately while the other child begged for it, move away casually, knocking down a small block structure in the process, and then sit down on the edge of someone's book so that the pages could not be turned."

"Bullying comes in many forms. Sometimes it shows up in small and covert ways and includes behaviors such as those I mentioned above. It is the act of deliberately trying to annoy or upset another. Some of the solutions that I have tried to incorporate in my classroom are reminding children to treat each other with respect, making certain that the rules are clear, encouraging the victim to speak up, and holding a class meeting. One topic was 'How to be a good friend.'"

Conflict Strategies for Sixes to Eights

Primary-age children have a growing repertoire of more complex strategies for responding to conflict. They develop resolution processes and negotiation strategies in two ways: They develop strategies on their own, and they learn them as a system from adults.

Strategies That Children Use on Their Own

Primary-age children's physical responses to simple possession conflicts are more often accompanied by words than among younger, less verbal children. Physical coercion and aggression, if used, could be more serious. These responses can lead to violence if the conflict escalates. Verbal strategies, like arguments, are more common than physical fighting.

Primary-age children are more likely to use verbal strategies, fortunately. Most children have a range of verbal skills to choose from: negotiation and reasoning, persuasion, and threats or name-calling, which are forms of verbal aggression. These children are more verbal and are able to name their feelings. They understand the effect of words and actions, and they can know "what hurts others." Threats may be real ("I'll break your pencil if you don't quit that!"), or unrealistic ("I'll never play with you ever again"), or even fanciful ("I'll make your nose turn green if you keep doing that"). Depending on the cognitive equality between children, these threats may be taken seriously or may have the effect of defusing the situation through humor. Name-calling can be an instigation, a retaliatory strategy, or game-playing. Katch cites Barney and Brower's apt image of boys "throwing insults back and forth to a worthy opponent" (2001, p. 95).

TEACHER QUESTION FOR THOUGHT

Should you follow up on friendship threats? (Katch, p. 80)

Other children may join in as spontaneous peer mediators. Sometimes children in conflict may call on peers as allies to support their side. A sense of loyalty and of right and wrong may result in children standing up for others and intervening on behalf of another. We can relate this response to the topics of friendship and a positive onlooker intervention in bullying.

Primary-age children may exhibit independence in resolving conflicts instead of calling on adults for issues of rules and territory. However, if an adult is nearby, children are accustomed to seeing the teacher as an authority figure whose judgment is the last word. Also, by now they are used to having adults intervene and tell them how the conflict will be resolved, or perhaps tell them what to say as a way of guiding them through it. Children, in their deference to adults, are doing *exactly what they think the adults want and expect them to do*, which is to cede authority to the adult. What teachers need to do is to give children a voice, literally as well as figuratively, in mediating a conflict. Whose voice is heard doing the talking? Is it the teacher's voice or the children's?

DISCUSSION: A TEACHER'S QUESTION

It's easy to just say, "No fighting," but is there a better way? (Katch, 2001)

Strategies Learned from Adults in a Systematic Way

At school, children learn systematic and intentional strategies (more about teacher intervention in Chapter 10, and more about conflict resolution programs in Chapter 12). Steps for resolving conflicts and problem-solving may be presented to children by a teacher or guidance counselor, posted in the classroom, and practiced in group sessions. Shared language and acronyms used as mnemonic devices provide cues for children and are reminders to follow the steps for resolution. Although these strategies have not originated spontaneously with children, the goal for teachers is to help children learn to use the strategies and resolve conflicts on their own.

What most of the processes have in common are these basic steps:

1. Stop and take a breath so that no more words or actions keep the conflict going.
2. Identify the problem and figure out exactly what the conflict is about.
3. Listen openly to each other and hear all points of view. Exchange perspectives on the situation.
4. Generate a number of alternatives, examining each suggestion for its effects on each person.
5. Choose one solution that meets each person's needs equitably.

There may be other steps or refinements, such as labeling feelings, making a commitment to the solutions, and following up on the solution. Generally, teachers stick with something simple, easy to remember, with clearly labeled steps and cues.

Example

Here is an example of a conflict resolution process developed by a first-grade teacher using the easily remembered acronym SETS (Charney, 1997, p. 58). The steps this teacher and the children use are as follows:

Stop and get cool

Explain what you are unhappy about

Talk at the table

Shake hands

The goal of these strategies is to help children develop habits of social problem-solving, building on the social and cognitive abilities that teachers have tried to nurture in a caring classroom (perspective-taking, generating alternative solutions, etc.). Charles (2000) stresses an openness to the idea that there can be a third alternative, that something else exists out there.

Example: Wheel of Choice

A first-grade teacher describes an approach that she introduced to help children resolve conflicts. Referring to a large "Wheel of Choice" poster, children could consider and select from a number of alternative strategies such as "wald away," "talk it out," "share and take turns," and "count to ten to cool off." Browning, L., Davis, B., & Resta, V. (2000). What do you mean "Think before I act?": Conflict resolution with choices. Journal of Research in Childhood Education, 14, 232–238.

Another strategy that children may learn from adults in school is systematic peer mediation. Children learn to bring a dispute to a mediator or peacemaker who has been trained in guiding those in conflict through stating the problem and creating solutions. The mediator follows specific steps in the process, and the children engaged in the conflict may have steps to follow in the process as well. There are examples of peer mediation program models in Chapter 12.

An additional strategy involves ignoring a behavior that may provoke a conflict. This ignoring sometimes takes the form of the Turtle technique. One teacher uses the Turtle technique almost exclusively, with the idea that it develops self-control and defuses conflicts. Another teacher disagrees, saying that this approach teaches avoidance and creates missed opportunities for developing conflict-resolution skills. Her point is that, in this situation, the message to children is that we are not confident in their ability to resolve conflicts. Their conversation is below. What do you think?

TEACHERS TALK

Teacher A: *"I use Ignoring for K-2 ('the Turtle technique'). When one child is trying to pay attention to a lesson and does not want to be bothered by another student, they put their hands near their head, put their feet together, and keep their head near their desk. This will tell the other student that they are trying to work and not to bother him or her. This is taught at the beginning of the year."*

Teacher B Response: *"I do not fully agree with Ms. A that children should avoid conflict. I don't believe that anyone should go searching for confrontations. However, conflicts are going to happen from time to time. Children need to learn that conflict is a normal part of life, and that it's all right to experience conflicts with others. Children also need to learn how to approach conflict in a constructive, non-violent way."*

CLASSROOM ENVIRONMENTS FOR COOPERATION: WHAT TO DO

Physical Environment in Primary Classrooms

Room arrangement is a factor in children's conflicts in primary as well as preschool classrooms. Decisions for teachers include seating arrangement, space, and arrangement of desks or tables. Physical space is needed for bigger children. Teacher and children may prefer table groups to traditional rows of desks. What do you think about desks in a circle? Is there any reason that children in first, second, and third grade need to have desks in a row facing the teacher? Are they too old for tables? In one elementary school, the primary grades chose tables. The next year, the fourth-, fifth-, and sixth-grade teachers all requested tables too, for community building in their classrooms. How about rocking chairs and soft places to sit and get away to think and regroup quietly? (Chapter 13's case study compares several classroom arrangements.)

With overcrowded classrooms, traffic patterns and space are important. Congestion and crowding can set off conflict. Accessibility for children and adults with physical impairments is needed as well.

TEACHERS TALK

"At the beginning of the school year, I establish patterns with the children in my classroom. To come from their seats to the front of the room, they go straight over to the window side of the room and walk up the side. To go back, they go to the opposite wall. It's like a one-way street, I guess. I just started doing this last year because I had a class of 29 and they needed specific traffic patterns to avoid conflicts, and I have continued because it was so successful."

Do you have any other ideas? Do you think that this teacher figured out this traffic flow system as a community problem-solving activity with the children?

Materials

Collaborative materials, blocks, and shared supplies are still important in the primary grades. Children can take a more active role in deciding how to organize shared materials to provide access. In this decision-making process, ownership of the classroom community, consensus-building, and concern for the needs of all can be embedded. There is less focus in the classroom on what is "mine" and more on what is "ours."

TEACHERS TALK

"In the back of the classroom, I have a basket of pencils and a huge box of crayons. Whenever the children are missing a supply, they are allowed to go back to the basket and take what they need."

Technology

Computer access presents an equity issue that primary teachers must address. With equitable access for children with disabilities and others, the computer's use in cognitive development, as well as social and emotional development, will be of great benefit in the classroom. Potentially, working at a computer with good software can provide all those positive experiences we have mentioned about conflict resolution and peacemaking. As two or more children work together at the computer, there are excellent opportunities for caring encounters (Noddings).

DISCUSSION QUESTIONS

What role does technology play in your early childhood setting? How does it fit in your caring classroom? (This is not just a question for the primary children.) You may also think more about the computer equity issue. Which children have access to computers at home, in the classroom, or in the library? Do age, ethnicity, language, or family structure make a difference, or do all children have equal access and opportunity?

Special Spaces to Support Conflict Resolution

Primary children also need a space away from it all. Creative teachers can find such a spot in the most crowded classrooms. In addition, there may be a Peace Table and other designated areas where children may go to discuss and resolve a conflict. Many teachers are incorporating Peace Tables and have developed a variety of rituals and practices that work in their classrooms (starting small). The basic idea of the Peace Table is that it is a space apart. There are ground rules for conflicts and positive interactions. There may be prompts, cues, a script, or props to help children on their negotiation. Finally, children will be expected to transfer Peace Table skills to wherever conflict occurs.

Playground

Playground time and recess is an opportunity for social development. It is a fluid, less controlled, "child-owned" environment in which both positive and negative interactions occur. The playground is a place for bullying opportunities, but also for development of a rich, positive peer culture (Thompson, 1997). Teachers in a caring environment are aware of the range of possibilities. Unless they have duties elsewhere, teachers do not see recess as their free time. There are opportunities for mutual caring encounters (caring for and by). Teachers can anticipate playground issues and work with children to set expectations. (Begin with, "We all want to enjoy recess, so let's see how we can share the equipment.") Our classroom community extends to the playground. Parent volunteers and paraprofessionals are often involved in playground time, and they also need to understand the social opportunities of recess.

Teachers may plan interventions to address individual playground conflicts. In some cases, managing conflict will become a whole-class responsibility. Recess can be a fun, relaxing time for large-motor exercise and getting brains going for later indoor-classroom learning. It can provide independent play choices and time with friends.

Recess can also be a dreaded, stressful time of the day, full of chaos, teasing, aggression, and bullying. Do children feel physically and psychologically safe? Recess conflict issues include space on equipment, limited play materials like balls, and territory. The social context is often changing and unpredictable, with several classes on the playground at one time and children of different ages and sizes. Do teachers go to the playground? There can be a lack of accountability and suspension of indoor rules. Solutions to the recess dilemma include class meetings or recess meetings (Thompson, 1997), rehearsal, perhaps inter-classroom meetings, or a buddy in another class. Teachers need to know what is going on, and children need to know that teachers know.

Beyond the classroom, there are more spaces where conflicts may occur and other parts of the school day that affect children. There may be conflicts on the bus or in the lunchroom (Roberts, 2002). Why might these areas be places for conflict, teasing, and bullying? Who owns the spaces? What can be done? An example in *Kids Taking Action* (Roberts, 2002) describes a 2-year school-service learning project, involving younger and older children and bus drivers, to stop bullying in the bus.

Social Environment in Primary Classrooms

Routine Times, Scheduling, Transitions, and Grouping

Routine times include arrivals and dismissals, morning meetings, snacks and lunch, and those other pieces of daily life in the classroom. Morning meetings provide for daily connectedness and can be used for specific issues or problems to be solved. Class meetings can be held on an ad hoc basis, as well as when there is group decision-making to do. They provide a time for both making agreements and connecting. The increasing cognitive ability and rule orientation of this age group may make class-decided agreements powerful and binding with ownership. Class meetings provide a time to demonstrate that all children are heard and issues can be discussed peacefully (Charney, 2002; Vance & Weaver, 2002). Class agreements compare to Katch's (2001) class rules about violence in play and stories. The "how to be a friend" discussion is another example of a class meeting about a problem to be solved.

The daily *schedule* should provide ample free "non-work" time. In one school, "breathing in" and "breathing out" are times at the beginning and end of the day when children can relax, chat with friends, and make the transition from home to school and then from school to home. Teachers find that after morning "breathing in," children are ready to attend and participate, having already chatted with their best friends.

Transitions are also important for primary-grade children. Reminding children to look at the clock before it is time for an activity to end makes for a smoother transition and signals respect for children and value for what they are doing.

Grouping practices are part of the social environment. Decisions you need to make include small group versus large group, how to group boys and girls, grouping by ability and interest, and how often to change groups. There should be a balance of grouping approaches throughout the day, as well as different groups and different sizes of groups. Other variations include homogeneous/heterogeneous, different tasks, and rotating groups so that everyone can spend time with everyone else (See the examples in Chapter 8, Chapter 13, and the Appendix). Children with special needs should be included in groups for conflict learning by all children. Make sure that grouping decisions do not send an unintended message to children. Do certain groups always go first or seem to have a favored status?

TEACHERS TALK

> "*I never thought how grouping makes a difference. It is a bias issue to always separate the girls and boys.*"

TEACHERS TALK

> "*Flexible grouping promotes conflict resolution. Get children to understand their own feelings first, and work through who they are and why they feel the way they do, before they deal with others. Teach children problem-solving skills, and help them get to know themselves and one another. Give them a chance to work with everyone in the class so they can see they have so much in common. Hold class meetings and teach the children 'I' statements.*"

Adults in the setting are an important part of the social environment, providing models and guiding children in powerful ways. As Eisner (AERA annual meeting, April, 1999, Montreal, Canada) has said, "Children learn both more and less than we intend for them to learn." For instance, children may not master all of the intended objectives of a math lesson, but they will learn things that were not lesson objectives, like the fact that the teacher hates math. They may also be learning that, whatever happens, the teacher cares about them. Trust is at the center of what Charles describes as the "synergistic classroom." Ethics lead to this trust with seven components: kindness, cooperation, faith, helpfulness, fairness, honesty, and potential (Charles, 2000, p. 23).

QUESTION FOR SELF-REFLECTION

Do you really trust that children want to do the right thing, and that perhaps with guidance they will do the right thing?

TEACHERS TALK

"Another technique is to link up with a buddy teacher. This teacher or administrator would be someone who the teacher would send the child to when there is a good paper or assignment completed by the student. This way, the child receives extra praise and it raises their self-esteem."

(Note: This strategy for affirming a child within the school community by sending the child to visit another classroom offers a strong contrast to the assertive-discipline technique of sending a child to another classroom to give the teacher a break from that child's behavior.)

Language in the Environment

To support an environment for conflict resolution and peace-building, teachers must choose mutually understood words and phrases. A positive expectation may be set in the classroom, both by the children and by teacher, in an inclusive way. An example is the "Fantastic Frogs" at the beginning of the chapter. Understood shared language provides for clear communication and increases the sense of community and group identity.

The following is an example of what a teacher believes and is strongly committed to.

TEACHERS TALK: A COMMITMENT TO MANNERS

"There is more to conflict resolution than just solving problems. The basic ideas of character and respect, learning how to socialize with each other, and how to get along with others comes into play. Children do not always come into the classroom knowing how to socialize and share, and conflicts occur. This is why I make it a point to begin each year with learning manners as well as rule, and routines. I told my principal at the beginning of the year, 'If there is one thing the children will come away with this year, it would be manners.' I firmly believe that, and I felt it was important for me and for the children, to maintain a peaceful classroom."

Collaborative Learning Centers

Children can practice collaborating, problem-solving, and perspective-taking in centers designed for learning and working together. Independent of adult direction, children also have an opportunity for self-assessment. Integral to curricular learning objectives, these centers are not "something to do when (if) you finish your work." They are part of the physical, social, and curricular aspects of the child's classroom experience. These questions provide accountability for children's participation in the learning center: What did I do with someone else at the center today? What did I help someone do? What did someone else help me do or understand?

The following are a few examples of collaborative learning centers:

- Integrated thematic learning centers: An inventors' corner or a newspaper or a travel center, possibly for a specific locale, can be used.
- The following curriculum areas can be used in the centers:
  - Math: Collaborative learning where children learn how to share a pie.
  - Science: Collaboration in center activities—Can you build it together? Children generate alternative solutions.
  - Social Studies: Children learn all about people—perspective-taking (people live in different houses).

Collaborative learning contributes to a caring community in a primary classroom.

- Literacy cooperative book-making: Children learn by working on add-on stories with words and/or pictures (wordless books are especially valuable and books in other languages).
- Arts: Children play instruments together improvising, making emotion faces, and using a "story can." (A story can can be a coffee can with small figures or props that teachers or children use as they tell a story.)

Safe Places and Caring Spaces

The whole classroom should be a safe and caring place, but there should be special spots for comfort, reorganizing oneself or conflict resolution, working things out with others, and sharing thoughts or worries. These areas should be equipped with a soft place to sit or lie down, quiet music, writing materials, and other comforts.

Balance Center: This area is a room or corner where children can calm down, recenter, and decompress. Materials in the center may include music from tribal or Eastern cultures with calming tonalities and tempo as well as nature sounds.

Worry Box: Children write down their worries and thoughts and put them in the container, a safe place to put troubling thoughts.

Journaling: Another form of secure communication, journaling should offer both privacy and psychological safety.

TEACHERS TALK

"I mentioned my Tree of Virtues that I use in my classroom, where I catch people being responsible, respectful, caring, or honest and give them a leaf on my tree that represents that virtue. Would this be considered a classroom strategy?"

TEACHING AND LEARNING: CURRICULUM MODELS AND ACTIVITIES

Curriculum Models

Here we will look at ways that teachers can support children's conflict resolution and peacemaking as integral parts of the school experience. First, we will think about what we mean by "curriculum." In the preschool years, we are very comfortable with the idea of curriculum as "all the happenings in a child's day." The hidden and unintentional, or *implicit,* curriculum is usually purposeful: teacher interactions at child's level, room arrangement, snacks or lunch planned with intentionality. In the primary grades, curriculum is likely to be a set of learning objectives and instructional strategies, with an emphasis on academic content areas. These may be called *implicit* and *explicit* curriculum and include all content areas and the arts, as well as conflict resolution, peacebuilding, and violence prevention.

We will explore classroom organizing approaches and activities as a framework for specific curriculum content and learning objectives, beginning with cooperative learning and multiage classrooms.

Cooperative Learning

Formal Cooperative Learning Models   Cooperative learning is not a single approach, but has many forms and variations (Slavin, 1990; Johnson et al, 1994). Implementation by teachers in real-world classroom contexts adds further variability. (See Ramsey, 1991; Johnson et al; Circles of Learning.) Cooperative learning is often implemented as a mixture of cooperation within groups and competition between groups. For primary-age children, the fully cooperative approaches are preferable, and can be modified by classroom teachers to meet the needs of their children. Collaboration relates to the idea of the more capable peer and to multiple intelligences (Johnson, Johnson, & Holubec, 1994). Vyogotsky's theories support collaborative learning.

There are five essential components of cooperative learning according to Johnson, Johnson, & Holubec (1994):

- Face-to-face promotive interaction
- Group processing
- Interpersonal and small-group skills
- Individual accountability/personal responsibility
- Positive interdependence (goal interdependence, reward interdependence, resource interdependence, role interdependence, task interdependence)

Learning Cooperatively in the Primary Grades   Which of these components can work in a primary classroom? Most of them may be incorporated in primary settings. "Think, pair, share" is a form of cooperative learning. Children in primary classrooms often work together in face-to-face seating. They have an opportunity to fully attend to one another and to collaborate more naturally, developing mini-communities in table or desk groupings. Primary-age children can experience positive resource interdependence and are capable of discussing how they worked as a group. Primary teachers may be more comfortable with the idea that children are "learning cooperatively," instead of using the term "cooperative learning" in its more formal sense.

How Cooperative Learning Relates to Conflict Resolution   In the cooperative learning framework of Johnson, Johnson, Holubec (1994), all children are peacemakers. The processes and components of pure cooperative learning are consistent with the caring, listening, and perspective-taking that lead to peaceful resolution of children's conflicts.

Multiage Grouping

Another effective strategy for constructive conflict resolution and peacebuilding is multiage grouping, also known as multi-grade grouping or ungraded primary. Teachers at a school where multiage grouping was adopted in the primary grades, and later in all grades, found that children experienced opportunities for nurturing and empathy, an outcome not anticipated by the teachers or families. There has been little formal research on multiage grouping and children's social and emotional development, but there is a strong theoretical base and anecdotal evidence to support the connection.

Multiple Intelligences

Are you "word smart" or "body smart" or "people smart?" Applying Howard Gardner's theory of *multiple intelligences* in the classroom helps create an inclusive community where everyone is "smart" in one way or another. Children and adults find their own strengths in knowing the world and communicate their understanding through eight intelligences: *logical-mathematical, linguistic, visual-spatial, bodily kinesthetic, musical, interpersonal, intrapersonal,* and *naturalist*. In classrooms where teachers talk about multiple intelligences with young children, there may be an "MI Pie" on the wall, divided into eight sections to help children identify and label their own intelligences and those of their peers. This basis of empathy, understanding, and respect for all contributes to children's conflict resolution and peacebuilding where everyone is valued. The curriculum and the classroom environment are planned to "fit" all intelligences (Armstrong, 1994; Gardner, 1983, 1993).

Schoolwide Programs for Conflict Resolution

Curriculum models for schools and classrooms have been designed for the express purpose of helping children develop conflict resolution and peace-building. These programs will be the focus of Chapter 12. One that we noted briefly in this chapter is a program called Quit It! This program provides lessons and materials to combat hurtful teasing and bullying. Can you think of other ways to deal with bullying in your setting?

Group Activities for Learning Conflict Resolution

Thinking Games

Thinking games are as effective with primary children as with younger children. These more verbal children can explain more complex reasoning in these games, generate more solutions, and can think of even more ways to solve problems. Children can expand their understanding of their differences. Thinking games can involve puppets, video, media, and books. Leo Lionni books are fine starting places for thinking games if you cannot think up your own story. Again, our resources for thinking games are Edwards (1984) and Ramsey (1991).

Thinking Game Example

In a small group or whole class discussion, the teacher explores consequences and alternatives to physical retaliation.

Teacher: What would you do if someone hit you?

Child: I would hit back.

Teacher: What do you think would happen next after you hit back?

Children offer ideas.

Teacher: What else could you do?

The conversation continues as children suggest alternatives.

Another way to think through conflicts with a group of children is a version of role-play. Replay the conflict, freeze it, play it in slow motion, and rewind and go backward. Children explain their feelings, responses, and alternatives along with each "freeze frame." This method can even be incorporated with other ways to defuse conflict, as one of a number of physical prompts that serve to lower the intensity of emotion, distance the players, and allow them to rehearse alternatives. This can be done on the spot with real-time conflicts or used in a role-play in a class meeting or whole group time. Children can use this approach to generate alternatives (what could they do differently?) and predict consequences (if they try it that way, what do you think would happen?).

More Ideas for Understanding Cause-and-Effect, Perspective-Taking, and Generating Alternatives: Using Puppets and Books. Scenarios for discussion: After reading a book or story, ask "what else could they do in the story?" or "what else could they say?" This works very naturally with literacy learning at all levels and can be especially effective as a primary writing experience. For instance, children can make a new ending to the story.

TEACHERS TALK:

Here are two more literacy connections in which children can exercise the abilities needed for conflict resolution and peace building that we have been discussing:

TABLEAUX:

In this literacy-through-drama activity, children pose in a still representation of a scene in a book or a page in a picture book. Their body language and facial expressions communicate to the audience, and the other class members, what is happening in the story. The children who are actors need to interpret the feelings and behaviors of the story characters and represent them. The audience needs to understand and interpret what the actors are trying to portray.

FLAT STANLEY:

Children have been sending paper cutouts of this book character to people and places both far and near for many years. As a class activity, following Flat Stanley's travels with Stanley creates a sense of community within the classroom and a sense of community in the world. Children experience new perspectives as Flat Stanley travels the world. Flat Stanley *was written by Jeff Brown (Harper Collins New York, 1964).*

Creativity and the Arts

Creativity and the arts exist in an environment that is psychologically safe and risk-free, the components of our caring classroom. Creativity leads to safety in communicating feelings in meaningful and alternative ways that are inclusive for all. This includes music, drama, dance and movement, and the visual arts. By learning about the arts and through the arts with a community of artists and audiences, all are included. Sharing the experience and learning about the performing arts at the same time will set the stage for conflict resolution and peace-making.

From Thinking Games to Story Drama   Through role-play, children confront conflicts. As in good literature, conflicts are both internal and external. In story drama, children are guided in an enactment of a familiar story and may create characterizations and make plot changes as they go along.

For example, in a story drama of Rumplestiltkin, children become advisors to the queen in her dilemma of what to do about the strange little man who has asked for her baby. Another example using a book is *The Great Kapok Tree* (Cherry, 1990). Rules for drama in the classroom include no laughing, showing respect for everyone, and making the classroom a safe place.

Singing, dancing and moving, and creating visual and three-dimensional art as performers, and experiencing it as an audience, can create community and trust as well as alternative forms of expression in the primary classroom.

Cooperative Games for Primary Children

Game themes described by the Children's Creative Response to Conflict include cooperation, affirmation, and communication (Prutzman et al, 1988). The authors stress that conflict-resolution skills by themselves will not work. They must have the context of the community and cooperative environment.

Categories of games for conflict resolution:

1. Getting acquainted—name games
2. Cooperation
3. Communication: listening, observing, speaking
4. Affirmation (both group and individual)

5. Creative conflict resolution (skills and alternatives)

6. Sharing, trust-building

Ground rules for games are these: Participation is voluntary, and players may pass a turn. Everyone will have a chance to participate. Everyone must respect the contributions of others (Prutzman, 1988, p. 11).

To extend the idea of cooperative games, introduce games that children in other countries play. Children can explore what is the same and what is different in the hopping, running, jumping, and catching games played by children in many lands. Why do children around the world play different kinds of games? As children learn variations on familiar games, they can ask what's alike and what's different? Why do the games have different names? How can the games help us understand each other? What is the weather like, as well as animals, plants, things that children see, and the environment? How can we make them more cooperative?

A good resource is *Children's Games from Around the World* (Kirchner, 2000). Considering how children in different countries play the same or different games can be a first step in building global understanding. Although not all of the games in this book are cooperative games, the author provides ways to adapt games and make your own cooperative games.

Here is some advice on using games. Luvmour (1990) suggests first putting friends together in a game that involves cooperation and a physical challenge, like a three-legged race. Then put together two non-friends. At this point, the challenge should motivate the two non-friends to work together peacefully.

There are games listed at the end of this chapter. More physically challenging games will tap into primary-age children's desire to accomplish new tasks. Some of these games are harder than they look, require teamwork and problem-solving, and may make children, and adults for that matter, laugh together as they make their attempts. (Try the Standing Together task with an increasing number of people and see what happens.) It is also useful for adult group-building!

Primary-age children enjoy cooperative word play, such as word games, Mad Libs, and word searches (for older children). Teachers or children can even make up their own Mad Libs. Take a familiar story and leave out crucial words: "three little pigs" becomes "three little teacups." Extend the word game to creative drama and act out the new story.

IDEA FOR YOUR CLASSROOM: PEACE PEBBLES

Everyone paints a pebble to make a mountain: "A pebble is to a mountain as peaceful acts and attitudes are to a peaceful world. A peaceful world is made up of many small peaceful acts and attitudes." (Whitener, personal communication, 2002)

Caring and Social Action

A social action curriculum for children moves them to act for change and make the world a better place, not only for themselves, but mainly for others. This goal is described in Banks' transformative/social action model of multicultural education (1999), and in Derman-Sparks' Anti-Bias Curriculum (1989). Primary-age children can act on behalf of others in meaningful ways. The premise of community service learning is that through serving others, children will learn caring and principles of service to others while they are addressing content learning in a meaningful way (Roberts, 2002). Social action projects are most meaningful when children see a need and generate the ideas themselves. Projects may last for a few weeks, or a year or more.

The Dog Care Project
Third-grade children noticed stray dogs in the neighborhood, looking hungry and not cared for. Worried that they will be run over in traffic, the children began a year-long project to teach everyone about caring for dogs and finding ways to keep the dogs safe.

Curriculum Content Areas

Integration of content areas is a natural way for children to learn and for teachers to plan for learning. Project learning has cooperation and the negotiating of multiple points of view built in. Building on the Chapter 7 curriculum layer, project learning falls into place quite naturally, with collaborative learning embedded into each curriculum content area.

Examples of Project Topics

Food and Hunger: A caring theme with clear content area connections. A few questions to guide the project: Where does food come from? How does it help our bodies? How do we prepare it? What do different people eat? What happens if we don't have enough to eat? How can we help others get enough to eat?

Fabric: How we are all connected, woven together as part of a tapestry, is one of several figurative ways to think about this topic. The content area connections are abundant. This is a good place for Tar Beach, quilts, science, math, social studies, and culture. How about making a quilt and giving it to a family in need instead of decorating the school walls?

Here are just a few ideas to get you started.

Literacy: There are many books with themes related to caring, peace and conflict resolution, collaborative and reflective writing, and tableaux. (See "Peace Scholars" in Chapter 12.)

Science: Caring for the environment, plants, animals, and the earth offers many topics and avenues for learning.

Math: This includes community graphing and learning about the needs of others. How many people live in different places?

Social Studies: Make things work as a group or community. "Let's decide how these early settlers would build a house." Make economic decisions about meeting possibly conflicting needs.

Physical Education: Learn about games from children around the world. Physical challenges should be solved by the group, not necessarily by those with the greatest size, strength, or speed.

TEACHERS TALK

"I want to instill in them, even as young children, that their environment can't stop them from succeeding. I tell the kids to try and find those quiet places in their lives. I read them biographies about Ben Carson, Ruby Bridges, and other role models for the kids to look to as they face such drastically hard circumstances."

Themes of Caring in the Curriculum

The idea of themes of caring in the curriculum has been described in the work of Nel Noddings (1995). Themes include topics like food/hunger, fabrics, and intentional themes that lead to concrete actions, or "caring-for" actions, such as kindness. Older children may explore themes such as injustice or the negative concepts of war. In early childhood, we see how children and teachers can experience acts of caring. In the same way, the themes of caring and social action in the preceding example will include caring as envisioned by Noddings (Goldstein, 2001).

Connecting conflict resolution to caring activities and other learning experiences, additional ideas include pen pals (or e-mail pals), international or cross-town school partners, matching classrooms within the school (older and younger children), and activities from Teaching Tolerance/Starting Small (Southern Poverty Law Center).

TEACHERS TALK: PENNY DRIVE AFTER 9/11

"My school has started a penny drive. The response has been great, considering most people do not have much extra money. My classes filled up a gallon jug in 4 days. My kids and I discussed what it was for. Actually, they told me. They seemed to want to help children affected by this tragedy. It was very heartwarming. Many of the older children have been taking turns singing patriot songs over the loudspeaker. It is very uplifting. It brings tears to my eyes."

TEACHERS TALK: SANDWICHES FOR THE SOUP KITCHEN

"The students at our school make sandwiches each month for the community soup kitchen using the money students donate on 'Giving Wednesday.' One Wednesday a month, each child brings a small envelope with a donation. It is stressed that this money

---

CELEBRATIONS FOR THEMES OF CARING

Peace Week: Children, families, schools, and communities have celebrated a Day of Peace or Week of Peace at different times of the year, such as remembrance of a world tragedy, the beginning of a new millennium or even a new year, or in hope at the coming of spring. These celebrations are meant to share a clear message of peace with creative and colorful peace banners, poles and other displays in the community, song and dance, multicultural celebrations, and plans to reach out in understanding to others. Many of the celebrations have involved connecting with other children across the world, making the celebrations global ones. A search of the Internet will provide background on peace celebrations, activities, books for children, and more.

Earth Day: Since 1970, Earth Day has been celebrated on April 22 to raise awareness of the importance of protecting the environment. Earth Day celebrations can be expanded to a week or an entire month, as children learn about caring for the earth and its resources and acting on behalf of the environment. An accessible theme for children and families, Earth Week activities are easily available on many Web sites, and they lend themselves to action projects that are immediate and meaningful to children.

---

should come from the child and not from the parent, and each child brings whatever they can. We usually make about 300 sandwiches, which takes about an hour if two classrooms are working together. Each class signs up for which month they want to participate at the beginning of the year. This has been a positive experience that the students remember long after they move on to middle school."

ALL CHILDREN

This book is written with all children in mind and describes a culturally responsive and inclusive classroom community. Consideration of all children is an integral part of this book. Some of the diversity issues we will continue to consider include *culture and language, gender*, and *ability*. A few additional points:

Curriculum should be "a mirror, not a wall." This statement from King, et al (1994) provides a yardstick for judging the responsiveness of our classrooms. Do children see themselves reflected in the curriculum or is the curriculum an impenetrable barrier like a wall?

Adults and children should focus on two-way communication and ask how other people understand us and how we understand other people. In classrooms, teachers share with children the idea that each person is a unique part of a whole. Be aware that primary-age children can understand and share in your basic commitment to respect, caring, and inclusion.

In the next chapter, we will look extensively at relating to families. Home *culture and language* are key elements. Teachers should remember that it is important to support authentic verbal and non-verbal communication between children in the class whose home languages are not the same, and clearly and explicitly make them aware of the differences in what people say and do. *Gender* issues were discussed earlier and remain an important consideration. Connecting gender to our discussion of moral decision-making will help us see both girls and boys as leaders in a culture of peace, speaking with "different voices" (Gilligan, 1982).

Ability differences in an inclusive primary classroom lead to the idea of solidarity: how people reach out to make connections. In an inclusive classroom, children are asked, "What do you have in common with the child in the wheelchair or the child who is visually impaired?" Teachers provide ways for children to establish commonality and share experiences. Using sign language with all children in the class is one way in which children and adults in the class communicate. Technology, both assistive/adaptive and mainstream, can provide opportunities for community-building, shared experiences, and alternative communication in your caring classroom. Planning the environment for children with a variety of special needs who find stress in day-to-day classroom peer interaction may include spaces for self-control and emotional regrouping (Mrug, et al, 2001).

COMFORT CORNER

The Primary Intervention Program (PIP) has a place called the Comfort Corner where children may go and work out their feelings. It is a comfortable, homelike space where there is a sense of security for the children. The space may be used by a child and an adult to work together through troubling issues (Novick, 1998).

RESOURCES FOR THE CARING CLASSROOM

Finding, Evaluating, and Adapting Materials

The principles for locating and evaluating materials for primary classrooms are the same as those for preschool and kindergarten children. Primary teachers will find the discussion of program models in Chapter 12 to be of interest.

Books for Children

When looking for books for primary children, there are valuable resources with lists of books, such as *Teaching Conflict Resolution Through Children's Literature* by William Kriedler, and web sites such as Ways To Use Children's Literature (http://www.csmp.org/family/ways.htm). The Council on Interracial Books for Children offers criteria for evaluating books for bias and stereotype (Derman-Sparkwm, 1989; Ramsey, 1998). Teachers will find picture books valuable in helping children discuss issues and emotions related to conflict resolution and peace-building. Picture books are not just for preschoolers. They provide a complete experience and offer rich opportunities for exploring interpersonal issues, feelings, and more. Chapter books that are well-chosen, with positive character models and prosocial themes, can help maintain a conversation in the classroom about peace, caring, decision-making, and revisiting issues over time.

More Games and Activities

As in Chapter 8, there is a chart of games (Table 9–1) for primary children in this chapter. Teachers will notice that primary-age children enjoy games with rules and often invent their own. Observing the nature of these games is important. If there is a high degree of competition in the games, and a trend where one or more children always win and others always lose, teachers may call a class meeting to see if there is another way to play the game.

>>

SUMMARY

Primary-age children, from 6- to 8-years-old, are becoming more capable in many ways and are finding themselves with many other children in their daily lives. They are now interested in accomplishing things and making friends. In the caring classroom, teachers can help children build on these new capabilities and interests and use them to strengthen their ability to resolve conflicts and work toward becoming peace-builders.

>>

SUPPLEMENTARY MATERIALS FOR CHAPTER 9

Research Focus Teacher Research

We have discussed how primary-age children try to "make things work" and "be friends." What about the games that 6- to 8-year-old children play? In a classic example of ethnographic interviewing techniques with young children, Sue Parrott asked second-grade boys to explain their play at recess. They described "games, tricks, and goofing around." If you could have conversations with primary-age children over time, what would you learn about their play?

What may have changed in the 30 years since Parrott's study? How much is this like your setting? Parrott, S. (1972). *Games children play: Ethnography of a second grade recess.* In I. Spradley & D. McCurety (Eds.), *The cultural experience: Ethnography in complex society.* Prospect Heights, IL: Waveland Press.

TABLE 9–1 GAMES FOR PEACE-MAKING AND COMMUNITY-BUILDING: PRIMARY GRADES (DETAILS OF HOW TO PLAY THE GAMES ARE FOUND IN THE APPENDIX)

Game	Ages	Group Size	Materials	Activity Level 1= most active)
Standing Together: Holding hands while sitting in a circle, all stand at once (Luvmour)	8 +	4 +	None	2
Rope Raising: Holding a rope, all try to stand up together (Luvmour)	8 +	10 +	Large rope tied into a circle	2
Spaghetti: Holding hands with others not standing beside them, children try to form circle	6 +	6 +	None	3
A What?: Coordination of question and answer sequence; try not to get mixed up!	7 +	8 +	Two small balls or simple objects	4
Inuit Ball Pass: Pass ball around using only open palm of hand (Luvmour)	8 +	8 +	Sand-filled balls or similar	3
Cooperative Story Telling: Everyone contributes a part	All	8 +	Props may be used	5
Sleeper: "It" secretly winks, puts people to "sleep" till someone figures out who "it" is	7 +	10 +	None	4
Cooperative Juggling: Throw 2 or more balls across circle at once	8 +	5 +	Balls	2
Human Jigsaw Puzzle: Make a people puzzle and try to recreate it (Prutzman)	6 +	8 +	None	4
Honey, I Love You, But I Just Can't Smile: Try not to smile when you answer	8 +	8 +	None	5
Pantomime Games: Try many variations, acting out in pairs or teams (Prutzman)	6 +	6 +	None	4
Machine Building: Enact a machine with group body sculpture (Prutzman)	8 +	6 +	None	4
Cooperative Monster Making: Everyone contributes part of the creation (Prutzman)	7 +	Small groups	Paper, crayons, scissors, masking tape	4

Luvmour, S., & Luvmour, J. (1990). *Everybody wins*. Philadelphia: New Society Publishers.

Prutzman, P., Stern, L., Burger, M. L., & Bodenhamer, G. (1988). *The friendly classroom for a small planet*. Philadelphia: New Society Publishers.

Wichert, S. (1989). *Keeping the peace: Practicing cooperation and conflict resolution*. Philadelphia: New Society Publishers.

>>

APPLICATION EXERCISES

1. Create a chart called "Peace Education/ Conflict Resolution Strategies and Ideas," and exchange ideas with others in your setting or in your class to help build your repertoire. Use these headings:
   - Creating a Caring Community for All Children
   - Arranging the Physical Environment for PE/CR
   - Children's Books, Games, and Activities for PE/CR
   - Ideas About What to Do When Conflicts Happen
   - PE/CR with Families, Community, and Other Professionals
2. Visit a primary classroom. Observe the environment and ask the teacher for more ideas and strategies for your chart.

>>

THINKING ABOUT ALL CHILDREN

1. Evaluate your primary classroom, or a primary classroom where you have permission to visit and observe, using the "mirror or wall" question as you did in Chapter 8 with a preschool-kindergarten classroom. Do you think this is a greater challenge in the primary grades?
2. Compare what you see in the primary classroom to what you have seen in the preschool or kindergarten classroom you have observed. Do you notice different types of conflicts, different ways that children work things out, or different types of interactions between boys and girls? Can you connect what you see to the discussion in this chapter?

10

Adult Intervention in Young Children's Peer Conflicts

"I don't care who started it! I'm taking this ball and putting it away for the rest of the day!"

Chapter 10 Objectives: Chapter 10 represents the top layer of the cake, the role of the adult in situations when the inevitable conflict does arise. Readers will explore effective approaches for observing, intervening and supporting children during their conflicts. Appropriate adult intervention provides scaffolding and the tools that children need in order to learn to resolve their conflicts on their own.

Chapter 10 Outline
> When to Intervene: Observing Children
> > What to Look for Before Stepping in
> > Individual and Cultural Differences in Response to Conflict
> > A Question of Time

Example: "I Didn't Know How Till the Teacher 'Splained It to Me!" Two preschoolers were each attempting to look in a small mirror as both held it. They started tugging back and forth.

Samantha (shouting): *"Let me have it!"*
Jack: *"I want it!"*

The teacher calmly came over and took the mirror. She put it on the table and showed the children that they could both see themselves in the mirror if they stood back a little. The two children seemed content with this solution and played happily together for the next several minutes as they both looked in the mirror. Later, Jack mentioned the incident to his mother. She asked him why he had not shared the mirror with his friend in the first place. "Well, I didn't know how till the teacher 'splained it to me."

WHEN TO INTERVENE: OBSERVING CHILDREN

In our journey so far, we have explored ways to observe what is happening in children's interactions (Chapter 3), and we have discussed characteristics of children's conflicts (Chapter 4). We have also recognized that conflict-resolution ability contributes to children's development (Chapters 5 and 6). We have looked at ways to create classroom environments where children have the desire to resolve conflicts in a caring community (Chapter 7) and have acquired the tools to do so (Chapters 8 and 9). Finally, we realize that conflicts between children will still occur. In this chapter, we will address the decisions that teachers make as they encounter children in conflict. When should teachers intervene, and what should they do? First, observe and assess.

What to Look for Before Stepping In

Assessing Safety

First things first: If there is an immediate threat to children's safety, teachers must intervene without hesitating. This directive not only makes sense to adults who care for children, but also is the first principle of NAEYC's Code of Ethical Conduct and Commitment (2001). When teachers intervene, they should be clear to children about their commitment to all children's safety and protection from physical harm and hurtful words.

Assessing Intent and the Progress of the Conflict

Observe and listen carefully as you assess the situation. Here are some considerations that will guide your decision-making.

- *Intent:* Is the conflict an issue to be resolved or a ritual or pretend dispute that is not intended to solve a dispute? Pretend and ritual conflicts are not likely to need adult intervention. There is no issue to resolve as long as good humor and pretend status is maintained.
- *Bias, prejudice, or discrimination:* Teachers in caring, culturally responsive, and socially active classrooms are committed to fairness and inclusion and will confront prejudice and bias. In such a situation, teachers will intervene to protect children from harm, guide children away from bias, and model social action.
- *Affectivity:* Is this conflict constructive or destructive? Is there increasing potential for harm, either physical and psychological? Teachers may decide to intervene and invite the conflict participants to cool down and collect themselves before returning to negotiate the issue.
- *Progress of the conflict:* Does it seem that the conflict is escalating, or does it look as if the children will be able to resolve the problem without help? Is the conflict issue something that can be negotiated, or is it beyond children's control? Are the initial issues giving way to retaliation? The answers to these questions will determine whether—and how—adults should intervene.

Assessing the Conflict Structure

As we discovered in Chapter 4, the structural characteristics of children's conflicts may predict the outcomes. Observing these characteristics, teachers may decide whether to intervene. Strong predictors of mutually agreeable child-generated outcomes are as follows:

- Children's interaction before the conflict: Children who are friends, or who are playing together before a conflict arises, are more likely to resolve the conflict and continue to play together afterward.

Young children who use reasoning and negotiation are likely to resolve conflicts on their own.

• Type of strategy: Children who use strategies of reasoning are more likely to resolve conflicts than those who use physical strategies or simple verbal insistence.

Example A: *The "turf war," a conflict about a place in line or on the playground. No prior play or social interaction between children; strategies are verbal insistence deteriorating to physical conflict; the interaction escalates as children become angry.*

Example B: *Roles in dramatic play. "Who gets to be the mother (daddy)?" Children in cooperative, sociodramatic play; use negotiation and reasoning to create more parts to play that are equally appealing; the play continues with children in good humor.*

What do we know about these two conflicts? What does the teacher do? In Example A, the teacher is more likely to monitor the interaction and, anticipating shoving and pushing, will be ready to intervene. In Example B, the adult observer is likely to make note of the children's creative solutions to the problem.

Assessing Yourself and Your Goals

As you observe children's conflicts to determine whether to intervene, identify your goals for intervening. Are you hoping to restore or maintain peace and harmony in your classroom? Are you intervening for the safety of the children? Are you intervening to support children's social competence and conflict-resolution ability? Be certain to make an informed decision, based on your observation of the situation and your knowledge of children. Be sure that you are intervening for the right reasons. A further step in your self-assessment is to define your role or roles in children's classroom conflicts. Possible roles include facilitator, guide, director, provider of information, scaffolder, and mediator. What other roles could you suggest?

TEACHERS TALK: YOUR ROLE

"I feel my role is to be a mediator. I encourage children to solve conflicts on their own as long as violence doesn't occur."

Individual and Cultural Differences in Response to Conflict

As we have seen throughout this book, individual and cultural differences come into play as children engage in conflicts with their peers. Adults need to consider these differences as we interpret what is happening in children's conflicts and decide about intervening (see Figure 10–1). Individual and cultural differences in children's reactions to disputes may include differences in communication style, including the speed and intensity of words and language. Loud voices may mean anger for some, but for others it is a normal way of speaking. We must remember issues that may arise as a result of varying cultural norms about property and space. These issues have a bearing on defining what is an agreed-upon solution as well.

Reciprocal understanding and considerations of culture and communication are also required as teachers intervene to guide children's conflicts to resolution. Teachers should not always insist on eye contact, and may find that directive statements make more sense to children than indirect requests. As you will recall, children also share a culture apart from that of adults. As adults guide children toward resolution, it is important to know if children have actually negotiated a mutually agreeable solution or if their resolution is a matter of acquiescence or compliance with an adult's wishes.

Our discussions in earlier chapters about children with special needs also are applicable here. For instance, children with special needs or developmental delays often have more problems with group entry. Successful group entry depends on learning the rules of the ongoing play and the ability to pick up social cues. Teachers observing group-entry conflicts can help in decoding cues and rules of play for the child with special needs. They may also help make typically developing peers aware of the need to clarify the rules. For a professional perspective on specific

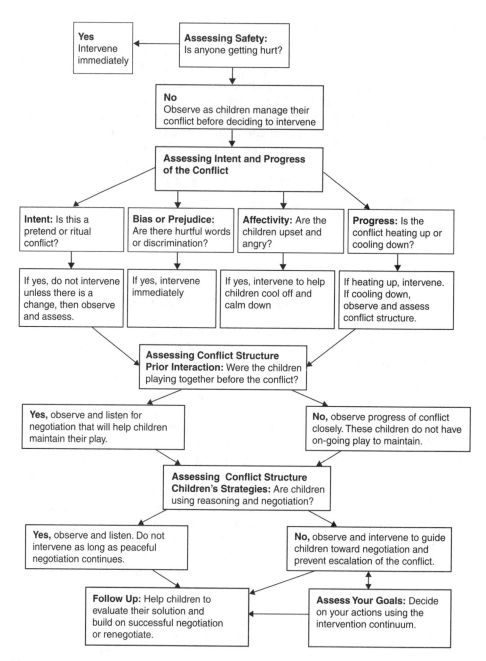

Figure 10–1
Adult intervention decision tree.

behavioral issues, the DEC/CEC position statement on challenging behaviors is included as a resource at the end of this chapter.

A Question of Time

Children's conflicts happen quickly and rarely last very long. Teachers frequently need to make on-the-spot decisions. A pertinent question is whether teachers have time for all of the observing and decision-making described here. Teachers need to be comfortable with an easily retrieved repertoire of strategies and words to support and guide children in conflict. This may mean retraining yourself to naturally use a set of words, just as you are working with children to adopt some of the same words as tools in their conflicts. In our Chapter 5 example, Mrs. Stone prompts, "Who can be the bigger person?" and the children are reminded to negotiate a resolution. Teachers guide children as young as 2 years old using "I Care Language" in their conflicts, or simply, as you saw earlier in this book, "It's not okay to use bodies. Use words."

TEACHERS TALK ABOUT QUICK FIXES AND TEACHABLE MOMENTS

"I have been guilty of 'quick fixing' conflicts because of time or energy constraints. Many situations that arise lead themselves to a 'teachable moment' where a valuable lesson can be learned by those involved. It is impossible to do this for every conflict that arises. We can only do our best and make the most of as many of these moments as possible."

HOW TO INTERVENE: WHEN YOU DECIDE TO STEP IN

Intervention as Guidance or Interference

Adult intervention in children's conflicts can take the form of guidance, scaffolding, or modeling at appropriate developmental levels. In a supportive environment, children can learn through and about conflict.

TEACHERS TALK: WHEN CONFLICTS POP UP

A kindergarten teacher says: *"I feel that the first step in dealing with the conflicts that pop up is to attempt to take the time to listen to each side and be an active mediator when necessary. I try to encourage children to maintain open communication with each other. If a cooling-down time is necessary, I find it helpful to take the time to sit and discuss the situation with the angry child, and help him/her find some strategies to help successfully solve similar situations that might happen another day."*

In the contrasting example that follows, we see intervention as interference. Children experience something quite different from the guidance described previously. With their second-grade teacher as a model, children learn that authority and power rule. There is no opportunity for, or demonstration of the value of, problem solving, mutual understanding, or conflict management.

On the Playground with the Second Graders

Teacher: "That is enough!! I don't care who started it! I'm taking the balls and putting them all away!"

Moving from Adult to Child Control: A Continuum of Involvement

When conflicts arise, teachers have a range of available intervention strategies. These strategies exist on a continuum, with adult control of the conflict on one end and child control on the other. Although teachers may find themselves intervening and solving problems for children quickly and firmly, the goal of conflict resolution is for children to resolve disputes in a mutually agreeable way, independently (without adult help). In a particular conflict episode, teachers should begin with the least controlling and intrusive strategy on the continuum and move along as needed. Over time, as children become more adept at negotiating and problem-solving, the least adult intervention will be all that is needed.

This continuum is similar to the Teacher Behavior Continuum, described by Oken-Wright (1992).

Beginning with greatest adult involvement and control, and moving to full child control, the continuum includes the following:

- *Physical intervention and adult direction of the outcome:* The teacher tells children what to do, perhaps physically removing children or objects. In the example with the second-graders in conflict over the ball, the teacher is at this end of the continuum.

- *Restating rules:* If there are rules in place, the teacher invokes them to decide the issue. Let's continue with our second-graders and create some class rules for our example: *"The rule is five minutes with the ball, Jerry. You've had your five minutes. Here, Samantha."*

- *Offering choices or suggesting what to do:* The teacher offers an adult-generated solution or a choice of solutions to children. *"Here's an idea. Jerry, you can have two more minutes, and then give the ball to Samantha. Or perhaps you can both play with the ball?"*

- *Supporting children's negotiation:* The teacher offers prompts and encouragement as children work on developing a solution, demonstrating confidence in the children's ability to solve the problem. *"Let's see if you can work this out. What's your idea, Jerry? What's your idea, Samantha?"*

- *Restating the problem:* The teacher, in an active listening stance, clearly identifies the issue with reminder cues or prompts about conflict-resolution tools or words that are in the children's repertoire: *"I see that you both want the ball. Can you use I Care language to work on the problem?"*

- *Looking on:* Using the least involved mode, the teacher may find that being nearby and watching is a "silent prompt" for children to remember to use negotiation and problem-solving. Non-verbal communication from the teacher must signal interest, but not involvement or any implied suggestion that the teacher is about to step in. *Saying nothing, the teacher looks from Jerry to Samantha with a calm but interested expression on her face, clearly paying attention to what they are saying and doing. The children notice her watching, their faces and bodies relax, and they begin negotiating with their shared conflict-resolution language.*

Example: Conflict on the Blacktop

Two 5-year-olds fight over the preferred riding toy and always race to the blacktop to claim possession. This situation has become a daily occurrence. Where on the continuum might these teacher suggestions be found?

1. *The teacher asks, "Can you think of a way that you can work it out so that you can both use it?"*
2. *The teacher offers the children two concrete options and asks them to choose.*
3. *The teacher chooses a solution for the children, but tells them to change the solution if it doesn't work.*
4. *As a follow-up, the next day, before the children head out to the playground, the teacher says to them, "Let's see if you can remember what you did yesterday."*

TEACHERS TALK: THE POLAR BEAR

"A common conflict in my room is arguments over our stuffed polar bear, which is our classroom mascot. Everyone loves to play with it, and there are often fights over who gets it. In an idealistic situation, I ask each of the children involved to state the problem, and then give each of them a chance to come up with a fair solution. Due to lack of time, I have been known to take the bear away, stating, 'If you guys can't share it, no one gets it.'"

TEACHERS TALK ABOUT INTERVENING

These teachers describe different perspectives on intervening in children's conflicts. What strategies in the continuum do you think these teachers might use? What does their language suggest to you about the environment for conflict resolution and peacemaking in their classrooms?

Pre-K Teacher: *"I have started to really listen to myself as I help children through conflicts. I used to like to settle the disputes so that the children would resume play, but I have learned how to walk them through peacefully to a resolution. I now see how important it is for children to learn these skills in order to grow up and work cooperatively with others."*

Kindergarten Teacher: *"The rules are simple. If you get hit, you come and tell me immediately. I will punish the hitter. However, if you hit back, both students will be disciplined. I believe that this will curtail some of the fighting that can take place in middle school. These children must learn this early."*

Pre-K Teacher: *"We discuss the conflicts, and I make them express their feelings with guidance from me. I make them own the conflict themselves."*

Third-Grade Teacher: *"I have learned more about myself as a mediator/disciplinarian. I know that often children can work out their own differences, yet in other cases they may require intervention. I want my students to feel comfortable and realize that, in some situations, it's okay to seek outside help."*

What to Do When Intervening in Conflicts

The following recommendations will guide teachers as they encounter children in conflicts.

• When children are emotionally engaged, intense, or clearly expressing anger, help them disconnect long enough to calm down and regain control. Let children know that this is not a time-out or a punishment, but simply a chance to regroup and collect themselves before calmly working to solve the problem. Children may need a few moments in a place away from the conflict site. When children are well in control and relaxed, talk through what happened together and discuss ways to solve the conflict. If these intense conflicts occur frequently,

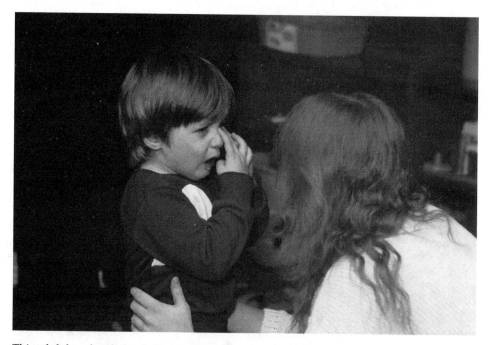

This adult has decided to help the child collect himself before guiding a resolution to the conflict.

it would be helpful to have some shared language that children can use to signal a need for a cool-down time, such as "cool off," "slow down," "thinking space," or other understood word cues. Or have a designated spot in the classroom where children can go to regain control.

- Give children time and physical space to work things out on their own. Keep your presence at a distance so that as children are attempting to negotiate they do not turn to you for help prematurely. Children will often turn to authority figures and expect them to take control. It is interesting to note that researchers have discovered that children are more likely to resolve conflicts agreeably on their own if an adult is not present.

- Make sure that children's words and attention are directed toward each other. Ask them to look for cues and responses from one other and not the teacher. As they negotiate, help children listen to each other. Make sure that each person has a chance to state the problem, as they see it, talking *to each other* and not *about each other to the teacher*. Encourage them to collaborate as they explore consequences, generate alternatives, and work for solutions in which all children in the conflict have shared ideas. Ask them to review the final solution from the perspective of each child.

TEACHERS TALK: SAYING SORRY

"Instead of saying 'I'm sorry' when we do something to hurt one another, we have to find a way to make that person feel better. ('I'm sorry' is too easy in my book!) For example, you can get a piece of ice to put on a boo-boo that you caused, you can rub it, or you can give them a hug. If it was feelings that got hurt, they need to find a way to fix that as well. Sometimes they make a happy picture, or give a compliment, or invite a child to play with them."

- Be willing to accept children's mutually agreed-upon solution to a conflict issue if it has been generated by all those in the conflict. As mentioned in an earlier chapter, children's ideas of a solution, based on fairness, rights, or needs, may not be the same as adult ideas of a solution based on justice and fairness. Remember that children's perspectives and values may be different from those of adults. Accepting children's decisions is also a question of respect, trust, and sharing control.

TEACHERS TALK: THE BULLDOZER AND THE OSTRICH

"Some adults use the ostrich method, where they try to ignore the conflict, hoping it will resolve itself. A far greater number use the bulldozer method, where they use their authority as adults to decide who is right and who is wrong and then dole out their idea of justice. Being unable or unwilling to see children's disagreements as opportunities to deal with feelings and cooperate with peers to solve problems usurps children's ownership of conflicts and prevents children from developing autonomy."

WHAT ABOUT TIME-OUT?

The traditional time-out removes children from the classroom activity for a specified period of time. When they return to the group, they will be expected to behave in accordance with the teacher's expectations. Time-out advocates describe the approach as a logical consequence and an opportunity for a needed "cooling off" period. Critics argue that children see nothing logical about being placed in a time-out chair, and that this adult-imposed discipline is a public punishment that makes no changes in behavior.

NAEYC makes a distinction between traditional classroom discipline, which is a punishment-oriented stance, and guidance, which is a learning and problem-solving stance. Suggestions in Part II of this book reflect the guidance approach. Alternatives to time-out and other discipline-based models have been widely published in recent years. Recommendations include a number of books by Vivian Paley and two articles by Daniel Gartrell in *Young Children*:

Gartell, D. (2001). "Replacing time-out: Part one—Using guidance to build an encouraging classroom." *Young Children*, 56(6), 8–16.

Gartell, D. (2001). "Replacing time-out: Part two—Using guidance to maintain an encouraging classroom." *Young Children*, 57(2), 37–43.

WHAT DO WE MEAN BY TIME-OUT?

Is the following time-out or a safe place to go? Mrs. Stone says: "I have two places for time-out in my classroom. I have two chairs with signs above them that read, 'I need time to think.' I give children time to think and get themselves together."

Supporting Children's Conflict Management

Scaffolding to Encourage Negotiation

Once they are "inside" a conflict, teachers have an opportunity to provide scaffolding and opportunities for learning. Here are more recommendations for teachers to help children grow in their ability to resolve conflict.

Encourage children's independent problem-solving in the context of conflict just as you would with any other problem or new skill, like using scissors or thinking about numbers. Resist the temptation to provide your own solution. Validate children's efforts, and celebrate their willingness to pursue a solution. Failing to acknowledge children's efforts will suggest that adult intervention is the only real answer.

TEACHERS TALK: LEARNING THROUGH MISTAKES

"Although we do not like to admit it, the most important part of learning is the making of mistakes! When children make mistakes in how they approach situations of conflict with others, they should be entitled to learn from the mistake. A conflict should be treated

as a learning experience for both the children involved and the teacher. How the child handles a conflict can give the teacher many insights about a child's social, emotional, and cognitive development."

As children work through conflicts, teachers can support their learning by providing scaffolding. Help them reason and negotiate at a slightly higher level than they might do on their own. Provide prompts and cues to help them to the next step. We have learned much from Vygotsky's theories. The notion of learning from adults and more capable peers and of thinking, with help, at a level just beyond where we can think on our own is a powerful one for our topic. Teachers can talk young children through conflict, giving them words to practice and guiding them through the process of negotiating. Children can learn moral reasoning and practice the tools of language in conflict.

Steps in the Process of Conflict Resolution   There is a common core of steps in the process of resolving conflicts, and there are many published versions. Teachers should choose one that seems to make sense to adults and children, and that can be remembered and followed consistently, and adapt it to their setting. The process you choose may even have some type of mnemonic device or memory aid.

As we explore conflict resolution programs in Chapter 12, we will find additional process models. Here are a few examples developed over a number of years. Compare them and look for common elements. You may want to try them out and find one that "fits" with you and the children, or you can develop your own set of words for the basic steps.

The conflict resolution process includes the following, according to Wichert (1989, p. 54):

1. Calming and focusing
2. Turning attention to parties concerned
3. Clarification/stating problem
4. Bargaining/resolution/reconciliation
5. Prevention
6. Affirmation

Here is the basic process in 4 steps (Adams & Wittmer, 2001, p. 10–11):

1. Defining the problem
2. Generating alternative solutions
3. Agreeing on a solution
4. Following through to determine if the chosen solution is successful

In a social problem-solving approach, children ask themselves questions that mirror these steps (Adams & Wittmer, 2001, p. 11):

1. *What Is the Problem?* Naming, labeling, expressing, and listening to other points of view; talking about feelings; perspective-taking activities, books, and games.

2. *What Might Happen If?* Actually the same as the name of a thinking game described in Chapter 8 (Crary, 1984); many ways to incorporate a cause-and-effect way of thinking.

3. *Choose a Solution and Use It.* Make a decision about a solution and try it out.

4. *Is It Working?* If not, what can I (we) do now?

Finally, Gartrell proposes a five-step approach, counting each step on one finger (2001, p. 37):

1. Cool down (thumb)

2. Identify the problem (pointer)

3. Brainstorm solutions (tall guy)

4. Go for it (ringer)

5. Follow-up (pinky)

Follow-Up: What Happens Next?

Each of the preceding conflict resolution processes includes some form of follow-up. In one of the strategies in the Conflict on the Blacktop example discussed earlier in this chapter the teacher reminded the children on the following day about the solution that they used the day before. When children have achieved an agreed-upon resolution, they have accomplished something worthy of recognition and even celebration. Teachers should affirm children's work and results.

The next part of the follow-up is to see if the solution is indeed workable and actually resolve the issue in a mutually agreeable and sustainable way. It is important for children to know that not every solution will be successful, and it is all right to try again and "renegotiate." (That may even become a word that children adopt in their process.) Primary-age children may notice examples of adults negotiating and renegotiating in real life. When resolutions are successful, children can use them to guide future interactions and to build new resolutions or defuse future conflicts as they arise.

TOOLS FOR CONFLICT RESOLUTION ON THEIR OWN

Peace Tables and Other Tools for Resolving Conflicts

Tools and sources of support for children as they develop independent conflict-resolution skills include designated spaces and props, words to use, and help from peers.

A Peace Table, Peace Corner, or Peace Rug is a place for peacemaking where children in conflict may go to work out their problems. A specific setting in neutral ter-

This teacher is intervening in a lunchtime conflict. What will she do next?

ritory, away from the activity of the classroom, may be equipped with posters, books, puppets, and writing materials to help the resolution process: Children value these peace spaces and learn peacemaking skills these that can be used in other settings.

Dream Catcher Corner: In a quiet corner of the room, children may sit and spend time sharing their thoughts with a dream catcher, an American Indian item easily found in stores and catalogs. The web of the dream catcher captures children's fears and worries, freeing them for peaceful play with their peers. The observant teacher who has created the Dream Catcher Corner notices the children who feel a need to unburden their worries, and will try to provide particular support to that child.

Talk About It Town: This peacemaking space is described by a teacher: "Talk About It Town is an area that is in my classroom. It is two chairs covered by an awning with an emotions poster inside. There are emotion words and a mirror inside. Talk About It Town is the area that children go with an adult to discuss their feelings. It is used for all types of situations, ranging from the children that are so energetic and can't stop talking to the behavior conflicts. The children respond well to it, to the point that children would ask if they could 'talk' during center time. They would role-play and help each other work through problems. The children were acting as therapists without knowing they were doing the job."

Talking Stick: Teachers can use the talking stick to help children speak wisely, and to practice listening respectfully to all members of the group. The talking stick has been used for centuries in many American Indian tribes when a council is called. It allows all council members to present their points of view. The Talking Stick is passed from person to person as they speak and only the person holding the stick is allowed to talk during that time period.

The talking stick recognizes the value of each speaker. Every member of the meeting must listen closely to the words being spoken, so when their turn comes, they do not repeat unneeded information or ask impertinent questions. Indian children are taught to listen from age 3 forward; they are also taught to respect another's viewpoint. This is not to say that they may not disagree, but rather they are bound by their personal honor to allow everyone their time to speak. A talking Stick can be made from any type of Standing Person (tree). The Talking Stick may be used when they teach children, hold Council, make decisions regarding disputes, hold Pow-Wow gatherings, have storytelling circles, or conduct a ceremony where more than one person will speak.

Slow-Motion Replay: A technique for clarifying issues and outcomes of a conflict is the Slow-Motion Replay. Children re-enact the conflict slowly, step by step, pausing to identify and label actions, discuss reasons for what they did or said, point out the effects of actions, and generate alternatives. The slow-motion "stop action" process calms children, and it even introduces some humor as children move in slow motion or freeze to hold poses.

Conflict Escalator: This image is "a technique used to diagram conflicts in a step by step manner. Each behavior of the disputing individuals is a step on the escalator either up or down. Children use the escalator to record this behavior and learn why conflicts escalate" (Kriedler, 1994).

Wheel of Choice: This visual reminder in the classroom, described in Chapter 9, shows children their options for responding to conflict. Sections of the wheel include Talk It Out, Offer Your Help, Tell Them to Stop, Use an I Message, Class Meeting Agenda, and others. The Wheel of Choice can be created by children and adults together, and they can explore and practice all the strategies that will become part of the wheel. First-graders who were learning to use the Wheel of Choice also kept journals to record positive strategies (Browning, Davis, & Resta, 2000).

Warm Fuzzies and Cold Pricklies

A teacher remembers: "One of my most vivid memories of elementary school came to me last week, when Enid was talking about 'teddy bear words' and 'porcupine words.' The school counselor came into my third-grade class to talk about Warm Fuzzies and Cold Pricklies. I still remember the multicolored cotton ball I made to represent the kind words we use with friends, and the sweet gum ball (those prickly balls that come from a tree), which showed us what hurtful Cold Prickly words felt like. It had been quite a while since this had appeared in my mind, but I clearly remember it had an impact on my behavior, especially toward my younger siblings."

Do Children Have Words to Use?

We have discussed the importance of shared language as tools for children's mutual understanding and conflict resolution. Words for conflict resolution and peacemaking should have the following characteristics:

- Meaningful to children; ideally created by them, but words that come from books or conflict resolution programs can be made meaningful and effective for the classroom
- Shared by both children and adults
- Appropriate and adaptable to fit a number of situations; enough different words or phrases to make sense, but not so many as to distract or confuse children
- Easily remembered and quickly retrieved and articulated
- Shared and used throughout the grade-level team and school
- Shared with families

Children use shared language to label feelings and help develop understanding. Thinking games and other aspects of the curriculum from Chapters 8 and 9 are tools that provide the groundwork for what children do when conflict occurs. Teachers use these tools to help children learn how to talk through conflicts before they occur. Incorporating these key words and phrases into the culture of your classroom will help children communicate with each other directly. Some simple phrases for young children:

"I didn't like that."

"Are you okay?"

"Can I help you fix it?"

"Let's work it out."

Together with the children, decide on your own useful words and phrases based on what works in your setting. In this book, teachers have shared what they do in their classrooms: "We have two rules: 'Use words' and 'Don't hurt.'" Another teacher adds, "Be gentle."

TEACHERS TALK: WORDS WORK!

A kindergarten teacher tells children to "use their words" to express when someone or something is bothering them. "I find that when the students do this, they really end up solving things fairly and without violence."

Examples of Shared Language in the Classroom

"It's okay, it's not okay; use words not bodies; listen to his words," Jonathan tells his 3-year-old friends Julia and Billy.

"You can't say you can't play." Vivian Paley (1992) makes this a rule for kindergarteners, to eliminate rejection and exclusion of some children in the class and help others become more accepting of peers who want to play.

TEACHERS TALK

A teacher describes the experience of adopting the language tools in this published curriculum resource. "Last year, I unknowingly solved all their problems for them and was very frustrated and exhausted all the time. I didn't realize what I was doing wrong. This year, my students know that they need to use 'I Care' language to try to solve their problems themselves. They also know that they need to, at the very least, talk to the other person before they come to me with the problem. They are comfortable with this routine now and know the expectations." (We will include "I Care" materials in the Chapter 12 evaluation of curriculum models.)

Peer Mediation: A Little Help from My Friends

Help from peers can be another tool for children in resolving conflicts. Peers can be powerful in children's authentic engagement in the negotiation. Young children are more likely to simply comply with an adult's wishes, rather than understanding the other child's point of view and "owning" the resolution. Classmates and friends can act as peer mediators, either in a systematic way or informally.

Spontaneous Peer Mediators and Peer Encouragers

In an example in an earlier chapter, 3-year-old Jonathan engages in an act of spontaneous peer mediation. There is no formal peer mediation training in his preschool, but there is a context of caring and friendship, and all children in the preschool have words to express expected behaviors. "It's not okay to use bodies! Use words!" In other cases, children in conflict may be working for resolution and trying to negotiate. Other children may act as "peer encouragers," offering support and suggestions and generally validating the peaceful negotiation process.

A number of settings for preschool and primary-age children have more formal peer mediation programs. Children learn specific steps, strategies, and words to use in their roles as peer mediators. Children who are engaged in conflicts also learn how to call on a peer mediator, and how to follow the guidance offered by the mediator. There is wide variety in these peer mediation programs, and we will include some of them in our Chapter 12 discussion. One major distinction among these programs is how the mediators are selected. In some programs, a few children are selected for special training and become designated peer mediators. In other programs, all children learn the skills and strategies, and any child can be called upon to mediate between peers in conflict. In the Head Start Fussbuster Program, the peer mediator is called a Fussbuster. A mutual friend of the disputants is called to help children resolve differences at the class Peace Table (Gillespie & Chick, 2001).

A third opportunity for peer mediation occurs in the group. Children may bring their issues to class meetings for group problem-solving. Class meetings and morning meetings are good opportunities for these discussions (Charney, 1992, 2002; Vance & Weaver, 2002).

TEACHERS TALK

"My biggest issue is stepping back from the issues. I have to have the children voice their issues and encourage them to speak for themselves. Children get more when they hear it from a child and not an adult."

A Plan in Your Setting

Finding What Works for Your Setting

Throughout this book, we have investigated a number of ways to develop a caring classroom for conflict resolution and peacemaking. In Chapter 12, we will explore curriculum models available for schools and centers. Teachers are encouraged to evaluate, select, and try out approaches and strategies to find what works in your setting.

"I try to incorporate the team concept in my classroom. We do a lot of our work in small groups. I'm trying to teach the children to be responsible for themselves and their behavior. They are young, but they are old enough to understand the difference between right and wrong. If there is a problem in the group, the whole group is responsible for getting themselves back on track. I try not to step in too often, because I want them to learn how to work things out. I also utilize the Peace Table in my classroom. If two children are having a disagreement, they are directed to the Peace Table. They must use 'feeling words' to solve their problem. ('I feel sad when you do this.')"

Trying out Something Different

We have stressed conflict resolution strategies that fit the needs of the children and adults in each setting. The following intervention examples show slightly different approaches to intervening in children's conflicts.

Here Comes "Trouble!"   A group of 4-year-old girls is trying to keep another classmate from joining them. As she approaches, one of the group announces, "Here comes trouble!" The girls move away from their classmate, continuing to exclude her. Seeing this, the teacher moves closer to the group and announces, "My name is Trouble. Who wants to play Follow the Leader with me?" All the girls are happy to fall in line behind the teacher. The excluded girl joins the game.

Through the teacher's indirect intervention, exclusions and alliances have been redefined, and the name-calling has been defused because the name "Trouble" now has status.

The Good Old-Fashioned Guilt Trick   "I know you are such a good friend to _____ that you would never mean to hurt his feelings. He must have misunderstood and thought you said something else. Could you explain to him what you were really trying to say? And ask him if he accepts your apology?"

This approach could be described as "a strategy of positive restatement" rather than "a guilt trick," but those are the words that the teacher used. Without absolving the child from the consequences of using hurtful words, the teacher offers her a chance to make amends and replay the situation positively with alternative words.

Celebrating Successes with Children

A final but important note is to celebrate children's success in learning conflict resolution and peacemaking. Teachers and families celebrate success in all areas of learning and development, and conflict resolution should be no different. Children can share their successes with posters in the classroom and the halls, school assembly presentations, letters to family, and articles in the school newsletter or even in the community newspaper. Sharing their success may mean mentoring other children in learning conflict resolution and peacemaking.

Taking our work with conflict resolution and peacemaking out of the classroom leads us to the next few chapters of this book. We will develop ways to collaborate on conflict resolution, with families and community members as partners and advocates.

SUMMARY

When conflicts arise, as they inevitably will even in our caring classrooms, teachers need to make decisions about whether, when, and how to intervene in order to support and guide children in positive resolutions. We have explored a continuum of intervention strategies, from the teacher in control to children solving the issue independently. Using the three-layer cake image, teacher intervention is the top layer. Our hope is that, with firm bottom and middle layers, the teacher's role in the top layer will be that of an onlooker or cheerleader and not a judge or referee.

TEACHERS TALK: A STUDENT TEACHER LEARNS ABOUT CHILDREN'S CONFLICTS

"There are many conflicts that occur daily in a second-grade classroom among 7- and 8-year-olds. It is amazing to watch and to learn how they solve their differences and resolve their issues. Some need assistance, either mere coaxing to tell the other child how they felt about what happened or a friendly reminder to use their words to help the issue.

"What is interesting to observe is that most of the children can resolve their problems on their own, with little or no intervention by the teacher. Some children are quick to let the problem go, not to confront the problem fully until it is resolved. It seems to me that it is easier for the children to solve their problems in an appropriate way if it is first modeled by the teacher. During instruction, some time is devoted to handling problems in an appropriate manner. It is then apparent to me which children are ready to handle problems in a 'mature' way and which children were just quick to give up or act out.

"My conclusion is that all children handle conflict in different ways. It is the role of the teacher and the parent to teach children and students the skills that are necessary for them to confront their problems with themselves and other children."

SUPPLEMENTARY MATERIALS FOR CHAPTER 10

Research Focus/Teacher Research

Here is a classroom research question to investigate: Do teachers look at children's developing conflict ability in the same way that they see other areas of development and learning? In a typical classroom, two children are trying to figure out how to make a tower of blocks balance. Another child is working a difficult puzzle. Another is reading a book that is a stretch beyond his mastery level. What does the teacher do? What should the teacher think about before offering help: perhaps first, observe, think about problem-solving tools available to the child, what the teacher knows about the child and the nature of the task, and how the teacher sees her/his role (e.g., facilitator, guide, director, provider of information, Vygotsian mediator of learning)?

How are these children's activities alike or different from the arguing? The difference is that, in the conflict situation, teachers may see potential for harm and hurt, but in the developmental task, the teacher sees collaborative learning. Observe yourself or another teacher in a "traditional" learning situation/developmental task and in a conflict situation. How are the teacher responses and behaviors the same or different?

APPLICATION EXERCISES

1. Role play: Develop examples of intervention along the continuum. Use cards with scenarios, varying them by mixing them up with teacher perspective factors and aspects of cultural understanding or misunderstanding.
2. Discuss the Teacher Intervention Continuum with other teachers in your school or in a school where you may visit. How do the teachers approach conflicts in their classroom and on the playground? Is there a difference between teacher intervention indoors and outdoors or between boys and girls? How do these teachers decide whether and how to intervene?

THINKING ABOUT ALL CHILDREN

1. Consider the children in your setting who have diverse cultures, family customs, and languages. Do your current approaches to intervening, mediating, and guiding children in their conflicts seem to you to be culturally responsive? Are there aspects of touching, personal space, eye contact, or rules of possession and ownership or assertiveness that make some children and families uncomfortable?

   For a greater understanding of cross-cultural communication, teachers may refer to a number of sources and authors (Delpit, Ladson-Billings, Lynch & Hanson).
2. Read the DEC Position Statement and reflect on its implications for your current and future experiences with young children and families.

THE DIVISION FOR EARLY CHILDHOOD

DEC POSITION STATEMENT ON INTERVENTIONS FOR CHALLENGING BEHAVIOR

Adopted: April 1998
Reaffirmed: June 2001
Endorsed by: NAEYC

> Many young children engage in challenging behavior in the course of early development. The majority of these children respond to developmentally appropriate management techniques.

Every parent, including parents of young children with disabilities, wants his or her child to attend schools, child-care centers, or community-based programs that are nurturing and safe. Many young children engage in challenging behavior at various times during their early development. Typically, this behavior is short-term and decreases with age and use of appropriate guidance strategies. However, for some children these incidences of challenging behavior may become more consistent despite increased adult vigilance and use of appropriate guidance strategies. For these children, the challenging behavior may result in injury to themselves or others, cause damage to the physical environment, interfere with the acquisition of new skills, and/or socially isolate the child (Doss & Reichle, 1991). Additional intervention efforts may by required for these children.

> DEC believes strongly that many types of services and intervention strategies are available to address challenging behavior.

Given the developmental nature of most challenging behavior, we believe that there is a vast array of supplemental services that can be added to the home and education environment to increase the likelihood that children will learn appropriate behavior. A variety of intervention strategies can be implemented with either formal or informal support. Services and strategies could include, but are not limited to: (a) designing environments and activities to prevent challenging behavior and to help all children develop appropriate behavior; (b) utilizing effective behavioral interventions that are positive and address both form and function of a young child's challenging behavior; (c) adopting curricular modification and accommodation strategies designed to help young children learn behaviors appropriate to their settings; and (d) providing external consultation and technical assistance or additional staff support. In addition, all professionals who work with children in implementing IEPs or IFSPs must have opportunities to acquire knowledge and skills necessary for effective implementation of prevention and intervention programs.

> DEC believes strongly that families play a critical role in designing and carrying out effective interventions for challenging behavior.

Given the family-focused nature of early childhood education, we acknowledge the critical role that families play in addressing challenging behavior. Often times, challenging behavior occurs across places, people and time, thus families are critical members of the intervention team. A coordinated effort between family members and professionals is needed to assure that interventions are effective and efficient and address both child and family needs and strengths. All decisions regarding the identification of a challenging behavior, possible interventions, placement, and ongoing evaluation must be made in accordance with the family through the IEP, IFSP, or other team decision-making processes.

Doss, L. S. & Reichle, J. (1991). *Replacing excess behavior with an initial communicative repertoire. In J. Reichle, J. York, & J. Sigafoos (Eds.),* Implementing augmentative and alternative communication: Strategies for learners with severe disabilities. *Baltimore: Brooks Publishing Co.*

IV

Supporting Children's Conflict Resolution Beyond the Classroom: Understanding and Collaboration in Family, School, and Community

11 Working with Families and Communities for Conflict Resolution

"I have grown to realize that conflict resolution is much more than something that would occur in my classroom. There are conflicts that occur everywhere and anywhere, from a classroom to a playroom, from a parking lot to a freeway, from the bathroom to the bedroom. They are everywhere."

Chapter 11 Objectives: Children learn about conflicts and aspects of social behavior at home and in the neighborhood, as well as in school. Teachers and families wonder whether children will carry their prosocial attitudes and behaviors into their lives beyond school and home. Therefore, this final part of the book looks at children's conflict experiences beyond the classroom. In Chapter 11, we will look at children's conflict experiences at home, with siblings, adults, and neighborhood peers. We will explore ways that families and schools can collaborate in support of children's conflict resolution and peace-making. Finally, we will look at ways in which families and schools work together in the community. This chapter will stress home/school communication and understanding of the culture and language of the family and community. This chapter also looks at the power of the many adult models in

Family/School Connections

Conflict Resolution

Curriculum Ideas and Activities

Your Commitment to a Peaceful Classroom

children's lives. In this chapter, we will hear the voices of families, as we have heard voices of teachers throughout the book.

CHILDREN'S CONFLICTS OUTSIDE THE CLASSROOM

The Icing on the Cake

Children experience conflict at home, in the family and the neighborhood, not only in the school or center. In this chapter, we will look at the "icing on the cake" in our image of children's conflict resolution and peacemaking. The "icing" describes the family and community that surround the experiences of children and teachers in early childhood settings. In this book, we have stressed the idea of understanding children in the context of the family and home culture. The questions that we will address at this point are as follows:

1. How can we understand and support children and families in conflict resolution and peacemaking at home?

2. How can we make sure that teachers and families are working together?

3. How can families, schools, and the community join together to create safe environments for all?

We know that children learn about conflicts both at home and at school. Do children deal with conflicts the same way at school as they do at home? Do they hear the same messages from adults at school as at home? Is there carry-over to school from what children learn at home, and from what they learn at school to home? To support this carry-over, as early childhood professionals, we need to address the larger issue of home-school continuity in approaches to child rearing and understanding children's behavior, discipline, aggression, conciliation, and other aspects of conflict resolution.

Theory Note: As we consider whether children's responses to conflict are generalized across contexts, the question is what is internalized within a child's own framework for conflict and peace. We are guided by Vygotsky's concept of internalization, learning first on a social level and then internally.

New Images: Nesting and Overlapping Spheres

In addition to the idea of the three-layer cake, there are other ways to visualize relationships between home, school, and community where children grow and learn. In this chapter, we can add other visual images of what children learn at home and at school in the worlds, or spheres, in which they grow and learn.

Concentric Circles or Spheres

This image draws on the nested ecological systems described by Urie Bronfenbrenner (1979). Child and family interact with the school in the center circles, and respond and grow with the community in the outer circles (see Figure 11–1). (We discussed Bronfenbrenner's theory earlier.) The child and family are in the center microsystem. In the mesosystem, the child and family interact with school and neighborhood. And in the exosystem, they interact with the community, local government, adult workplaces, and media.

Overlapping Circles or Spheres

An image that looks more like a Venn diagram describes areas where a child's experiences at home and school are congruent and where they are not (see Figure 11–2). This model has been used to demonstrate cultural congruence, and we will use it in that way, as well as in conflict learning, child rearing, etc., drawn from the area of diversity studies and multicultural education (Smith, 1998). Surrounding both of the overlapping circles, we will draw a larger circle representing the community.

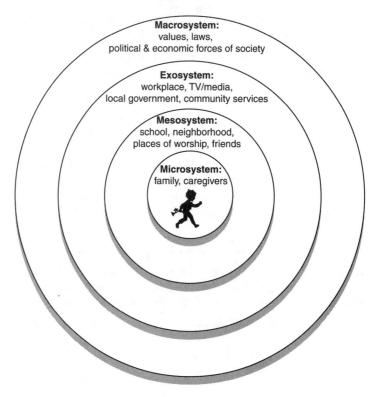

Figure 11–1
Home, school, and community: Concentric circles.

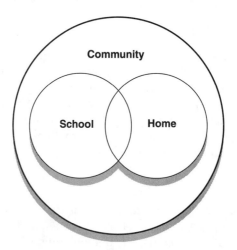

Figure 11–2
Home, school, and community: Overlapping circles.

The two circles will not completely overlap because there are normal and necessary differences between home and school. However, the greater the overlap the better, because it shows greater consistency and congruity between school and home. If the circles do not touch at all, the child is then living in two separate worlds that not only do not support each other but that may provide actively conflicting messages to the child. One way to view these interrelated influences in children's lives is to think about who are the "important people in your life" (Fallin et al., 2001).

CHILDREN'S CONFLICTS IN THE HOME AND FAMILY

How Children Experience Conflict in the Home and Family

We have looked closely at the conflicts that children experience with their peers in Early Childhood settings. In this chapter, we will explore the nature of conflicts that occur in other settings, with family and friends at home.

What Is Universal Among Children's Home and Family Conflicts?

We can make assumptions about a few things that all children share in their conflicts at home. First, as at school, conflicts at home arise naturally and frequently, and also have a structure (issues, strategies, and outcomes). As with peers, conflicts within the family can be constructive as well as destructive. Sibling conflicts are complex and perhaps even more varied than those with peers. Before we go further, we will stop to make clear what we mean in this chapter by "family" and "home."

Definitions of "Family" and "Home"   What is "family?" We will define family as people who are bound by affection and caring. Family is defined by the U.S. Census Bureau in terms of people related by birth, marriage, or adoption, who live in the same household. Sociologists define families by their function: those who "live together and care for one another," specifically, "to protect and prepare children" (Fuller & Olsen, 1998, pp. 2–3). There are a number of expectations and roles that usually describe families and have a bearing on relationships among family members. One is that parents and adult family members are authority figures in decision-making and passing on knowledge. Children are those cared for with growing apprenticeship in the family. Another assumption is that siblings will outlive parents, and the sibling relationship will last longer than the parent/child relationship.

What is "home?" In this context, the word "home" means wherever children and families are together, living and caring for one another, not necessarily a physical structure. We are not excluding families who are "homeless," in that our sense of "home" may apply to that domain where a family gathers for mutual care even if they are transient. Our discussion will include conflicts that occur at "home" among non-family friends, as well as those among siblings and other family members.

Note: In this book, the choice has been made to use the more inclusive tern "family" rather than "parents." In some cases, however, the words "parent" or "parenting" are used for semantic clarity to mean "adult family members." A further reminder is that "parents" and "family" include fathers, often invisible in the face of unspoken assumptions that the mother is the primary caregiver.

What Is Different About Family Relationships?

Differences between the conflicts that children experience at home and the ones that occur at school are due in part to the relationships and roles within the family. Bonds of kinship make family relationships different from those of peers at school or in the neighborhood. Family relationships are *obligatory*, as children have not chosen, and are not free to leave, their families. *Voluntary* relationships with peers are those that children choose to have and may abandon.

In addition, relationships may be described according to *closeness* (Maccoby, 1996; Vespo, 1997). Both family members and friends may be close or not close. Children may work harder to resolve conflicts with close friends because conflict resolution is required to keep the relationship intact. For siblings, the permanence of the relationship is not threatened by conflict, and the option of abandoning the relationship is not available as it would be for peers, especially those who are not close friends. The possibility of longer-lasting effects of destructive conflicts may be a concern because the sibling relationship is ongoing.

Conflicts with siblings may be more intense and more physical, and may last longer. This phenomenon makes sense because children may feel a need to persist to a conclusion, but do not need to be as conciliatory in their conflict strategies as with friends. Not all those who study children's conflicts are in agreement about the effects of relationship differences on children's conflicts because of the variations in age, gender, birth order of the siblings, and the types of conflict issues.

Diversity in Family Conflicts   What we can also say with certainty is that all families are not the same and their ways of approaching conflicts also differ. There are too many variations to begin to list them all, but teachers need to be responsive to each family without assumptions or generalizations. Among the ways in which families differ are culture, family structure, and parenting styles.

The Role of Culture in Children's Home and Family Conflicts   The culture of the family includes aspects of language, religion, national origin, and ethnicity, and a mixture of these cultures exists within many families. Studies on cross-cultural child rearing give us insight into variations in family relationships. Diversity studies describe differences in approaches to a range of social interaction, including conflicts (DeLoache & Gottlieb, 2000; Lynch & Hanson, 1998; Whiting & Edwards, 1988).

The culture of the family also includes ways of understanding and behaving that develop within families. Rituals, routines, and behaviors adopted as the family norm are often quite unique to one family, and may be very different from other families.

Family Structures and Roles   Families come in a variety of structures and sizes, and there are different roles and relationships. There are multigenerational families of different ages, single-sex couples, single-parent households, large extended families, adopted children, foster children, adults and children with special needs, blended families, only children, multiples and close-in-age "stair steps," and spread-out "gap babies." Primary care responsibilities can be assumed by mother or father, grandparents, and home or center care. Just think of your own family and those of several people that you know. How much variety do you see? When we talk about "young children and their families," it is a varied image.

Conflicts with Siblings

General Perceptions of Sibling Conflicts: "I Hate My Sister!"

How common is the assumption that children in a family just will not get along with each other? Powerful messages in the media affect children's ideas about what a sibling relationship looks like. Portrayals in children's literature are often negative, or begin as negative and then the family works things out. Portrayals of adults usually show sibling conflict resolved by adult authority or power (Kramer et al., 1999). Sibling relationships are presented as problematic and conflictual, not as opportunities for caring and friendship. Changing this perception is an important task for parents and teachers.

Consider your own experiences. Do you remember your experiences with siblings as happy or as conflictual, or both? Do parenting books present a "no-win" situation and assume siblings do not get along, or do they show strong and caring relationships? The parenting literature often presents only the problems: rivalry, arguments, and aggression. It is true that some siblings will get along better than others. Sibling relationship quality has been described in six categories. The three positive categories are 1) warmth and affection, 2) involvement, and 3) conflict resolution and relationship maintenance. The three other categories are negative: 4) antagonism, 5) control, and 6) rivalry and competition (Kramer et al., 1999). As with peer interactions, adults can communicate their expectations for, and notice, positive sibling interactions.

Sibling Relationships and Sibling Culture

As with children in a classroom, children in a family create a sibling culture with its own rules, shared language, and humor. For children close in age, this peer culture can be very strong. Siblings widely separated in age may not share their growing-up years, and their relationship and the nature of conflicts will be very different. In this discussion, we will focus on siblings close enough in age that there are shared times, spaces, experiences, and parenting.

Typically Developing Children   Age, gender, and birth order all offer variations and contexts for issues and strategies in sibling conflicts. We can be guided in our

---

A FAMILY STORY: MESSAGES FROM BOOKS

Eight-year-old Annie has been reading Judy Blume's novel *Superfudge* (1980), a humorous story told from the point of view of an older brother suffering from the misbehavior of a younger brother named Fudge. Annie's mother has noticed that Annie has started to pick on her own 5-year-old brother Ben, even though the two have always had a close and supportive relationship. Ben, by the way, is now at the same school as Annie and is now learning to read. Annie has always considered herself to be the "reader." Mother suspects that two things may be happening and decides to have a talk with the children. She makes two unequivocal pronouncements: "Ben is not Fudge!" and "Everyone in this family will be a reader!" Peace returns to the household.

---

understanding of sibling conflicts in several themes from established research and practice. First, we can see that older siblings may act as a "more capable peer," extending the thinking and strategies of the younger sibling in an argument (Vygotsky, 1978). We can also look to the classic work of Rudolph Dreikurs (1964, 1990), who describes children seeking a place or special niche within the family. Having a safe turf may avoid rivalry disputes, but it may be a source of conflict if the territory is invaded. An understanding of issues and differences in moral reasoning, often gender-related, may cause conflict or impede resolution (Gilligan, 1982).

Siblings with Disabilities   Families that have children with special needs are not exempt from sibling conflict issues. Disabilities and developmental delays bring added family stress, even in loving and harmonious families. Typically developing children experience mixed feelings about their "special" siblings, from loving and protecting to impatience and resentment. These children will need support from teachers and from parents. In turn, teachers will need to support parents, children, and school peers. In addition to the age, gender, and birth order, the nature of the special need or disability influences sibling interaction (Kostelnik et al., 2002; others). Constructive conflict between siblings with and without disabilities can be evidence of a sense of equality in the relationship and respect for the sibling with a disability as a "person first." Conflict that occurs in a situation where there is a "level playing field" (a child in a wheelchair can argue about a game of checkers!) emphasizes the ability, not only the disability.

Non-disabled siblings often have been overlooked in intervention programs that attend to children with special needs and families, but now are often included. Children need information and knowledge about their sibling's condition to ensure their own understanding and to be able to respond to those outside the family who ask, inappropriately at times. Children whose brothers or sisters have a disability often display greater tolerance, patience, and compassion for others, and are often proud of the accomplishments and abilities of their disabled siblings (Fuller & Olsen, 1998). These attributes, as we would expect, contribute to children's conflict resolution and peacemaking skills with their peers.

What Happens in Sibling Conflicts?

There are some things about sibling conflicts that are the same as conflicts with peers, and some things that are different. We can see that conflicts occur naturally; can be constructive or destructive; and are structured encounters with issues, strategies, and outcomes. There may be differences in what these issues, strategies, and outcomes look like; the boundaries of time and place are different; and the relationships with adults in the setting differ from peer conflicts in classrooms and centers. We will explore issues, outcomes, strategies, and in the following sections.

Conflict Issues: Why Do Siblings Argue?   First of all, is the conflict serious, a "real" conflict, or non-serious, a companionship interaction? Children often are heard squabbling. Is it really an argument, or is it verbal play? Sibling quarrels, verbal non-issue conflicts, and squabbling can act as a safe place for rehearsal and testing. If there is hurtful teasing or one-sided mischief, the situation may not be healthy, but a case of sibling bullying. (See Chapter 9 on bullying.)

Here are some underlying causes that may set the stage for sibling conflicts. Immediate instigating issues may be possession of an object or space, not unlike peer disputes.

Parental attention: Children often engage in a conflict to gain attention from adult family members if they feel that it is the only way. Similar to a situation in a classroom, children will behave in ways that they know will work. Parents need to find ways to provide the attention that children so desperately seek in ways that are positive. By creating a special time for children, parents can help children find their uniqueness and feel secure in their place in the family, and secure in their parents' love. Rivalry and resentment may be prompted by a real or perceived difference in attention and time for one sibling who's participating in a sport or achieving in school.

FAMILY INTERVIEW: DIFFERENCES BETWEEN CHILDREN, PARENTAL ATTENTION

Mother of a boy (age 8) and a girl (age 4): "Jon is so hard to manage. He doesn't listen to me, he can't be quiet, he constantly needs my attention. I know Ali creates conflict just so that she can get my attention."

Power/control over the situation: Children may engage in conflict to gain power or control. Dominating a sibling through conflict, and even just the act of cresting conflict, is one of few areas where children can have some control in their young lives. Families should provide appropriate areas for children to make choices and feel respected as individuals. Agree on family rules and expectations instead of simply saying, "Do as you're told!" In conflicts, adults should not assign blame but provide affirmation of positive resolution, guide children in negotiation with awareness of others, and set age-appropriate limits.

EXAMPLE TO DISCUSS

An interesting example of a sibling conflict, perhaps related to birth order, power, or parental attention and favor: 6-year-old Micah and 4-year-old Jenna argue loudly and often over who will get to play with their new baby sister. Can you suggest reasons for this conflict?

Sibling relationship and identity issues: For the most part, children innately value their relationships with siblings, and at the same time are working to develop their own identities (Erikson). Frequently, children are not on the same wavelength at any point in time.

• A need for separateness, space, identity, and individuality may cause conflict when one sibling wants to be alone, or alone with age-mates, and the other sibling wants to connect.
• A desire for another sibling's attention, wanting connectedness, may be at the root of teasing, mischief, or annoyance. Adults can help siblings generate alternative solutions, find compromises in time and place to play together or alone, and help siblings express caring for each other even when they are not together.

Finally, because most siblings (except twins) are not age-mates, an *age or developmental mismatch* may cause a different understanding of a situation, or a difference in attention span or physical coordination, leading to disagreement, misunderstanding, and conflict. Parents can help by working with children on perspective-taking and listening.

FAMILY INTERVIEW: "THE MAIN CONFLICT ISSUES AMONG THE CHILDREN"

Mother of boys (ages 10, 6, and 3) and a girl (age 9): "The worst problem I have is with the kids is their constant *nudging* (rhymes somewhat with 'pudding' and can mean anything along the lines of teasing, bothering, annoying, or irritating someone else). There are also territorial issues. They get upset if one of the other children walks into their room without permission. Possession issues are big also, usually toys, but it could be anything, really. They are also big on correcting each other in many different situations. They each like to be right and to prove the other one wrong. The majority of the conflict centers around the 6-year-old. He annoys, often deliberately, the two older ones. They have absolutely no patience with him. There's not much conflict with the 3-year-old. He generally gets along well with the others."

Sibling Strategies and Responses   As with children's peer conflicts, children's conflicts with siblings include physical strategies and verbal strategies (calling on adults for help). How do these strategies look in sibling conflict?

Physical strategies may include the same sorts of non-aggressive strategies we have seen among peers, such as push-pull, holding on to an object, and taking things away. Siblings may also use aggressive physical strategies, such as hitting. Verbal strategies include insistence, as well as negotiation and reasoning. The basis for negotiation may be different among siblings than among peers. Siblings may use different threats and promises. The friendship threats and promises heard with peers, such as "I won't invite you to my birthday party" or "Pleeeease! You'll be my best friend forever!" do not apply to siblings. Much more powerful is the "I'm telling!" threat, and the ability to make threats, promises, and bargains that will last further into the future than among peers. ("I'll let you use my special baseball glove!") Threats of telling are more persistent effects and different bargaining tools.

The strategy of calling on adult help lends itself to unique sibling situations; the idea of "framing" or deflecting guilt. Another issue at home is that more than one adult may be an authority figure, leading to the famous "shopping around" strategy, or setting up one parent to agree by saying that another has already agreed.

Outcomes and Consequences for Children: Responses to conflict also can be seen as a continuum from understanding to violence (see Figure 11–3). Children receive powerful messages from the responses to conflict that they experience at home, as well as at school.

Outcomes to immediate conflict situations include both child-generated and adult-controlled outcomes. Child outcomes parallel those among peers: mutually agreeable resolutions, one-sided dominance, dropping the issue (described in a grown-up memory as "letting it evaporate"), or mediation by another sibling or even a peer. Compromising among siblings may involve complex negotiations of privileges over time. Children can anticipate with certainty that some situations will recur, such as trips in the car (who sits in front), chores that need to be done routinely, and so forth. Children can bargain for future privileges ("Let me pick now and you can pick next time"), for example, or make threats of future reprisal ("If you mess my game up now, just wait till it's your turn").

Adult-imposed solutions are more likely to take into account children's ages, past history, and differential expectations for children based on age, gender, or previous behaviors. A wide variety of sanctions or punishments can be imposed by family with effects over time and space: till bedtime, all week; stay in your room, yard; extra chores, etc. Consequences can be more enduring and sometimes

Violence   Avoidance   Cooperation   Acceptance   Understanding

Figure 11–3
Continuum of responses to conflict (applies to both children and adults).

remembered for years as "family lore." ("Remember the year when you ate my Halloween candy but never admitted it?" "Well, that was the same year you ate my chocolate bunny.")

FAMILY INTERVIEW: SHOPPING AROUND

Mother and father (boy, age 7, and girl, age 4): "We try to be of one mind with regard to conflicts that arise in the family. Both children use the age-old technique of children everywhere, asking one parent something and, when denied, going immediately to the other parent. Our approach is to try to bring harmony and mutual understanding to the situation without overriding each other. By this, I mean we communicate with each other to understand each other's true reaction."

Conflicts with Neighborhood Peers at Home

Children also have conflicts at home with friends, as well as with non-friend neighborhood peers. Friends share some characteristics of siblings in their motivation to resolve conflicts in a long-term relationship. Neighborhood friends have the option to leave and go home, but conflicts can extend beyond the school day and even from one day to the next. Adult intervention and household rules are different from teacher intervention and school or classroom rules. There also may be more escape routes in home settings. Between friends and non-friend neighborhood peers, one question is whether children have a motivation or reason to resolve conflict. Other questions are whether the conflict takes place on home territory or neutral turf, and whether the conflict occurs during peer play or in a group (Kramer et al., 1999). Neighborhood peer conflicts occur not only in dyads, between two children, but also in groups. In a multi-party dispute, children may act on their own behalf as individuals. For example, three children may argue about which one of them will have the first turn. In a different situation, children may argue on behalf of others, acting as a member of a group. To a newcomer, one of a group of children insists, "You can't play in our space!" (Does this remind you of the chapter about sociology?) Although group conflicts are interesting and very common in neighborhood play, most of the writing and study on children's conflicts has been in the context of pair conflict, or conflict between two children.

Children's Conflicts with Adults in the Family

Children and adults in the family also have disagreements. These disagreements are in a different context because the relationship between adults and children is not the same as with peers or siblings. Disputes occur between adults and children, but the question is: Are these disagreements actual conflicts and a prolonged response to a child's behavior, such as wanting a toy at the store, or not wanting to clean up, go to bed, or do homework? Conflict management in these cases is a parenting issue.

FAMILY INTERVIEW

Mother of boys (ages 10, 6, and 3) and a girl (age 9): "Oh, yes, quite a bit of conflict there! And it's different with each one, probably because I have different expectations for each child. With the 3-year-old, it's mostly oppositional behavior. With the others, it's issues like respect, attitude, the way they talk, time management, etc."

Differences of perception, understanding, and need are opportunities for learning and guiding, not the same as adult/adult or child/child conflict. If there is a disagreement, what are the ground rules? What are adult roles and responsibilities when there is a disagreement with children? The following are guidelines or "do's and don'ts":

Do:

1. Remain calm, and do not assume a combative stance.
2. Use the disagreement as a chance to say "let's decide."
3. Use the situation as an opportunity for modeling problem-solving, listening, generating alternatives, and finding a mutually agreeable solution in a respectful and caring way.
4. Remove any child or adult who is out of control.

Don't:

1. Engage in an argument with children.
2. Use physical power or coercion, of threats or physical, verbal, or emotional violence.

This does not mean parents do not have discussions with children or listen to each other's points of view (see authoritative parenting).

FAMILY INTERVIEW

Mother of boys (ages 10, 6, and 3) and a girl (age 9): "I try to encourage them to work it out by themselves whenever possible. I have to admit that my biggest problem is dealing with my own anger when these situations arise. I can't seem to pull myself back from the situation and act like the parent. Sometimes, I feel like I'm not showing any more self-control than my 10-year-old. And then I expect him to control himself with his little brother. It can be disheartening."

How Families Deal with Conflict

What Families Can Do to Support Conflict Resolution and Peacemaking

What is the family culture of interaction and environment for daily living? Just as we have discussed classrooms with a climate of caring and kindness, families can create a climate of caring. Families provide support for children by setting aside a special time for children, individually and as a family; respecting each child an individual; teaching negotiation skills; and creating a safe and caring environment. Children need the ability to listen and understand consequences; adults need to hear children's viewpoints without imposing adult perceptions. (Much of what has been discussed in earlier chapters will apply to families as well as teachers.)

Types of Parenting Styles: What Do They Teach Children About Conflict Resolution?   Adult response to children's conflicts is closely related to types of parenting styles. The ways parents deal with children's conflicts are strong models for children:

- Authoritative: Democratic, encourages problem solving, stresses communication, provides appropriate limits and expectations for behavior but engages children in decision-making, is both demanding and responsive.
- Authoritarian: Sets arbitrary rules, applies punishment, restricts children's environment, expects conformity, is demanding but unresponsive.
- Permissive: Few if any rules or expectations for children's behavior, may be either overly indulgent or neglectful, unwilling to set limits, is undemanding but generally responsive.
- Uninvolved: Neglectful, undemanding, and unresponsive.

Berger adds dysfunctional parenting as an overlay to any of the other styles, where family conditions include debilitating mental illness, substance abuse, or abuse of children (Berk, 2000; Berger, 2000).

The following examples offer contrasts in family approaches to children's conflicts.

FAMILY INTERVIEW: PARENTING STYLE

Mother of boy (age 8) and girl (age 4): "We (husband and wife) grew up with similar backgrounds, and so we agree on most child-rearing issues. We have high expectations, perhaps even more so than our own parents. The children rarely argue because we always talk about treating everyone with respect, and I think that the whole family has respect for each other. Being 4 years apart, and one is a boy and the other a girl, may play a part in the lack of confrontation. When they do argue, we sit them down and discuss the conflict. We have them resolve it with some prompting. There is not a set of rules, but we want the children to learn what is right and what is wrong."

FAMILY INTERVIEW: PARENTING STYLE

Mother of two boys (ages 6 and 8), and two girls (9 and 12): "All of my children have their own bedrooms where they keep their own things. Their brothers and sisters must ask for permission before going into each other's rooms or using each other's things. We also have a game room, which has toys and games that the children share. We have toys that are used outside that are shared as well. If someone breaks a toy that didn't belong to them, they are expected to replace it using money from their own allowance."

Family Climate and Expectations

Once again, we are reminded that caring and harmony do not look the same from one family to the next, and that peace is not the absence of conflict. There is no single right way to resolve a conflict. Families define and communicate rules and expectations for what each family member is expected to do: chores, schoolwork, work outside the home, being there, and cultural and individual family differences, as well as consequences for when expectations are not met.

FAMILY INTERVIEW: EXPECTATIONS, NOT RULES

Mother of three (boy age 14, girl age 12, and boy age 2): "Expectations come from discussion with the children. When the children were smaller, we did not use behavior charts, we used praise. When the children did well, they called their grandparents. We worked at keeping expectations for behavior at school and outside the home consistent. Now that the children are older, we are seeing the children becoming more consistent with their follow-through."

FAMILY INTERVIEW

Mother of boys (ages 12 and 11), girl (age 13): "We don't have rules, more like guidelines. We often talk about the Golden Rule. Respect is not so much a rule but an attitude that is expected no matter what the situation. Our biggest rule that we state to children is this: Before you do or say anything, ask yourself if you would do or say it if your father or mother were standing right there."
    (This mother is a teacher and uses this in her classroom as well.)

Rules and expectations for children may include the types of play allowed (violent play, weapons, loud or active play indoors, with whom each child may play, where and how long).

TO HELP FAMILIES: CHOOSING TOYS FOR NON-VIOLENT PLAY

Teachers Resisting Unhealthy Children's Entertainment (TRUCE) is an organization to promote healthy, non-violent play. The Web site has toy selection information, media violence guides, and other resources and links for families and teachers.
TRUCE Web site: *http://truceteachers.org*

Consistency Within the Family   Do all adults agree on what the family rules are, when and how to intervene, and what consequences should occur? Is there consistent or equitable treatment for all children? Shared language and understood strategies are valuable at home as well as at school.

FAMILY INTERVIEW

Tom (father) and Beth (stepmother) have 5-year old twins (boy and girl) and a 3-year-old girl.
   How do you promote conflict resolution?
   Beth: "I ask each one involved to explain in their own words what happened within the conflict. Depending on how harmful the conflict is, I will intervene and resolve the situation. Otherwise, I will encourage them to solve their own conflicts using their own solutions. I seek first to understand and have them solve it themselves. It is important to have each one see the other's perspective."
   Tom: "I promote conflict resolution by getting control of the situation, staying calm, and letting them feel as though everyone is winning, through teaching fairness. I think it is important to validate their feelings and teach them there may not be a right or wrong or a 'first' in certain circumstances, or it may not be the time. For example, they may need to listen to Daddy, and there is no negotiation."
   Is there consistency between parents?
   Beth: "In our family, I would say no. However, there has been improving consistency. It is more important for me to have consistency with the children and future conflicts. In my opinion, it is more important to Tom to solve the conflict immediately, with or without future ramifications. For example, if the 3-year-old grabs a toy from the 5-year-old, Tom will try to pacify the 5-year-old and let the 3-year-old keep the toy, explaining that she is just a baby. I would rather have the 3-year-old learn that what she did was wrong, even if it means that she cries."

Adults as Models in the Family   Adult modeling at home establishes and strengthens a culture of caring and gives children examples of how to negotiate and resolve conflicts. Adults demonstrate positive social interactions in their fair, caring, and respectful behaviors with children, and with other adults. Consistent, respectful behavior demonstrates an authentic "This is who I am," not "This is who I am with adults, but I am a different person with children," or communicating that it is important to treat some people well but not others, such as those who are younger or smaller. Children see that adults solve conflicts with peaceful listening and reasoning, rather than using power and might to resolve conflicts through domination. Parents may also make explicit statements of their commitment to caring and conflict resolution. Children then carry this attitude into interactions with siblings and peers.

FAMILY INTERVIEW

Father of a girl (age 3): "Conflict is a problem between two or more parties that needs to be resolved. When my wife and I have a conflict and Alisha is present, we try to be sensitive to that. We use calm voices, we listen to each other, and we try to compromise. When Alisha is not around, we still try to model these behaviors, but I think we kind of take advantage of the situation. Conflict is hard for everyone to deal with. It's better to learn to deal with it at an early age."

FAMILY INTERVIEW

Mother of boys (ages 12 and 11), girl (age 13): "Our rules do not conflict because we support each other's decisions in front of the children. However, there are times when we disagree with one another's discipline. We tell each other our feelings, but not in front of our children."

Family Thinking Games   Thinking games are effective in family settings as well as in classrooms. Teachers may share some of the basic classroom thinking games from Chapters 7, 8, and 9 with families to support conflict resolution and peacemaking at home (Crary, 1984; Edwards, 1986). In choosing, adapting, or creating thinking games, families should focus on what their children may need for problem-solving and conflict resolution:

1. Listening
2. Using language to express their thoughts
3. Understanding and labeling feelings and consequences
4. Generating alternative solutions
5. Perspective-taking
6. Understanding of cause and effect, consequences of actions

Creating Family Thinking Games   A thinking game to help children explore feelings involves magazine or book pictures of people with a variety of facial expressions. The adult can ask, "How do you think this person is feeling? Can you tell a story about what this person has been doing?" Guide children in labeling feelings and emotions and in taking the perspective of the person in the picture. In another thinking game about feelings and emotions, adults and children make various facial expressions in a mirror.

To generate alternatives, describe a common conflict scenario, such as a possession issue, and ask children, "What else could they do?" For each alternative suggested, adults can follow up with, "What would happen next?" This extends the thinking game to exploring consequences and effects.

For perspective-taking, the questions to ask are, "How do you think you would feel if ...?" And then, "How do you think this person would feel?" Then discuss why the responses are the same or different.

In a thinking game that explores children's moral decision-making called Dividing the Cookies, (Edwards, 1986), children decide how many cookies each person in the story should have based on how many each has made, strict equality, age, or need. Books that can be used with this theme are *The Doorbell Rang* (Hutchins), *The Grouchy Ladybug* (Carle), and any version of *The Little Red Hen*.

Thinking games can be adapted from published sources (Crary, 1984; Edwards, 1986), or families can create their own or develop them from stories in children's books or invented stories. Puppets, pictures, and props may be used in thinking games. Thinking games can be done with one child, and are especially effective with a group of siblings. In inventing stories, adults can decide how closely the characters should resemble their own children. If the story scenario is too close to reality, the children may not be able to distance themselves. In other cases, children may be thrilled to have someone in the story "just like me!"

In sibling conflicts, adult family members recognize each child as an individual and listens with respect.

Intervention, Outcomes, and Consequences

What Families Do About Children's Conflicts   Family meetings are one strategy for dealing with chronic, recurring conflicts. Similar to class meetings, families can meet to share issues as well as news, and to make family decisions. These meetings can address specific conflict issues or ways to deal with conflicts in general. Families can use thinking games for families and read books that have kind and caring themes at bedtime, or whenever there is a time for a book. Similarly, families can share and discuss television programs, movies, and video games.

FAMILY INTERVIEW

Ted (father) and Betty (stepmother) have 5-year-old twins (boy and girl) and a 3-year-old girl.

Betty: "The children and I were going to the office supply store and, before we were even out of the car, there was conflict about who was going to ride in the cart. I asked calmly if anyone had any ideas. They had brilliant ideas and solved the conflict on their own. They were open and owned the problem."

FAMILY INTERVIEW

Mother and stepfather (boy, age 7, and girl, age 4): "While it is seldom that all the younger members of the family are able to be together, when this does occur, both children are expected to behave and interact in a friendly manner."

Should Parents Intervene?   We have seen that in classroom peer conflicts, there are times when children's independent conflict management is more effective than teacher intervention. Children do learn from generating their own resolutions in constructive conflict situations. Adults intervene when destructive conflicts escalate and become dangerous. In non-harmful conflicts, there are contrasting views. The effectiveness of parental intervention depends on variations and factors such as the type of intervention and parental gender, and the ages and spacing of children. Adults may consider these aspects and decide which ones apply in the situation at hand.

Parental intervention may be positive when children of different ages are in conflict, and parents may ensure that rules of fairness are understood in the same way by a 2-year-old and a 4-year-old. Intervention may help if children are able to learn and use more advanced negotiation when adults provide guidance and scaffolding. Researchers have suggested that there may be fewer conflicts as a result (Kramer et al., 1999).

FAMILY INTERVIEW

Mother and father of three children (7, 6, and 2):

Father: "We usually allow the children to work out their differences. We try only to step in when they fail to come up with a solution."

Mother: "We will stop them if they look or sound like they are going to start hitting each other. We really want them to work their problems out themselves, so we tell them that if we get involved, they will not like the solution we come up with. For example, if they argue over a toy and they won't share, well, we'll just take the toy. None of them like that."

Conversely, parental intervention can be negative because it may upset the balance of power among siblings when parents side with the younger child. Parental intervention may seem to be differential treatment. If conflicts are intended to gain adult attention, then adult intervention will increase conflicts. Adult intervention may deprive children of the opportunity to learn to resolve conflicts on their own. General Categories of Interventions, described by Kramer et al. (1999), include the following:

Passive non-intervention, in which the adult appears to be completely removed from the conflict and is not involved in any way. This can also mean simply ignoring the situation.

Child-centered interventions, in which children and adults are actively working together toward a resolution. These interventions may include 1) collaborative problem-solving, exploring alternatives and compromises; 2) reasoning, guided explanation of the dispute and outcome; 3) active non-intervention, expecting children to resolve the conflict but being available to help; and 4) exploring feelings and emotions, and guiding children in examining the causes and effects of the conflict.

Adult-controlled interventions, in which the primary goal is to end the conflict without concern for children's involvement in the process or opportunities to learn how to deal with future conflicts. These interventions may include 1) directing or redirecting children's behaviors or activities away from the situation, 2) simple assertion of adult power through threats or punishment, or 3) verbal commands to stop fighting (Kramer et al., 1999).

FAMILY INTERVIEW

Mother and father (boy, age 7, and girl, age 4): "If a conflict arises, we allow them ample time to resolve any issue before any adult intervenes."

FAMILY INTERVIEW

Mother of boy (age 8) and girl (age 4): "I intervene almost always. If I don't stop the arguments, then it will never get taken care of. I swear, those two will just yell at each other for no reason other than to yell."

FAMILY INTERVIEW

Mother of boys (ages 10, 6, and 3) and a girl (age 9): "I try my best to use logical consequences, but I have to admit I'm not as consistent as I would like to be. So much of it depends on my mood, on what type of behavior has occurred previously that day. My first reaction is to separate the ones who are fighting. Violence is never acceptable. If it's an argument, I tell them to work it out. I try not to mediate. If they can't work it out, then I try other things. For the younger ones, I use time-outs. The older ones are sent to their rooms, which I guess is essentially a time-out. It's generally effective. The only time when it doesn't work is when the 'accused perpetrator' feels that he or she is actually innocent or feels victimized."

When and How to Intervene: The Continuum for Families   The interventions that parents use fit within the same continuum of intervention that teachers use. Families will benefit from understanding the range of available interventions as they work toward the same goal of children as independent problem-solvers and peacemakers at home. (See Chapter 10.) The continuum from greatest adult control to child control includes these strategies, which apply similarly to adults in the family:

- Physical intervention and adult direction of the outcome
- Restating rules
- Offering choices or suggesting what to do
- Supporting children's negotiation
- Restating the problem
- Looking on

Knowing what they are seeing is important for adults as they determine their intervention in children's conflicts. The guidelines are the same as for teachers: look for prosocial and not just antisocial behavior. As we mentioned in Chapter 3, adults more often notice, and sometimes expect, children's antisocial behaviors, overlooking the many prosocial behaviors that happen throughout the day. The same expectation and "noticing" takes place in the family setting as well. Let us watch for, and celebrate with children, the acts of caring, cooperation, support, empathy, and mediation that we find.

FAMILY INTERVIEW

About consistency and ownership, parenting style:
"Both of us try to enforce the same set of rules and consequences for all three children. We also try to keep the children busy as often as possible to reduce the number of conflicts that occur. We try to have lots of things in the house for them to do. We also encourage them to play with their friends and have their friends over. If one child has a friend over, I like for each of them to have a friend over. If one has a friend over but one does not, I try to keep the others occupied so they do not bother each other."

FAMILY INTERVIEW

Mother and father of three children (7, 6, and 2):
Father: "We believe that the children have to be taught that their actions will bring consequences. They must follow rules and control their behavior. We also believe that this takes time."
Mother: "Children must follow rules at home in order to follow rules outside of the home. (No hitting, respect other people's property, no foul language, no disrespect to elders, no spitting.) These are rules we believe they will have to follow in order to function properly in society."
Interviewer who talked to children in the family: "I was amazed by their candor and understanding of their household rules and expectations, as well as consequences. They discussed how they worked out their differences with each other, as well as with peers. They discussed being able to come up with their own solutions rather than having the adults decide the solution. They said it gave them a 'grown up' feeling."

Intervening with Neighborhood Peers   While intervening in an on-the-spot conflict among siblings and neighborhood peers, families need to be aware of issues of fairness. Do parents hold their own children as hosts to a different standard of fairness than friends as guests? Parents may expect their children to share and divide toys with guest playmates according to a rule of fairness and equality, but guest playmates are not expected to share with hosts. In other cases, the "house rules" apply to all children, from a desire for consistency, as a matter of adult control of children's behavior, or perhaps as a sense of shared responsibility for neighborhood children (Kramer et al., 1999; Ross & Conant, 1992; family interviews, 2000).

When to Ask for Extra Help   When children and adults in the family are frustrated and a variety of strategies they have tried have not made a difference, there may be a need for additional help. It is important to address chronic family conflicts that are destructive and lead to antagonism, extreme frustration, and even violence. Teachers should be familiar with resources in the community, such as Parents Anonymous, Child Find, and others, and make the referral information

---

FAMILY INTERVIEW

Mother of six (18, 15, 12, 9, 6, and 3); home-schooled her children; eldest now away at college: "I would separate the children and put the one who did something wrong in time-out. I would discipline another child by putting them in time-out. I would never hit another person's child, and I wouldn't want another parent to hit my child, but they can put my child in time-out."

FAMILY INTERVIEW

Mother and Father of three children (7, 6, and 2):

   Father: "I have no problems disciplining other people's children, especially if they are in my house. I want my children to be productive in our society, not end up incarcerated. I believe my friends and associates want the same things. I expect them to keep my kids in line also. Remember the old African proverb, 'It takes a village to raise a child.' For some reason, this philosophy has died in the communities. It is one we truly need to hold on to. As parents, we need to watch out for other children and let them know when they are doing wrong."

---

available to all families, before, as well as when, it is needed. Teachers need to have a resource file for local contacts and agencies on-hand.

Open sessions for families to share concerns can be an effective first step in needed family peace-building interventions. Parent education meetings and family support groups can be valuable. Often, what families need is an understanding of typical child social and emotional development. Teachers and schools can provide families with information and tools for better understanding their children's behaviors. A number of assessment tools have been designed for families to use at home with minimal training, such as the Ages & Stages Questionnaires: Social-Emotional (ASQ:SE) (Squires, Bricker, & Twombly, 2001).

Families Supporting Children in Troubling Times

Increasing exposure to violent confrontations in conflict, and the stress and uncertainty noticeable in the adults who care for them can take a toll on children. Teachers and caregivers can play an important role in giving families information and resources, as well as understanding, to support their children in troubling times. Many professional organizations, such as NAEYC, provide practical resources for families and teachers in responding to current events. (Refer to resources in Chapter 2.)

HOW ADULTS CAN FACILITATE PROBLEM-SOLVING WHEN INTERVENING

Crary's Steps for Families (1984, pp. 21–22) are similar to the steps for children and teachers in the classroom (Chapter 10):

1. Gather data: Listen and understand perspectives, label feelings.
2. Define the problem: Together, identify the basic issue to be resolved.
3. Generate alternatives: Brainstorm ways to resolve the issue.
4. Evaluate alternatives: Talk about the consequences of each alternative.
5. Ask for a decision: Ask children to come to a consensus about which alternative to try out. (Adults must respect this choice, even if it is not the one that they would choose.)

RESEARCH NOTE: TEACHERS AS RESEARCHERS/FAMILY AS RESEARCHERS

Offer the idea of action research to families. Here are two choices:

1. Observe children and keep track of their prosocial behaviors. How often do they occur? Can you find any patterns: time of day, children's activities, what happens afterward?
2. Observe sibling conflicts, practice the Problem-Solving Steps, and observe some more sibling conflicts.

What other home action research topics can you plan with families?

What Teachers Can Do to Support Families: Sibling Issues

• In the classroom, integrate children's books where family conflicts are resolved peacefully. These books can be shared with families in accessible and appropriate ways. Evaluate books carefully for portrayal of sibling relationships, children's conflict resolution, and adult intervention. If children are reading books where siblings are portrayed as rivals or as not getting along, or where conflicts are ended by adult authority, discuss why this should not be the norm. Ask them, "How could this story be different?"

• Work to create family-building activities, like family projects where each child and adult can contribute in some way, or games where cooperation helps everyone win.

• Provide information to families about supporting positive interactions among siblings. Books, brochures, parent education meetings, and parent support groups can help families learn how to help brothers and sisters get along. Some suggestions follow.

WHAT CAN PARENTS DO WHEN CHILDREN ARGUE?

• Take immediate action if the situation is unsafe to either child.

• Ignore the quarrelling and give attention to the appropriate behavior. Consider your body language as well as not speaking or looking. Sometimes you might even leave the area if the conflict is an attention-seeking behavior.

• Restructure the environment so that conflicts are less likely. Keep most of an older child's toys out of a toddler's reach. Mealtime squabbles and "turf battles" can be the result of power issues. Parents can help by creating mealtime rituals and table manners and by planning household traffic patterns.

• Direct children's behavior: There are three criteria for what to say in constructive directing:

1. The statement focuses on the behavior, not the person.

2. The statement tells children how to succeed rather than fail.

3. The statement expects children to succeed in the future.

• Only offer choices to children that you are willing to accept. This approach respects children's decision-making and offers them a sense of control ("You can decide how to take turns or you can choose something else to do.")

• Encourage children's negotiation: Identify the problem, generate alternative solutions, predict consequences, and make decisions collaboratively. This approach takes more time, but it will save time in the long term. Children need experience in conflict resolution. In *Kids Can Cooperate*, Crary (1984) suggests thinking games for parents to use with their children in addition to these strategies.

Ways to Prevent Destructive Quarreling

In the early chapters of this book, we defined conflict as being either constructive or destructive. As teachers work to keep destructive conflicts from happening, so do families want to avoid destructive sibling conflicts. Here are some parenting tips that have been shared often. There are cultural variations in family expectations of children's behavior and in children's role in the family, but these suggestions can apply in most situations:

• Give each child some special time as an individual each day. This time can be part of the daily routine, but take advantage of moments like bath time, going to the bus stop, etc. Pay attention to being together. You should both enjoy it.

• Recognize children as individuals. Each child has something special. Avoid judgmental comparisons. (Remember the *Superfudge* story. Children will often work to make sure that you see them as someone of value, even in a non-competitive cultural context.)

• Give children the tools to ask for attention constructively. One of these tools is learning to read the signals or social cues of the other person.

- Teach children how to negotiate with others using the negotiating steps we have described.
- Set up the play and living spaces to reduce destructive conflicts (but not all conflicts). Providing space and activities for playing together give children a chance to practice working things out. Children also need a place where they can sometimes be alone.
- Communicate to children your positive expectation that they care for one another as you care for each of them and that they will be able to resolve their conflicts.

FAMILIES AND SCHOOLS WORKING TOGETHER FOR CHILDREN'S CONFLICT RESOLUTION

Importance of the Home/School Connection in Children's Conflicts

"The way schools care about their children is reflected in the way schools care about the children's families" (Epstein, 1995, p. 701). We now turn our attention to how families and schools can work together to support children's conflict resolution. This section includes notes on general family collaboration and on specific ways to work together on the issue of children's conflicts.

The importance of strong home/school connections is unquestioned. A top concern among practitioners is family involvement. According to the National Educational Goals (U.S. Department of Education, 1994) report, relationships between family and school contribute to children's social, emotional, and academic growth. Reasons for family involvement include increased academic achievement, creating effective schools, improving attendance and graduation rates, and fewer remedial placements and special education referrals. This involvement is one foundation of Head Start and other comprehensive and full-service school models. *Strong Families, Strong Schools: Building Community Partnerships for Learning* (Ballen & Molles, 1994) offers clear rationale and solid research support for school/family/ community partnerships.

There are equally compelling reasons for collaboration in the area of conflict resolution. Conflicts are something that children learn about naturally in all contexts of their lives. Children learn at both home and school, and they learn powerful messages if there is consistency and continuity in models and messages. It is important to connect children's learning in both contexts in a meaningful way. Adults are also powerful in the way they deal with potential family/school conflict.

What Is True Home/School Collaboration?

Authentic home/school collaboration means that home and school work together as partners to support children's learning and development. This collaboration requires active, two-way communication and a sense of mutuality: both family and teacher are experts about the child in different and complementary ways. The whole child should be seen not only in terms of all domains of development, but also in terms of all contexts and roles. Early Childhood professionals use the word "children" instead of "students," "to reflect the focus on all aspects of development and learning, and to remind us that children have identities outside of their class-room roles" (NAEYC, 2001).

"Effective collaboration is based on the ongoing participation of two or more individuals who are committed to working together to achieve common goals" (Walther-Thomas et al., 2000, p. 5). Such collaboration is voluntary and is based on equality of status, mutual respect for the contributions of all, and a willingness to share information (Walther-Thomas et al., 2000). True home/school collaboration meets the needs of both partners, is appropriate for all families, and works to find common ground and mutual respect.

Ways to Develop Home/School Collaboration

General Guidelines for Family Involvement

Meaningful family involvement is the basis for working together on all issues, including issues related to conflict and conflict resolution. The first step in creating this involvement is to establish authentic home/school communication. Communication is continuous and ongoing. It flows in both directions and is mutually understood. Teachers must maintain continuous home/school communication, both oral and written, formal and informal. They begin communication at the

Effective collaboration requires authentic communication between individuals working together toward shared goals.

beginning of the school year, establishing a positive relationship before it is time for report cards or reports of problems. Home/school communication is two-way. Teachers need to keep families informed about children's progress and school activities and procedures, but equally important is the information that families provide to teachers about their children. Communication must be accessible and understood, and must be presented in different ways to reach all families (written notices, phone calls, home visits, e-mail, and gatherings at school).

How are families involved? Teachers must realize that all families will not be involved in the same way, and should use a variety of approaches to include all families. They will consider each family's situation and needs and offer meaningful support for families in their involvement. Sharon Lynn Kagan (Ready at Five Conference, Baltimore, MD, December, 2000) describes an institutional view of the 1950s model of parent involvement with families of 2002: Family involvement is now more than bake sales and PTA meetings.

Institutional assumptions about what it means to be a parent who cares about children's education have generated expectations about time and resources that many families lack. Teachers and school administrators should ask, "What do our families look like? What do our families need?" What teachers and schools can do includes: sharing good news, not just bad; finding out what parents can do effectively as volunteers in the school, and what they can do to support children's learning; offering services that families need in the school; and including parents as decision-makers in what happens in schools. Families can provide input in a number of forums and are listened to. In a Kentucky school where this type of involvement takes place, "'parents are equal to teachers and the principal' in the decision-making process" (ASCD, 1998, p. 1).

Epstein's (1995) classic model of involvement gives us a framework for finding involvement that matches the needs and abilities of a variety of families, and it offers a way for families to grow in their involvement and power as parents and advocates for children, schools, and families.

QUESTIONS FOR REFLECTION

Consider this self-assessment attitude check: Do you see families as sources of strength, help, and partnership, or in need of external help? Are they powerless, not competent or inexpert, or perhaps even uncaring or dysfunctional? Do you see families as children's "first teachers," or do you see families as a barrier to your teaching goals? What criteria do you look for in family involvement? What are your assumptions about what that involvement should be? One parent, a university professor, admits that she rarely is able to attend parent meetings at her child's school and could not be there on conference day. She asks, "Does that mean that I am an uninvolved parent? I'm sure the teacher thinks so."

Let's consider families of children with special needs, delays, and disabilities. Teachers need to be advocates for families in IEP meetings to facilitate collabora-

---

EPSTEIN'S FRAMEWORK FOR FAMILY INVOLVEMENT

1. Parenting: Basic parent education about children's development and learning and support for families at home.
2. Communicating: Effective two-way communication about the school or center program and children's progress.
3. Volunteering: Multiple ways for families to help in the school or center.
4. Learning at home: Ways for families to help children in their learning.
5. Decision-making: Involving families in school governance.
6. Collaborating with the community: Community help for families and partnerships for children, families; and schools, providing services to support the family (first aid, literacy, finance).

---

tion with related service providers (Walther-Thomas et al., 2002). Family involvement is mandated by PL94–142, IDEA, and IEP and IFSP regulations. What is important is to make the involvement meaningful. What are families of children with special needs facing day-to-day? Understanding the family's experiences and avoiding assumptions about what should be done are critical in supporting children and families, especially where there are special needs or disabilities.

Continuity Between Home and School in Conflict Resolution

Continuity between home and school means that children are receiving consistent messages. This consistency is particularly important in conflict resolution. Many teachers have experienced conflicting home and school rules and have responded with a statement of fact: "Those may be the rules for you at home, but these are the rules that we use at school." How much more effective and meaningful would it be if the rules were the same? Children can rightly question why there are differences. In true collaboration, families and teachers share what works at home and at school. What can we do that is consistent, and what are the underlying reasons for what we do?

Another area for teachers to consider involves parenting style and teaching style. How do parenting styles match the classroom teaching style? Is this a source of conflict and misunderstanding?

TEACHERS TALK

One teacher who works for this continuity asks children to have a consistent framework for the decisions that they make with their peers. Her question also communicates and models respect for family rules.

Teacher to child: "Would you say (or do) that if your mom/dad were standing here right now?"

Conditions for effective continuity and strategies include a school environment that supports the home language. Teachers demonstrate responsiveness to language and communication styles. First needed is an awareness of the differences in communication and learning between home and school. Shirley Brice Heath (1983, 1999) describes common disconnects in communication style between home and school. Other language differences may even lead to misunderstandings and misperceptions as families and teachers talk. There may be differences in what is considered polite or impolite forms of address, or aspects of conversational style such as turn-taking, pacing, and interrupting (Lynch & Hanson, 1998; Tannen, 1990).

NAEYC publications and position statements emphasize continuity of care, respect for family culture and home language, and collaboration with families, communities, and other professionals. The *Position Statements on Linguistic and Cultural Diversity* call for this kind of collaboration and stress the developmental value of continuity (NAEYC, 1995).

Knowing the community is another condition of effective continuity. Not all teachers live in the community where they teach, but children attending neighborhood schools and centers do. It is important for teachers to know what is happening, know the landmarks, and make connections to the daily lives of children and families. (If you ask children to go to the library, have you been there yourself? Is there one nearby? Where do families shop for food? What transportation is available for families? How do children experience the natural world in their community?)

Understanding the Role of Family and Community Culture

The role of family and community culture is important in creating the collaboration and continuity we have been discussing. Specific guidelines and key points include the following:

- Provide children with continuity between home and school by respecting and welcoming their home culture and language.
- Learn about and respect each family's cultural and communicative norms. Does the family value compliance rather than collaboration? Responsiveness to language and communication styles helps us avoid conflicts with families and allows us to understand diverse conflict management styles.
- Knowing and examining your own assumptions is a first step in recognizing and valuing the culture of each family. One teacher practices a role-reversal mentally: What are these parents experiencing? What would I do if …? (Are you picturing your own "ideal" parenting?)
- Do all families share the same approach to child rearing? Valuable insights are found in cross-cultural child rearing.
- Each family thrives within a cultural community and creates its own culture within a community. Responsive teachers will not rely on a list of "Characteristics of Asian-American Families" (Lynch & Hanson, 1998). Avoiding cultured generalizations, they will see each family as unique.

An example: According to one Hispanic mother in Chicago to be *bien educado*, or well-educated, a child must know how to act, to be well-behaved and respectful. She did not use the words to be well-educated in the sense of academic learning (Carger, 1997). Without understanding that value, a teacher would mistakenly assume that the family is not concerned about their child's education because they are not spending time on literacy and numeracy skills at home.

TEACHERS TALK: WORKING WITH FAMILIES, CONTINUITY AND DISCONTINUITY BETWEEN SCHOOL AND COMMUNITY

In this example, the culture of the community where Tomas lives is not the same as the culture of the school. The teacher's story:

"Tomas' mom told me that she is concerned about what will happen when he goes to kindergarten at the neighborhood school in the fall. Here he is used to using words when there is a conflict. Next year, the neighborhood boys will expect him to fight. He looks like them and they will expect him to act like them."

Identifying and Overcoming Barriers to Partnerships/Connections/Communication

A school or center where families are involved in authentic collaboration and partnership is one that is accessible. We can understand barriers to family involvement in terms of types of inaccessibility. When we learn what is causing the inaccessibility, we can work toward making our schools and centers accessible.

Social and psychological inaccessibility may result from a family's feelings of intimidation and a lack of confidence. Those with little or no formal education, education in other countries, or unhappy memories of their own school experiences may be reluctant to become involved. Other barriers are status issues and perceived inequality. Families may not feel comfortable or welcome among teachers and other families who differ from them in income, language, color, culture, or ethnicity. To create accessibility, teachers must work to make all families welcome. Sharing family stories (telling yours and listening to theirs) helps build bridges. Attending to spoken language and body language, using active listening, and conveying honesty all contribute to a sense of safety and respect. Educational jargon not only can be a barrier to communication, but can create a status gap. Parents should be equal in the decision-making process for children. Teachers can greet and introduce families to each other, thus creating good will, familiarity, and common goals among families.

Communication and language inaccessibility may come from barriers of language or dialect. Informed and two-way communication is vital. To confront these barriers, teachers and schools may use translation services, have interpreters for conferences, and offer workshops and classes in the family's home language. Cultural understanding can be developed through home/school liaisons. In an example of a systematic approach to accessible communication, one school partnered with a local radio station to provide school announcements and information in the Navajo language (U.S. Department of Education, 2001).

Physical inaccessibility involves basic issues of time, place, and transportation. Conferences, meetings, and workshops are often held when families cannot be there because of work schedules or family caretaking responsibilities. Scheduling at different times of the day and days of the week, providing child care or elder care, providing meals, offering transportation, or meeting at an alternative site such as a library may make activities more accessible. Schools and systems may encourage businesses to give employees at all levels time off, without loss of income, to attend conferences and school functions.

Institutional accessibility may need to be addressed by school-wide or center-wide efforts. Training and information can be provided for families and school staff. Restructuring of school policies may be needed to bring families into the decision-making process at the school level. Are there policies in place that marginalize some families, such as required forms or information available only in English? Schools and centers may need to seek external support for funding and resources for partnership efforts (Fuller & Olsen, 1998; USDE, 2001).

Common Ground in Approaches to Conflict Resolution

Inevitably, there will be issues that create conflict between school and family. The steps for resolving conflicts that we have described for children are the same as those when teachers and families do not agree. Here are some ways to find common ground:

• Establish a team approach based on mutual respect. Work toward home/ school continuity and a consistency of expectations for children's approach to conflicts.

• Keep families informed of your class or school peace/violence prevention programs. Ask for their input and ideas. Develop a shared language that children can use at school and at home to defuse or resolve conflicts with peers and siblings.

• When confronting specific issues about violent behavior in the classroom, discuss the behavior, not the person. Work on alternatives to violence for families. (Note: Be clear about your responsibility to protect children from child abuse.)

• Listen openly to all points of view to hear the rationale for each person's position. Work backward in each party's thinking to find a common understanding or goal. All will agree that we want what is best for children. The next step is defining what we mean by "what is best for children." Perhaps our ideas of "best" are different. Why? How can we create consensus?

• Support family integrity and maintain the wholeness and sense of identity of the family.

Practical Points for Developing Home/School Communication

- Reach every family at the beginning of the year and find out how and when to communicate. Create a sense of welcome and belonging, and ask for family input from the beginning.
- In the school or center, have signs in many languages (welcome, library, office, exit). Use translation services for what is sent home. Provide interpreters at meetings for speakers of different languages and the deaf.
- At conference time, ensure communication and comfort. Conferences are about "being on the same page" and offer a valuable opportunity for meaningful communication. There are many excellent resources on effective conferences found in books, articles, professional organization web sites and at workshops.
- Continue to build cultural continuity between home and school by providing workshops for families on meaningful topics, and invite families to share their experiences and cultures in the school or center.
- Consider how families in the school or center may benefit from different types of family involvement, as in Epstein's model.

FAMILIES, SCHOOLS, AND THE COMMUNITY: CREATING SAFE AND CARING PLACES FOR CHILDREN

Communities Where Children Live

The children we work with in early childhood settings live in a variety of urban, rural, and suburban communities. We have noted that the overlapping circles of family and school both exist inside the community circle. The communities in which children and families live form the next circle of the sphere of influence. As the teacher in Chapter 1 remarked, "Every day on my way to school, I see what my children see." Teachers, whether or not they live close by, are aware of the community in which children live. In developing an environment that supports conflict resolution, families and schools work together in the community for conflict resolution, peace, and violence prevention.

Adults as Models in the Community

Other adults in the community, in addition to family and teachers, populate children's worlds. As individuals, adults in the community are models for children in their interactions with others and add to children's growing construction of social understanding and dealing with conflicts. Adults can also model caring and group decision-making. They can provide both positive and negative models. Adult models are in sports clubs, places of worship, scouts, recreation and community centers, libraries, and other places. Police officers and firefighters work actively to offer positive models for children. The familiar saying "It takes a village to raise a child" is a powerful reminder of the importance of home, school, and community commitment and collaboration on behalf of children.

Individual adults have an opportunity to offer models to children in amicable resolution of disputes in the community or neighborhood. For example, neighbors may need to agree on where to build a fence or about sharing parking spaces on the street and in parking lots. Collectively, adults model conflict resolution and decision-making through involvement in civic groups and participation in the political system by voting. Children do not need to understand specific issues being voted on or the details of the electoral system, but they can understand the democratic principle of making a decision together in a peaceful, responsible, and informed way.

Teachers can find examples in the child's world of community caring and collaboration and point them out to children. Just as adults need to notice the positives in children's interactions, children need to notice the positives in the adult world as well. There are the everyday small kindnesses and organized efforts in response to others in need, such as adding coins to a Salvation Army kettle, holding a door for someone whose arms are full, or giving a seat to someone on the subway.

SUGGESTED FAMILY ACTIVITY FOR COMMUNITY CARING

Keep a list or log of all the kind, caring, and helpful things that you see each day in the community. Be open to discovering kindness and peaceful actions by others.

Community Partnerships That Support Children's Conflict Resolution

Businesses in the community may join families, schools, and civic groups to work for violence prevention and peace, and for issues such as literacy, health, a clean environment, and safety. What business partnerships can offer, in many cases, are funding, materials, meeting spaces, and personnel to help community initiatives take place (U.S. Department of Education, 2001). For example, "adopt a highway" groups take responsibility for keeping a section of road clear of litter, helping the environment and keeping the community clean and pleasant to be in.

Community collaborations have developed in a wide variety of ways. For example, the New York City Board of Education joined with a group called Educators for Social Responsibility to bring the Resolving Conflict Creatively Program (RCCP) into schools throughout the city. Themes include peace and conflict, assertive mediation, and diversity. The program involves both teachers and families (Lantieri & Patti, 1996). In Italy, the city of Reggio Emilia has made a commitment to young children since the end of World War II, and created its municipal centers and schools for infants and preschoolers. (This compelling story is told in the book, *Brick by Brick*, Barazzoni, 2000). In Baltimore, Maryland, Ready at Five, a partnership of business leaders, is working with schools, libraries, Early Childhood organizations, and service agencies state-wide to provide resources to support children and families. Throughout the United States, communities have adopted programs such as Character Counts (to be described in Chapter 12).

Ways to Create and Sustain Community Collaboration

Creating community collaboration requires a mutually identified purpose or goal, basic advocacy skills, the ability to identify appropriate and meaningful ways for each party in the collaboration to contribute, and the same mutual respect and communication as is needed with home/school collaboration.

To sustain partnerships, successful collaborations among families, schools, and communities are guided by a number of factors (USDE, 2001). There is not a "one size fits all" approach to collaboration. Each one is developed in a way appropriate to the local situation. Preparation, training, and staff development are needed to support the partnership. Communication among all partners is vital. Collaborators should be flexible and open to many different approaches and viewpoints. External resources may be needed to sustain the collaboration over time. Patience is key: "Change takes time." Assessing the project on a regular basis informs the group about what works and what could be changed, and may offer a cause for celebrating and sharing the partnership's accomplishments.

Community Response in Troubling Times

Some collaborations arise from a particular need or time of crisis. Communities are quick to ask, "What can we do?" Ironically, it is often in such times that we see the most widespread mutual help and collaboration. (Further discussion in Chapter 1.) Can we apply what we learn from our efforts in times of crisis to what we can do day-to-day?

What Teachers Can Do: Practical Points for Community Partnerships

In addition to other strategies discussed in this chapter, teachers can do the following:

• Encourage connection with positive adult models in the community. Caring leaders work with children in churches, sports teams, scout groups, and other community activities.

• Support your school in providing space in your school building for these activities, if possible.

- Develop partnerships with community businesses. Volunteers from local businesses have made regular visits to schools to work with student partners as tutors and reading buddies.
- Provide important information and resources about conflict resolution and peace-building.
- Act as a point of contact for community partnerships.

We will look further at program models that include community partnerships in Chapter 12, and at advocacy strategies in Chapter 13.

RESOURCES FOR FAMILIES

Recommended for the Family Bookshelf

Brazelton, T. B., Greenspan, S. I., & Sparrow, J. (2001). *Touchpoints three to six: Your child's emotional and behavioral development.* Cambridge, MA: Perseus Publishing.

Brazelton, T. B., Sparrow, J. A., & Sparrow, J. D. (2001). *The irreducible needs of children: What every child must have to grow, learn, and flourish.* Cambridge, MA: Perseus Publishing.

Carlsson-Paige, N., & Levin, D. (1990). *Who's calling the shots? How to respond effectively to children's fascination with war play and war toys.* Philadelphia: New Society Publishers.

Dreikurs, R., & Cassell, P. (1973). *Discipline without tears* (2nd ed.). New York: Dutton/Plume.

Dreikurs, R., & Zuckerman, V. S. (1991). *Children the challenge.* New York: Dutton/Plume.

Elkind, D. (1987). *Miseducation: Preschoolers at risk.* New York: Alfred A Knopf.

Elkind, D. (1998). *Reinventing childhood: Raising and educating children in a changing world.* Rosemont, NJ: Modern Learning Press.

Elkind, D. (2001). *The hurried child: Growing up too fast, too soon* (3rd ed.). Cambridge, MA: Perseus Publishing.

Greenspan, S., & Salmon, J. (1991). *Challenging child: Understanding, raising, and enjoying the five "difficult" types of children.* Cambridge, MA: Perseus Publishing.

Levin, D. (1998). *Remote control childhood: Combating hazards of media culture.* Washington, DC: National Association for the Education of Young Children.

Organizations With Resources for Families

National Association for the Education of Young Children (NAEYC)
  Journal: *Young Children*
  Web site: *www.naeyc.org*
Association for Childhood Education International (ACEI)
  Journal: *Childhood Education*
  Web site: *www.acei.org*

Council for Exceptional Children/Division of Early Childhood (CED/DEC)
 Journal: *Exceptional Children*
 Web site for the Council for Exception Children (CEC): *http://www.cec.sped.org/*
 Web site for the Division for Early Childhood (DEC): *http://www.dec-sped.org/*.

Web Resources to Share With Families

Be sure to use information from creditable sources or professional organizations.

TRUCE: Teachers Resisting Unhealthy Children's Entertainment (*http://www .truceteachers.org/*)
 Includes action guides on toy selection and media violence and flyers about current concerns, such as *Guidelines for Helping Children During the War.*

Ask ERIC (*http://www.askeric.org/*)
 At this site, network information specialists have compiled over 3,000 resources on a variety of educational issues. This collection includes Internet sites, educational organizations, and electronic discussion groups. Through this site, you can even e-mail your own question to the information specialists.

ERIC Digests (*http://www.ed.gov/databases/ERIC_Digests/index/*)
 One sheet each, these digests offer a summary of issues and research on a particular topic. At this URL, you can search for digests on a topic of interest.
 Here are some examples:

- **Aggression and Cooperation: Helping Young Children Develop Constructive Strategies**
 http://www.ed.gov/databases/ERIC_Digests/ed351147.html
- **Bullying in Schools**
 http://www.ed.gov/databases/ERIC_Digests/ed407154.html
- **Young Children's Social Development: A Checklist**
 http://www.ed.gov/databases/ERIC_Digests/ed356100.html
- **Youth Aggression and Violence: Risk, Resilience, and Prevention**
 http://www.ed.gov/databases/ERIC_Digests/ed449632.html

Other Resources

Family Communication, Inc. Mr. Rogers Neighborhood (web site) includes anger management, self-control, prejudice prevention, and the Safe Havens Project described in Chapter 1.

Faber, A., & Mazlish. E. (1998). *Keeping peace at home: Parenting skills that work.* [Parent and child video]. Pleasantville, NY: Sunburst Communications. Available at *www.sunburst.com.*

Janke, R. A., & Peterson, J. P. (1995). *Peacemaker's A, B, Cs for young children: A guide for teaching conflict resolution with a peace table.* (16542 Orwell Rd. North, Marine on St. Croix, MN 55047).

Letts, N. (1997). *Creating a caring classroom: Hundreds of practical ways to make it happen.* New York: Scholastic Press. (Includes chapter for parents.)

Ages & Stages Questionnaires: Social-Emotional (ASQ:SE) subtitled *A Parent-Completed, Child-Monitoring System for Social-Emotional Behaviors,* by Jane Squires, Ph.D., Diane Bricker, Ph.D., & Elizabeth Twombly, M.S., with assistance from Suzanne Yockelson, Maura Schoen Davis, & Younghee Kim. This assessment tool is a user-friendly way for parents to observe and understand their children's social and emotional behavior.

>>>

SUMMARY

Children's conflicts in the classroom are not isolated from the rest of their world. We know, as Early Childhood teachers, that families are children's "first teachers" and are vital partners in our work with young children. In this chapter, we have followed children from the classroom into the family and neighborhood in order to learn about the other conflict experiences they are learning from. We have provided information to share with families who will ask us for guidance in sibling relationships at home. Finally, we have explored ways to develop authentic collaborations with families and with communities as well, in our goal of supporting young children's conflict resolution and peacemaking.

>>>

SUPPLEMENTARY MATERIALS FOR CHAPTER 11

Research Focus/Teacher Research

Are schools and early childhood centers meeting the needs of poor urban families? Have schools and teachers marginalized some families? Find out the demographics of your community and consider the family involvement expectations of your school. Do they seem to match? Arrange for some interviews of teachers and families to ask what they feel involvement means. Background reading includes the following:

Delpit, L. (1995). *Other people's children: Cultural conflict in the classroom.* New York: The New Press.

Fadiman, A. (1998). *The spirit catches you and you fall down: A Hmong child, her American doctors, and the collision of two cultures.* New York: Farrar, Straus and Giroux.

Heath, S. B. (1983). *Ways with words: Language, life and work in communities and classrooms.* New York: Cambridge University Press.

Kozol, J. (1995). *Amazing grace: The lives of children and the conscience of a nation.* New York: Crown Publishers.

Kozol, J. (2000) *Ordinary Resurrections: Children in the years of hope.* New York: Crown Publishers.

>>>

APPLICATION EXERCISES

1. Consider your own experiences. Do you have a "favorite sibling story," positive or negative? How did you feel, and what did your parents do? Why do you think that you remember this particular episode?

2. Brainstorm sibling issues, strategies, and outcomes. What does this suggest about the nature of sibling conflict that may or may not be similar to peer conflict (friend and non-friend)?

3. Develop a resource list of books for families. Try these to start with:

   Dreikurs, R. (1990/1964). *Children: The challenge.* New York: Plume.

   Faber, A., & Mazlish. E. (1995). *How to talk so kids can learn at home and at school.* New York: Rawson Associates.

   Faber, A., & Mazlish, E. (1998). *Siblings without rivalry: How to help your children live together so you can live too* (10th ed.). New York: Avon Books.

>>>

THINKING ABOUT ALL CHILDREN

What do families feel is important in preschool? Do families have the same goals as those of teachers? Resources for discussing these issues of cultural continuity and cross-cultural child rearing can be found in *Zero to Three* (Nugent, 1994) and Lynch and Hanson (1998). *Preschool in Three Cultures* (Tobin et al, 1989) includes a survey of teachers and families about what they believed was important for children and teachers in preschool. You may have an opportunity to ask families and teachers, and to compare the responses. If they are different, can you suggest why and how the results will guide you in your teaching? How can kindergarten and primary teachers learn from this kind of survey?

12

Program Models for Conflict Resolution

"I see children trying to use the techniques when conflict arises."
"I don't see the children using the things that they have learned in the program. They can tell me what they should do, but do not do it in a real situation."

Objectives for Chapter 12: Chapter 12 examines the growing number and diversity of programs for schools and classrooms that are being developed in response to concerns about widespread violence and destructive conflict in schools and communities. We will explore ways to evaluate programs and curriculum models based on what we know about children's development and their approach to conflicts, and we will consider ways to select, adapt, and create models in our own settings.

Chapter 12 Outline

PROGRAM EVALUATION FORM

Scenario: The principal or the center's governing board announces that everyone will begin using "The Brand New Character Education Model!" How can you object to such an obviously important project? At the same time, you are asking yourself, "Will this be appropriate for my children and my classroom?"

In this chapter, we will explore different types of conflict resolution programs and discuss criteria that we can use to evaluate them. Practitioners may hesitate to seem critical of the worthwhile objectives of these programs. We agree with the idea of learning conflict resolution skills, just as we agree that children should learn reading and math. In the same way that we evaluate a new reading or math curriculum, we can also evaluate program models for conflict resolution, character education, and peacemaking.

TYPES OF PROGRAMS

There are more and more programs for schools and classrooms that are designed to help children learn and grow as strong and peaceful individuals in a world of violence. These programs vary greatly and represent a continuum based on their primary focus, with *Violence Prevention* at one end and *Peace Education* at the other. The continuum of the types of models that we will discuss in this chapter is shown in Figure 12-1.

Define and Describe Program Models

Program models can be defined according to their primary themes, purposes, and desired outcomes for children, what we can call *focus* and *function*. Program models can be further described by the *form* that they take. Many models share the same outcomes, goals, and strategies, but have different underlying assumptions about children and the world. We will define these types according to their use in settings with young children, although many models have been designed for older children. In this discussion, we will not look at general models of discipline and classroom management. These models may include conflict resolution components, but their primary purpose is generally to develop child behaviors for classroom teaching and learning rather than life-long conflict resolution and peace-building.

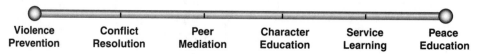

| Violence Prevention | Conflict Resolution | Peer Mediation | Character Education | Service Learning | Peace Education |

Figure 12–1
Peace education to violence prevention: A spectrum of program models.

Focus, Functions, and Forms

Focus is the primary purpose or motivation for creating the program. This *focus* can be understood as a response to a perceived need. For instance, a program may be described as a response to "children's aggressive behavior in the classroom," or as "a need for building peace through understanding of other cultures." Looking at the words we use to label these models also gives us a hint: *resolution, mediation,* and *prevention* are words that describe processes or actions; *education* and *learning* are related to change and growth.

Function encompasses the scope of the program: the intended age range of children, the location (classroom, school, community, in the United States and abroad), and ownership (teachers, families, administrators). *Function* includes the expected outcomes: What is the program supposed to do for children, classroom, school, community, and society? One element of *function* is the change process: Do you need to name and extinguish the negative in order to replace it with the positive?

Form: What does the program look like? Does it take the *form* of an extra in-class "special" by the teacher or a visit from a guidance counselor, or is it an integrated part of the ongoing curriculum and routine of the classroom? *Form* is the "what, who, where, when, how" of the model. Elements of *form* include the approaches and strategies for teaching and learning (scripted lessons, class meetings, steps to follow in peer interaction, words to use, music, songs, props, role-play, video, pictures, stories, games, projects, family connections.)

Categories of Models

Our models include *conflict resolution, peer mediation, violence prevention, character education, peace education,* and *service learning.* Some programs label themselves as one model or another, and the labels may be more or less arbitrary. There is often a great deal of overlap, hybrid, and carry-over across the types we have identified. There is also nesting, with multiple model types embedded in the more comprehensive programs. We must remember that there are many effective classrooms where the approach is not a "program model" but a day-to-day way of life in a caring classroom, as described in Chapter 7. One such example is the Responsive Classroom (Charney, 2002; Horsch et al., 2002).

Conflict Resolution

These programs are designed to give children an understanding of peer conflicts and strategies for resolution. They may be narrowly focused and only teach children steps of what to do when conflicts occur, or they may be broader to include the whole classroom or become a school-wide theme.

Focus: The conflict event is the focus. The assumption is that conflicts will happen and that these tools will enable children to resolve things without adult help. The

Conflict resolution curriculum models often include whole class learning time and special books and other materials.

program may be targeted or part of a comprehensive program. The interactive focus is two children in conflict.

Function: Children will be able to resolve conflicts without adult direction by using words, steps, and/or props as they have learned in the program.

Form: Children learn steps to follow and words to use. There may be props or special places for conflict resolution. Teaching often takes place in a group setting, with posters and environmental cues, and often is presented by a guidance counselor.

Examples: *Peacemaking Skills for Little People.* (A number of programs such as this one describe themselves as conflict resolution, but the focus extends beyond the conflict event.) Many classrooms use a *Peace Table*, even if it is not part of a more extensive conflict resolution program.

Peer Mediation

These programs are related to conflict resolution programs, but the emphasis is on resolution through mediation by peers, often a designated and specially trained child or children. Other children may also learn steps for how to seek mediation or how to take their disputes to a peer mediator.

Focus: The conflict event is the focus. Peer mediation programs have a targeted focus rather than a comprehensive focus. The assumption is that conflicts will happen and that a peer mediator can help children resolve them effectively without adult help. The interactive focus is three children (two children in conflict and one mediator).

Function: The outcome is that children will recognize the need for peaceful alternatives and will turn to a peer mediator for help. The peer mediator takes the place of the adult in guiding the resolution process. One question to ask about a peer mediation program is, "Does it work toward children's unmediated resolution?" In other words, does the mediator eventually step aside?

Form: These models emphasize the steps in the mediation process and may include a formula for words to use, a contract for agreement, a place to go to for mediation, or a way to identify the children designated as mediators. The form includes selection and training of mediators, and training for disputants in the process. The model may be implemented by a guidance counselor or classroom teacher, and is most frequently used in elementary schools, but is also used in preschool settings.

Examples: *Fussbusters, Resolving Conflict Creatively Program (RCCP).*

Violence Prevention

These programs are a response to violence in the community and in society, and they address school violence as a precursor to later violence. Concerns include school safety and violence.

Focus: The focus is on conflict events, and also on a more generalized climate of alternatives to violence. The assumptions are that all children are exposed to violence and, to varying degrees, are learning violent responses; that conflict will lead to violence; and that violence is learned and can be unlearned. The programs teach alternative responses and address anger management and self-control in defusing and de-escalating conflict. The focus is on the individual child, the self, and internal response.

Function: Children learn alternatives to violent responses, and ways to avoid conflict and withdraw from confrontation.
Form: In addition to specific conflict resolution steps, children develop internal control strategies: calming, anger management, self-regulation, understanding, and expressing feelings. Role-play and practicing responses to situations are common teaching strategies and are often taught by a guidance counselor.

Examples: *No Put Downs, Second Step, I Can Problem Solve (ICPS). Resolving Conflict Creatively Program (RCCP)* identifies itself as a violence prevention program, but is comprehensive and includes conflict resolution, cultural understanding, and peacemaking.

Character Education

These programs are intended to be comprehensive, and the broad goal is to develop multiple aspects of what is defined by the specific program as "character." A major contributor to the character education movement in the 1990s, Thomas Lickona (1991), defines character as "knowing the good." The "good" is defined by families and schools in many different ways, but Lickona feels that universal components are respect and responsibility, which come from moral knowing, moral feeling, and moral action. Character education is "the intentional, proactive effort to develop good character" (Lickona, 1997, p. 46). Lickona's model consists of nine classroom strategies and three school-wide strategies. The Six Pillars of Character used in the Character Counts Coalition are respect, responsibility, trustworthiness, caring, fairness, and citizenship (ASCD, 1997; Pastor, 2002).

Focus: Universal values guide children to do what is right and good. The model assumes these universals are a necessary context for conflict resolution, violence prevention, and peacemaking. These programs are comprehensive and not targeted to specific events, but emphasize the learning of a shared language of values. Unlike a focus on interactions between two or three children, these models involve the whole class, school, or community.

Function: The outcome is to have children internalize assorted values or components of character that will guide their behavior and decision-making in any situation.

Form: These comprehensive programs may be based on modules, with a particular value as the school-wide theme of the month. There are usually age/grade-level variations in each theme. In collaboration with others in the school, the classroom teacher usually implements the program. Universals may be defined differently from those at home but are consistent within the school.

Examples: *Character Counts, Discover Understanding of Self and Others (DUSO).*

Peace Education

These programs may have a local or global focus. The objective is to develop greater understanding of others and a motivation for working toward peace. The field of peace education is broad and diverse, and it has a long history in the United States and internationally (Harris, 2002; Reardon, 1988, 2002). Even with locally focused activities, peace education programs look beyond the immediate time and place. Young children can make sense of global conflict, according to Kathy Bickmore (1999), a peace educator and reseacher. Children's ability to negotiate with other children seems to grow with their understanding of conflict between groups.

Focus: Peace education involves understanding, action, collaboration, and over-coming differences that lead to conflict and negative feelings. The focus is not the specific event, although peace education supports children's individual interactions. Cross-cultural understanding and empathy are critical components.

Function: Children, as individuals and as a group, will develop empathy, other-orientation, and the motivation to make changes for peace, beginning with themselves and working with others.

Form: These programs may take many forms and often include collaboration, action projects, and symbolic representations of peace, unity, and understanding, extending beyond the borders of classrooms and schools. Features may include peace words and other communication mechanisms, awareness-building, and advocacy. Projects include peace quilts, peace poles, pen pals, and connecting and learning online. Many peace education programs are locally developed or are shared by a network of peace education advocates worldwide. Usually not published programs, these models are usually implemented by teachers or school teams. Peace education is often integrated into social studies (Bickmore, 1997, 1999).

Examples: *Peace Scholars*, local initiatives such as the Ward School's Global and Peace Education, participation in Peace Week projects, peace education integrated into social studies.

Service Learning

This action-oriented program model may be one project, or it may be an encom-passing commitment to service that is integrated throughout the school or center. Service learning refocuses existing academic learning in school to something that will benefit others. It provides children an opportunity to "learn by doing" and develop social, moral, and ethical understanding by doing (Roberts, 2002).

Focus: These models involve project-based learning where the project provides service to others. The assumption is that, through action, children will internalize an ethic of caring, helping, other-awareness, problem-solving, and fairness, all of which contribute to conflict resolution. Children will see the needs of others and develop perspective-taking and empathy.

Function: Children will develop action-oriented advocacy as a way of thinking. They will work as a group for change. As an additional outcome, children will internalize many of the skills and dispositions needed for day-to-day conflict res-olution and peacemaking.

Form: This model is designed to be part of an integrated, project-based curriculum. Project goals may be to solve a problem or to meet the needs of others. Such as what to do about bullies on the bus (Roberts), stray dogs in the neighborhood, or litter in the local park? Goals may be to provide access for those with disabilities, or to help provide for the hungry and homeless. Usually not a published program, service learning is implemented by teachers or school teams.

Examples: Community Service Learning. In Kids Taking Action, Roberts, (2002) describes several examples of community service learning. In one project, children worked with an organization called Kids Feeding Kids and the Empty Bowls, a national anti-hunger effort.

Program Model Example in Practice: Peacemaking Skills for Little People

This program uses shared language and rules to help children remember prosocial actions and avoid destructive conflicts. Children have learned I Care Rules through group lessons featuring the I Care Cat puppet. Teachers and children incorporate these rules and words into the everyday life of the classroom.

I Care Rules (on classroom poster):

1. We listen to each other.

2. Hands are for helping, not hurting.

3. We use I Care language.

4. We care about each other's feelings.

5. We are responsible for what we say and do.

Concerns About Program Models

Counterpoint: A Prepackaged Curriculum?

The Children's Creative Response to Conflict (CCRC) program is designed to help children and teachers create an environment for caring and cooperation that supports non-violent responses to conflict. The CCRC book, *The Friendly Classroom for a Small Planet* (Prutzman et al., 1988), includes background materials, planning strategies, games, songs, and activities. In the preface to the book, the authors describe their reluctance to "turn the CCRC program into a standardized curriculum" (1988, p. vii) because of the importance of adapting the material to the needs of each particular class or group of children. This approach may take time and energy, but the result will be "a new sense of community" and learning that is aligned with existing classroom objectives.

TEACHER STORY: USING I CARE LANGUAGE IN THE CLASSROOM

Janelle has instigated this conflict, interfering with Marcus as he tries to write his name. Marcus is responding by escalating the conflict rather than using I Care language to defuse and resolve it. He retaliates by squeezing Janelle's arm.

Janelle: Marcus, stop!

Teacher: Marcus! Are you using helping hands?

Marcus: She is trying to mess up my name!

Teacher: Are you using helping hands? Do we ever touch people like that?

Marcus: No. (to Janelle) Stop it!

Teacher: Are you using I Care language?

   The teacher's reflection: "Although 'Stop it!' may not be I Care language, at least Marcus is now using a verbal instead of a physical strategy. What is the I Care language for Marcus to use to ask Janelle to leave his paper alone?"

Counterpoint to Character Education

David Elkind (1998) asks, "Is character education an ineffective luxury?" He describes the difficulty of defining "character" and questions the selection and definition of the values, or constructs, that make up "character." A further concern is that character education attempts to solve problems that have originated elsewhere. Elkind also points out that children's meanings of constructs such as honesty may be different from those of adults. Remembering earlier chapters, we can consider our practice in children's meanings of fairness.

Other questions have been raised about character education:

- Alfie Kohn (1997) suggests that there are two kinds of character education: one is a constructivist model, focusing on generalized universals such compassion, and the other one presents a transmission model, with a narrow focus on certain defined "values of the week" and a stance that children need to be "fixed." He asks, "Who selects and defines these values?" and "Are these definitions the same for adults and for young children?"

- Geneva Gay (1997) questions the compatibility of character education and multicultural education. Honesty and truth are key concerns in both of these efforts, but the question persists about the meaning of honesty and truth. In multicultural education, those values include the hard truths of history and the current and persistent reality of racism, as well as the idea of bringing diverse perspectives and experiences to the table. A valid concern seems to be that character education as a general model needs to be defined before it can be understood (Lockwood, 1997). These points suggest that, as we will see in this chapter, teachers should look carefully at program models that are proposed in their schools and centers.

Considering Families

Early childhood professionals should examine these varied programs in terms of what we know about children and families. Questions to consider: What messages do these programs send? How do they portray families? Do character education programs send the message that families are ineffective and even failing in supporting children's social and moral development and that schools must take on that role? Or is there the more positive message that professionals respect families and consider them to be partners and models?

WAYS TO EVALUATE AND SELECT PROGRAM MODELS

Let's return to our chapter's opening scenario. This time, though, you have been asked to select which program model to adopt. As an administrator, teacher, or member of an advisory group, you have been asked to evaluate a program in order to decide whether to adopt it. Your first task is to make a list of your objectives, both short-term and long-term, and compare your list to the stated objective of the program you are evaluating. The following criteria will give you additional questions to ask in your evaluation.

Criteria for Evaluation: What to Look For

Descriptive Items: Is This Designed for Your Situation?

1. Scope of the program: Is it designed for a classroom, school, community, or school district? Which adults in school or at home are involved? Does the program fit with the type of Early Childhood setting that you have?

2. Age of children: What is the age of the intended child "audience" of the program?

3. Major features of the program: Does the overall approach, general goal, and style of the program fit with your goals and classroom style and with the needs of the children, school, and community?

4. Assumptions about children: What assumptions does this program make about children, learning, and the world? This information should be clearly stated in the program's materials or documentation. These assumptions should be consistent with your own understanding.

5. Prior testing and piloting: Has the program been tried out before? Information about pilot testing should be available in the program's documentation or descriptive material.

Practical Aspects: How Will It Work?

1. Cost: This is a basic but important question to ask. The cost of published programs varies tremendously.

2. Practical and useable materials: Materials that are hard to use or inconvenient can become a barrier to implementing the program.

3. Renewable and easily available materials: Does the program include materials that will be used up and will need to be reordered, or does it use everyday materials that are readily available, inexpensive, and easy to find?

4. Easy to learn: Is the program fairly easy to understand and put into place, both for teachers and for children?

5. Training and instructions provided for teachers: Even the "easy to learn" programs should include clearly written instructions and implementation strategies. Mechanisms for training and orientation sessions should be provided as well.

Substantive Concerns: Will It Work Well?

1. Knowledge base: Is the program based on what we know about children from theory, research, and best practices?

2. Consistent philosophy: Are the basis of the program, its goals and objectives, and its implementation approach consistent with your understanding of children and learning?

3. Developmentally appropriate: Does the program reflect age, individual, and cultural appropriateness?

4. Responsiveness to children: Does the program allow you to start where the children are? Is there a pre-assessment component to help you begin in the right place?

5. Integration: Does the program work with your existing curriculum? Can it be integrated throughout all content areas and embedded into the routines of the day?

6. Adaptable: Does the program allow you to make adjustments for the needs and interests of children, for the timetable of the day, and for special events?

7. Multiple learning modes: Does the program offer a variety of ways for children to encounter learning (visual, kinesthetic, and auditory modes, as well as multiple intelligences)?

8. Cultural responsiveness: Does the program respect and address diversity in children's culture and home language?

9. Children of all abilities: Is the program designed for children of all abilities in an inclusive setting?

10. Child-relevant, fun, and meaningful: Will children truly enjoy the program activities?

11. Home/school connections: Does the program connect with families by sharing information, and by drawing on family knowledge, perspectives, and needs? Is the basic view of families a positive one (as mentioned above)?

12. Child-oriented outcome: Does the program move from adult-directed or structured processes to intrinsic, natural, child-controlled resolutions?

13. Transferable learning: Are the processes for conflict resolution and peacemaking context-specific, or are they generalizable, portable skills? For instance, can you make peace on the playground, or only at the Peace Table?

14. Peacemaking for all children: Does the program call for designated children as peer mediators, or are all children seen as peacemakers? Which of these approaches seems better for your setting? Can you rotate the mediation role among children? Will you encourage spontaneous peer mediation?

15. Evaluation: Is there an evaluation component that allows you to determine the effectiveness of the program and make adaptations as needed?

TEACHERS TALK

> "This is a great program, but it's been on a shelf for 2 years. It was just handed to us during the first week of school, and I didn't have time to read it. Once I finally took the time to sit down and read it, I found out that it would really help. I am using some of the ideas now, and they do work. I can see a difference."

TEACHERS TALK

> "This is a really good program, but the problem is that it is supposed to be part of the social studies lesson. In first grade, we team-teach at our school, and I teach reading, so I never get to see what my children are learning in this program. I'd love to reinforce it during the rest of the day, but I don't know what they are doing."

DISCUSSION

"Teacher-proof" package versus teacher autonomy? Some programs are structured so that teachers follow the plan precisely and do not need to develop anything or make decisions on their own. The idea is that there is uniformity and less work for teachers. Teachers who value autonomy in their practice may prefer programs that provide for adaptation and their own decision-making. What do you think?

USING PROGRAM MODELS IN YOUR SETTING

Adapting a Program Model in Your Classroom

As with any new curriculum or materials, knowing your children is the key to using and adapting a program for conflict resolution and peacemaking. Is the program a good match with your practice, your philosophy, your curriculum, and most of all, your children? Is there alignment with what you are already doing that you can build on? As you examine the new program, what seems to be missing, and how can you fill in the gaps?

HOW DO DEVELOPERS AND RESEARCHERS EVALUATE PROGRAM MODELS?

How are programs evaluated? How are results determined and measured? According to Knowles (2001), there has not been a great deal of systematic research on the effectiveness of these programs. It will be helpful to ask how programs have been formally evaluated and to understand the evaluation methods and findings. Are there ways to measure effectiveness? Is measurement the best way to determine effectiveness? How else can it be done? Evaluators have looked at teacher ratings of children's positive social behaviors and emotional control, academic achievement, children's self-report data, and the number of disciplinary actions taken.

To learn more, look for evaluation reports for published programs in documentation materials or online. Another source is the ERIC Digest on *Practitioner Assessment of Conflict Resolution Programs* ED 451277, by Moron Deutsch (2001).

To locate ERIC Digests, try *http://www.ed.gov/databases/ERIC_Digests/index/*.

Teachers have identified common gaps and have suggested what may need to be added or changed. Plan new activities, create alternatives, or find different materials. Here are some suggestions:

- Invent adaptations in order to include children with different abilities, special needs, disabilities, and developmental delays.

- Respond to culture and language. Address sexism and other stereotypes in materials and processes.

- Create examples that relate to children's experiences.

- Add ways to engage many learning and communication styles.

- Develop family connections.

- Look for curriculum connections and build on them.

- Modify steps or vocabulary to be consistent with existing classroom practices and routines.

- Respond to particular events and local needs.

- Work with a guidance counselor to connect the program the rest of the day.

Creating Your Own Program

Is there no conflict resolution program in place in your school? Many Early Childhood programs are not part of large school systems. There are also schools where programs have not been adopted and schools that have not found a program that works. There are a number of basic steps to follow to create your own program: conducting a needs assessment, establishing goals and objectives, collecting input from all stakeholders and even an advisory group, and developing procedures,

WHAT ABOUT TIME?

Is this just "one more thing" to fit into your busy day? Another unit, another lesson? Does it need to be "extra?" Perhaps the adaptation you need is to creat a way to incorporate the learning into activities and experiences already in place. There are opportunities to integrate aspects of the program throughout the day using literature, center, morning meetings, writing prompts and story dictations, pictures in the room, partners, transitions, and grouping. These strategies are described in Chapters 7, 8, and 9.

Creating your own program may include collaborating with children to develop the steps they will use to resolve conflicts.

evaluation, a budget, and a timeline. These items, as well as the scope and alignment with philosophy, the needs of children, and the context of family and community, are things to consider in program development. (There are a number of excellent sources available on program development and evaluation. There are also notes in Chapter 11 about community program development.)

What will make the program work?

1. Ample teacher training
2. Ownership of all stakeholders

3. Integration throughout the day

4. Authenticity and connections to real life

5. Broad base of support including the community

6. Willingness to stay the course over time

If your plan is only for your classroom, you will follow the same steps as for a whole-school plan but on a smaller scale. Decide what your goals are and who else will be involved (another class, the whole school). Learn what ideas are already out there, and examine what you are already doing in your classroom. Then begin to develop your plan. Consider books and online sources that will be helpful. An effective program approach will be consistent, authentic, and ongoing. Concepts will be embedded as a way of doing and thinking, in the implicit/hidden curriculum, and with intentionality in routines, transitions, and grouping.

Three Examples of Program Development

Courtesy and Respect

TEACHERS TALK

"Our school has developed its own program. We decided that if children can use good manners, then other positive behaviors will follow. We are using the title Having Courtesy and Respect in Every Situation. The program acronym, HCARES, is the same as the initials of the school, another way to see ourselves as a school community. All of us, children and adults, use polite words and thoughtful actions. It is making a difference in my classroom in the way children treat each other."

Global and Peace Education

An example of a school-wide program development process is the school-wide initiative at the William B. Ward Elementary School (Grantham-Campbell personal communication, July, 2002). In developing the school's Global and Peace Education program, a site-based committee spent 3 years moving from discussion to a fully developed report to the school district. According to Grantham-Campbell, "We the Ward schooling community are giving serious attention to the challenges of student safety and campus security, but within a framework of mutual respect and global peace. The thematic curriculum focus includes both a local understanding of ourselves, our conflicts, and our community, and a "global" understanding of other continents, cultures, and languages. Our mission in developing this program is to have a schooling community that cares for our planet, shares the bounty of our earth, appreciates many perspectives, and listens to many voices, including the voices of children."

Empathy and Community

Our third example traces the development and implementation of another three-year process, this one in a child care center where the director's leadership and commitment brought about conflict resolution through a peaceful, caring, and compassionate environment, rather than a defined curriculum for conflict resolution. The complete story, shared by the director, is part of the "Case Studies and Stories from the Field" section of Chapter 13.

This is the basic process and outcome: "The first step was training the teachers and assistants to model feelings and to use only positive techniques in dealing with behavior, always focusing attention on the child in need and involving the perpetrator in the follow-up. The next step was implementation, with teachers using caring and empathic language such as, 'I see you are sad. Can we make you feel better?' or 'I feel mad sometimes too. Can I tell you what I do when I am mad?' After a few months, the language and environment completely changed among the children. They were much less violent when solving conflicts, they were more in tune with their emotions, and they worked more effectively as a community. Conflicts are resolved with patience and understanding, with the knowledge that every child is capable of empathy. We just need to guide them in their understanding of it. I often tell my teachers how much our children could teach many adults in society about understanding each other's feelings. How fortunate our children are to be in an environment of understanding and positive conflict resolution!"

Using Elements from Other Sources to Support Your Plan

Teachers can effectively combine approaches that are consistent with their goals and consistent with each other. If you are combining programs, be sure to decide on one set of vocabulary to use and one set of steps or procedures. Some elements to support your conflict resolution and peace-building plans may include the following:

1. Literature-based models can support a number of other models. Examples are *Teaching Conflict Resolution Through Children's Literature (K-2)*, by William Kreidler (1994), and *Peace Scholars*.

2. The social curriculum in Charney's *Habits of Goodness* (1997) refers to "intentional efforts to develop the social and ethical capacities of each individual, and to build respectful, inclusive, and safe community life" (p. 10).

3. Anti-bias education goals (Derman-Sparks, 1997) are clearly consistent with conflict resolution and peacebuilding: nurturing each child's self and group identity, promoting comfortable empathetic interaction with people from diverse backgrounds, fostering critical thinking about bias, and cultivating the child's ability to stand up for self and others in the face of bias.

4. Activities from *The Friendly Classroom for a Small Planet* (Prutzman et al., 1988) can replace competitive and individualistic activities.

Evaluating the Program in Your Practice

How is your program working? Evaluation is an important component of the plans for your new program. Include both *formative evaluation*, checking on what is happening throughout the year to make needed changes as you go, and *summative evaluation*, a final assessment of the whole project, in order to report to others and plan for next year. Develop your own strategy for evaluation based on the specifics of your program. Here is a framework with guiding questions for planning the evaluation:

1. What are your objectives?
2. What have children learned, and what can they do? Find out by:
   a. Observing children, both what can they do alone and with help.
   b. Interviewing children.
   c. Can you count or measure something? (Remember the strategies for observing and interviewing in Chapter 3.)
3. What are your own responses to children and situations? Has your teaching changed through the program and/or through children's changed behaviors?
4. How will you share your reflections with others (teachers, families)?

TEACHER TALK

"The best way to assess whether or not children are utilizing these peaceful strategies is simply to watch how they behave. For example, if there is a lesson involving an argument over a pencil, hopefully we will see children resolve a similar argument in class the way the lesson showed them. We can also assess how successful the program is by how the children react to other stories with similar plots and problems. If they recognize similar issues, as pointed out in the Peace Scholars literature, and connect them to solving conflicts, then most likely the program is successful."

ACTION RESEARCH: CONFLICT RESOLUTION AND PEACEBUILDING IN YOUR CLASSROOM

Develop your plan and use the steps in this chapter (or in another source on action research) to investigate the effectiveness of your plan.

EXAMPLES OF PROGRAM MODELS

A quick search of the Internet will demonstrate the growing number of programs for conflict resolution, violence prevention, character education, peace education, peer mediation, and service learning. The following list offers examples of some programs in use at the time of this writing. Programs are frequently revised and contact information may change. Each program is identified as conflict resolution (CR), character education (CE), violence prevention (VP), peer mediation (PM), or service learning (SL).

1. **Character Counts** is a "nonprofit, nonpartisan, nonsectarian coalition of schools, communities, and nonprofit organizations working to advance character education by teaching the Six Pillars of Character: *trustworthiness*, *respect*, *responsibility*, *fairness*, *caring*, and *citizenship*." This program is comprehensive, and its scope is not limited to schools. Towns and small cities have adopted Character Counts as a community project. Character Counts National Office, Josephson Institute of Ethics, Marina del Rey, CA 90292-6610. Source: *http://www.charactercounts .org*. (CE)

2. **Discover Understanding of Self and Others (DUSO)** is a "developmental guidance program" for kindergarten through third grade is based on the rationale that children's feeling of self-worth is critical to social and school success. The three units are Understanding Self, Understanding Others, and Making Choices. The DUSO approach incorporates listening, discussion, dramatic play, stories, guided fantasies, puppetry, role-play, feeling word activities, career awareness, music, and art. First introduced in 1970, DUSO has met with criticism by certain religious groups for its emphasis on self-esteem and use of guided imagery. American Guidance Service, 4201 Woodland Road, Circle Pines, MN 55014-1796. (CE)

3. **The CARES Model: Building Social Skills and Reducing Problem Behaviors in Early Childhood Classrooms** offers "strategies to reduce problem behaviors while promoting prosocial skills. In the CARES Model, one key strategy used to teach social competence to young children is the use of class meetings. (CR/ CE) Through class meetings, children gain a better understanding of their own feelings and behavior and develop a heightened sensitivity toward the feelings and perspectives of others. Topics include using a safety rule, understanding and expressing emotions, promoting positive social skills, learning a problem-solving process, introducing calming down steps and practicing stress reduction." (CR)

4. **Fussbusters**, a peer mediation program used by some Head Start programs, is in alignment with Head Start's program goals and is based on peer mediation at Peace Tables/rules. Gillespie and Chick (2001) describe their informal research on the positive responses to the program demonstrated by one difficult child. (PM)

5. **High/Scope Problem-Solving Approach to Conflict** targets children's conflicts and provides a six-step mediation process for adults, and specific steps for children in conflict. Training workshops and book: Evans, B. (2002). *You can't come to my birthday party: Conflict resolution with young children*. Ypsilanti, MI: High/Scope Press. (CR)

6. **I Can Problem Solve: Interpersonal Cognitive Problem-Solving Intervention (ICPS)** includes three age/grade levels: Pre-K, Kindergarten/Primary, and Elementary/Intermediate. (VP) The focus of ICPS is helping children find solutions to interpersonal problems with an emphasis on intervention for children at risk for behavioral dysfunctions. Pictures, role-playing, and puppets are used to help children learn problem-solving.

7. **No Putdowns** addresses children's violent responses in a negative encounter. "No Putdowns is a comprehensive, school-based curriculum that can meet your needs for work in violence prevention character development, substance abuse prevention, and life-skill building." The five basic steps are *think about why, stay cool, shield myself, think about a response, build up*. Mailing address: CONTACT Community Services, Syracuse, NY. (VP) Source: *http://www.noputdowns.org*

8. **Peace Education Foundation.** This organization provides a number of programs and publications for preschool, elementary, secondary, and home school that address the dynamics of conflict and promotes peacemaking. See *http://www.peace-ed.org/*. Here are two of the Peace Education Foundation programs:

   • **Peace Scholars Through Literature,** Jim Trelease. This model integrates the theme of peace and conflict resolution into stories already used in classroom. It is teacher-friendly and can be readily differentiated to meet the needs of all learners and adapted to create a family connection. A similar literature-based model is Kriedler's *Teaching Conflict Resolution Through Children's Literature*. (PE/CR)

   • **Peacemaking Skills for Little Kids,** F. Schmidt and A. Friedman. Another program from the Peace Education Foundation, this one offers grade-level specific classroom-tested I Care curricula for Pre-K through 2. "These user-friendly materials incorporate activities that foster school norms of cooperation and problem-solving rather than violence and aggression. Through role-plays, group work, and other interactive techniques, students are taught pro-social skills such as anger management, perspective taking, peer resistance, effective communication, and problem solving." (PE/CR)

9. **Quit It! A Teacher's Guide on Teasing and Bullying for Use with Students in Grades K-3.** This program addresses abusive teasing and bullying behavior. It provides lessons, activities, modules, reading suggestions, and family connections. Educational Equity Concepts, New York. (www.edequity.org) (VP)

10. **Resolving Conflict Creatively Program (RCCP),** K-12. Aggression and violence are learned and can be unlearned. This prevention program stresses conflict resolution and intercultural understanding. Used in an extensive network with 9,000 students in 60 public schools in NYC and in 12 other systems around the U.S. Educators for Social Responsibility: Lantieri, National Center for Children and Poverty. (VP)

11. **Second Step.** A comprehensive program of empathy training and anger management, Second Step: A Violence Prevention Curriculum is a "universal intervention designed to be used with all students in a school." Through use of the Second Step program, students begin to raise their self-esteem rather than their fists. Second Step consists of 20 scripted lessons. The lessons are taught for about 45–50 minutes a day to teach development of empathy, problem-solving skills, and anger-management techniques. Center for Effective Collaborations and Practice, Washington, DC. (VP)

12. **Skillstreaming** "addresses the social skill needs of students who display aggression, immaturity, withdrawal, or other problem behaviors. It is designed to help youngsters develop competence in dealing with interpersonal conflicts, learn

to use self-control, and contribute to a positive classroom atmosphere." There are three levels: Pre-K to grade 1, grades 2–5, and grades 6–12. Developers: A. Goldstein, E. McGinnes. Research Press, Champaign, Illinois. (VP)

13. **Service Learning.** As described in this chapter, service learning is not a specific program model, two Web sites are listed here. Also refer to Kids Taking Action (Roberts, 2002):

> Empty Bowls Projects: *http://www.emptybowls.net/*
> Kids Can Make a Difference: *http://www.kidscanmakeadifference.org/*

SUMMARY

With growing concerns about pervasive violence in schools, communities, and the world, teachers are being asked to address these issues in their classrooms, either on their own or with a mandated curriculum for conflict resolution, violence prevention, or character education. In this chapter, we have discussed types of program models, and ways to evaluate and adapt them for appropriate and effective use in early childhood settings. The most effective program may one that you, as a teacher or as a member of a team in your school or center create yourself.

SUPPLEMENTARY MATERIALS FOR CHAPTER 12

Research Focus

Research on the Fussbusters Program offers a model for evaluating the effectiveness of a program model on a small scale (Horsch et al, 2002). You may want to try an evaluation of a program already in use at your own site or elsewhere, using the approach in the Horsch study or another teacher research or action research model.

APPLICATION EXERCISES

1. Do you think that character education is an "expensive luxury," as Elkind (1998) suggests? What would you say to address his concerns? What characteristics would you like to have in a character education, conflict resolution, or peace education program?

2. Let's create a hypothetical classroom program called A Classroom Builds for Caring. Here are some possible strategies:

- Find caring actions in the classroom and celebrate what you find.
- Help children experience caring.
- Help children understand caring.
- Share ways of caring with others. What else would you consider in developing your program?

>>>

THINKING ABOUT ALL CHILDREN

Considering the types of program models discussed in this chapter, which would fit in an inclusive, culturally responsive classroom? If you are currently at a site where there is a conflict resolution/violence prevention/character education program in place, do you have questions about adaptability, cultural responsiveness, appropriateness for children with special needs, and so forth?

PROGRAM MODEL EVALUATION

Name of Model: _____

Source: _____

Recommended by:_____

Reviewer:_____

Date: _____

Descriptive Items: Is This Designed for Your Situation?	
1. Scope of the program: Is it designed for a class-room, school, community, or school district? What adults in school or at home are involved? Does the program fit with the type of early childhood setting that you have?	
2. Age of children: What is the age of the intended child audience of the program?	
3. Major features of the program: Do the overall approach, general goals, and style of the program fit with your goals and classroom style and with the needs of the children, school, and community?	
4. Assumptions about children: What assumptions about children, learning, and the world does this program make? This information should be clearly stated. These assumptions should be consistent with your understanding.	
5. Prior testing and piloting: Has the program been tried out before? Information about pilot testing should be available in the program's descriptive material.	

Practical Aspects: How Will It Work?	
1. Cost: This is a basic but important question to ask. The cost of published programs varies tremendously.	
2. Practical and usable materials: Materials that are hard to use or inconvenient can become a barrier to implementing the program.	
3. Renewable and easily available materials: Does the program include materials that will be used up and will need to be reordered, or does it use everyday materials that are readily available and easy to find?	
4. Easy to learn: Is the program fairly easy to understand and put into place, both for teachers and children?	
5. Training and instructions provided for teachers: Even the "easy to learn" programs include clearly written instructions and implementation strategies. Mechanisms for training and orientation sessions should be provided as well.	
Substantive Concerns: Will It Work Well?	
1. Knowledge base: Is the program based on what we know about children from theory, research, and best practices?	
2. Consistent philosophy: Are the basis of the program, its goals and objectives, and its implementation approach consistent with your understanding of children and learning?	
3. Developmentally appropriate: Does the program reflect age, individual, and cultural appropriateness?	
4. Responsiveness to children: Does it allow you to start where the children are? Is there a pre-assessment component to help you begin in the right place?	
5. Integration: Does the program work with your existing curriculum? Can it be integrated throughout all content areas and embedded into the routines of the day?	
6. Adaptable: Does the program allow you to make adjustments for the needs and interests of children, for the timetable of the day, and for special events?	

7. Multiple learning modes: Does the program offer a variety of ways for children to encounter learning (visual, kinesthetic, and auditory modes, as well as multiple intelligences)?	
8. Cultural responsiveness: Does the program respect and address diversity in children's culture and language?	
9. Children of all abilities: Is the program designed for children of all abilities in an inclusive setting?	
10. Child-relevant, fun, and meaningful: Will children truly enjoy the program activities?	
11. Home/school connections: Does the program connect with families by sharing information and by drawing on family knowledge, perspectives, and needs?	
12. Child-oriented outcome: Does the program move from adult-directed or structured processes to intrinsic, natural, child-controlled resolutions?	
13. Transferable learning: Are processes for conflict resolution and peacemaking context-specific, or are they generalizable, portable skills? For instance, can you make peace on the playground or only at the Peace Table?	
14. Peacemaking for all children: Does the program call for designated children as peer mediators, or are all children seen as peacemakers? Which of these approaches seems better for your setting? Can you rotate the mediation role among children? Will you encourage spontaneous peer mediation?	
15. Evaluation: Is there an evaluation component so that you can determine the effectiveness of the program?	

13

Reflection and Action: Conflict Resolution with Children and Adults

"I have also observed and evaluated that many conflicts occur in my life, and there is not one set way for me to deal with them. Each conflict seems to be different, and there are different strategies that I use to conquer each conflict. I also noticed that there are many conflicts that I can deal with on my own, and there are some where I need help or need to ask for some type of intervention by a second or third party."

Chapter 13 Objectives: To summarize and fully apply new knowledge, in this final chapter we will reexamine and reflect on our understanding of children's conflicts. With continuing self-assessment, we will develop and prioritize our goals for helping young children understand, manage, and resolve their conflicts. Chapter 13 also provides advocacy tools, case studies for further analysis, and an appendix on conflicts with other adults in the professional setting.

Chapter 13 Outline
Reflection and Re-Examination
    Reflecting on Your Approach to Conflict Resolution
    Self-Assessment Tools
    Identifying and Articulating Your Goals for Conflict Resolution
Advocacy, Action, and Growth
    Advocacy Basics
    How to Be an Advocate for Conflict Resolution
Summary
Chapter Appendix: Case Studies and Stories from the Field
Head Start Education Coordinator
Center Director
Itinerant Reading Resource Teacher
First Grade Teacher
Reflections on Building Empathy and Community in the Classroom:
    A True Story
Teacher of Threes in an Urban Parish Center: A Self-Awareness Exercise and
    Statement of Commitment to Children

REFLECTION AND RE-EXAMINATION

Reflecting on Your Approach to Conflict Resolution

Early childhood professionals are well-acquainted with the idea of reflective practice. Reflection helps us make sense of each day and makes explicit what we understand intuitively about children, learning, and teaching. The value of reflective practice clearly applies to our understanding of children's conflicts. In addition, we know that teachers' attitudes have a bearing on their practice. Therefore, reflection and awareness of our beliefs are important. Is there a gap between teachers' beliefs and teachers' actions in children's conflicts? Some research has suggested that such a gap exists (Chen & Smith, 2002). Continual self-assessment and understanding of our responses to conflicts, both among children and among adults, may reduce the likelihood of such a gap.

Attitudes Toward Children's Conflicts

What do you think about children's conflicts? If you did a self-awareness activity at the beginning of this book, this would be a good time for a "Self-Awareness Revisited" activity. Ask yourself questions such as

Are conflicts inevitable?

Are they harmful?

What is peace?

Are children capable of resolving their conflicts?

What is the value of classroom harmony?

Is it better to stop conflicts or to intervene immediately?

As a teacher, what is your role in children's conflicts?

The answers to these questions will draw a clear picture of your attitudes toward children's peer conflicts. Although your natural comfort level with interpersonal conflict may not have changed, you may have a new understanding of the nature

---

A TEACHER'S REFLECTION

Do teachers sometimes have preconceived notions about particular children or types of children? One teacher tells a story about a child who always seemed to be on the scene when a conflict was happening. The teacher developed a hypothesis: "This one is a troublemaker." After taking some time to observe the children's conflicts and listen to what was going on, the teacher began to realize that this child was an active peacemaker. She was drawn to the site of every class conflict in order to mediate, and therefore was always on the scene when the teacher arrived.

Teachers continually reflect on their attitudes and practices.

of children's conflicts and of appropriate adult intervention. Current knowledge, reflection, and self-assessment will guide you to informed professional practice.

ANOTHER TEACHER REFLECTS

"It's not fair of me to feel sorry for children and have lower expectations because of conditions in home and community. The reality is that my children can and will do it if you offer them the net of support they will need, and the celebration of their accomplishments when they make it."

Attitudes Toward Conflicts Among Adults

Another area of self-reflection is your response to conflict among adults. Most likely, your natural response to adult conflict will be similar to your response to children's conflicts in the classroom.

TEACHERS TALK

"People in general tend to perceive conflict as always being a negative event, because they are not emotionally able to conduct conflicts in an appropriate manner."

"Conflicts are inevitable in life. They are not the bulk of the problem, though. I think it is how you deal with that conflict that makes it peaceful or disastrous."

As mentioned in Chapter 11, response to conflicts with adults is an important part of the discussion. A consistent approach to conflicts in and out of the classroom helps ensure authenticity in your approach with children. Modeling conflict and collaboration with other adults provides a powerful model for children and families. Interactions with families, colleagues, other teachers, coworkers, staff, those you supervise, and those who supervise you all provide opportunities to present positive models for children.

Conflicts Among Adults: Staff Issues Conflicts arise among adults just as inevitably as they do among children. As with children, adults have an opportunity to confront and resolve conflicts in positive and cooperative ways. Children observe the adults in their world closely. The way that those adults interact and confront conflicts provides a powerful model and a window into the ways of the adult world, which children will then practice with their peers.

Relationships among teachers, and between teachers and principals or administrators, can be positive and support a sense of community, or they can be negative and create a sense of isolation. The nature of adult/adult interaction, and adults' approach to their own peer conflict, is an important factor in creating a positive sociomoral classroom environment (DeVries & Zan, 1994). Adults model positive social interaction and conflict resolution through collaboration, listening to opposing viewpoints, and arriving at a mutual agreement. The process occurs regularly among teachers in the schools in Reggio Emilia, as described by Edwards et al. (1998, p. 191):

"Intellectual conflict is understood as the engine of all growth in Reggio. Therefore, teachers seek to bring out, rather than suppress, conflicts of viewpoints between children. Similarly, among themselves they readily accept disagreement and expect extended discussion and constructive criticism; this is seen as the best way to advance. The teachers' pleasure in teamwork and acceptance of disagreement provides a model for children and parents."

Self-Assessment Tools

Continual Reflection in Practice

Teachers use reflection as a tool for continual self-assessment. As described previously, reflective journals and periodic self-awareness checks are accessible and always-available forms of self-assessment. Using reflection as a tool, teachers can ask "why," "how," and "what next?" Reflection can be a valuable component of action research.

ACTION RESEARCH: CARING IN YOUR CLASSROOM

A teacher has discussed with children and has modeled acts of caring-for and caring-by, as described by Nel Noddings (1992). Asking children to help her notice these caring acts in the classroom, the teacher wonders if this awareness of acts of caring will lead children to engage more purposively in these caring encounters. A busy classroom teacher, she makes anecdotal records of what she sees, and during class meetings, she asks children to confirm and add to her observations.

   Could you try this approach in your setting?

TEACHERS TALK

"I have just been reading Habits of Goodness: Case Studies in the Social Curriculum, by Ruth Sidey Charney (1997). The book includes case studies by six teachers who describe real-life strategies of instilling a sense of community in their classrooms and creating an environment where acts of caring and goodness are the norm among students. The other thing about this book is that this book offers a case study outline that could be helpful for a reflective teacher research project."

Develop a Checklist and Self-Assessment Inventory

Checklists and inventories can also provide self-assessment. Researchers have developed an inventory to assess teachers' beliefs about children's peer conflicts in order to examine the alignment of beliefs and practices. The Social Conflict Inventory (SCI) examines three areas: general orientation toward conflicts, beliefs about stopping conflicts, and beliefs about facilitating conflicts (Chen & Smith, 2002). Chapter 1 included a description of four types of teacher approaches to classroom conflict: no-nonsense, problem-solving, compromising, and smoothing (Kriedler, 1984). Doubtlessly, you made a quick self-assessment and assigned yourself to one of the categories. As an informal inventory, document your reactions to conflicts that occur during the day and reassess yourself according to these types. You can develop your own checklist and use it periodically.

   In addition to evaluating your attitudes and beliefs, reassess your teaching and the social, physical, and learning environments that support conflict resolution, peacemaking, and caring in your setting.

A Teacher Checklist of Attitudes and Responses to Classroom Conflict   These statements may help you see how you feel about conflicts, children's conflict management, and your role. Ask yourself which of the following statements you agree with most of the time:

1. It is important to have peace and harmony in the classroom at all times.

2. It is important to allow children to learn how to get along with others.

3. Unless an adult intervenes to stop a conflict, someone will probably get hurt.

4. Children are usually able to resolve conflicts on their own.

5. A teacher's role is to maintain order and prevent conflicts from occurring.

6. A teacher's role is to mediate children's conflicts when they occur.

7. A teacher's role is to provide children with words and strategies for resolving conflicts when they occur.

8. It is important for adults to intervene when children have conflicts about possession of objects.

9. It is important for adults to intervene when children have conflicts about rules.

10. It is important for adults to intervene when children are teasing or calling names.

11. The best way for a teacher to approach children's conflicts is to separate children and punish the child who started the conflict.

12. The best way for a teacher to approach children's conflicts is to tell children what to do to end the conflict.

13. The best way for a teacher to approach children's conflicts is to help children find ways to end the conflict on their own.

14. Conflicts among children are harmful and destructive and should be prevented or stopped immediately.

15. Conflicts can be constructive and can contribute to children's development.

Identifying and Articulating Your Goals for Conflict Resolution

Developing Your Goals

Based on your self-assessment, you can begin to develop goals to support children's conflict resolution that are consistent with your professional growth and with what is important to you. After reading this book, you may have developed goals such as learning more about children's conflicts in your setting; planning time to observe; developing strategies for the physical and social environment and the curriculum; reconsidering your approach to your intervention; creating opportunities for greater family involvement; evaluating your setting for cultural responsiveness; drafting your own classroom model for conflict resolution and peacemaking; looking closely at an existing model in your school; and reading in the professional literature about children's conflicts.

Using the Three-Layer Cake to Plan Your Goals   The three-layer cake analogy can provide a framework for building specific goals and actions (see Figure 13–1). Identify at least one action that you can take in each layer: Commitment to a Peaceful Classroom, Curriculum Ideas and Activities, and Intervening in Conflicts and Family/Community Connections. Determine which will be long-term or short-

Figure 13–1
The final appearance of the cake.

term goals. Be sure to include at least a few short-term goals in your plan, and be prepared to be patient with the long-term ones.

Sharing What You Know   Sharing what you have learned with other professionals can be an important goal. Teaming with another teacher for your classroom strategies can enrich both classrooms and further extend your caring community. Another possible goal could be to develop and share your self-assessment tools.

Priorities for Change

Local Change   The first step in making changes for conflict resolution and peacemaking is to find what you can do that is close at hand. When you are considering your possible goals, you may include changes that will affect your classroom, children, families, colleagues, and yourself. Keeping others engaged in the process of change is important. Even local change often takes time, patience, persistence, and flexibility.

Societal Change   Thinking more globally, working toward societal change may be a long-term goal. Difficult but nonetheless worthwhile, your work toward societal change fits within our models of peace education, service learning, and a curriculum of caring. A model for involving children in social change has been the

Anti-Bias Curriculum, in which children learn to identify and confront bias and stand up for themselves and others (Derman-Sparks, 1989). Social change is based on the idea of global mutual well-being, that all people are connected in some way in a borderless world community, and that helping others not like ourselves makes the world better for all of us. Grass roots efforts for social change have led to voting rights, the eight-hour day and other labor laws, environmental and health protections, domestic violence laws, and more.

ADVOCACY, ACTION, AND GROWTH

Advocacy Basics

Early childhood advocacy means standing up for young children and their families and articulating their needs (Lombardi & Goffin, 1988). The first steps are to understand the importance of advocacy and, consistent with our definition of social change, to make a commitment to action as professionals, beyond our classrooms, offices, and homes.

Early childhood professionals have valuable knowledge and experiences to share. Our contributions as advocates include giving voice to what we know and reclaiming the importance of childhood for its own sake, not as a time of preparation for a future workforce. Advocacy challenges include defining the professionalism of the field, creating a space for families to be heard, and widening the circle of those who will speak for children and families to include businesses and other service professionals, among others (Jensen & Hannibal, 2000; Robinson & Stark, 2002). Jonah Edelman (2002) recommends organizing a team of advocates for greater effectiveness. As he suggests, you can use the image of *Swimmy* (1963), in the story by Leo Lionni, to enlist others to add their voices on behalf of children. Swimmy, one very small fish, joins with many other small fish to become one very large fish.

How to Be an Advocate for Conflict Resolution

What You Can Do to Make Change for Conflict Resolution

Becoming an advocate is a developmental process. You may begin your journey as an advocate for children's conflict resolution with small steps, such as sharing lists of non-violent television programs with families. You can make a commitment to continue growing as an advocate and plan to take actions at a later date, such as visiting your legislator to ask for support for violence prevention issues.

Here are some ideas for supporting young children's conflict resolution, now or at a later time:

- Write an article in a school or classroom newsletter for families.

- Visit a web site for resources on conflict resolution or violence prevention and share what you find.

Teachers can be advocates by sharing information and speaking to others on behalf of conflict resolution.

- Write a letter or send an e-mail message to a toy manufacturer or retailer about violent or stereotypical toys or games (or write to a sponsor of inappropriate television programming).
- Ask your local bookseller about children's books with prosocial and anti-bias themes.
- Evaluate the books and materials in your classroom for caring, prosocial themes.
- Plan a family night, workshop, or parent education meeting on community violence prevention or conflict resolution.
- Join an advocacy organization at the local or national level, such as Action Alliance or Stand for Children. (There is information about these organizations later in this chapter.)
- Testify on behalf of violence prevention issues at your state legislature.

Targeting Your Advocacy Efforts

To begin your advocacy on behalf of conflict resolution and peacemaking, you can follow the steps for "targeting your advocacy efforts" described by Lombardi & Goffin (1988).

First, choose an area of concern or focus: What aspect is your most pressing concern? Is it media violence, or a need for safe after-school care in the community?

Next, gather facts so that you will know who else is affected, what the effects are on children and families, and who may agree or disagree on the issue. Collect facts, figures, and compelling stories. Locate position statements and current statistics online.

The third step is to focus your response with fact sheets and talking points that are responsive to the current political climate.

Finally, you are ready for action. Refine your message for your target audience and develop an advocacy style that is comfortable for you.

Resources for Advocacy and Change

The following are resources for your advocacy tool kit:

Position Statements from Professional Organizations   NAEYC, Association for Childhood Education International (ACEI), Southern Early Childhood Association (SECA), and others. NAEYC Position Statements are available online at *http://www .naeyc.org/resources.*

These statements offer brief explanations of issues and practical recommendations for what can be done to help. A few examples of NAEYC position statements are as follows:

Media Violence in Children's Lives

Prevention of Child Abuse

Responding to Linguistic and Cultural Diversity

Respuesta a la Diversidad Lingüística y Cultural

Standardized Testing of Young Children

NAEYC Code of Ethical Behavior

ERIC Digests   The ERIC Web site has many resources to offer. You may select the tab "ERIC Digests" for two-page full-text articles that summarize the latest information on a particular topic. See *http://www.ed.gov/databases/ERIC_Digests/ index/.* Enter search terms such as conflict resolution, peace education, character education, violence prevention, working with families, and social competence.

Aidman, A. (1997). *Television violence: Content, context, and consequences.* (ERIC Digest ED414078)

Bruns, D. A., & Corso, R. M. (2001). *Working with culturally & linguistically diverse families.* (ERIC Digest ED455972)

Flannery, D. J. (1998). *Improving school violence prevention programs through meaningful evaluation.* (ERIC Digest 417244)

Grosse, S. J. (2001). *Children and post traumatic stress disorder: What classroom teachers should know.* (ERIC Digest ED460122)

Johnson, M. L. (1998). *Trends in peace education.* (ERIC Digest ED417123)

Lu, M. (2001). *Children's literature in a time of national tragedy.* (ERIC Digest ED457525)

Marion, M. (1997). *Helping young children deal with anger*. (ERIC Digest ED414077)

Massey, M. S. (1998). *Early childhood violence prevention*. (ERIC Digest ED424032)

McClellan, D. E., & Katz, L. G. (2001). *Assessing young children's social competence*. (ERIC Digest ED450953)

Moore, S. G. (1992). *The role of parents in the development of peer group competence*. (ERIC Digest ED346992)

Otten, E. H. (2000). *Character education*. (ERIC Digest ED444932)

Schwartz, W. (1999). *Preventing violence by elementary school children*. (ERIC Digest ED436602)

Wallach, L. B. (1994). *Violence and young children's development*. (ERIC Digest ED369578)

Wheeler, E. J. (1994). *Peer conflicts in the classroom*. (ERIC Digest ED372874)

Current Statistics

Children's Defense Fund (annual state of America's children) *http://cdfweb.vwh.net/*

Annie Casey Foundation (annual Kids Count reports) *http://www.aecf.org/*

U.S. Department of Education *http://www.ed.gov/index.jsp*

Books About Being an Advocate

Jensen, M. A., & Hannibal, M. A. (2000). *Issues, advocacy, and leadership in early education* (2nd ed.). Boston Allyn, and Bacon.

Lombardi, J., & Goffin, S. G. (1988). *Speaking out: Early childhood advocacy*. Washington, DC: National Association for the Education of Young Children.

Robinson, A., & Stark, D. (2002). *Advocates in action: Making a difference for young children*. Washington, DC: National Association for the Education of Young Children.

More Advocacy Resources

C.E.A.S.E. (Concerned Educators Allied for a Safe Environment), 55 Frost Street, Cambridge, MA. Network of parents, teachers, and others working for a safe world for children. Newsletter with lists of books for children and adults, web sites, articles, and other resources.

Children's Defense Fund, 25 E. Street NW, Washington, DC 20001 (*childrensdefense.org*). Links through this site to reports on children's health, safety, and economic issues, as well as many others.

Southern Poverty Law Center, 400 Washington Avenue, Montgomery, AL 36104 (*splcenter.org*). Involves resources, publications, and advocacy. Publications include *Ten Ways to Fight Hate* and *Starting Small*, a free resource for teachers described below.

Stand for Children, 1420 Columbia Road, N.W., Washington, DC 20009 (*www.stand.org*). A "nationwide grassroots voice for children" with advocacy at the national, state, community, and neighborhood levels.

Action Alliance. These regional, state, and local organizations bring together advocates for children and families and provide information about current issues, sponsor advocacy events, and provide materials in print and online. Check for an Action Alliance group in your state.

TEACHERS TALK

Names
There is only one child in the world;
And the child's name is All Children.
Carl Sandburg

"I found this quote in my collection of Things to Save. It seems to capture what we mean when we speak of being an advocate for children. Advocacy can be as close to home as what you do to help a particular child in your care receive the services he or she may need. Advocacy is making neighbors aware of the needs of the children and families in the community. Advocacy happens at the national and global level as well, but you can start in your own backyard."

SUMMARY

This chapter has been another step on our continuing journey as early childhood professionals in support of young children's conflict resolution and peacemaking. As with any area of our practice with young children, it is vital to reflect on our understanding of children's conflicts and to be aware of how that understanding guides us in our work with children, families, and colleagues. That awareness leads us to setting goals for future professional growth. Finally, we will include in those goals a plan to carry what we know beyond our immediate setting as advocates for young children and families, and for a safe and peaceful world.

SUPPLEMENTARY MATERIALS FOR CHAPTER 13

Research Focus

What do teachers think about children's conflicts, and how does what they think influence what happens in the classroom? Chen and Smith (2002) have piloted a

Let's communicate!

research tool to help answer these questions. You may want to conduct your own informal research by asking first yourself and then others in your setting about children's conflicts. Compare what you find to what other researchers have found.

APPLICATION EXERCISES

1. Repeat the web activity from the first chapter: Does it look different now?

2. Make a peace quilt with classmates, children, or friends. Each square will have a peace message designed by a different person.

3. Design a bumper sticker with a peace or non-violence message.

4. Practice your advocacy by developing a one-minute Public Service Announcement (PSA). Find out how to have a PSA on your local television or radio station.

THINKING ABOUT ALL CHILDREN

In this book, we have used NAEYC's definition of "all children" as "children with developmental delays or disabilities, children whose families are culturally and linguistically diverse, children who are gifted and talented, children from diverse socioeconomic groups, and other children with diverse learning styles and needs" (NAEYC, 2001). Now that you have come to the end of the book, do you find that your understanding of children's conflicts fits with this definition? Does your advocacy plan include all children?

>>

CHAPTER APPENDIX: CASE STUDIES AND STORIES FROM THE FIELD

Head Start Education Coordinator

"I have gained a wealth of knowledge about my child during this project and throughout her two years at Head Start. I've learned that Head Start is a safe haven for Brianne. This is her home away from all of the pressures of violence in her home and neighborhood. This is the place where she is comfortable enough to cry out for help. I've also learned, more importantly, that she is depending on the Head Start staff to seek the help she needs. Therefore, we vow to fulfill those needs with all our resources. I know Brianne is a 4-year-old who needs love, guidance, and a safe environment. At her age, Brianne should be beaming with questions and engaging in fun-filled activities. She should be working those little muscles, running, jumping, and hopping all over the school. Yet, oftentimes I see Brianne angry and aggressive. She comes to school and talks about her responsibilities at home, which are washing her little brother, changing his diaper, and putting covers on him. These are not age-appropriate tasks for a 4 year old. This is what they imagine when they play in housekeeping, not for Brianne. The next step for Brianne and her family is counseling. The center was very pleased when her mother called to say she wanted help. My hope is that Brianne's mother uses the wealth of resources that Head Start will give the family. The Head Start staff has volunteered to escort her to all related appointments. My greatest fulfillment would be knowing that these resources will assist in easing Brianne's transition into the public school setting."

Center Director

"I know that, in the past, this has been one problem in the child care setting. My current position is one where I do not have issues such as this to deal with, but in the most recent past, I felt like all I did was adult management. By saying this, I mean that the teachers sometimes forget where they are and that little ears are listening. I am sorry to say that I have had teachers get into arguments in front of the children until I separated them and told one to leave. Also, I don't think parents are aware of some of the things that they say in front of their children. I had to deal with a few parents who were upset about a situation that happened in their child's classroom, and they raised their voices and used inappropriate words in front of their child.

"I think that teachers should have to attend training on conflict resolution and how to conduct themselves in and around children if a conflict arises. Wow, maybe I can develop a workshop for teachers myself?"

Itinerant Reading Resource Teacher

"In visiting and observing several preschool and primary classrooms, I have discovered that room arrangement can make all the difference in the learning and behavioral environment. I found that large, open amounts of space encouraged negative behavior, while strategically placed furniture routed children through an organized and orderly day. I also found that messy, unorganized classrooms tended to have more conflict than orderly and organized classrooms. Classrooms that provided children with a place to work in small groups and individually seemed to have less conflict than those that forced children to remain in one seat and next to the same children for most of the day.

"In Classrooms One and Two, the children could move about the room, but they were not able to create conflict by running throughout the classroom. Also, in these classrooms, the students could work with small groups, with a partner, or alone, which seemed to create a pleasant and low-conflict atmosphere. While Classroom Two was organized, it was somewhat crowded, which seemed to foster more conflict than the room arrangement in Classroom One.

"In Classroom Three, the teacher has the room set up in a very organized and orderly fashion. Every toy and learning tool has a place, and the children are provided with cozy and calming areas. This classroom was especially low-conflict. Upon entering this classroom, there is a feeling of what is expected, as well as feelings of security, calm, and comfort.

"Classroom Four is an organized classroom, but it is set up in such a way that it is obvious that the teacher is in charge of everything. The children's desks are arranged in a U shape with the teacher in the front and center. This classroom does not provide much room for the children to move around and interact with one another. In this classroom, when the children line up or sit as a group, there tends to be more conflict among the students than in classrooms where the children are constantly working together and interacting with one another.

"Classroom Five is a classroom with many discipline problems and conflict among the students. This is similar to Classroom Four in the way that the desks are in a U shape with the teacher in charge of everything. The difference in Classroom Five is the way the desks are all crowded toward the front of the room, which leaves the back of the classroom with a large empty space where children get themselves into trouble. The students in this classroom always sit next to the same one or two people, which provides them minimal interaction. When these children are asked to work together, there is a great deal of conflict.

"Throughout my visits in these five classrooms, it has become very obvious to me that the way a classroom is set up has a great effect on the amount of conflict and negative behavior that exists in that classroom. When children are given an environment in which they are allowed to move about the room and work with one another, there is less conflict among the students. When classrooms are organized and comfortable, and when they give children some ownership of the room and the items in it, students tend to behave in a positive manner."

First-Grade Teacher

Josh's voice comes from the reading rug. He is breathing heavily. From across the room, the teacher asks him what is wrong. "He threw his notebook at me and it hit me in the eye and it hurt!" At this point, the teacher walks over to the rug and kneels down next to Josh. Mike, the student Josh points to, does not say a word. Josh becomes more agitated by the minute and repeats his accusations: "He threw his notebook at my eye and he meant to do it!" The teacher turns to Mike and asks if what Josh is saying is true. Mike immediately begins crying and says, "He punched me in the back and it hurt!" Then neither of them says anything. Josh continues his heavy breathing and Mike continues crying. After a few minutes with the teacher watching them, Mike cries out, "It was an accident!" Josh replies, "You meant to do it!" Mike then says, "No, it was an accident. I'm sorry." Josh begins to calm down at this point, but Mike is still crying. The teacher turns to Josh and asks if he thinks he owes Mike an apology for punching him in the back. He replies, "I did that already but he didn't listen!" (He actually hasn't apologized.) Mike tells him that he didn't hear it. Josh then says, "Sorry." The teacher asks each child what he could have done differently. Mike says he would not throw his notebook again. Josh says, "Not get in a fight to work it out."

Reflections on Building Empathy and Community in the Classroom: A True Story

Ruby F. Martin, Director

Daniel steps on Zachary's the finger in block area. Zachary, obviously hurt, begins to cry. A look of genuine concern washes over Daniel's face. "Are you okay?", he asks. Zachary, holding onto his finger, nods his head but continues to cry. Daniel kneels next to Zachary, places a hand gently on his back, and asks, "Would you like some ice?" Zachary again nods. Daniel looks to the teacher who is close by and watching the situation. "Can we get Zachary some ice, I stepped on his finger." The language, compassion, and concern for others is an everyday occurrence in the center I direct. Daniel and his friend are 3 years old, and the modeling and empathy-building start at 6 weeks.

We do not use any defined curriculum for peaceful conflict resolution, and we do not force children to apologize. What we do is to gently guide children from a very young age to try to understand their feelings. The teachers model compassion and the children follow their lead. It is a simple, effective process that in 3 years has shown wonderful results.

The first step in obtaining a peaceful environment for us was training the teachers and assistants that showing emotion is completely appropriate. We need to focus on guiding the children to make good choices and giving them the tools they need to help each other.

We use only positive techniques in dealing with behavior, always focusing attention on the child in need and involving the perpetrator in the follow-up.

Once the teachers were trained, the next step was implementation. I began to hear teachers using language such as, "I see you are sad, can we make you feel better?", "I feel mad sometimes too, can I tell you what I do when I am mad?", "I understand that you are frustrated, it is never okay to hurt someone, so let's talk about some things we can do instead," "Can you see that your friend is hurt? Let's find out what they need to make them better." After a few months, the language and environment completely changed among the children. They were much less violent when solving conflicts, they were more in tune with their emotions, and they worked more effectively as a community.

Our ultimate goal in this process was to give children a place where they would always feel safe to say or do anything without judgment, being reprimanded, or being treated harshly. We want them to learn that when you work together and understand each other's feelings, things are positive and days run smoothly. There is more time for exploration, experimentation, and play when we get along with others. Have we met our goal?

Last week I overheard Jayne in our kindergarten telling Kevin, "When people boss me around I feel like I don't matter, could you try not to boss me so much?" Kevin pondered her request for a second, and his response was, "I can try really hard, cause you do matter."

Dominic, in the twos, was obviously distraught by the actions of one of his friends. In tears, he expressed, "You made me feel sad!" The other child immediately went over and started rubbing Dominic's back, saying, "Feel better?" Just getting children to understand the effect they have on others impacts their emotions makes me think that yes, we have reached our goal. It is a constant practice, and the teachers have to always keep in mind that the children see and hear everything around them. The children need to mentor new students when they arrive at the center. The outcome is amazing. If we need to model compassion and language for children while obtaining these outcomes, I can see no negative in this kind of environment. Make the commitment to make change as directors or administrators, and the employees will follow your lead. It has been a year and a half since I have had a child in my office for negative behavior. Everything is handled within the classroom community as a team. Conflicts are resolved with patience and understanding, with the knowledge that every child is capable of empathy, and we just need to guide them in their understanding of it. When others tour our center or come in for training, I often hear that they do not hear negative noise. Not only do the teachers blend into the environment, but the children are talking to one another in a pleasant and respectful manner and solving conflicts calmly. I am a firm believer that setting up environments in appropriate ways and training your teachers in appropriate practices instantly reduces the number of conflicts among children that need to be dealt with. However, adding the next step of building empathy in children has made our environment even more effective.

I often tell my teachers how much our children could teach many adults in society about understanding each other's feelings. How fortunate that our children get to be in an environment of understanding and positive conflict resolution! (Note: In this story, as in the rest of this book, names of children and teachers have been changed.)

Teacher of Threes in an Urban Parish Center: A Statement of Commitment to Children

Our final story from the field is the following list created by a teacher as a self-awareness exercise following her study of the subject of children's conflicts as presented in this book. Her words demonstrate her clear commitment to young children and her dedication to supporting their conflict resolution and peacemaking in a safe and caring environment.

- Every child has the right to a safe and loving family.
- Every child has the right to an education, to be given a chance to one day give back to his or her society.
- Every child has the right to absolute safety, to be free from the terror of abuse and chains of neglect.
- Every child has the right to live without fear, unhindered by the threat of rampant drugs, violence, and alcohol.
- Every child has the right to have respect and be free from exploitation.
- Evaluate the classroom, the curriculum, and yourself for progress and necessary changes.
- Be a role model, exhibiting behaviors that you expect to see demonstrated by children.
- Allow children the space and opportunity they need to resolve problems. Don't be too quick to intervene.
- Teach and demonstrate values, respect, and problem-solving skills.
- Reflect on your body language, tone of voice, and attitudes with children.
- Don't overreact to situations. Be patient and understanding, always forgiving.
- Am I an advocate and supporter of organizations that promote peace, non-violence, and safety?
- Am I aware of what's happening through the technological media, such as computers, music, etc.?
- Am I kept abreast of what is affecting the community and children, such as gangs, guns, drugs, etc.?
- Do I know what resources are available for dealing with conflict resolution? What works best in my classroom?
- Do I encourage and support those children who come to me for help? Do I work with parents and supply them with resource materials?
- I believe that every child is special and has the right to be given the chance to one day make the world a better place.

Appendix A
Observation Tools: Play Scales

These play scales are based on an understanding of children's play in the cognitive and social domains of development. Piaget (1962) describes the cognitive levels of play and Parten (1932) provides the types of social play. Both of these lenses on play provide a context for children's interactions in conflicts.

PIAGET'S COGNITIVE PLAY

1. *Functional Play:* This level of play involves repetitive movement with or without objects—also known as practice play. Functional play could be hopping and jumping, hammering, stacking cubes, pouring sand back and forth, and so on.

2. *Constructive Play:* This level of play involves the use of objects to build, create, or construct; combines functional and symbolic play, as children stack blocks to build towers or create images with a variety of media.

3. *Symbolic Play:* Also described as dramatic play, pretend play, or imaginative play, in this level of play children use their role-play and imagination, to transform themselves, others, objects, or places. Examples include a child using a block as a telephone or a group of children in an extended dramatic play sequence about a pirate ship and buried treasure.

4. *Games with Rules:* This level of play involves a pre-determined set of rules that players accept and follow, and it may include competition and goal-orientation. Outdoor games such as races and tag and indoor games such as board games are familiar examples.

PARTEN'S SOCIAL PLAY CATEGORIES

1. *Onlooker:* In this type of social play, a child observes others with interest, close enough to hear what is said, but without participating or interacting with the children at play.

2. *Solitary:* In this type of play, a child plays alone, independently, without interaction with others nearby and with different materials. Children at any age may engage in solitary play.

3. *Parallel:* In this type of play, children play alongside others with the same or shared activity, but they play independently and do not share toys or materials or comment about the activity.

4. *Associative:* In this type of play, children play independently near others in the same or similar activity, but they comment about what the others are doing.

5. *Cooperative:* In this type of play, children play with others in a common activity with agreed-upon roles and shared goals in sociodramatic play, co-construction, or group game.

Non-Play Activities

After observing children in an Early Childhood setting, you will note that not all activities are a form of play. Some are teacher-directed activities, routine times, classroom transitions, movement from one activity to the next, or simply unengaged, unoccupied "down time."

HOW TO USE THE PLAY SCALE OBSERVATION TOOLS

1. You may use a simple checklist to record the types of social play or levels of cognitive play that you observe in your setting.
2. You also may use the combined Parten/Piaget Observation Record to record both dimensions of children's play at the same time. Use tally marks to record the type of

social and cognitive play that you observe. Until you become familiar with analyzing children's play, you may want to make brief notes of the activity in the blocks on the form.

SOURCES

Isenberg, J. P., & Jalongo, M. R. (2001). *Creative expression and play in early childhood* (3rd ed.). Upper Saddle River, NJ: Merrill/Prentice Hall.

Johnson, J., Christie, J., & Yawkey, T. (1987). *Play and early childhood development*. Glenview, IL: Scott-Foresman.

Parten, M. (1932). Social participation among preschool children. *Journal of Abnormal Psychology*, 27(2), 243–269.

Piaget, J. (1962). *Play, dreams, and imitation in childhood*. New York: Norton.

PARTEN/PIAGET OBSERVATION RECORD
NAME OF CHILD: _____

DATE/TIME OF OBSERVATION: _____

		Cognitive Play			
		Functional	Constructive	Dramatic	Games with Rules
Social Play	Solitary				
	Parallel				
	Associative				
	Cooperative				

Non-Play Activities	
Unoccupied or onlooker play, transition between play activities	
Other non-play activities: Classroom routine and transition times, teacher-directed activities	

Adapted from J. Johnson, J. Chistie, and T. Yawkey (1987)

Appendix B
Observation Forms and Resources

OBSERVATION FORMS

Here are a few examples of observation tools that you may use or develop yourself in order to learn more about their approach to conflicts with their peers.

NARRATIVE OBSERVATION FORM

Child's Name: _____ **Date/Time:** _____

Purpose of the Observation: _____ **Setting:** _____

Observations:	Notes/Interpretations:

Recommendations and Plans for Follow-up:

CONFLICT OBSERVATION RECORD

This recording sheet may be used to record information as interactions are occurring or to analyze interactions after they have occurred.

Social Context		Physical Context	Issues		Strategies		Outcomes	
Type of Social Play		Play Activity and Location	Physical	Social	Physical	Verbal	Child-Generated	Adult Control
Onlooker, Solitary, or Parallel	Associative or Cooperative		Objects or Territory	Group Entry Rules, Superiority, etc.	Physical: Aggressive or Non-Aggressive	Simple Insistence or Reason and Negotiation	Mutual, Dominance, Withdraw, or Peer Help	

PROSOCIAL AND SOCIOMORAL COMPETENCE RATING SCALE

This rating scale was developed by teachers to learn more about the children in their classrooms. What might you add or change to use this observation tool in your setting

	No Evidence	Occasionally	Frequently	Consistently	Comments
Empathy Recognizes feelings of others Consoles others Shows concern for the welfare of others					
Conflict Resolution Solves conflicts without adult help Uses reasoning and negotiation Demonstrates self-control					
Prosocial Behavior Makes appropriate behavior choices Collaborates with peers Shows understanding of role as part of the community					
Communication Verbalizes details of conflict Uses words to resolve conflict Listens to what others have to say Communicates feelings					

OBSERVATION RESOURCES

Beaty, J. J. (1998). *Observing development of the young child* (4th ed.). Upper Saddle River, NJ: Merrill/ Prentice Hall.

Bentsen, W. R. (1985). *Seeing young children: A guide to observing and recording behavior*. Albany, NY: Delmar.

Losardo, A., & Notari-Syverson, A. (2001). *Alternative approaches to assessing young children*. Baltimore: Paul H. Brookes.

McAfee, O., & Leong, D. J. (2001). *Assessing and guiding young children's development and learning* (3rd ed.). Boston: Allyn & Bacon.

Project Zero & Reggio Children. (2001). *Making learning visible: Children as individual and group learners*. Reggio Emilia, Italy: Reggio Children.

Ramsey, P. G. (1991). *Making friends in school: Promoting peer relationships in early childhood*. New York: Teachers College Press.

Wortham, S. (2001). *Assessment in early childhood education* (3rd ed.). Upper Saddle River, NJ: Merrill/ Prentice Hall.

Appendix C
Children's Books for Caring, Conflict Resolution, and Peace-Building

These are a few suggested books, old and new, that can be used to support children's caring, conflict resolution, and peace-building. The list includes books for a range of children, from toddlers and young preschoolers to primary-grade children. Please choose as you would with any list of recommended books or materials to find those most appropriate for the children in your setting. The themes and applications to topics related to caring and conflict resolution include

Feelings and emotions

Families and friends

Perspective-taking and empathy

Kindness and compassion

Diversity and affirmation

Social justice, activism, and anti-bias

Caring for the earth and environment

Experiencing and resolving conflict

Teachers can find one or more of these themes in most children's books. The characters in any story interact with each other in a number of ways that can be the basis of discussion with children. Using concept or information books, teachers can also provide opportunities for problem-solving, perspective-taking, and other abilities for conflict resolution and understanding of others. Themes related to caring and conflict resolution are listed for each book:

Bang, M. (1999). *When Sophie gets angry—really, really angry.* New York: Blue Sky Press.

Themes: Feelings and emotions, anger, families and friends.

Bourgeois, P. (1993). *Franklin is bossy.* Toronto: Kids Can Press.

Themes: Feelings and emotions; friendship.

Bruchac, J. (1993). *First strawberries: A Cherokee story.* Dial: New York.

Themes: Families and friends; experiencing and resolving conflict; adult conflict.

Bunting, E. (1991). *Fly away home.* New York: Clarion Books.

Themes: Resilience and perspective-taking, economic diversity.

Carle, E. (1977). *The grouchy ladybug.* New York: Harper Collins.

Themes: Kindness, sharing, alternatives to violence.

Carlsson-Paige, N. (1998). *Best day of the week.* St. Paul, MN: Redleaf Press.

Themes: Experiencing and resolving conflict. This picture book is written to accompany the teacher's guide, *Before Push Comes to Shove: Building Conflict Resolution Skills with Children.*

Cheltenham Elementary School Kindergarteners (1991). *We are all alike we are all different.* New York: Scholastic.

Themes: Diversity and affirmation, friendship.

Cherry, L. (1990). *The great kapok tree: A tale of the amazon rain forest.* San Diego, CA: Harcourt Brace Jovanovich.

Theme: Caring for the environment.

Clifton, L. (1976). *Three wishes.* New York: Viking.

Themes: Experiencing and resolving conflict among friends.

Coleman, E. (1996). *White socks only.* Morton Grove, IL: Albert Whitman.

Themes: Community action, social justice, activism, anti-bias.

Coles, R. (1995). *The story of Ruby Bridges.* New York: Scholastic.

Themes: Social activism, courage in the face of prejudice.

Crary, E. (1996). *My name is not dummy.* Seattle: Parenting Press.

Themes: Bullying, problem-solving.

de Paola, T. (1980). *The knight and the dragon.* New York: Putnam.

Theme: Peaceful alternatives to fighting.

Feelings, M. (1971). *Moja means one: A Swahili counting book.* New York: Dial Books.

Jambo means hello: A Swahili alphabet book. New York: Dial Books. (1974)

Themes: Diversity, affirmation, perspective-taking.

Feeney, S. (1980). *A Is for aloha.* Honolulu: University of Hawaii Press.

Themes: Diversity, affirmation, perspective-taking. Alphabet and counting books in a variety of languages and signs communicate both diversity and commonality.

Greenfield, E. (1973). *Rosa Parks.* New York: Crowell.

Themes: Social activism, courage in the face of prejudice.

Greenfield, E. (1976). *First pink light.* New York: Black Butterfly.

Themes: Families: conflict and resolution between parent and child.

Greenfield, E. (1978). *Honey I love and other poems.* New York: Crowell.

Themes: Diversity, feelings, affirmation, family and friends.

Grimes, N. (1994). *Meet Danitra Brown.* New York: Lathrop, Lee & Shepard.

Themes: Friendship, feelings, facing adversity.

Guback, G. (1994). *Luka's quilt.* New York: Greenwillow.

Theme: Conflict resolution in the family.

Hamanaka, S. (1994). *All the colors of the earth.* New York: Morrow Junior Books.

Themes: Diversity and affirmation.

Henkes, K. (1991). *Chrysanthemum.* New York: Greenwillow.

Themes: Diversity and affirmation, feelings and emotions, response to name-calling.

Henkes, K. (1996). *Lily's purple plastic purse.* New York: Greenwillow.

Themes: Feelings and emotions, family and friends, consequences of hurtful actions, restitution.

Herron, C. (1997). *Nappy hair.* New York: Knopf.

Themes: Diversity and affirmation.

Hoffman, M. (1991). *Amazing grace.* New York: Dial Books.

Themes: Diversity and affirmation, overcoming limitations of color and gender.

Hoose, P., and Hoose, H. (1998). *Hey, little ant.* Berkeley, CA: Tricycle Press.

Themes: Perspective-taking and empathy; kindness and compassion; emerging social conscience; care for those in nature; bullying.

Hutchins, P. (1986). *The doorbell rang.* New York: Greenwillow.

Themes: Sharing, negotiation, problem-solving, concern for others.

Jeffers, S. (1991). *Brother eagle, sister sky.* New York: Dial Books.

Themes: Respect for the earth, perspective-taking.

Jones, R. (1995). *Matthew and Tilley.* New York, Dutton.

Theme: Conflict and resolution among friends.

Keats, E. J. (1968). *A letter to Amy.* New York: Harper.

Pet show (1972). New York: MacMillan.

Peter's chair. (1967). New York: Viking.

Whistle for Willie. (1964). New York: Viking.

Themes: Feelings, family and friends, affirmation, diversity. Each of Keats' books offers a real child-world situation for children to experience along with Peter and his family and friends.

Kraus, R. (1971). *Leo the late bloomer.* New York: Windmill Books.

Themes: Feelings, family and friends, diversity and affirmation.

Leaf, M. (1936). *The story of Ferdinand.* New York: Viking Press.

Themes: Peace, kindness, compassion, feelings and emotions, being different.

Lionni, L. (1963). *Swimmy.* New York: Parthenon.

Theme: Cooperation and working as a group.

Little blue and little yellow. (1959). New York: Astor.

Themes: Diversity and friendship.

It's mine. (1996). New York: Knopf.

Themes: Conflict and learning together.

A color of his own. (1975). New York: Parthenon.

Themes: Diversity and affirmation.

All of Lionni's books have prosocial themes.

Morgan, P. (1990). *The turnip: An old Russian folk tale.* New York: Philomel Books. There are several versions of this old story about cooperation, including the following: Tolstoy, Aleskey. (2002). *The enormous turnip: A classic folk tale.* San Diego, CA: Harcourt.

Naylor, P. (1994). *King of the playground.* New York: MacMillan.

Themes: Problem-solving when confronted with bullying.

Pfister, M. (1992). *Rainbow fish.* New York: North-South Books.

Themes: Sharing, kindness, friendship.

Ringold, F. (1991). *Tar beach.* New York: Crown Publishers.

Themes: Family, diversity and affirmation.

Ringold, F. (1995). *Aunt Harriet's underground railroad in the sky.* New York: Crown Publishers.

Theme: Courage and helping others in the face of hardship and suffering.

Sciescka, J. (1989). *The true story of the three little Pigs by A. Wolf.* New York: Scholastic.

Themes: Perspective taking, dealing with conflict.

Sendak, M. (1963). *Where the wild things are.* New York: Harper.

Themes: Feelings and emotions, comfort.

Seuss, Dr. (1984). *The butter battle book.* New York: Random House.

Theme: Experience with intergroup conflict that escalates.

The lorax. (1971). New York: Random House.

Theme: Caring for the environment.

Horton hears a who. (1954). New York: Random House.

Themes: Caring for others, respect, equality, standing up for others.

Sharmat, M. (1980). *Gila monsters meet you at the airport.* New York: Aladdin.

Themes: Diversity, dealing with stereotypes.

Surat, M. (1983). *Angel child, dragon child.* New York: Scholastic.

Themes: Feelings, family, diversity, cultural conflict and understanding.

Viorst, J. (1972). *Alexander and the terrible, horrible, no good, very bad day.* New York: Atheneum.

Themes: Feelings and emotions, encouragement, empathy, family.

Williams, V. B. (1982). *A chair for my mother.* New York: Greenwillow.

Themes: Families, kindness, compassion, perspective-taking and empathy.

Zolotow, C. (1976). *The hating book.* New York: Harper Trophy.

Themes: Communication skills and friendship, feelings and emotions.

Appendix D
Books for Teachers— Activities and Classroom Ideas

Carlsson-Paige, N., & Levin, D. E. (1998). *Before push comes to shove: Building conflict resolution skills with children.* St. Paul, MN: Redleaf Press.

Charles, C. M. (2000). *The synergistic classroom: Joyful teaching and gentle discipline.* New York: Longman.

Crary, E. (1984). *Kids can cooperate: A practical guide to teaching problem solving.* Seattle, WA: Parenting Press.

Kreidler, W. J. (1984). *Creative conflict resolution: More than 200 activities for keeping peace in the classroom K-6.* Glenview, IL: Scott, Foresman.

Kreidler, W. J. (1994). *Teaching conflict resolution through children's literature.* New York: Scholastic Professional Books.

Levin, D. E. (1994). *Teaching young children in violent times: Building a peaceable classroom.* Philadelphia, PA: New Society Publishers (2nd edition, 2003, Washington, DC: NAEYC).

Luvmour, S., & Luvmour, J. (1990). *Everybody wins! Cooperative games and activities.* Philadelphia: New Society Publishers.

Pelo, A., & Davidson, A. (2000). *That's not fair!: A teacher's guide to activism with young children.* St. Paul, MN: Redleaf Press.

Prutzman, P., Stern, L., Burger, M. L., Bodenhamer, G. (1988). *Friendly classroom for a small planet: A handbook for creative approaches to living and problem solving for children.* Philadelphia: New Society Publishers.

Roberts, P. (2002). *Kids taking action: Community service learning projects K-8.* Greenfield, MA: Northeast Foundation for Children.

Smith, C. A. (1993). *The peaceful classroom: 162 easy activities to teach preschoolers compassion and cooperation.* Mt. Ranier, MD: Gryphon House.

Vance, E., & Weaver, P. J. (2002). *Class meetings: Young children solving problems together.* Washington, DC: National Association for the Education of Young Children.

Wichert, S. (1989). *Keeping the peace: Practicing cooperation and conflict resolution.* Philadelphia: New Society Publishers.

York, S. (1991). *Roots and wings: Affirming culture in early childhood programs.* St. Paul, MN: Redleaf Press.

York, S. (1992). *Developing roots and wings: A trainer's guide to affirming culture in early childhood programs.* St. Paul, MN: Redleaf Press.

Appendix E
How to Play the Games in Chapters 8 and 9

GAMES AND ACTIVITIES FOR PEACEMAKING AND COMMUNITY-BUILDING: PRESCHOOL, KINDERGARTEN, AND PRIMARY GRADES

There are many variations of these games and a number of them are very familiar. Feel free to adapt and modify these and other games, as long as the new versions are still based on cooperation, community-building, and mutual support of all players. Individual competition, material rewards, and outcomes based solely on physical size, strength, or ability should be avoided. Most of the games below have been collected and adapted from multiple sources, but the references provided in some cases may be helpful.

- *Animal Acting:* Children choose an animal to pantomime while others try to guess what they are acting out (Luvmour, 1990, p. 38).

- *A What?:* This game involves coordination of a question-and-answer sequence. Try not to get mixed up!

  Child 1 hands an item to Child 2 and says, "This is a ball" (or whatever the item is)

  Child 2 asks, "A what?"

  Child 1: A ball.

  Child 2: Oh! (turns to Child 3) This is a ball.

  Child 3: A what? (and so forth)

Now, what makes this fun and challenging is to pass two items in opposite directions around the circle. A variation for older children (or even grownups) is to pass the items one right after the other so that players are engaged in two conversations at once. You may use inherently humorous items, like bananas, or use a ball or block and call it something else.

- *Blanket Toss and Catch:* Children work to-gether, holding onto a blanket so that they can toss one or more balls in the air and catch them again in the blanket. There are many other ideas for cooperative games with blankets, as well as with parachutes.

- *Body Sculpture:* Children work in pairs or teams to pose themselves or each other into statues or sculptures (Wichert, 1989, p. 67).

- *Cooperative Juggling:* Children play catch, throwing two or more balls across a circle at once. Paying attention is important! Again, there are many variations.

- *Cooperative Monster Making:* This is a group art activity in which everyone contributes part of the creation of an imaginary monster, outer space creature, or fantasy animal. Children take turns adding multiple body parts, and may end by naming the creature or telling a group story about it (Prutzman, 1988, p. 28).

- *Cooperative Musical Chairs:* This is a familiar cooperative version of what used to be a very competitive game. Seats are gradually removed, but not players, and all pile onto one another on the remaining seats. Floor pillows may be safer than chairs.

- *Cooperative Spider Web #1:* Children sit on the floor in a circle and make a web by rolling a ball of yarn back and forth across the circle, remembering to keep holding onto the yarn. Children may use their turns to say something nice about each other, tell a piece of a story, rhyme words, etc.
- *Cooperative Spider Web #2:* A team of children, each with a ball of yarn or string, works together to create a room-sized spider web. Another team untangles the web. There may be a treat, surprise, or message attached to the end of each string.
- *Cooperative Story Telling:* Everyone contributes by adding a part to the story. The storytelling may proceed around the circle or follow a ball of yarn from person to person. Storytellers may pass an item or prop to use in the story. Many variations are possible.
- *Favorite Things Chart:* A language experience can become a cooperative community-building opportunity by making a group list of everyone's favorites. Children discover how alike and different their favorites are, exploring commonalities and differences and getting a feel for who they are as a group.
- *Find Your Animal Mate:* Each child is secretly told the name of an animal, and they all act out their animals until they find another child acting out the same animal (Luvmour, 1990, p. 27).
- *Gyrating Reptile:* A favorite! Children make one long snake that moves by "tummy power." Children lie on the floor in a long line, holding the ankles of the child ahead of them. The child at the head may use hands and the child at the tail may use feet, but everyone else just wriggles along (Luvmour, 1990, p. 39).
- *Honey, I Love You, But I Just Can't Smile:* This is a "try not to smile" challenge! Player 1 says to Player 2: "I love you, Honey!" Player 2 attempts to keep from smiling while answering, "Honey, I love you, but I just can't smile." Then Player 2 gets to try it out on Player 3, and on around the room. (It gets harder and harder not to smile!)
- *Hot and Cold:* This is a well-known whole group activity. An object is hidden, and everyone but one child (or a small team) knows where it is.

The group gives clues, hot (getting close) and cold (getting farther away), until the seeker or seekers locate the object.
- *Human Jigsaw Puzzle:* In this activity, children make a people puzzle by lying close together on the floor, intertwining their arms and legs as interlocking puzzle pieces. After a few minutes, they get up, walk around, and then try to recreate the puzzle as it was (Prutzman, 1988, p. 24).
- *Inuit Ball Pass:* Children pass a ball from one to another around the circle, using only the open palm of one hand. The idea is to pass the ball as quickly as possible without dropping it or using the thumb and fingers to hold on (Luvmour, 1990, p. 46).
- *Lemonade:* In this team pantomime game, one team acts out an action, object, animal, etc. As soon as someone on the other team guesses correctly, the pantomime team runs to base, chased by the guessing team. Anyone tagged changes teams (Luvmour, 1990, p. 15).
- *Machine Building:* In this variation of creative drama, children use group body sculpture to represent a real or imaginary machine (Prutzman, 1988, p. 30).
- *Pantomime Games:* There are many variations to try, as children act without words in pairs or teams, making letters of the alphabet, tableaux or scenes from stories, and so forth (see creative drama sources as well as ideas in Prutzman, 1988).
- *Popcorn Balls:* As the teacher orchestrates the action in this activity, children begin by sitting on the floor as popcorn kernels. As they pretend to heat up, they pop up and hop around, eventually all sticking together in one big popcorn ball (Luvmour, 1990, p. 16).
- *Rolling Along:* Children lie on the floor with the bottoms of their feet together and roll along, trying to stay connected (Luvmour, 1990, p. 17).
- *Rope Raising:* This is much harder than it looks. Children sit in a circle holding a rope that is tied together at the ends. All try to stand up together (Luvmour, 1990, p. 17).
- *Sleeper:* One player is secretly designated as "it." As "it" secretly winks at other players, they pretend to fall asleep until someone figures out who "it" is.

- *Spaghetti:* Children stand in a circle and hold hands with others who are not standing next to them. Children will need to work patiently and cooperatively to un-tangle the spaghetti and make a circle without letting go.
- *Standing Together:* Another group physical challenge! Children sit in a circle holding hands and work together to stand up all at once (Luvmour, 1990, p. 16).
- *This Ain't No Piano:* Children lie next to each other on the floor to form a keyboard. Each child chooses a unique sound. Children produce their own sounds as the teacher or a child piano player touches their feet (Wichert, 1989, p. 80).
- *Tracing a Friend:* Children trace each other's bodies on a large piece of paper on the floor. This is a cooperative alternative to having the teacher do the tracing. You may adapt this for all ages. Crayons are better than markers (Wichert, 1989, p. 70).
- *Wrap a Friend:* A great team effort and lots of fun! A few children work together to wrap another child in large pieces of news-print. When they are finished, the wrapped child breaks out of the paper. A few rules: Keep the face free, and don't use scissors. Masking tape may be used, but only on the paper, not on the child (Wichert, 1989, p. 85).

References

Aboud, F. (1988). *Children and prejudice*. New York: Blackwell.

Adams, S. K., & Wittmer, D. S. (2001). "I had it first": Teaching young children to solve problems peacefully. *Childhood Education, 77*, 10–16.

Adults and Children Against Violence. (2002). *Violence prevention in early childhood: How teachers can help*. Washington, DC: American Psychological Association and National Association for the Education of Young Children (NAEYC).

Alat, K. (2002). Traumatic events and children: How early childhood educators can help. *Childhood Education, 79*, 2–8.

American Academy of Pediatrics. (2001). Organized sports for children and preadolescents. *Pediatrics, 107*, 1459–1462.

American Psychological Association. (1993). *Violence and youth: Psychology's response. Volume I: Summary report of the American Psychological Association Commission on Violence and Youth*. Washington, DC: Author.

American Psychological Association & the National Association for the Education of Young Children. (2002). *Violence prevention in early childhood: How teachers can help*. Washington, DC: Authors.

Arcaro-McPhee, R., Doppler, E. E., & Haw-kins, D. A. (2002). Conflict resolution in a preschool constructivist classroom: A case study in negotiation. *Journal of Research in Childhood Education, 17*, 19–25.

Armstrong, T. (1994). *Multiple intelligences in the classroom*. Alexandria, VA: Association for Supervision and Curriculum Development.

Arnold, D. H., Homrok, S., Ortiz, C., & Stowe, R. M. (1999). Direct observation of peer rejection acts and their temporal relation with aggressive acts. *Early Childhood Research Quarterly, 14*, 183–196.

Association for Supervision and Curriculum Development. (1997). *Promoting social and emotional learning: Guidelines for educators*. Alexandria, VA: Author.

Association for Supervision and Curriculum Development. (1998). Making parent involvement meaningful. *Education Update, 40*(1), 1, 3, 8.

Ayres, B. J., & Hedeen, D. L. (2003). Creating positive behavior support plans for students with significant behavioral challenges. In M. S. E. Fishbaugh, T. R. Berkeley, & G. Schroth (Eds.), *Ensuring safe schools: Exploring issues—Seeking solution* (pp. 89–105). Mahwah, NJ: Lawrence Erlbaum.

Bakeman, R., & Brownlee, J. R. (1982). Social rules governing object conflicts in toddlers and preschoolers. In K. H. Rubin & H. S. Ross (Eds.), *Peer relationships and social skills in childhood* (pp. 99–111). New York: Springer-Verlag.

Bakly, S. (2001). Through the lens of sensory integration: A different way of analyzing challenging behavior. *Young Children, 56*(6), 70–76.

Ballen, J., & Moles, O. (1994). *Strong families, strong schools: Building community partnerships for learning*. Washington, DC: U.S. Department of Education.

Banks, J. A. (1999) *Introduction to multicultural education* (2nd ed.). Boston: Allyn & Bacon.

Barazzoni, R. (2000). *Brick by brick*. Reggio Emilia, Italy: Reggio Children.

Beaty, J. J. (1998). *Observing development of the young child* (4th ed.). Upper Saddle River, NJ: Merrill/Prentice Hall.

Bell, N., Grossen, M., & Perret-Clermont, A. (1985). Sociocognitive conflict and intellectual growth. In M. W. Berkowitz (Ed.), *Peer conflict and psychological growth. New directions for child development, 29* (pp. 41–54). San Francisco: Jossey-Bass.

Berger, E. H. (2000). *Parents as partners in education: Families and schools working together* (5th ed.). Upper Saddle River, NJ: Merrill/Prentice Hall.

Berk, L. E. (2000). *Child development* (5th ed.). Boston: Allyn & Bacon.

Berkowitz, M. W. (Ed.). (1985). *Peer conflict and psychological growth. New directions for child development, 29.* San Francisco: Jossey-Bass.

Bernat, V. (1993). Teaching peace. *Young Children, 48*(3), 36–39.

Bernstein, J., Zimmerman, T. S., Werner-Wilson, R. J., & Vosburg, J. (2000). Pre-school children's classification skills and a multicultural education intervention to promote acceptance of ethnic diversity. *Journal of Research in Childhood Education, 14,* 181–192.

Bickmore, K. (1997). *Teaching conflict and conflict resolution in school: (Extra-) curricular considerations.* Paper presented at Connections '97 International Social Studies Conference, Sydney, Australia.

Bickmore, K. (1999). Elementary curriculum about conflict resolution: Can children handle global politics? *Theory and Research in Social Education, 27,* 45–69.

Blanchard, K., & Johnson, S. (1982). *One minute manage.* New York: Berkley.

Blume, J. (1980). *Superfudge.* New York: Dutton.

Brenneis, D., & Lein, L. (1977). "You fruithead": A sociolinguistic approach to children's dispute settlement. In S. Ervin-Tripp & S. Mitchell-Kerman (Eds.), *Child Discourse* (pp. 49–65). New York: Academic Press.

Bronfenbrenner, U. (1979). *The ecology of human development.* Cambridge, MA: Harvard University Press.

Bronfenbrenner, U., & Morris, P. A. (1998). The ecology of developmental processes. In R. M. Lerner (Ed.), *Handbook of child psychology: Vol. 1. Theoretical models of human development* (5th ed., pp. 535–584). New York: Wiley.

Bronson, M. B. (1995). *The right stuff for children birth to 8.* Washington, DC: National Association for the Education of Young Children.

Brown, M., & Bergen, D. (2002). Play and social interaction of children with disabilities at learning/activity centers in an inclusive preschool. *Early Childhood Education Journal, 17,* 26–37.

Brown, V., & Pleydell, S. (1999). *The dramatic difference: Drama in the preschool and kindergarten classroom.* Portsmouth, NH: Heinemann.

Browning, L., Davis, B., & Resta, V. (2000). What do you mean "Think before I act?": Conflict resolution with choices. *Journal of Research in Early Childhood, 14,* 232–238.

Bruner. J. (1986). *Actual minds, possible worlds.* Cambridge, MA: Harvard University Press.

Bullock, J. R. (2002). Bullying among children. *Childhood Education, 78,* 130–133.

Burton, R. A., & Denham, S. A. (1998). "Are you my friend?" How two young children learned to get along with others. *Journal of Research in Early Childhood, 12,* 210–224.

Byrnes, D. A., & Kiger, G. (Eds.). (1992). *Common bonds: Anti-bias teaching in a diverse society.* Olney, MD: Association for Childhood Education International.

Campbell, P. H., McGregor, G., & Nasik. E. (1994). Promoting the development of young children through use of technology. In P. L. Safford (Ed.), *Yearbook in early childhood education: Vol. 5. Early childhood special education* (pp. 192–217). New York: Teachers College Press.

Carger, C. L. (1997). Attending to new voices. *Educational Leadership, 55,* 39–43.

Carlsson-Paige, N., & Levin, D. (1990). *Who's calling the shots?: How to respond effectively to children's fascination with war play and war toys.* Philadelphia: New Society Publishers.

Carlsson-Paige, N., & Levin, D. E. (1992). Making peace in violent times: A constructivist approach to conflict resolution. *Young Children, 48*(1), 4–13.

Cazden, C. (1988). *Classroom discourse: The language of teaching and learning.* Portsmouth, NH: Heinemann.

Chapman, M., & McBride, M. L. (1992). The education of reason: Cognitive conflict and its role in intellectual development. In C. Shantz & W. Hartup (Eds.), *Conflict in child and adolescent development* (pp. 36–69). Cambridge, UK: Cambridge University Press.

Charles, C. M. (2000). *The synergistic classroom: Joyful teaching and gentle discipline.* New York: Longman.

Charney, R. S. (1992). *Teaching children to care: Management in the responsive classroom.* Greenfield, MA: Northeast Foundation for Children.

Charney, R. S. (1997). *Habits of goodness: Case studies in the social curriculum.* Greenfield, MA: Northeast Foundation for Children.

Charney, R. S. (2002). *Teaching children to care: Classroom management for ethical and academic growth k-8.* Greenfield, MA: Northeast Foundation for Children.

Chen, D. W., & Smith, K. E. (2002). The Social Conflict Inventory (SCI): A measure of beliefs about classroom peer conflicts. *Journal of Early Childhood Teacher Education, 23,* 299–313.

Children's Defense Fund. (2002). *The state of America's children yearbook 2002.* Washington, DC: Author.

Cicourel, A. W. (1970). The acquisition of social structure: Toward a developmental sociology of language and meaning. In J. D. Douglas (Ed.), *Understanding everyday life* (pp. 136–168). Chicago: Aldine.

Clarke, S. H., & Campbell, F. A. (1998). Can intervention early prevent crime later? The Abecedarian Project compared with other programs. *Early Childhood Research Quarterly, 13,* 319–343.

Clayton, M. K. (2001). *Classroom spaces that work: Strategies for teachers series.* Greenfield, MA: Northeast Foundation for Children.

Coles, R. (1986). *The moral life of children.* Boston: Atlantic Monthly Press.

Coles, R. (1990). *The spiritual life of children.* Boston: Houghton Mifflin.

Collins, E. N., & McGaha, C. G. (2000). Create rewarding circle times by working with toddlers, not against them. *Childhood Education, 78*(4), 194–199.

Corsaro, W. A. (1981). Entering the child's world: Research strategies for field entry and data collection in a preschool setting. In J. Green & C. Wallat (Eds.), *Ethnography and language in educational settings* (pp. 117–146). Norwood, NJ: Ablex.

Corsaro, W. A. (1985). *Friendship and peer culture in the early years.* Norwood, NJ: Ablex.

Corsaro, W. A. (1986). Discourse processes within peer culture: From a constructivist to an interpretive approach to childhood socialization. In P. A. Adler & P. Adler (Eds.), *Sociological Studies of Child Development* (pp. 81–103). Greenwich, CT: JAI Press.

Corsaro, W. A., & Eder, D. (1990). Children's peer cultures. *Annual Review of Sociology, 6,* 197–220.

Corsaro, W. A., & Rizzo, T. A. (1988). *Discussione* and friendship: Socialization pro-cesses in the peer culture of Italian nursery school children. *American Sociological Review, 53,* 879–894.

Corsaro, W. A., & Rizzo, T. A. (1990). Disputes in the peer culture of American and Italian nursery school children. In A. D. Grimshaw (Ed.), *Conflict talk* (pp. 21–66). Cambridge, England: Cambridge University Press.

Corsaro, W. A., & Schwartz, K. (1991). Peer play and socialization in two cultures: Implications for practice and research. In B. Scales, M. Almy, S. Nicolopoulou, & S. Ervin-Tripp (Eds.), *Play and the social context of development in early care and education* (pp. 234–254). New York: Teachers College Press.

Coser, L. (1956). *The functions of social conflict.* New York: Free Press.

Covey, S. R. (1989). *Seven habits of highly effective people: Restoring the character ethic.* New York: Simon and Schuster.

Crary, E. (1984). *Kids can cooperate: A practical guide for teaching problem solving*. Seattle, WA: Parenting Press.

Crick, N. R., Casas, J. F., & Mosher, M. (1997). Relational and overt aggression in preschool. *Developmental Psychology, 33,* 579–588.

Crosser, S. (1992). Managing the early childhood classroom. *Young Children, 47*(2), 23–29.

Crosser-Tower, C. (2002). *When children are abused: An educator's guide to intervention*. Boston: Allyn & Bacon.

D'Amato, J. J. (1989). Rivalry as a game of relationships: The social structure created by boys of a Hawaiian primary school class. In M. N. Bloch & A. D. Pellegrini (Eds.), *The ecological context of children's play* (pp. 245–281). Norwood, NJ: Ablex.

Damon, W. (1977). *The social world of the child*. San Francisco: Jossey-Bass.

Danby, S., & Baker, C. D. (2001). Escalating terror: Communicative strategies in a preschool classroom. *Early Education and Development, 12,* 343–358.

DeGaetano, Y., Williams, L. R., & Volk, D. (1998). *Kaleidoscope: A multicultural approach for the primary school classroom*. Upper Saddle River, NJ: Merrill/Prentice Hall.

DeLoache, J., & Gottlieb, A. (2000). *A world of babies: Imagined childcare guides for seven societies*. Cambridge, UK: Cambridge University Press.

de Marquez, T. M. (2002). Creating world peace, one classroom at a time. *Young Children, 57*(6), 90–94.

Delpit, L. (1995). *Other people's children: Cultural conflict in the classroom*. New York: The New Press.

Derman-Sparks, L., & the A.B.C. Task Force. (1989). *Anti-bias curriculum: Tools for empowering young children*. Washington, DC: National Association for the Education of Young Children.

DeVries, R., & Zan, B. (1994). *Moral classrooms, moral children: Creating a constructivist atmosphere in early education*. New York: Teachers College Press.

Dewey, J. (1938). *Experience and education*. New York: Collier.

Division for Early Childhood. (1999). *DEC concept paper on the identification of and intervention with challenging behavior*. Reston, VA: Author.

Donaldson, M. (1978). *Children's minds*. New York: Norton.

Dreikurs, R. (1990/1964). *Children: The challenge*. New York: Plume (1990).

Dunn, J., & Cutting, A. L. (1999). Understanding others and individual differences in friendship interactions in young children. *Social Development, 8,* 201–219.

Edelman, J. (2002). Want early childhood education to be a political priority?… Start organizing! *Young Children, 57*(2), 75–77.

Edwards, C. P. (1986). *Promoting social and moral development in young children: Creative approaches for the classroom*. New York: Teachers College Press.

Edwards, C., Galdini, L., & Forman, G. (Eds.). (1998). *The hundred languages of children: The Reggio Emilia approach—advanced reflections* (2nd ed.). Greenwich, CT: Ablex.

Eisenberg, A., & Garvey, C. (1981). Children's use of verbal strategies in resolving conflicts. *Disourse Processes, 4,* 149–170.

Elkind, D. (1998). Character education: An Ineffective Luxury? *Child Care Information Exchange, 124*(6), 6–9.

Epstein, J. L. (1995). School/family/community partnerships: Caring for the children we share. *Phi Delta Kappan, 76,* 701–712.

Epstein, J. L. (2001). *School, family and community partnerships: Preparing educators and improving schools*. Boulder, CO: Westview Press.

Erikson, E. (1963). *Childhood and society*. New York: Norton.

Erwin, E. J., Alimaras, E., & Price, N. (1999). A qualitative study of social dynamics in an inclusive preschool. *Journal of Research in Childhood Education, 14,* 56–67.

Essa, E. (2003). *A practical guide to solving preschool behavior problems* (5th ed.). Albany, NY: Delmar.

Evans, B. (2002). *You can't come to my birthday party: Conflict resolution with young children*. Ypsilanti, MI: High/Scope Press.

Faber, A., & Mazlish, E. (1995). *How to talk so kids can learn at home and at school*. New York: Avon Books.

Faber, A., & Mazlish, E. (1998). *Siblings without rivalry: How to help your children live together so you can live too* (10th ed.). New York: Avon Books.

Fallin, K., Wallinga, C., & Coleman, M. (2001). Helping children cope with stress in the classroom setting. *Childhood Education, 77*, 17–24.

Fillipini, T. (1998). The role of the pedagogista: An interview with Lella Gandini. In C. Edwards, L. Galdidni, & G. Forman (Eds.), *The hundred languages of children: The Reggio Emilia approach—advanced reflections* (2nd ed., pp. 127–137). Greenwich, CT: Ablex.

Fine, G. A. (1985). The strains of idioculture: External threat and internal crisis on a Little League baseball team. In G. A. Fine (Ed.), *Meaningful play, playful meaning*. Champaign, IL: Human Kinetics Publishers.

Forman, E. A., & Kraker, M. J. (1985). The social origins of logic: The contributions of Piaget and Vygotsky. In M. W. Berkowitz (Ed.), *Peer conflict and psychological growth. New directions for child development, 29*, 23–29. San Francisco: Jossey-Bass.

Froschl, M., & Gropper, N. (1999). Fostering friendships, curbing bullying. *Educational Leadership, 57*, 72–75.

Froschl, M., & Sprung, B. (1999). On purpose: Addressing teasing and bullying in early childhood. *Young Children, 54*(2), 70–72.

Fuller, M. L., & Olson, G. (1998). *Home-school relations: Working successfully with parents and families.* Boston: Allyn & Bacon.

Furman, W., & McQuaid, E. L. (1992). Intervention programs for the management of conflict. In C. Shantz & W. Hartup (Eds.), *Conflict in child and adolescent development* (pp. 402–429). Cambridge, UK: Cambridge University Press.

Gandini, L. (1998). Educational and caring spaces. In C. Edwards, L. Galdidni, & G. Forman (Eds.), *The hundred languages of children: The Reggio Emilia approach—advanced reflections* (2nd ed., pp. 161–178). Greenwich, CT: Ablex.

Garbarino, J. (1995). *Raising children in a socially toxic environment.* San Francisco: Jossey-Bass.

Garbarino, J. (2000). CAN reflections on 20 years of searching. In M. A. Jensen & M. A. Hannibal (Eds.), *Issues, advocacy, and leadership in early education* (2nd ed., pp. 89–91). Boston: Allyn & Bacon.

Garbarino, J., Kostelny, K., Dubrow, N., & Pardo, C. (1992). *Children in danger: Coping with the consequences of community violence.* San Francisco: Jossey-Bass.

Gardner, H. (1983). *Frames of mind: Theory of multiple intelligences.* New York: Basic Books.

Gardner, H. (1993). Multiple intelligences: The theory in practice. New York: Basic Books.

Gartrell, D. (2001). Replacing time-out: Part one—Using guidance to build an encouraging classroom. *Young Children, 56*(6), 8–16.

Gartrell, D. (2002). Replacing time-out: Part one—Using guidance to maintain an encouraging classroom. *Young Children, 57* (2), 36–43.

Garvey, C., & Shantz, C. U. (1992). Conflict talk: Approaches to adversative discourse. In C. Shantz & W. Hartup (Eds.), *Conflict in child and adolescent development* (pp. 93–121). Cambridge, U.K.: Cambridge University Press.

Gay, G. (1997). Connections between character education and multicultural education. In A. Molnar (Ed.), *The construction of children's character* (pp. 97–109). Chicago: University of Chicago Press.

Genishi, C., & DiPaolo, M. (1982). Learning through argument in the preschool. In L. C. Wilkinson (Ed.), *Communicating in the classroom* (pp. 49–68). New York: Academic Press.

Gillespie, C. W., & Chick, A. (2001). Fussbusters: Using peers to mediate conflict resolution in a Head Start classroom. *Childhood Education, 77*, 192–195.

Gilligan, C. (1982). *In a different voice: Psychological theory and women's development.* Cambridge, MA: Harvard University Press.

Gilligan, C. (2001). *The birth of pleasure.* New York: Knopf.

Goldstein, L. S. (1998). More than gentle smiles and warm hugs: Applying the ethic of care to early childhood education. *Journal of Research in Childhood Education, 12*, 244–261.

Goldstein, L. S. (2002). *Reclaiming caring in teaching and teacher education.* New York: Peter Lang.

Goodman, J. (2000). Moral education in early childhood education: The limits of constructivism. *Early Education and Development, 11,* 37–54.

Goodwin, M. H. (1990). *He-said-she-said: Talk as social organization among Black children.* Bloomington, IN: Indiana University Press.

Goodwin, M. H., & Goodwin, C. (1987). Children's arguing. In S. U. Philips, S. Steele, & C. Yanz (Eds.), *Language, gender, and sex in comparative perspective.* Cambridge, U.K.: Cambridge University Press.

Graue, M. E., & Walsh, D. J. (1998). *Studying children in context: Theories, methods, and ethics.* Thousand Oaks, CA: Sage.

Greenman, J. (2001). *What happened to the world? Helping children cope in turbulent times.* Watertown, MA: Bright Horizons Family Solutions.

Grimshaw, A. D. (Ed.). (1990). *Conflict talk.* Cambridge, U.K.: Cambridge University Press.

Groves, B. M., Leiberman, A. F., Osofsky, J. D., & Fenichel, E. (2000). Protecting young children in violent environments—A framework to build on. *Zero to Three, 20*(5), 9–13.

Guralnick, M. J. (1994). Social competence with peers: Outcome and process in early childhood special education. In P. L. Safford (Ed.), *Yearbook in early childhood education: Vol. 5. Early childhood special education* (pp. 45–71). New York: Teachers College Press.

Guralnick, M. J. (1996). Immediate effects of mainstreamed settings on the social interactions and social integration of preschool children. *American Journal on Mental Retardation, 100,* 359–377.

Guralnick, M. J., & Connor, R. T. (1996). The peer relations of preschool children with communication disorders. *Child Development, 67,* 471–489.

Harris, I. (2002, April). *Peace education theory.* Paper presented at the meeting of the American Educational Research Association, New Orleans, LA.

Hartup, W. W. (1992). *Having friends, making friends, and keeping friends: Relationships as educational contexts.* Urbana, IL: Clearinghouse on Elementary and Early Childhood Education. (ERIC Document Reproduction Service No. ED345854)

Hartup, W. W., & Laursen, B. (1989, April). *Contextual constraints and children's friendship relations.* Paper presented at the biennial meeting of the Society for Research in Child Development, Kansas City, MO (April 27–30, 1989). (ERIC Document Reproduction Service No. ED310848)

Hartup, W. W., & Moore, S. G. (1990). Early peer relations: Developmental significance and prognostic implications. *Early Childhood Research Quarterly, 5,* 1–17.

Hartup, W. W., Laursen, B., Stewart, M. I., & Eastenson, A. (1988). Conflict and the friendship relations of young children. *Child Development, 59,* 1590–1600.

Hay, D. F. (1984). Social conflict in early childhood education. *Annals of Child Development, 1,* 1–44.

Hay, D. F., & Ross, H. S. (1982). The social nature of early conflict. *Child Development, 53,* 105–113.

Heath, S. B. (1983). *Ways with words: Language, life and work in communities and classrooms.* New York: Cambridge University Press.

Heft, T. M., & Swaminathan, S. (2002). Effects of computers in the social behavior of preschoolers. *Journal of Research in Childhood Education, 16,* 162–174.

Horowitz, S. V., Boardman, S. K., & Redlener, I. (1994). Constructive conflict management and coping in homeless children and adolescents. *Journal of Social Issues, 50*(1), 85–98.

Horsch, P., Chen, J., & Wagner, S. L. (2002). The responsive classroom: A caring, respectful school environment as a context for development. *Education and Urban Society, 34,* 385–383.

Isenberg, J. P., & Jalongo, M. R. (2001). *Creative expression and play in early childhood* (3rd. ed.). Upper Saddle River, NJ: Merrill/Prentice Hall.

Kamps, D. M., Tankersly, M., & Ellis, C. (2000). Social skills interventions for young at-risk students: A 2-year follow-up study. *Behavioral Disorders, 25*(4), 310–324.

Jensen, M. A., & Hannibal, M. A. (2000). *Issues, advocacy, and leadership in early education* (2nd ed.). Boston: Allyn & Bacon.

Johnson, D. W., Johnson, R. T., Dudley, B., & Burnett, R. (1992). Teaching students to be peer mediators. *Educational Leadership, 50* (1), 10–13.

Johnson, D. W., Johnson, R. T., & Holubec, E. J. (1994). *The new circles of learning: Cooperation in the classroom and school*. Alexandria, VA: Association for Supervision and Curriculum Development.

Johnson, J., Christie, J., & Yawkey, T. (1987). *Play and early childhood development*. Glenview, IL: Scott-Foresman.

Kaiser, B., & Rasminsky, J. S. (1999). *Meeting the challenge: Effective strategies for challenging behaviours in early childhood environments*. Ottawa, Canada: Canadian Child Care Federation.

Katch, J. (2001). *Under deadman's skin: Discovering the meaning of children's violent play*. Boston: Beacon Press.

Katz, L. G. (1984). The professional early childhood teacher. In J. F. Brown (Ed.), *Administering programs for young children* (pp. 23–30). Washington, DC: NAEYC.

Katz, L. G., & Chard, S. C. (1989). *Engaging children's minds: The Project Approach*. Norwood, NJ: Ablex.

Katz, L. G., & McClellan, D. E. (1991). *The teacher's role in the social development of young children*. Urbana, IL. (ERIC Document Reproduction Service No. ED331642)

Kelker, K. R. (2003). Resolving conflicts in schools: An educational approach to violence prevention. In M. S. E. Fishbaugh, T. R. Berkeley, & G. Schroth (Eds.), *Ensuring safe schools: Exploring issues—Seeking solutions* (pp. 69–86). Mahwah, NJ: Lawrence Erlbaum.

Killen, M., & Turiel, E. (1991). Conflict resolution in preschool social interactions. *Early Education and Development, 2*, 240–255.

King, E. W., Chapman, M., & Cruz-Jansen, M. (1994). *Educating young children in a diverse society*. Boston: Allyn & Bacon.

Kirchner, G. (2000). *Children's games from around the world* (2nd ed.). Boston: Allyn & Bacon.

Klahr, D., & MacWhunney, B. (1998). Information processing. In D. Kuhn & R. S. Singer (Eds.), *Handbook of child psychology: Vol. 2* (5th ed., pp. 632–678). New York: Wiley.

Kneese, C., Fullwood, H., Schroth, G., & Pankake, A. M. (2003). Decreasing school violence: A research synthesis. In M. S. E. Fishbaugh, T. R. Berkeley, & G. Schroth (Eds.), *Ensuring safe schools: Exploring issues—Seeking solutions* (pp. 38–57). Mahwah, NJ: Lawrence Erlbaum.

Knowles, C. R. (2001). *Prevention that works! A guide for developing school-based drug and violence prevention programs*. Thousand Oaks, CA: Sage.

Kohn, A. (1991). Caring kids: The role of the school. *Phi Delta Kappan, 72,* 496–506.

Kohn, A. (1997). The trouble with character education. In A. Molnar (Ed.), *The construction of children's character* (pp. 154–162). Chicago: University of Chicago Press.

Kohn, A. (2001). Five reasons to stop saying "good job." *Young Children, 56*(5), 24–28.

Kostelnik, M., Onaga, E., Rohde, B., & Whiren, A. (2002). *Children with special needs*. New York: Teachers College Press.

Kozol, J. (1995). *Amazing grace: The lives of children and the conscience of a nation*. New York: Crown.

Kozol, J. (2000). *Ordinary resurrections: Children in the years of hope*. New York: Crown Publishers.

Krall, C. M., & Jalongo, M. R. (1999). Creating a caring community in classrooms. *Childhood Education, 75,* 83–89.

Kramer, L., Noornam, S., & Brockman, E. (1999). Representations of sibling relationships in young children's literature. *Early Childhood Research Quarterly, 14,* 555–574.

Kramer, L., Peroszynski, L. A., & Tsai-Yen Chung. (1999). Parental responses to sibling conflict: The effects of development and parent gender. *Child Development, 70,* 1401–1414.

Krcmar, M., Cooke, M. C. (2001). Children's moral reasoning and perceptions of televi- sion violence. *Journal of Communication, 51,* 300–316.

Kreidler, W. J. (1984). *Creative conflict resolution: More than 200 activities for keeping the peace in the classroom*. Glenview, IL: Scott Foresman.

Kreidler, W. J. (1994). *Teaching conflict resolution through children's literature (k-2)*. New York: Scholastic, Inc.

Ladd, G. W. (1990). Having friends, keeping friends, making friends and being liked by peers in the classroom: Predictors of children's early school adjustment. *Child Development, 61,* 1081–1100.

Ladson-Billings, G. (1994). *The dreamkeepers: Successful teachers of African-American children.* San Francisco: Jossey-Bass.

Lantieri, L., & Patti, J. (1996). *Waging peace in our schools.* Boston: Beacon Press.

Laursen, B., & Hartup, W. W. (1989). The dynamics of preschool children's conflicts. *Merrill-Palmer Quarterly, 35,* 281–297.

Levin, D. (1994, 2003). *Teaching young children in violent times: Building a peaceable classroom.* Philadelphia: New Society Publishers. (Revised edition forthcoming, to be published by NAEYC in 2003.)

Levin, D. E. (1998). *Remote control childhood? Combating the hazards of media culture.* Washington, DC: National Association for the Education of Young Children.

Lickona, T. (1991). *Educating for character: How our schools can teach respect and responsibility.* New York: Bantam.

Lickona, T. (1997). Educating for character: A comprehensive approach. In A. Molnar (Ed.), *The construction of children's character* (pp. 45–62). Chicago: University of Chicago Press.

Linder, T. (1994). The role of play in special education. In P. L. Safford (Ed.), *Yearbook in early childhood education: Vol. 5. Early childhood special education* (pp. 72–95). New York: Teachers College Press.

Lipsitt, L. P. (Ed.). (1994). *Violence: Its causes and cures: An edited transcript of a national symposium.* Providence, RI: Manisses Communications Group.

Lockwood, A. L. (1997). What is character education?. In A. Molnar (Ed.), *The construction of children's character* (pp. 174–185). Chicago: University of Chicago Press.

Lombardi, J., & Goffin, S. G. (1988). *Speaking out: Early childhood advocacy.* Washington, DC: National Association for the Education of Young Children.

Losardo, A., & Notari-Syverson, A. (2001). *Alternative approaches to assessing young children.* Baltimore: Paul H. Brookes.

Lubin, D., & Forbes, D. (1984). Children's reasoning and peer relations. In B. Rogoff & L. Lave

(Eds.), *Everyday cognition: Its development in social context* (pp. 220–237). Cambridge, MA: Harvard University Press.

Luvmour, S., & Luvmour, J. (1990). *Everybody wins! Cooperative games and activities.* Philadelphia: New Society Publishers.

Lynch, E. W., & Hanson, M. J. (1998). *Developing cross-cultural competence: A guide for working with children and their families* (2nd ed.). Baltimore: Brookes.

Maccoby, E. E. (1996). Peer conflict and intrafamily conflict: Are there conceptual bridges? *Merrill-Palmer Quarterly, 42,* 165–176.

Malloy, H. L., & McMurray, P. (1996). Conflict strategies and resolutions: Peer conflict in an integrated early childhood classroom. *Early Childhood Research Quarterly, 11,* 185–206.

Mandell, N. (1986). Peer interaction in day care settings: Implications for social cognition. In P. A. Adler & P. Adler (Eds.), *Sociological studies of child development* (pp. 55–79). Greenwich, CT: JAI Press.

Mann, J. (2000, May 19). A scientist's insights into gun violence. *The Washington Post,* p. C11.

Marshall, C. S. (1998). Using children's storybooks to encourage discussions among diverse populations. *Childhood Education, 74,* 194–199.

Marshall, H. H. (1995). Beyond "I Like the Way …" *Young Children, 50*(2), 26–28.

Maynard, D. W. (1985a). How children start arguments. *Language in Society, 14,* 1–30.

Maynard, D. W. (1985b). On the functions of social conflict among children. *American Sociological Review, 50,* 207–223.

McCarthy, C. (1992). Why we must teach peace. *Educational Leadership, 50*(1), 6–9.

McGinnis, J., & McGinnis, K. (1981). *Parenting for peace and justice.* Maryknoll, NY: Orbis Books.

Menacker, J., Hurwitz, E., & Weldon, W. (1988). Parent-teacher cooperation in the schools: Serving the urban poor. *Clearing House, 62*(3), 108–111.

Miller, P. M., Danaher, D. L., & Forbes, D. (1986). Sex-related strategies for coping with interpersonal conflict in children aged five and seven. *Developmental Psychology, 22,* 543–548.

Mish, F. C., et al. (2001). *Merriam-Webster's collegiate dictionary* (10th ed.). Springfield, MA: Merriam-Webster.

Molnar, A. (1992). Too many kids are getting killed. *Educational Leadership, 50*(1), 4–5.

Morris, V. G., Taylor, S. I., & Wilson, J. T. (2000). Using children's stories to promote peace in classrooms. *Early Childhood Education Journal, 28*, 41–50.

Mrug, S., Hoza, B., & Gerdes, A. C. (2001). Children with attention-deficit/hyperactivity disorder: Peer relationships and peer- oriented interventions. *New Directions for Child and Adolescent Development, 91*, 51–77.

Musatti, T. (1986). Early peer relations: The perspectives of Piaget and Vygotsky. In E. C. Meuller & C. R. Cooper (Eds.), *Process and outcome in peer relationships* (pp. 25–53). Orlando, FL: Academic Press.

National Association for the Education of Young Children (NAEYC). (1993). *Position statement on violence in the lives of children.* Retrieved December 1, 2002, from http://www.naeyc.org/resources/position_ statements/psviol98.htm

National Association for the Education of Young Children (NAEYC). (2001). Helping young children in frightening times. *Young Children, 56*(6), 6–9.

National Association for the Education of Young Children (NAEYC). (1995). *Position statement on linguistic and cultural diversity.* Retrieved December 1, 2002, from http://www.naeyc.org/resources/position_statements/psdiv98.htm

National Association for the Education of Young Children (NAEYC). (1997). *Code of ethical conduct and commitment.* Retrieved December 1, 2002, from http://www.naeyc .org/resources/position_statements/pseth98.htm

National Association for the Education of Young Children (NAEYC). (2001). *Standards at the initial licensure level.* Retrieved December 1, 2002, from http://www.naeyc.org/profdev/prep_review/preprev_2001.asp

National Center for Education Statistics (1993). *Student victimization at school: Statistics in brief from the National Household Education Survey (NHES).* Washington, DC: Author.

National Crime Prevention Council (n.d.). *Bullies: A Serious Problem for Kids.* Retrieved December 1, 2002, from http://www.ncpc .org/10adu3.htm

Nelson, J., & Aboud, F. (1985). The resolution of social conflict between friends. *Child Development, 56*, 1009–1017.

Neugebauer, B. (Ed.). (1992). *Alike and different: Exploring our humanity with young children.* Washington, DC: National Association for the Education of Young Children.

Noddings, N. (1984). *Caring: A feminist approach to ethics and education.* Berkeley, CA: University of California Press.

Noddings, N. (1992). *The challenge to care in schools.* New York: Teachers College Press.

Noddings, N. (1995). Teaching themes of care. *Phi Delta Kappan, 76*, 675–679.

Novick, R. (1998). The comfort corner: Fostering resiliency and emotional intelligence. *Childhood Education, 74*, 200–204.

Nucci, L. (1985). Social conflict and the development of children's moral and conventional concepts. In M. W. Berkowitz (Ed.), *Peer conflict and psychological growth. New Directions for Child Development, 29* (pp. 55–70). San Francisco: Jossey-Bass.

Nugent, J. K. (1994). Cross-culural studies of child development: Implications for clinicians. *Zero to Three, 15*(1), 1–8.

Oken-Wright, P. (1992). From tug of war to "Let's Make a Deal": The teacher's role. *Young Children, 48*(1), 15–20.

Okie, S. (2001, April 25). Survey: 30% of U.S. schoolchildren involved in bullying. *The Washington Post*, p. A8.

Paley, V. G. (1992). *You can't say you can't play.* Cambridge, MA: Harvard University Press.

Parrott, S. (1972). Games children play: Ethno-graphy of a second-grade recess. In J. Spradley & D. McCurdy (Eds.), *The cultural experience: Ethnography in complex society.* Prospect Heights, IL: Waveland Press.

Parten, M. (1932). Social participation among preschool children. *Journal of Abnormal Psychology, 27*(2), 243–269.

Pastor, P. (2002). School discipline and the character of our schools. *Phi Delta Kappan, 83,* 658–661.

Phinney, J. S. (1986). The structure of 5-year-olds' verbal quarrels with peers and siblings. *Journal of Genetic Psychology, 147*(1), 47–60.

Piaget, J. (1962). *Play, dreams, and imitation in childhood.* New York: Norton.

Pipher, M. (1994). *Reviving Ophelia: Saving the selves of adolescent girls.* New York: Random House.

Pollack, W. S. (1998). *Real boys: Rescuing our sons from the myths of boyhood.* New York: Random House.

Prince, D. L., & Howard, E. M. (2002). Children and their basic needs. *Early Childhood Education Journal, 30,* 27–31.

Prutzman, P., Stern, L., Burger, M. L., & Bodenhamer, G. (1988). *Friendly classroom for a small planet: A handbook for creative approaches to living and problem solving for children.* Philadelphia: New Society Publishers.

Puckett, M. B., & Black, J. K. (2000). *Authentic assessment of the young child: Celebrating development and learning* (2nd ed.). Upper Saddle River, NJ: Merrill/Prentice Hall.

Puckett, M. B., & Black, J. K. (2001). *The young child: Development from birth through age eight* (3rd ed.). Upper Saddle River, NJ: Merrill/Prentice Hall.

Ramsey, P. G. (1986). Possession disputes in preschool classrooms. *Child Study Journal, 16,* 173–181.

Ramsey, P. G. (1998). *Teaching and learning in a diverse world: Multicultural education for young children* (2nd ed.). New York: Teachers College Press.

Ramsey, P. G. (1991). *Making friends in school: Promoting peer relationships in early childhood.* New York: Teachers College Press.

Reardon, B. (1988). *Comprehensive peace education: Educating for global responsibility.* New York: Teachers College Press.

Reardon, B. (2002, April). *The changing facets of peace education.* Paper presented at the meeting of the American Educational Research Association, New Orleans, LA.

Reed, T., & Brown, M. (2000). The expression of care in the rough and tumble play of boys. *Journal of Research in Childhood Education, 15,* 104–116.

Rende, R. D., & Killen, M. (1992). Social interactional antecedents to conflict in young children. *Early Childhood Research Quarterly, 7,* 551–563.

Rinaldi, C. (1998). Projected curriculum constructed through documentation—Progettazione: An interview with Lella Gandini. In C. Edwards, L. Galdidni, & G. Forman (Eds.), *The hundred languages of children: The Reggio Emilia approach—Advanced reflections* (2nd ed., pp. 113–126). Greenwich, CT: Ablex.

Rizzo, T. A. (1989). *Friendship development among children in school.* Norwood, NJ: Ablex.

Roberts, P. (2002). *Kids taking action: Community service learning projects k-8.* Greenfield, MA: Northeast Foundation for Children.

Robinson, A., & Stark, D. (2002). *Advocates in action: Making a difference for young children.* Washington, DC: National Association for the Education of Young Children.

Ross, H. S., & Conant, C. L. (1992). The social structure of early conflict: Interaction, relationship and alliances. In C. W. Shantz & W. Hartup (Eds.), *Conflict in child and adolescent development* (pp. 153–1895). Cambridge, UK: Cambridge University Press.

Sacken, S., & Thelen, E. (1984). An ethological study of peaceful associative outcomes to conflict in preschool children. *Child Development, 55,* 1098–1102.

Saldana, J. (1995). *Drama of color: Improvisation with multiethnic folklore.* Portsmouth, NH: Heinemann.

Selman, R. L. (1981). *The growth of interpersonal understanding.* New York: Academic Press.

Shantz, C. U. (1987). Conflicts between children. *Child Development, 58,* 283–305.

Shantz, C. U., & Hartup, W. (Eds.). (1992). *Conflict in child and adolescent development.* Cambridge, UK: Cambridge University Press.

Shantz, C. U., & Shantz, D. W. (1985). Conflict between children: Social-cognitive and sociometric correlates. In M. Berkowitz (Ed.), *Peer conflict and psychological growth. New directions for child development, 29* (pp. 3–21). San Francisco: Jossey-Bass.

Sheldon, A. (1993). Pickle fights: Gendered talk in preschool disputes. In D. Tannen (Ed.), *Gender and conversational interaction* (pp. 83–109). New York: Oxford University Press.

Shepard, R., & Rose, H. (1994). The power of parents: An empowerment model for increasing parental involvement. *Education, 115*, 373–377.

Shoemaker, C. (2000). *Leadership and management of programs for young children* (2nd ed.). Upper Saddle River, NJ: Merrill/Prentice Hall.

Siegler, R. S. (1998). *Children's thinking* (3rd ed.). Upper Saddle River, NJ: Prentice Hall.

Singer, E., & Hännikäinen, M. (2002). The teacher's role in territorial conflicts of 2- to 3-year-old children. *Journal of Research in Childhood Education, 17*, 5–18.

Singer, E., & Hannikainen, M. (2002). The teacher's role in territorial conflicts of 2- and 3-year-old children. *Journal of Research in Childhood Education, 17*, 5–18.

Slaby, R. G., Riedell, W. C., Arezzo, D., & Hendrix, K. (1995). *Early violence prevention: Tools for teachers of young children*. Washington, DC: National Association for the Education of Young Children.

Smith, G. P. (1998). *Common sense about common knowledge: The knowledge bases for diversity*. Washington, DC: American Association for Teacher Education.

Spradley, J. P. (1979). *The ethnographic interview*. Fort Worth, TX: Holt, Rinehart, & Winston.

Soto, L. D. (Ed.). (2000). *The politics of early childhood education*. New York: Peter Lang.

Squires, J., Bricker, D., Heo, K., & Twombley, E. (2001). Identification of social-emotional problems in young children using a parent-completed screening measure. *Early Childhood Research Quarterly, 16*, 405–419.

Stanulis, R. N., & Manning, B. H. (2002). The teacher's role in creating a positive verbal and nonverbal environment in the early childhood classroom. *Early Childhood Education Journal, 30*(1), 3–8.

Stepp, L. S. (2001, November 11). Children's worries take new shape: Artwork reveals the effects of Sept. 11. *The Washington Post*, p. C1.

Straus, R. A. (2002). *Using sociology: An introduction from the applied and clinical perspectives*. Lanham, MD: Rowman & Littlefield.

Swiniarski, L. A., Breitborde, M., & Murphy, J. (1999). *Educating the global village: Including the young child in the world*. Upper Saddle River, NJ: Merrill/Prentice Hall.

Tamivaara, J., & Enright, D. S. (1986). On eliciting information: Dialogues with children informants. *Anthropology and Education Quarterly, 17*, 218–238.

Tannen, D. (1990). *You just don't understand:* Women and men in conversation. New York: Morrow.

Taylor, L. O., & Adeleman, H. S. (2003). School-community relations: Policy and practice. In M. S. E. Fishbaugh, T. R. Berkeley, & G. Schroth (Eds.), *Ensuring safe schools: Exploring issues—Seeking solutions* (pp. 107–132). Mahwah, NJ: Lawrence Erlbaum.

Teaching Tolerance Project. (1997). *Starting small: Teaching tolerance in preschool and the early grades*. Montgomery, AL: Southern Poverty Law Center.

Thompson, S. (1997). Helping primary children with recess play: A social curriculum. *Young Children, 52*(5), 17–21.

Thurston, L. P., & Berkeley, T. R. (2003). Peaceable school communities: Morality and the ethic of care. In M. S. E. Fishbaugh, T. R. Berkeley, & G. Schroth (Eds.), *Ensuring safe schools: Exploring issues—Seeking solutions* (pp. 133–147). Mahwah, NJ: Lawrence Erlbaum.

Tobin, J. J., Wu, D. Y. H., & Davidson, D. H. (1989). *Preschool in three cultures*. New Haven, CT: Yale University Press.

T.R.U.C.E. *Media violence and children action guide 2003–2003*. Retrieved December 1, 2002, from http://www.truceteachers.org/ TRUCE/ mediaviolence02.pdf

Turiel, E. (1983). *The development of social knowledge*. Cambridge, UK: Cambridge University Press.

U.S. Department of Education Office of Educational Research and Improvement. (2001). *Family involvement in children's education: Successful local approaches: An idea book* (abridged version of Publication No. AR 97-7022R) Jessup, MD: Author.

Upright, R. L. (2002). To tell a tale: The use of moral dilemmas to increase empathy in the elementary school child. *Early Childhood Education Journal, 30*(1), 15–20.

Van Ausdale, D., & Feagin, J. R. (2001). *The first R: How children learn race and racism.* Lanham, MD: Rowman and Littlefield.

Vance, E., & Weaver, P. J. (2002). *Class meetings: Young children solving problems together.* Washington, DC: National Association for the Education of Young Children.

Vespo, J. E. (1997). *The nature of sibling conflict during middle childhood.* Paper presented at the biennial meeting of the Society for Research in Child Development, Washington, DC. (ERIC Document Reproduction Service No. ED412003)

Vespo, J. E., Pederson, J., & Hay, D. F. (1995). Young children's conflicts with peers and siblings: Gender effects. *Child Study Journal, 25,* 189–212.

Vygotsky, L. S. (1978). *Mind in society.* Cambridge, MA: Harvard University Press.

Walther-Thomas, C., Korinek, L., McLaughlin, V. L., & Williams, B. T. (2000). *Collaboration for inclusive education: Developing successful programs.* Boston: Allyn & Bacon.

Washington, V., & Andrews, J. D. (1998). *Children of 2010.* Washington, DC: National Association for the Education of Young Children.

Watson-Gregeo, K. A., & Boggs, S. T. (1977). From verbal play to talk story: The role of routines in speech events among Hawaiian children. In S. Ervin-Tripp & C. Mitchell-Kernan (Eds.), *Child discourse* (pp. 67–90). New York: Academic Press.

Weiser, M. G. (1991). *Infant/toddler care and education* (2nd ed.). Upper Saddle River, NJ: Merrill/Prentice Hall.

Werner, E. E. (1992). *Overcoming the odds: High risk children from birth through adulthood.* Ithaca, NY: Cornell University Press.

Werner, E. E., & Smith, R. S. (1982). *Vulnerable, but invincible: A longitudinal study of resilient children and youth.* New York: McGraw-Hill.

Werner, E. E., & Smith, R. S. (2001). *Journeys from childhood to midlife: Risk, resilience, and recovery.* Ithaca, NY: Cornell University Press.

Wheeler, E. J. (1997). A qualitative study of preschool children's peer conflicts. *National Head Start Association Research Quarterly, 1,* 117–123.

Wheeler, E. J. (2000). Common questions and concerns about conflict resolution. In M. R. Jalongo & J. P. Isenberg, *Exploring your role: A practitioner's introduction to early childhood education* (pp. 340–342). Upper Saddle River, NJ: Merrill/Prentice Hall.

Whiting, B. B., & Edwards, C. P. (1988). *Children of different worlds: The formation of social behavior.* Cambridge, MA: Harvard University Press.

Wichert, S. (1989). *Keeping the peace: Practicing cooperation and conflict resolution.* Philadelphia: New Society Publishers.

Wilson, K. E. (1988). *The development of conflict and conflict resolution among preschool children.* Unpublished masters thesis, Pacific Oaks College, CA. (ERIC Document Reproduction Service No. ED304211)

Wortham, S. C. (2001). *Assessment in early childhood education* (3rd ed.). Upper Saddle River, NJ: Merrill/Prentice Hall.

York, S. (1992). *Roots and wings: Affirming culture in early childhood programs.* St. Paul, MN: Redleaf Press.

Zeece, P. D., & Stolzer, J. (2002). Creating literature safety zones for young children. *Early Childhood Education Journal, 30*(1), 47–52.

Zero to Three (2002). *Little listeners in an uncertain world: Coping strategies for you and your child after September 11.* Brochure available at www.zerotothree.org.

Name Index

Subject Index

Note: Boldface numbers indicate illustrations.